John Baker Hopkins, John Diprose

Some Account of the Parish of Saint Clement Danes

Vol. 1

John Baker Hopkins, John Diprose

Some Account of the Parish of Saint Clement Danes
Vol. 1

ISBN/EAN: 9783337336653

Printed in Europe, USA, Canada, Australia, Japan

Cover: Foto ©Lupo / pixelio.de

More available books at **www.hansebooks.com**

Some Account

OF THE

Parish

OF

Saint Clement Danes

(WESTMINSTER)

Past and Present.

COMPILED FROM VARIOUS SOURCES

By JOHN DIPROSE.

London:
DIPROSE AND BATEMAN, 13 & 17, Portugal Street, Lincoln's Inn.
1868.

DIPROSE & BATEMAN, PRINTERS, 13 & 17, PORTUGAL STREET, LINCOLN'S INN FIELDS.

PREFACE.

THE compiler of this volume of Topography and History of St. Clement Danes trusts that his book will be found of interest both to the antiquarian and general reader, as giving—so far as it goes—a faithful account of one of the most remarkable parishes in the metropolis.

At the present moment, when the character of the parish is being rapidly changed by the wholesale demolition of houses and streets, to make room for the erection of a Palace of Justice, it becomes the duty of the chronicler to record the ancient features of some of the houses and streets, once so intimately connected with the literary and political history of our country.

He cannot presume to offer it to the public as a History of St. Clement Danes, in the usual sense of the word History, but chooses rather to submit it (as its title bears,) as "Some Account of the Parish." A mere casual perusal of the various articles and notes here collected will show that St. Clement Danes is no mean parish. In it have been enacted some of the most noteworthy events in the history of our country; in it many great and worthy men, as authors, actors, statesmen, or lawyers, have been born, flourished, and died. On the other hand, time has unravelled in the parish many a plot against the Throne and the People, and it is not a little curious to find that on this very spot, which has been the scene of many a crime and deed of infamy, will be erected one of the most magnificent buildings ever dedicated to the great cause of justice.

In conclusion the compiler feels it his bounden duty to acknowledge the great services he has derived from the many authors whose able works he has consulted, and which he hopes, in all cases, are duly mentioned. He also desires to acknowledge the help afforded him by the London Newspaper Press; and, further begs to acknowledge, with feelings of the deepest gratitude, the valuable assistance he has received from many gentlemen both in and out of the parish. In particular his warmest thanks are due to the following:—J. W. Anson, D. Betts, D. Bruton, W. B. Brook, J. Bullock, W. Burnett, J. F. Clarke, G. Crossley, R. Dansie, E. Du Bois, C. L. Gruneisen, R. Hardwicke, F. Hart, J. B. Hopkins, J. F. Isaacson, J. Johnson, Rev. R. H. Killick, J. Kilner, T. C. Noble, J. Prout, J. Reddish, W. H. Spilsbury, T. M. Stone, A. Wilkinson and E. T. Wood, Esquires.

JOHN DIPROSE.

November, 1868.

The New Law Courts.

For many years there had been gradually forming in the minds of the members of the various branches of the legal profession, and perhaps still more in the minds of those whose fortune it is, more or less frequently, to become litigants before any of the superior tribunals, an impression of the desirability, which ultimately grew into a conviction of the necessity, of a concentration of the Law Courts of the Metropolis. Englishmen are proverbially fond of justice: therefore, if they think they have suffered wrong-doing of any kind, they are prone to repair to the fountain of English law; for they believe that its principles, precepts, and practice, constitute an embodiment of the primal foundations of justice. We have ever loved our Common Law—a term even more dear to us than our statutory glories of 1215 and 1688—since the day when Edward the Confessor devised the pregnant and significant term, to indicate the fusion of the three provincial codes which had hitherto held in the dominions of his much-loved and much-loving subjects. After his great act of codifying amalgamation, there was no longer one code for the Mercian, a second for the West Saxon, a third for him or her—whether of Teutonic or Scandinavian blood—who dwelt in those counties which retained most largely the Danish imprint.

Rough, but actuated by most just intent, were our Saxon ancestors in their notions of legal amercement and compensation. They bequeathed to us the animating spirit of our law—we have but improved upon its letter. No longer do we assess the fine for cutting off a human being's ear at the fixed sum of thirty shillings—a pecuniary penalty to be multiplied if the hearing were lost in consequence of the brutality. Nevertheless, the nice exactness of the statutory and other provisions which stipulate graduations of punishments in proportion to the heinousness of offences, is but a more civilised and improved expansion and outgrowth of the old root represented by the Saxon usage.

If Englishmen love Law—that is *their* Law—because they believe it to be just, another characteristic of our busy and frugal people is a dislike, which amounts to abhorrence, of needless waste of time and money. That such waste, in both senses, has been abundantly and painfully caused by the wide isolation and severance of our various Courts of Law and Equity over a considerable section of the metropolis—a section large enough to cover all but its suburban portions—is a fact too trite to demand more than passing reference. The truth of this fact having become recognised by all concerned, the only question which remained was—How, when, and where to set about the remedy? Cost, also, was an element of judicious consideration. And, accordingly, the legal profession, the nation, and its legislatorial representatives, acting on the truly national maxim, *festina lente*, spent a considerable, but not an excessive, period in deliberation ere the final details of the remedial plan were matured. The first step towards the conclusion ultimately arrived at, was the issuing, in 1858, a Royal Commission for the purpose of inquiring into the expediency of bringing together in one place or neighbourhood all the superior Courts of Law and Equity, the Probate, Divorce, and Admiralty Courts, with their various offices. The Commission was directed to investigate the means for providing a site, and for erecting suitable buildings. The inquiry ended in a recommendation that the site of the proposed edifice should be an area of ground lying between Lincoln's Inn and that part of the Strand between Temple Bar and St. Clement's Church. In 1861, a Bill was introduced for the purpose of carrying out the recommendation of the Commissioners; but, from causes on which it is not here necessary to dilate, it was thrown out in the House of Commons by the narrow majority of 181 to 180. The further consideration of the matter was postponed until 1865, in which year two Acts of Parliament were passed to carry out the well-matured recommendation. The first Act provided funds for the cost of the buildings, partly by a parliamentary grant, partly by a contribution of one million unclaimed interest on stock standing to the account of suitors in Chancery, and partly by a slight taxation of litigants in other courts. The second Act empowered Her Majesty's Commissioners of Works and Public Buildings to acquire the requisite site, to purchase the houses standing on it, and to provide the necessary accommodation for the New Courts and Offices.

Besides the authority given to the Commissioners of Works, Parliament called into existence another body, designated the "Courts of Justice Commission." By one of the enactments to which we have referred, the plan of the new buildings was to be determined upon by the Treasury, "with the advice of such persons as Her Majesty shall think fit to authorise in their behalf;" and the Queen, in the exercise of this power, issued her Royal Commission to that effect.

THE FOLLOWING ARE THE COMMISSIONERS:—

1. The Right Honorable the Lord Chancellor for the time being.
2. The Right Honorable the Lord Cranworth, 40, Upper Brook Street, W.
3. The Right Honorable the Chancellor of the Exchequer, Treasury, Whitehall.
4. The Right Honorable the Lord Chief Justice of England, 17, Park Lane.
5. The Right Honorable the Lord Chief Justice of the Common Pleas, 12, Prince's Gardens, Prince's Gate, Kensington, W.
6. The Right Honorable the Lord Chief Baron, Hatton, near Hounslow, W.
7. The Right Honorable Lord Justice Cairns.

COMMISSIONERS.—*(Continued).*

8. The Right Honorable the Judge of the High Court of Admiralty, 18, Eaton Place, S.W.
9. The Right Honorable Sir James P. Wilde, 2, Grafton Street, New Bond Street, W.
10. The Right Honorable the First Commissioner of Works, 12, Whitehall Place.
11. The Honorable Vice-Chancellor Stuart, 5, Queen's Gate, Kensington, W.
12. The Honorable Vice-Chancellor Wood, 31, Great George Street, Westminster, S.W.
13. The Honorable Vice-Chancellor Malins.
14. The Honorable Mr. Baron Martin, 75, Eaton Square, S.W.
15. The Honorable Mr. Justice Mellor, 16, Sussex Square, Hyde Park, W.
16. The Honorable Mr. Justice Smith, 119, Park Street, Grosvenor Square, W.
17. The Attorney-General, 11, New Square, Lincoln's Inn.
18. The Solicitor-General, 1, Mitre Court Buildings, E.C.
19. The Queen's Advocate, 5, Arlington Street.
20. Sir Roundell Palmer, Knight, M.P.
21. Hugh C. E. Childers, Esq., M.P.
22. James Clarke Lawrence (Alderman , 18, Cannon Street, Mansion House, E.C.
23. The President of the Law Society for the time being.
24. Pearce William Rogers, Esq., Registrar's Office, Chancery Lane.
25. George Hume, Esq., Taxing Master's Office, Staple Inn, Holborn.
26. C. F. Skirrow, Esq., Staple Inn, Holborn.
27. Charles Manley Smith, Esq., Master's Office, Temple.
28. William Morgan Benett, Esq., Common Pleas Office, Serjeants Inn, Chancery Lane.
29. William Henry Walton, Esq., 7, Stone Buildings, Lincoln's Inn.
30. H. Cadogan Rothery, Esq., Doctors' Commons.
31. Augustus Frederic Bayford, Esq., Doctors' Commons.
32. William George Anderson, Esq., Treasury, Whitehall.
33. Sir Alexander Young Spearman, Bart., National Debt Office, Old Jewry.
34. Henry Arthur Hunt, Esq., 44, Eccleston Square.
35. R. P. Amphlett, Esq., Q.C., 7, Old Square, Lincoln's Inn.
36. D. D. Keane, Esq., Q.C., 4, Brick Court, Temple.
37. Thomas Southgate, Esq., Q.C., 4, New Square, Lincoln's Inn.
38. H. Bliss, Esq., Q.C., 6, Paper Buildings, Temple.
39. John Young, Esq., 6, Frederick's Place, Old Jewry.
40. William Strickland Cookson, Esq., 6, New Square, Lincoln's Inn.

The Commissioners having instituted elaborate inquiries into the sufficiency of the proposed site, and the amount of the accommodation to be provided for the several courts and offices proposed to be concentrated, they were enabled to prepare instructions for the guidance of the architects who might be invited to send in designs for the new buildings. It became necessary at this stage to consider how the competitors were to be selected, and in what manner their designs should be adjudicated upon. It was ultimately determined to call a third body into existence, for the purpose of discharging these very important duties. It was decided that this third body should consist of five members, and that they should be designated "Judges of Designs." Two were nominated by the Treasury, viz., The CHANCELLOR of the EXCHEQUER, and WILLIAM STIRLING, Esq., M.P., now Sir WILLIAM STIRLING MAXWELL, Bart., M.P. Two were appointed by the Commissioners, viz., The LORD CHIEF JUSTICE of ENGLAND, and the ATTORNEY-GENERAL. The fifth member, and chairman of the body, was The FIRST COMMISSIONER of WORKS. In order, however, that a change of Ministry should not change the tribunal, all the members were appointed by *name* and not by *office*. It may as well be stated here, although not chronologically in order, that an addition of two members of the architectural profession was subsequently made to the body, at the repeated request of the competitors and the demand of the House of Commons. The Judges, therefore, as now constituted, are:—The Right Honorable W. COWPER, M.P.; The Right Honorable W. E. GLADSTONE, M.P.; The Right Honorable SIR ALEXANDER COCKBURN, Bart.; SIR ROUNDELL PALMER, M.P.; SIR WILLIAM STIRLING MAXWELL, Bart., M.P.; JOHN SHAW, Esq.; and GEORGE POWNALL, Esq.

The Judges of Designs nominated six architects whom the Commissioners invited to send in designs; more than one declined on the ground of large existing engagements. The number, however, was speedily made up and the competitors set to work, when the House of Commons interfered and required that the number of the competitors should be increased to twelve. Their names are as follows:—Mr. H. R. ABRAHAM; Mr. E. M. BARRY, A.R.A.; Mr. RAPHAEL BRANDON; Mr. W. BURGES; Mr. T. N. DEANE; Mr. H. B. GARLING; Mr. JOHN GIBSON; Mr. H. F. LOCKWOOD; Mr. J. P. SEDDON; Mr. G. G. SCOTT, R.A.; Mr. G. E. STREET, A.R.A.; and Mr. ALFRED WATERHOUSE. Each of the competitors to receive £800. One of the number—Mr. JOHN GIBSON—withdrew from the contest, reducing the number to eleven.

It was held by some, that only gentlemen directly responsible to the country, by virtue of their position of Cabinet Ministers, should be entrusted to discharge the duties of Judges of Designs. The question was, very properly, brought forward for discussion in the House of Commons. In March, 1867, in going into Committee of Supply, Mr. CAVENDISH BENTINCK moved in his place in the House—"That, in the opinion of this House, it is expedient that all arrangements respecting the building of the New Courts of Justice, should be effected under the sole responsibility of Her Majesty's Government." Mr. BERESFORD HOPE, a gentleman of equal eminence as a standard of architectural taste and an ensample of personal honour, rose to support (though not in every detail) the honorable and learned gentleman's proposition. Mr. COWPER, although not then an official, inasmuch as he had been Minister of Public Works when the bill was passed, justified the principle on which the selection of the Commissioners had been based. He disclaimed altogether the suggestion that the appointment of non-Ministerial Commissioners had either been intended to, or would have the effect of, relieving Ministers themselves of direct Parliamentary responsibility for every iota of their transactions. The Commission (said he) had been appointed "simply to consider and report on the subject." As it comprised judges and others specially interested in the successful issue, and acquainted with the exigencies, of the project, he could not but still justify the policy and utility of its appointment. Lord JOHN MANNERS, who had succeeded Mr. COWPER on the accession of Lord DERBY's Administration, expressed his entire concurrence with the opinion of Mr. COWPER, and with the considerations by which that gentleman had supported his views. He stated, distinctly, that Mr. BENTINCK's motion, if carried, would intercept altogether the action of the Commission, and constitute a "great misfortune." On this, Mr. BENTINCK at once withdrew his motion.

The architects having responded to the invitation given to them, the result is seen in the production of designs, which were hung in the temporary building erected for the purpose in New Square, Lincoln's Inn, designed and admirably arranged by the Architectural Clerk to the Commission, Mr. W. BURNET. The building of this fabric cost £1,500. All the architects exceeded in their estimates the costs contemplated by the Commissioners. The latter required that the building should not, if possible, exceed in cost £750,000. The lowest estimate is £1,074,278. The Commissioners specified the area on which the buildings were to be erected, but the architects require more space, thus adding probably £250,000 to the £750,000 already devoted to the purchase of the ground. The highest estimate for the buildings is £2,379,046, and the average excess over the stipulated amount is £570,506, irrespective of the quarter of a million extra for the additional land. The Commissioners require that there should be 1,100 courts and offices of certain dimensions, and for this they allow a space of about eight acres. The architecture contemplated is, in all instances, Gothic, unless we except one "alternative design."

So much for a brief narrative of the course of discussion and legislation which has eventuated in the result now so happily attained. Ere long, one of the most historically interesting and socially squalid localities of the Metropolis will have been cleared of every one of its ancient or recently built tenements—the latter but few in number; and gradually will there arise, on the now desolate waste, what can hardly fail to be the noblest and most truly imperial building in the Metropolis of the World—a Palace of Justice worthy of the premier amongst peoples.

Those traditionary and romantic feelings, which are as much English as are our oaks and elms, cannot fail to enable us to revere and cherish certain of the associations of this historic site—a site on which are centred some of the richest recollections of the City of Westminster, along with some of the most curious of those of the City of London. Old London is fast disappearing, and he who attempts to fix in letterpress some of its fading memories, ere they quite vanish, discharges a task neither thankless nor unpleasant.

The impending Law Courts have already so cast their shadow before their coming, as to clear away, not a rookery, but a very nest of rookeries. Above 400 houses in all have been destroyed, or are in rapid process of demolition; or, in the case of some few, are only awaiting their early doom. Above 4,000 persons have been rendered homeless; but of these, the great majority, wherever they may migrate with their families and slender household goods, must necessarily inhabit homes much more healthy than the houses in which they recently dwelt. In all, above thirty courts, lanes, and streets have been demolished. Even this will be only the beginning of the end; for it is a matter inevitable, that the existing approaches to the magnificent edifice must be entirely remodelled. Accordingly, many more houses must be ultimately cleared away. From every part of the town there must be direct approaches to the noble building.

The Government, which of course had to pay the amounts for legal or beneficiary compensation, was well represented by GEORGE POWNALL, Esq., their appointed surveyor, and his able assistant, Mr. WALKER. The best proof of the skill with which they discharged duties which to some seemed to partake of harshness, is the fact, of which we are well assured, that on reflection, everyone was satisfied. When the wrath occasioned by the removal from old haunts and habitations, and the too lamentable difficulty of acquiring new, had been appeased by the interval of a little time, every one, whether dwelling in street or alley, in high-rented shop or misery-haunted garret, acknowledged, not alone that justice had been done, but that it had been liberally tempered by dignity, integrity and gentlemanly consideration.

As may well be supposed, even by those who are the least personally acquainted with the habits and belongings of the lower strata of society, many pages of the most interesting character—half saddening, half amusing—might be written about the steps which were necessary to be taken to procure the eviction of the tenants ere the tenements were overthrown; and about the negotiations for pecuniary compensation in the cases of those inhabitants who had equitable claims for the loss incurred by compulsory removal. The whole of the intricate arrangements so involved were intrusted by the authorities to the eminent legal firm of FIELD, ROSCOE, FIELD and FRANCIS. These gentlemen discharged duties of the utmost difficulty in a manner which evoked admiration from all who were spectators, interested or otherwise, of their prolonged exercise. They also found fit representatives in Messrs. BROWNLOW and WHITE, of whom we say enough—and we could not in many sentences say more—when we state that they were worthy delegates to act for worthy principals.

A concrete example always brings most clearly to the mind's eye the general and generic statement of which it is the particular instance. How great, then, must have been the difficulties to encounter—how great the tact and delicacy necessary to the successful and harmonious conclusion of the operation—in rendering tenantless over 400 houses, considering that in one court alone—Yates' Court—there were six small houses, tenanted by no less than 48 families, including, besides the ordinary complement of adults, 150 children! Much of the rougher and more repellant work involved fell upon a Mr. WHATLEY, an able and judicious assistant of Messrs. FIELD and ROSCOE. He could many "a tale unfold" of the miseries disclosed to his necessarily close inspection and prying vision. He could tell our readers, for example, in terms more vivid than we could emulate, how the poorer class of tenants invoked blessings upon the heads of the donors of the liberal compensation which was given in all cases, even where, as in the case of weekly tenants, there were no legal claims. He could also tell how, when the donations so bestowed had been expended by some of the recipients in a few days of indulgence, the blessings were changed into cursings, and male and female mouths which erst had smiled beatifically, were now disfigured by imprecatory scowls. But all these subsequent and supervening difficulties were overcome by Mr. WHATLEY'S wonderful tact and good nature, for we can speak from our own observation of the many instances in which his good advice, humanity, and kindness aided him in performing his unpleasant duties in a manner which might well be considered worthy of the eminent firm he represented. Messrs. CAPES and HARRIS, the accountants, of Old Jewry, were retained by the Commissioners for the examination of the books and accounts of all parties claiming compensation; we believe we are correct in stating that the last 18 months' profits were allowed in most cases.

COURT OF CHANCERY.—The annual return relative to the funds of the Court of Chancery, issued March 16th, 1867, shows that the receipts, including the previous balance, of the Suitors' Fund in the year ending Oct. 1, 1866, amounted to £147,416 0s. 4d. in cash, and £4,451,739 11s. 5d. stock. The total payments were—cash, £93,988 4s. 7d., and stock, £232,750 9s. 9d. The largest item of payment (more than £200,000) was on account of the New Courts of Justice. The Suitors' Fee Fund account shows a total receipt of £141,286 2s. 2d., making with balance from previous year, £280,593 18s. 7d. The total payments for the year amounted to £194,932 17s. 11d., a considerable amount of which was spent under the Courts of Justice Building Act.

THE NEW LAW COURTS.

The Site of the New Law Courts is situate in three parishes, viz.—
St. CLEMENT DANES, LIBERTY OF THE ROLLS,
and St. DUNSTAN-IN-THE-WEST.

The following Table shews the Names of the Places forming the Site, and also the Number of Houses and Families occupying the same:—

NAME OF PLACE.	NUMBER OF HOUSES.	NUMBER OF FAMILIES LIVING THEREIN.
Bailey's Court	5	14
Bell Yard	28	49
Boswell Court (Old)	19	45
Boswell Court (New)	18	28
Boswell Yard	1	1
Brick Court	3	8
Carey Street	28	56
Chair Court	6	16
Clement's Court	4	10
Clement's Inn	7	17
Clement's Inn (Foregate)	6	5
Clement's Lane	28	102
Cromwell Place	7	7
Crown Court	11	16
Crown Place	6	3
Fleet Street	3	5
Hemlock Court	18	48
Horse Shoe Court	3	7
Horse Shoe Court (Little)	2	3
New Court	3	8
Newcastle Court	16	41
Pickett Place	4	6
Pickett Street	14	29
Plough Court	10	55
Robinhood Court	2	11
Sawyer's Yard	1	1
Serle's Place	22	60
Serle's Place (Lower)	29	101
Serle's Place (Middle)	20	88
Ship Yard	31	107
Ship and Anchor Court	2	1
Strand	13	17
Star Court	9	24
Yates' Court	6	48

Not having any official returns before us, we have given the best account of the Number of Families we are enabled to do from our own inquiries.

THE NEW LAW COURTS.

Clement's Lane, which is the western boundary of the extensive piece of London destined for the site of the new abode of the British Themis, was entered from the Strand, as everybody will remember, through an open gateway flanked by massive stone pillars. The main length of Clement's Lane round the back of King's College Hospital, and communicating, by more than one obscure outlet, with New Inn and Clare Market, is merged, further on, in a wretched thoroughfare called Gilbert Street, which leads, indirectly, to the south-west corner of Lincoln's Inn Fields. Such are the ways for passing from the latitude of the Strand and Fleet Street to the latitude of Holborn, between the west longitude of Drury and the east longitude of Chancery Lanes. Well may it be said that they manage these things better in Paris! It is not yet determined, we believe, what broad, straight, and commodious streets are to be opened from north to south, in connection with the building of the New Law Courts; this will be a question for the Metropolitan Board of Works. Mr. Dickens might have placed the scenes of his quaintest stories of cockney humble life a quarter of a century ago in the midst of this doomed quarter of London, which was the haunt of gaiety and pleasure in the reign of Charles II., and is associated with memories of the bloods and bucks of the Restoration, and the wits of the days of Queen Anne.

As far back as 1831 the Roll's Estate is mentioned in the "Legal Observer" as a desirable piece of land for the purpose of erecting the New Law Courts, and from the same work in 1837, we extract the following remark :—

"The recommendation for the New Law Courts has received additional strength, from the circumstance that the two last Masters nor the present Master of the Rolls have resided in the Roll's House. Sir Robert Gifford was the last lawyer who lived in the true professional air. Lord Lyndhurst could not resign the parish of St. George's, Hanover Square, for Chancery Lane. Sir John Leach would not exchange South Street, and his look out into Hyde Park, for the pleasing prospect of the Cursitor's Office, and Lord Langdale has shown a similar preference

VIEWS IN ST. CLEMENT DANES.

St. Clement Danes' Parish.

THE CHURCH.

THE present edifice was erected in 1682, from a design by Sir Christopher Wren, except the lofty and picturesque tower, which owes its present elevation, of one hundred and sixteen feet, to Mr. Gibbs, by whom it was added in 1719; and was repaired in 1839; it contains a fine peal of bells, which at the hours of 9, 12, and 5, chime the tunes of Hanover, and the Lass o' Gowrie. On the north and south sides are domed porticos, supported by six Ionic columns. The interior is handsome and commodious, lighted by two stories of windows; the altar is of carved wainscot, of the Tuscan order; and the chancel is paved with marble. The top of the communion table is a very fine specimen of marble, which is supposed to have belonged to the old church, and worth at least £500. The length of the Church is 64 feet; breadth 40 feet; altitude 34 feet. The galleries are very spacious, in which is one of Father Smith's organs. The Rev. R. H. KILLICK is the Rector at the present time; the Curates are the Rev. F. G. LITTLECOT, and the Rev. T. D. GRAY.

Over the poor box in the centre aisle there is an antique piece of carved wood, which most probably was taken from the old church, and used, as now, to excite the sympathy of the benevolent.

As you have opportunity,
Do good unto All, But Especially
To them of the houshold of ffaith.
For to do good and to distribute,
With such sacrifices, GOD,
is well pleased.

On the north and south sides of the communion table are placed three handsome tablets, the inscriptions of which are as follows :—

To the Memory
of
Richard Dukeson D. Deate Rector of this Parish
Fortie and four yeares
A Reverend and Learned Divine
Eminent for
His great devotion towards God
His firm zeal to the Church
His unshaken loyalty to the King
His unwearing endeavour for the good of his flock
From which he was separated by the iniquity of ye
Dureing the late unnatural rebellion (times
By near Seventeen yeares Sequestration
But being restored he continued to the end of great
a contrite preacher   (age
Both by his doctrine and life
He died Sepr. 17 Ann. Domin. 1678.
Ætat suæ 86.

and of his only wife
Anne the daughter of Anthony Hickman Esq.
Dr. of Lawes
She was a virtuous and goodly Matron
With whom he lived in holy matrimony 46 yeares
and had three sons and 12 daughters
She died Sepr. 22 anno Domini 1670
Ætat suæ 66.

Their bodies lye interred on the right side
of the Communion table.
In verbo tuo Spes mea.

TO THE GLORY OF GOD
And for ye solemn worship of his
Holy name this old Church being greatly decayed
was taken down in ye yeare 1680 and rebuilt and
finished in ye yeare 1682 by the pious assistance
of ye Reverend Dr. GREGORY HASKARD
Rector and ye Bountifull Contributions of ye
Inhabitants of this Parish & some other NOBLE
BENEFACTORS Sr. CHRISTOPHER
WREN, his Mtis. surveyor freely and generously
bestowing his great care & skill towards ye
contriving and building of it

WHICH GOOD WORK
Was all along greatly promoted and incouraged
by ye zeal & diligence of ye vestry

HUGH OWEN HALL JARMAN) CHURCH-
THOMAS COX, WILLIAM   }
THOMSON, JOHN PADFORD) WARDENS
[being

II. CHRONICLES XXIV. XIII.
So ye workmen wrought & ye work was perfected
by them, & they set the house of GOD in his
state, and strengthned it.

SOLI DEO GLORIA.
This was erected in ye yeare 1684.

ROGER FRANKLIN, JAMES { CHURCH-
PARMAN   { WARDENS

Opposite to this place near the wall lieth the body of
Sn. EDWARD LECHE of SHIPLEY in the Coy. of DERBY
Knt. a Master of Chancery & a Member of ye Hon. house of Commons.

He died ye 12th day of July
Ao. Dm. 1652. Ætet 80 fere.

In a front pew at the east end of the north gallery there is also a "silent record" of one of the brightest ornaments of the literary circle of his time, of which the following is an accurate copy :—

In this pew
and beside this pillar, for many years,
attended Divine Service,
The celebrated DOCTER SAMUEL JOHNSON
The Philosopher, the Poet,
The great Lexicographer,
The profound Moralist, and chief Writer
of his Time.
BORN 1709.   DIED 1784.

In remembrance, and Honour
of noble faculties, nobly employed ;
some Inhabitants of the parish
of St. Clement Danes
Have placed this slight Memorial
A.D. 1851.

ST. CLEMENT DANES' CHURCH.

The two following inscriptions are of minor importance; one is a curiously carved scroll tablet placed on one of the centre pillars, and facing the south aisle; and the other is a small octagon shaped brass let in the pavement of the centre aisle, and ornamented with a skull and cross bones :—

<table>
<tr><td>
NEAR
This pillar lyeth ye body
of SAMUEL TATHAM
Surgeon and Citizen of
London late of this Parish
who died ye 14th of Nober.
Anno Dom. 1691.
Aged 69 years.
</td><td>
Here lies interd the
Body of Elizabeth ye wife
Of Thomas Browne daughter &
Only child of Thomas & Blanch Benskin
Both of this parish who departed
This life October 25th 1705 in
The 23 year of her age.
If youth & virtue could not save
A virtuous woman from the grave
Reader prepare to follow for you know
The debt that she has paid
We all do owe.
</td></tr>
</table>

The following is a copy of a brass plate, placed in the entrance to the Church :—

```
            The Eight bells in this steeple
        were cast by Will : & Phill : Wight-
        man their Majties : Founders Ano Domi.
                1693 In the Tyme of
WM. DAVIS &   ⎫ CHURCH-        EDWD. CLARKE. and ⎫ CHURCH-
              ⎬            And finishied when                 ⎬
EDWD. CLARKE  ⎭ WARDENS.         HUGH MILLS were  ⎭ WARDENS
              T. C. Q. L.
        Weight Total 4. 13. 2. 8.   The gift of EDWD. CLARKE.
```

A very old stone in front of the principal entrance to the Church, which must have been put up at the building or some subsequent restoration, contained, previous to 1860, the names of the churchwardens at the time, under which is also inscribed the words: "Thou God seest me." The names of the old churchwardens have been erased and others of a very recent date substituted.

INSCRIPTION ON THE 1st BOOK IN LARGE BLACK LETTER
WITH FINE INITIALS.

A Register of Baptisms, Marriages, and Burialls in the parrish of St. Clement Danes without Temple barr.

from the fifte of June, 1558, being the fourth and fifte yeares of the reigne of King Philip and Queene Mary.

This booke was bought when Robert Thomas and Edward Ryce, weare Churchwardens.

Being injoyned to provide the same, by the Canons sett forth in ye VIth yeare of the reigne of or Souereigne lady Elizabeth.

ST. CLEMENT DANES' CHURCH.

After the above there follows in small hand—

"And was continued by me John Morecroft, mynister in the year of grace 1598. And continewed according to ye tyme limited by him who is beyond all tyme."

On the other side of the leaf is the following Latin acrostic to Queen Elizabeth :—

Floreat alma diu princeps precer
ELIZABETHA

R	Roscida solatur rutilans ut gramina Titan	N
E	Et radio exhilerat cuneta elementa suo	O
G	Grata velut nutrix sic Anglis numina prebes	S
I	Judith nostra (Deo preside) clara viget	T
N	Nobilis hæc valeat in scæna hæc femina semper	R
A	Ac nectar gratu libet in ætherea	A

ANGLIÆ.

One of the earliest entries of baptism is the following :—

"June 6, 1563.—Master Robert Cicill (Sic) the sonn of ye L. highe Threasurer of England."

A passage in "Stow's Survey of the Cities of London and Westminster," published in 1633, is interesting, in reference to this entry, and also to the state of the streets round the former church :—

"Here, about this Church, and in the parts adjoining, were frequent disturbances, by reason of the unthrifts of the Inns of Chancery, who were so unruly a nights, walking about to the disturbance and danger of such as passed along the streets, that the inhabitants were fain to keep watches. In the year 1582 the Recorder himself with six more of the honest inhabitants stood by St. Clement's Church to see the lanthorn hanging out, and to observe if he could meet with any of these outrageous dealers. About seven at night they saw young Mr. Robert Cecil, the Lord Treasurer's Son (who was after Secretary of State to the Queen) pass by the Church, and as he passed gave them a civil salute, at which they said, ' Lo ! you may see how a nobleman's son can use himself, and how he putteth off his cap to poor men. Our Lord bless him !' This passage the Recorder wrote in a letter to his father, adding, ' Your Lordship hath cause to thank God for so vertuous a child.' This 'child' rose to as high favour with the Queen as his father, Elizabeth's minister. As Sir Robert Cecil he sat for the City of Westminster in Parliament, became Secretary of State in 1596, and Prime Minister in 1599. Upon the decease of the Queen it was he who rode to Scotland to inform James I. of his succession. He was made by the latter monarch Viscount Cranbourne in 1604 and Earl of Salisbury in 1605, and he succeeded Sir Thomas Sackville as Lord High Treasurer in 1608. He died worn out with application to public business in 1612."

The parish registers, beginning thus in 1558, are continued in folio volumes up to the present date. They are kept in an iron safe in the vestry, and are in excellent preservation, much better than in most parishes. It is curious to observe the great variety of handwriting which takes place in the 300 years as the pen dropped from one hand after another. The style in the oldest book (a hundred and twenty years anterior to the present Church), that of "Francis Morecroft, Mynister," is very distinct and regular, rather like the print of the present day; but from 1602 to 1614 the old character, illegible to inexperienced eyes, succeeds, which again gradually gives way to the present italic letters. The names also are often very quaint in the early books. Such female Christian names as "Syrophenissa," "Venus," "Sapio," "Cicely," are gone out now, although, on the whole, appellations have not changed much, and we are startled by seeing on one page, among the baptisms, in 1567, the familiar names of "Richard Cobden," and "John Bright."

Bishop Berkely, celebrated by Pope as having "every virtue under heaven," was buried here; as also the poet Otway, interred under the Church, in 1685. Dr. Kitchener; — Oxberry, Sen.; and W. H. Oxberry were also buried here; Powell, of Lincoln's Inn, was buried here in 1714. From the burial register:—"1611, Sept. 2. Wm. Ewins, Esquier, from Boswell House." The last burials at this Church, according to the register, were those of Emma Young, of 20, Vere Street, and Susannah Buckland, of 11, Denzell Street, both dated June 19th 1853.

The vaults underneath the Church were much crowded with dead. Upwards of seventy years ago they were discovered to be on fire, and continued burning for some days, many bodies being destroyed. After the Order in Council for closing the vaults and burial grounds was received by the parish, in 1858, the coffins (many of which were very costly) were placed in one part of the vault, which was filled in, and the whole enclosed by a brick wall, at a cost to the parish of about £300. Many persons of distinction have been buried here. One gentleman, an Admiral, gave £250 for the privilege of having a small portion of the vault set apart for the members of his family, when deceased, about two years only before the closing of the vaults.

The St. Clement to whom the old Church was dedicated, is supposed to have been that St. Clement, a disciple of St. Peter's, who was the Christian Bishop of Rome about A.D. 73 ; and who suffered martyrdom A.D. 100. The word "Danes," is said to have been added because in the days of Canute and his immediate successors, it belonged to the Danes, who formed quite a colony in this neighbourhood. Many of their nobles found a last resting-place within its walls, not the least notable among whom was Harold, the eldest son and successor of Canute. He died at Oxford, and was first buried at Westminster, but after some few months the body was disinterred, beheaded, and thrown into the Thames, by order of Hardicanute, his half-brother and successor. It was subsequently recovered by some fishermen, and was re-interred within the Church in 1040. The Church was afterwards given by King Henry II. to the Knights Templars, and was finally included within the Liberty of the Duchy of Lancaster. The building was repaired in 1608, and again in 1633; but being much decayed, was pulled down in the year 1680, and the present noble edifice erected on the site.

On the side of the churchyard facing Temple Bar, a stone-built house may be seen, looking like a burial vault above ground, which an inscription informs us was erected in 1839, to prevent people using a pump that the inhabitants had put up in 1807 over a remarkable well, which is 191 feet deep with 150 feet of water in it. Perhaps this may be the "holy well" of bygone days, that gave the name to a street adjoining, once noted for old pictures, old clothes, and old books— a place that is fast going to decay.

King Henry IV., by his charter dated at Westminster on the 7th June, in the 7th year of his reign, granted to "Robert Palmer, Parson of the Church of St. Clement without Temple Bar, a certain void place adjoining the burial ground of the said church, containing towards the north in length 200 feet of land, and in width 24 feet at

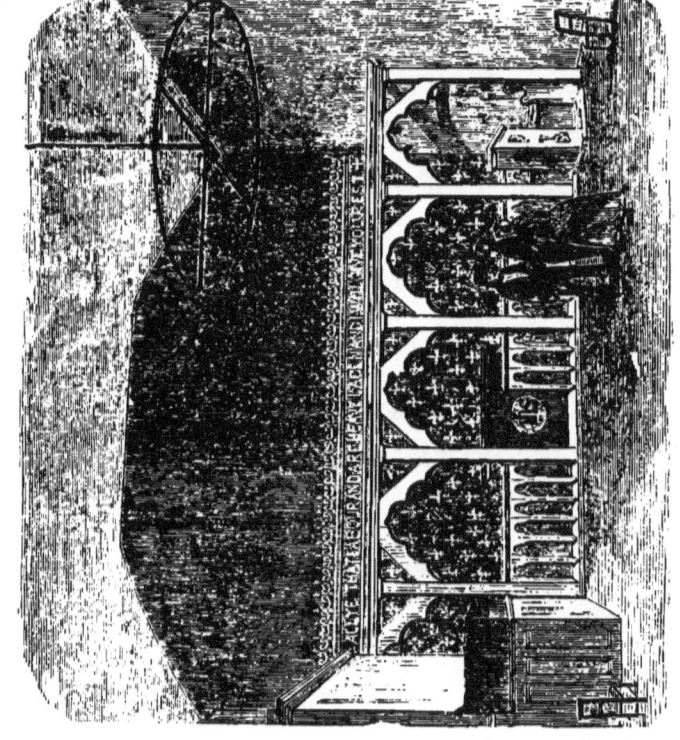

CLARE MARKET CHAPEL, Formerly Enon Chapel, afterwards converted to a Concert Room, Casino, Prize Fighting King, Penny Theatre, &c.; it is now well known as Clare Market Chapel.

the head towards the west, and 20 feet at the head towards the east, with license to enclose and build upon the same place, and the same so enclosed and built upon to hold to him and his heirs of the Lord the King; rendering, therefore, 2s. per annum for all manner of services: to hold the same in aid of the sustentation of a certain lamp before the Image of the Holy Trinity, in the church aforesaid, to be burning day and night; and in aid of other things for the use of the said church, according to the judgment of the keeper of the said church for the time being." This property cannot now be identified, and is consequently lost to the parish. It must have been about where the railway booking-office now stands, or where the street now is. The charter is enrolled among the charters of the period, and was accidentally discovered about five years ago.

THE ESSEX STREET CHAPEL.

THIS building, which was formerly an Auction Room, was planned and erected under the personal superintendance of a Mrs. Lindsey, of Richmond, Yorkshire, the wife of a Church of England minister; a lady who in her lifetime was well-known and highly esteemed for her energy and benevolence. It is almost unnecessary to state that it is supported by those professing Unitarian principles. The Rev. Mr. LINDSEY and the Rev. THOMAS BELSHAM were the former resident chaplains. The present minister is the Rev. J. P. HAM.

CLARE MARKET CHAPEL.

THE Parish of St. Clement Danes contains a population of about 14,000; and the Clare Market District consisting of upwards of 6,000 poor people, the necessity of the above Chapel can be well conceived. We are glad to find it continues to receive the liberal support of W. H. Smith, Esq.; Sir R. Palmer; Messrs. Twining; J. G. Stilwell, Esq.; Messrs. Essex; and a large number of ladies and gentlemen who take an interest in the Clare Market Mission.

The Rev. F. ROSE is the clergyman appointed, whose stipend

is partly paid from the Bishop of London's Fund, to whom the Chapel is leased, and partly by the Additional Curates' Society; the remainder, together with all other expenses connected with the Mission, is supplied by voluntary contributions. The seats in the Chapel are all free, likewise the schools, classes, &c., which are as follows:—Celebration of Holy Communion every Sunday at 9 a.m.; services 11 a.m. and 7 p.m.; school 3 p.m. Wednesday, Service 7 p.m. Day and Evening Schools. Bible Classes. Mothers' Meetings. Sewing School for Girls. Choristers meet every Saturday evening for practice.

TEMPERANCE HALL, PORTUGAL STREET.

SUNDAY ......Temperance Meeting for Religious Purposes.
MONDAY ......Friends of Labour.
TUESDAY ......Mrs. Stilwell's Mothers' Meeting; Band of Hope; Building Society; Temperance Meeting.
WEDNESDAY...Lady Radstock's Mothers' Meeting.
THURSDAY ...Temperance Meeting.
FRIDAY.........Prayer Meeting.
SATURDAY ...Benefit Society and Penny Savings' Bank.

The St. Clement Danes' Christian Total Abstinence Society is also held here, presided over by R. MOSELEY, Esq.

Many persons might pass up and down Portugal Street, and hardly notice the unpretending little building to which the above title has reference; but as has been stated by the Rev. R. H. KILLICK, a great work goes on there by means of Miss TWINING's energy and experience. The poor are well acquainted with the little building in question, and many have been dragged out of the mire of sin and misery, and helped into habits of temperance and thriftiness, through the unwearied zeal and gentle persuasion of that beneficent lady.

St. Clement Danes' Charities.

ALMER'S CHARITY, by will dated 1726, gave £500 for the benefit of twelve poor widows (housekeepers): the money is laid out in property in West Street, and produces £8 10s. 10d. for each, who receive it yearly on Lady Day.

LADY MIDDLETON (in 1690) left £200; Lady Bridgman (in 1694) £200; William Lawrence (in 1696) £300; Richard Shalmer (in 1698) £200—making a total of £900.

The monies derived from the four donors last named were laid out in the purchase of two houses on the north side of Saint Clement's Churchyard. Those houses were sold to the City of London under the provisions of various Acts of Parliament passed in and after 1793, for the improvement of the approaches to Temple Bar. The money received from the City was invested in the purchase of £1,797 15s. 4d. Three per cent. Consols, in the name of the Accountant-General of the Court of Chancery, to the credit of an account "Ex parte the Parish of St. Clement Danes." The dividends, amounting to £53 18s. 8d., are received by the trustees yearly. They have, from time to time, been apportioned agreeably to a recommendation of a committee appointed by vestry in the year 1816, and now amount (but varying with the rate of property tax) as follows:—

	£	s.	d.
To the Charities of Ladies Middleton and Bridgman ...	25	5	0
To that of William Lawrence	17	4	2
To that of Richard Shalmer	7	17	6
	£50	6	8

ST. CLEMENT DANES' CHARITIES.

The yearly sum of £25 5s., appropriated to the Charities of Ladies Middleton and Bridgman, is paid to the churchwardens, who distribute half on New Year's Day and half on Good Friday. Twenty-eight poor and deserving widows of the parish receive on each of these days sums of 8s. each, and one 8s. 6d.; 20s. are paid to the minister for preaching a sermon on New Year's Day, and another 20s. for preaching a sermon on Good Friday, of which a register is kept.

The sum of £17 4s. 2d., in respect of William Lawrence's gift, is given by the churchwardens on New Year's Day to poor and deserving housekeepers residing in that part of the parish which is in Westminster, in sums varying from 5s. to 2s. 6d., but subject to the payment of 6s. 8d. to the vestry clerk for reading the will of the donor on New Year's Day, and keeping the register of the Charities, and 20s. to the minister for a sermon.

The sum of £7 17s. 6d., in respect of Shalmer's gift, is carried to the overseers' general account for distribution amongst the poor at Christmas.

PETER WRAXALL, in 1663, gave £50 that "twenty poor widows or other poor people, not exceeding in the whole twenty in number, then being and from time to time thereafter to be, inhabitants of the said parish, might, every year, yearly for ever, receive and take of the churchwardens for the time being, upon every Christmas Eve at the church porch, the sum of £3, to be equally divided amongst the said twenty poor people, as a gift of him the said Peter Wraxall."

ANN WEBB, in 1807, left £25 to the little children chimney sweepers of St. Clement's, and also St. Dunstan's-in-the-West, the yearly income from which was to be spent on Christmas Day, as she had always on that day given them a treat. The stock (which was reduced by payment of legacy duty) now amounts to £38 9s. 4d. The small dividend is received by the churchwardens from the Accountant-General of the Court of Chancery annually, and since the abolition by statute of climbing boys as sweeps, has been distributed in money or tea amongst the inmates of the old parish almshouses.

ST. CLEMENT DANES' CHARITIES.

MUDFORD, date of will unknown, gave £3 per annum to be distributed to eight poor widows residing in Milford Lane, in sums of 5s. each; and 20s. to the minister for preaching a sermon on Good Friday.

RUPERTIA HILL, in 1818, left £400 Three per cent. Consols: To the clergyman who preaches the sermons in the parish church on Good Fridays and Christmas Days, £2 2s.; to the curate, for reading prayers, 10s. 6d.; to the clerk, 5s.; to the sexton and pew openers, amongst them, 7s. 6d., and the residue to the churchwardens, who first defray thereout the incidental expenses of lighting the Church upon those occasions, and distribute the balance annually amongst the deserving poor of the parish not receiving parochial relief.

RICHARD BEDDOE, of St. Clement Danes, by will, dated 3rd July, 1603, bequeathed to the churchwardens and feoffees of the said parish for the time being, for the maintenance of the poor of the said parish for ever, so many of his tenements as did then go for £20 per annum. He also bequeathed for the maintenance of the poor of the parish £100, to be lent to poor householders and young beginners, for two years a-piece, gratis, putting in good security to the feoffees and churchwardens for the time being. The £100 for loans to poor housekeepers appears to be lost. The overseers distribute the residue.

THE ALMSHOUSES* belonging to this parish are situate at the back of the Vestry Hall, entered by an iron gate from the "Foregate," or Clement's Lane. An inscription on the front reads:—

"These almshouses were repaired at the expense of the parish in the year 1850; William Webb Ellis, M.A., Rector; David Spencer, Robert Makin Bates, churchwardens; William Nex, Joseph Little, Charles Colwill, Robert Child, overseers."

DUCKETT'S CHARITY.—The parish is entitled, under the will of Isaac Duckett, who died 1620, to a moiety of the rents of a house

---

* In addition to these, there are some almshouses recently erected by the parish at Tooting, Surrey, consisting of 40 houses built in an elegant and most substantial manner, with a chapel and committee room, baths and washhouses; the supply of water is abundant from a fountain and artesian well. These are available for the reception of 40 poor persons, 20 of whom must be spinsters, or widows not less than 50 years of age, and the other 20 males of not less than 60 years of age. The male inmates must have been householders of the parish for five years, and the females must have been householders, or the widows or daughters of householders, for a like period. Official manager, W. Raimondi, Esq. The income for the year 1867 amounted to £4,000 from the Holborn Estate Charity.

and lands in the parish of Crayford, in the county of Kent, the house producing £20 per annum; and the lands held by Mr. Colyer for twenty-one years, at a rental of £52 per annum. The rents are to be divided equally between four maid-servants, two of the parish of St. Andrew, Holborn, and two of the parish of St. Clement Danes, at their marriage, upon certificate from their masters of their having faithfully served and inhabited with one master or mistress five years consecutively. The charity has derived a material accession of income during the past nine years by royalties on brick earth dug from a portion of the land on lease to Mr. Colyer, the proportion of St. Clement Danes now amounting to £2,500 stock.

JOHN SHAW, in 1649, left in trust to be distributed by ten discreet and honest men yearly for ever amongst the poor the rental of a small piece of ground on the east side of Addle Hill, near Thames Street, whereon a blacksmith's forge was erected, and produced £30 per annum. This charity property has since been taken by the Metropolitan Board of Works for public improvements in the city, and the purchase-money invested in the like trust.

There is also received from the following Charities, dividends, &c., as under:—

Stock purchased from sale of houses in Holywell Street and Butcher's Row, £31; Read's Charity, paid by Sadlers' Company (yearly), £1; Vale and Bissell's Charity, out of the Dog Tavern, Holywell Street (yearly), 10s.; Warner's Charity, out of 220, Strand (yearly), 13s. 4d.; Jacob's Charity, paid by Vintners' Company (yearly), £4; Price's Charity, out of house, Strand, £2 14s.; Blackhouse's Charity, out of house, 280, Strand, £1; Foster's Charity, out of house, 161, Strand, £1; Earl of Salisbury, £8; Hester Wright (biennially), £1 4s.: total, £51 1s. 4d.

This, together with the amount received from Beddoe and Shaw's Charities, is received by the overseers, and is annually expended by them in the purchase of coals, bread, and tea, which are given away by means of tickets at Christmas amongst the most deserving poor of the parish.

HENRY RUSSELL, in 1639, gave to the poor for ever £100 for their use, but there is no account of it extant.

LOST CHARITIES (ALL YEARLY).—Herman Price, date unknown, 13s. 4d.; Shoren, 1625, £1; Holford, 1659, £1; Lowman, 1661, 15s.

In 1786 a person of the name of DENNIE gave £200 to the poor, which also appears to be lost, likewise a sum of £60 given by the Duke of NORTHUMBERLAND. Several bequests of money to the parish, to be lent from time to time to poor tradesmen and young beginners, cannot now be found, and must have been lost from the insufficiency of securities or other causes.

ST. CLEMENT DANES' HOLBORN ESTATE CHARITY.

THIS Estate was, in 1552, purchased of one William Breton, in consideration of £160 paid him by the churchwardens of St. Clement Danes. It then consisted of twelve messuages and a void piece of ground, with a cottage and a tenement called the Slaughter House, and was conveyed to trustees to the intent that they should yearly pay the income to the churchwardens of the parish for the time being, to be distributed in alms amongst twelve poor parishioners, who had dwelt in the parish for twelve years and were of honest fame and opinion; the stipends were payable weekly or monthly, as should seem best by the discretion, consent and oversight of twelve honest, good, and decent parishioners, who had formerly borne the office of churchwardens of the parish. In the year 1647 the income of the Charity had so increased that the churchwardens were enabled to distribute it amongst the poor of the parish generally, who had been parishioners twelve years. The rental of this estate subsequently increased to such an extent, that in the year 1844 a scheme was settled by the Court of Chancery, directing the application thereof as follows:—

£300 for Parochial Schools, and £800 for Building ditto, when required.

£1,500 to be expended in building Infant Schools, Milford Lane, which were in 1851 erected on the site of the old Rectory-house: this property is held upon a lease for 99 years, from Christmas, 1850, at a rent of £27 13s. 4d. per annum, payable to the Rector. The School was opened 7th March, 1853. The other Infant School was subsequently erected in Houghton Street, and opened 4th August, 1862. £400 is allowed per annum for the support of these Schools.

ST. CLEMENT DANES' CHARITIES.

£300 is given to Kings' College Hospital, provided the Hospital receive all of the sick poor parishioners who are sent by the managers.

£100 is given to the Public Dispensary in Carey Street.

£50 to the Society for Relief of Lying-in Women.

£100 to the District Visiting Society.

£600 per annum is allowed for the support of the Grammar Schools, and £200 for the support of the Middle Class Girls' School.

In 1849 a large amount of money was expended by the managers in the purchase of eight acres of land, in Garrett Lane, Tooting, whereon they erected Forty Almshouses, with a Chapel, Committee Rooms, Baths and Laundry. In these almshouses forty poor persons, of whom twenty are females, not less than fifty years of age, and twenty are males, not less than sixty years of age, and who have been householders assessed to the poor-rates of the parish for five years, or widows or daughters of such persons, reside; the stipends of the inmates of these almshouses are £30 per annum for each inmate. In working the scheme with respect to these almshouses, the managers found that on the death of a married almsman, they were compelled to expel his widow from these almshouses, as the scheme provides that twenty of the almspeople must be males and twenty females; in order, therefore, to afford some relief to the widows of the almsmen, the managers determined to apply to the Court for the withdrawal of the sum of £200 per annum, which had been set apart by the original scheme for apprentice fees, and to apply annually out of the income of the Charity a sum not exceeding £100 per annum in payment of pensions to the widows of deceased almsmen. Several of these pensions are now received by the widows.

In the year 1860 the managers purchased the old Peacock Inn, and some houses in Houghton Street and New Inn Passage, on the site of which they erected the Grammar Schools, with Master's residence; a Middle Class Girls' School and an Infant School, with a residence for a Mistress to each of the latter; and also the Board Room and offices for the use of the managers. These schools were opened on the 4th August, 1862, and are now in full operation.

The property belonging to the Charity consists of freehold land and houses situate as follows, viz.: the southern boundary extends along the north side of High Holborn, from a mark in the footway pavement in front of the house No. 110, High Holborn, which is the south-western corner of the estate, to another mark at the south-eastern end of the house or shop No. 77, High Holborn, which is the south-eastern corner of the estate; the eastern boundary extends from the mark along the eastern side of the premises to a mark at the north-eastern end of the same premises, which is the north-eastern corner of the estate; the northern boundary is formed by an irregular line extending from the mark at the north-eastern corner of the estate, along the back of some of the houses in Eagle Street, to the north-western corner of the estate, where there are two marks; and the western side of the estate extends from that corner in nearly a straight line to the mark in front of the house No. 110, High Holborn.

On the site is erected the premises of the great blacking manufacturers, Messrs. Day and Martin, the cost of which was £12,000; and the Amphitheatre, the cost of which was £8,000.

ABSTRACT OF THE ACCOUNT OF THE MANAGERS OF
THE St. CLEMENT DANES' HOLBORN ESTATE CHARITY,
For the Year ending May 31st, 1867.

Dr.	£	s.	d.	Cr.	£	s.	d.
To Balance on 1st June, 1866	58	1	8	By Annual Donations	850	0	0
,, Rent from Trustees	4,122	14	10	,, Alms-Houses	1,670	9	6
,, Dividend on Accumulation Fund	31	10	7	,, Grammar School	1,013	3	4
				,, Middle Class Girls' School	241	1	5
,, Return of Income and Property Tax	74	6	7	,, Infant School, Houghton St.	159	4	3
				,, Ditto ditto, Milford Lane	173	14	7
,, Rent of Alms-Houses Field	13	8	6	,, Apprentice Fees	20	0	0
,, Grammar School Fees	367	5	0	,, Accumulation Fund	31	10	7
,, Middle Class Girls' ditto	172	0	0	,, Legal Expenses	148	7	8
				,, General Disbursements	471	2	0
				,, Balance	60	13	10
	£4,839	7	2		£4,839	7	2

Certified 11*th June*, 1867. W. RAIMONDI.

Audited 7*th June*, 1867, { S. H. TWINING, *Chairman.*
HENRY MASON.
GEO. ROSE INNES.

The Vestry Clerk (Mr. J. F. ISAACSON) has, for sixteen years, been the Receiver and Solicitor of the Charity Estate.

ST. CLEMENT DANES' BENEVOLENT PENSION SOCIETY.

This Society was instituted January 5th, 1835, for the relief of decayed housekeepers of the parish, by monthly pensions of twenty shillings, and was established at the late Mr. JAQUET's, of Clare Court, the Committee meeting by permission of the churchwardens, at the Vestry, the first Wednesday in every month. There are eight pensioners at the present time, seven of whom receive twenty shillings and one ten shillings, which is paid them by Mr. CROSSLEY, at his house, every month. The funded property of the Society is £1,500, the interest of which, together with the annual subscriptions of £30, being the total income. R. TWINING, Esq. kindly acts as Treasurer.

THE PEST HOUSE FIELD CHARITY.

This Charity was given conjointly to the parishes of St. Clement Danes, St. Martin's-in-the-Fields (with St. George, Hanover Square),* St. James, Westminster, and St. Paul, Covent Garden, by William, Earl of CRAVEN, in 1687, in consequence of the Great Plague, which began at the top of Drury Lane, in the winter of 1664, and continued to ravage London till July, 1666, as many as 12,000 persons dying in one week. De Foe declares that 100,000 perished. This was immediately followed by the Great Fire of London, which lasted four days and nights, and consumed 400 streets, 13,200 houses, St. Paul's Cathedral, eighty-nine churches, numerous chapels, and four of the City gates. The total loss of property was nearly ten millions.

The object of the Charity was to provide an hospital to give relief to the poor of the above four London parishes, suffering from contagious disorders. The present scheme for the management and application of the income was approved by an Order of the Court

---

* Only one-fourth of the Charity goes to St. Martin's and St. George's, in consequence of St. George's formerly being part of St. Martin's.

of Chancery, dated the 30th day of May, 1864, made in the cause of "Attorney-General *v.* Earl of Craven," and requires the management to be under the control of twenty-one trustees, elected from the above parishes, the incumbent from each parish being included. The scheme also provides that the income of the Charity (which is likewise in accordance with the recommendation of the Master of the Rolls), be paid to the Governors of King's College Hospital upon the following conditions :—That

> They shall set apart twenty-four beds for in-patients, sent by the Trustees of the Craven Charity; also shall receive and supply with advice and medicine, as out-patients, all poor persons, resident in the said several parishes, who shall be sent by the Trustees.

> All in-patients requiring surgical or medical aid, and being fit cases for hospital treatment, shall be received indiscriminately, whether suffering from contagious or infectious disorders or not (small-pox alone being excepted) and shall be treated, in all respects, in the same manner as the other patients received into the hospital.

During the year 1866, 256 patients had been received from the various parishes interested in the Craven Charity. The trustees of the Charity have appointed certain members of their body to visit the hospital once a month, and the committee of the hospital continue to receive the most gratifying assurances of the great satisfaction of the trustees with the care and attention bestowed upon the patients during their residence within the walls of the hospital. The amount received from the Charity in 1866 was £354 10s. 10d.

While the estate was in the hands of the Craven representatives, they, considering that the Charity was not a subsisting trust, let the Charity lands upon building leases, inserting a clause in such leases that if the Plague should return to either of the four parishes the tenants were to vacate their houses so as to allow the infected parishioners to be sheltered therein. When the present leases run out—about seventy years hence—the yearly income will be nearly £5,000, adequate to the formation of a great institution. At present the value of the "Pest House Estate" is as follows :—

ST. CLEMENT DANES' CHARITIES.

Situation of Property.	Rent now being paid for Occupation of the Buildings.			Ground Rent receivable by the Charity.			Term of Building Lease.
	£	s.	d.	£	s.	d.	
Lease No. 1.							
No. 14, Craven Hill	150	0	0	42	0	0	90 years from March 25, 1844.
,, 16, ,, ,,	150	0	0	42	0	0	
Lease No. 2.							
,, 18, Craven Hill	180	0	0	38	0	0	87 years from March 25, 1847.
,, 20, ,, ,,	180	0	0	5	0	0	
,, 22, ,, ,,	180	0	0	5	0	0	
Lease No. 3.							
,, 6, Craven Mews	40	0	0	6	10	0	83 years from March 25, 1851.
,, 7, ,, ,,	40	0	0	6	10	0	
,, 8, ,, ,,	40	0	0	6	10	0	
,, 9, ,, ,,	40	0	0	6	10	0	
,, 10, ,, ,,	40	0	0	6	10	0	
,, 11, ,, ,,	40	0	0	6	10	0	
,, 12, ,, ,,	40	0	0	6	10	0	
Lease No. 4.							
,, 30, Craven Hill Gardens	210	0	0	27	4	0	83 years from March 25, 1852.
,, 31, ,, ,, ,,	240	0	0	5	0	0	
,, 32, ,, ,, ,,	220	0	0	5	0	0	
,, 33, ,, ,, ,,	240	0	0	5	0	0	
,, 34, ,, ,, ,,	240	0	0	5	0	0	
,, 35, ,, ,, ,,	240	0	0	5	0	0	
,, 36, ,, ,, ,,	145	0	0	7	0	0	
,, 37, ,, ,, ,,	160	0	0	7	0	0	
,, 38, ,, ,, ,,	170	0	0	21	0	0	
,, 39, ,, ,, ,,	160	0	0	7	0	0	
,, 40, ,, ,, ,,	155	0	0	7	0	0	
,, 41, ,, ,, ,,	145	0	0	7	0	0	
,, 42, ,, ,, ,,	180	0	0	30	0	0	
,, 43, ,, ,, ,,	190	0	0	30	0	0	
Lease No. 5.							
Craven Hill Lodge	54	19	5	54	19	5	Held on Lease of which 21 years is unexpired.
Total £	3869	19	5	400	13	5	

A division of the parish of St James's, of 25 acres, has a population averaging 432 persons to the acre !!!—the most dense spot of all London. A division of St. Martin's-in-the-Fields, of 42 acres, has a population yielding an average of 287 to the acre. St. Clement Danes' parish, 54 acres, gives also 287 persons to the acre. This degree of density of population may be judged of when it is stated that the most crowded district of St. George's, Hanover Square, has but 95 to the acre, whilst of all London it is only 30.

ST. CLEMENT DANES' CHARITY SCHOOLS.

The Parochial School of St. Clement Danes is one of the earliest established on the principles first promulgated by the "Society for Promoting Christian Knowledge," and from the year 1700 to the present time the Institution has been an object of unceasing interest and utility to the inhabitants of the Parish.

The trustees, in the year 1778, introduced a new and important feature by the admission of eight girls into the school (as many as the funds would then permit), there to be wholly lodged, maintained, clothed, and educated, till they attained an age which fitted them for servitude. The number has since been increased to thirty.

In the other department, seventy boys are admitted, to be entirely clothed, instructed in the principles of the Christian religion, and taught reading, writing, arithmetic, geography, &c., that when of proper age, if of deserving character, they may be placed out as apprentices, or engaged in some useful employment.

With a view to promote a wholesome feeling of self-dependence both in parents and children, a weekly payment has been imposed recently of two-pence for every child attending the schools, except in cases where more than one child of the same family attends, when an extra penny is levied for every additional child.

KING'S COLLEGE HOSPITAL.

This Hospital was established in 1839, and is situate in Portugal Street; and lying as it does between Holborn and the Strand, it is in the midst of a densely crowded district. It is entirely dependent upon voluntary subscriptions and legacies. The entire cost of conducting the Hospital cannot be estimated at less than £10,000 per annum. The annual subscriptions, we regret to say, do not amount to more than £2,000; and the total income from all sources last year amounted to only £6,882 2s. 7d.

The Hospital receives liberal local support from the legal profession, Holborn Estate and Pest House Charities, also from a number of the most influential inhabitants of the parish.

Since the opening of the Hospital there have been 36,697 in-patients, and 657,131 out-patients, making a total of 693,828. About 2,000 in-patients are admitted every year, and nearly 40,000 out-patients receive advice and medicine. In addition to the best medical and surgical skill, the patients have the benefit of the services of the sisters and nurses of St. John's House, this Hospital having been the first in London to recognize the advantages of the improved system of nursing afforded by that Institution. Ten beds are set apart, under the auspices of Miss NIGHTINGALE, and at the charge of the Nightingale Fund, for the reception of poor married women, of whom 148 were confined within the Hospital in 1866; and thus, in addition to the direct benefit conferred upon the poor, midwife-nurses are, by this means, specially trained for the important object of attending married women at their own homes, under the direction of medical men. A most important addition to the usefulness of the Hospital was made last year by the opening of a special ward for the diseases of young children, which was founded by Mr. PETER PANTIA RALLI, in memory of his deceased father, for which purpose he contributed the munificent donation of £6,000. The ward was opened on the 5th of October, and contains ten beds.

This noble institution affords much relief to the neighbourhood. The patients are attended by the most eminent members of the medical profession, and nurses are provided to administer to every want; surgeons are in constant readiness to give immediate attention to cases of accident or emergency, the doors being open night and day. We regret to find the Hospital is so much in need of support. The Secretary, Mr. JAMES S. BLYTH, will thankfully receive subscriptions.

ANCIENT HOSPITALS.—The earliest Hospitals were probably nothing more than houses on the roadside, at which the chance traveller might obtain refreshment. Of this original design some traces were preserved until a late period. For instance, in the Hospital of St. Cross, near Winchester, the porter is still furnished, according to statute, with a certain quantity of bread and beer, of which any traveller who knocks at the lodge and calls for relief is entitled to partake gratis. At the time of HENRY VIII. the number of these hospitals mentioned are 387.

LIFE AND TIMES OF JOE MILLER.

THE ground on which the King's College Hospital now stands was formerly one of the burial-grounds of the parish.

One of the most remarkable persons interred in this burial-ground was the celebrated JOE MILLER, the actor, and father (by repute) of all modern jokes. He died of pleurisy, in the year 1738, and was buried under part of the site of the present Hospital. A modest stone was erected by his friends over the spot, and the epitaph written by STEPHEN DUCK, the thresher poet of Charlton, was engraved thereon, a copy of which is here given :—

JOE MILLER'S TOMBSTONE.

" Here lie the remains of honest JOE MILLER, who was
A tender husband, a sincere friend,
A facetious companion, and an excellent comedian.
He departed this life the 15th day of August, 1738, aged 54 years."

"If humor, wit, and honesty could save
The humorous, witty, honest from the grave,
His grave had not so soon its tenant found,
With honesty and wit, and humor crown'd.
Or, could esteem and love preserve our health,
And guard us longer from the stroke of death ;
The stroke of death on him had later fell,
Whom all mankind esteemed and loved so well."

Time, the devourer of all things, gradually gnawed and crumbled away the stone, and rendered the epitaph almost illegible, when Mr. JARVIS BUCK, one of the churchwardens of St. Clement Danes, in 1816 had a new stone, engraved with the above epitaph, &c., placed over the grave of the illustrious Joe, which stone may still be seen (though the grave has been swept away by improving time), in the King's College Hospital.

A few remarks on the life of the renowned Joe Miller, of facetious memory, may not be uninteresting to the rising generation. All that is known of his birth is, that he was born about the year 1684, but who or what were his parents, or where they resided, there is nothing left on record to enlighten us. His education appears to have been very scant, if any, for it is said that he took a wife to have somebody to read his parts to him. How he came to take to the stage is all conjecture, but when princes and other quality visited Bartelmy Fair, Smithfield, as was the case in the beginning of the 18th century, perhaps Joe's bold voice got him the trumpet part in front of some booth, to invite and coax in an audience to see the many wonders, or to remind the people that they "Could tumble up and have the fun of the fair all for one penny—babbies half price, and old ladies for nothing!" There was no disparagement in all this to Joe, for Thespis mounted a cart, and Kean played tumbler and harlequin before Richardson's Show.

The first appearance of Joe Miller on the London boards seems to have taken place on Saturday, April 30th, 1715, when he played at Drury Lane the part of Young Clincher, in Farquhar's comedy of "The Constant Couple; or a Trip to Jubilee," for the benefit of Bowen the actor; and on the following Saturday night, May 7th, Joe and a Mrs. Cox had a benefit, when he acted the part of Old Wilful, in Cibber's comedy of the "Double Gallant; or, the Sick Lady's Cure."

Joe soon after this took his stand as a useful actor—his talents lying among heavy fathers, countrymen, and idiots; he also played broken French and Irish parts. His salary attests his merit, which began at three and rose to five guineas per week—not very bad pay in those days, considering all things. On April 25th, 1717, Joe had a benefit all to himself, a venture for any one, as it oftener led to the Fleet than to fortune. He got Hogarth (then a young artist unknown to fame) to engrave the card-plate of admission; it was a scene taken from Congreve's comedy of the "Old Bachelor," the play chosen by Joe for the occasion, and in which he performed the part of Sir Joseph Whittol. When one of the cards was shown to Spiller, the comedian, he was so pleased with it, that he exclaimed, "That's the Ticket!"—a phrase which has been in use ever since when anything is produced which is exactly the thing required.

In 1736, Dodsley brought out his farce of "The King and the

Miller of Mansfield," and Joe had the part of the Miller assigned to him. This piece is the parent of "Charles II.; or, the Merry Monarch," and of "Cramond Brig." But the favourite character of Joe was Teague, in "The Committee; or, the Faithful Irishman," though he played many other parts equally well, and was considered a most respectable actor in his line of business.

Although Joe was a comedian, his style belonged to the jocoserioso school,—

"Ex gravita fecit fun,
Till the tears, thro' laughing run ;"

for his face was of the most imperturbable mould, full of gravity and solemnity, and evidently not intended for laughter in itself, though it was admirably adapted to cause laughter in others. In private life he was the dullest of the dull, scarcely ever speaking; and his friend Mottley, a merry wag of the time, used to poke fun at him and make him his butt whenever opportunity offered, which Joe took all in good part, for there was a kindly nature in him, even in his stolidity.

At the Old Black Jack Tavern, in Portsmouth Street, Lincoln's Inn Fields, the actors and dramatists of those days were wont to assemble, and here Joe used to pass his evenings, puffing away at his pipe in solemn silence, and communing with his own thoughts, if he had any; but Mottley declared that Joe had only one idea—and that was a wrong one.

This Black Jack Tavern was once a very noted house, and even is now much frequented by those sons of Galen, the students of King's College Hospital. For many years it was called the "Jump," because the notorious Jack Sheppard, being in the house and sought for by Bow-street officers, leaped out of the first-floor window and got clear off. In one of the attics is a sort of false chimney, where gentlemen in difficulties were often secreted till arrangements could be made with their creditors. As to the sign "Black Jack," that was taken from a leathern drinking-vessel formerly much in use and often covered with pitch, and thus called a pitcher; such were the drinking cups preceding the use of pewter pots.

As Joe was of a taciturn and saturnine disposition, his boon companions were for ever quizzing him, or making him their laughing stock, so that when anything droll or funny was said, it was instantly declared to be Joe Miller's, with — "That's another Joe Miller!" though Joe never made but one joke in the whole course of his life, and that was as he was sitting one day near the window at the Sun Tavern, in Clare Street, Clare Market, a fishwoman and her girl passing by, the woman cried her fish, saying—"Buy my soles, buy my maids!" "Ah! you wicked old creature," exclaimed honest Joe; "what! are you not content to sell your own soul, but you must sell your maid's also?"

And Joe was quite as poetical as he was witty, for he has only left us one solitary distich, viz.—

"The only Comedian now that dare
Vie with the world, and challenge the fair;"

referring, no doubt, to Bartelmy Fair, for Joe cannot surely mean the ladies fair, who, Dr. Johnson says, are only captivated through the ears; and Joe's loquacity was silence personified.

Although Joe was neither a jester, a poet, nor a vocalist, his solemn gravity was the cause of much fun and merriment in others, and gave rise to many a good joke and happy saying. And Jack Mottley made the most of his friend in every way, not only whilst alive, but turning him to account when dead—for he collected all the repartees and smart sayings made in the parlour of the Black Jack, purloining not a few from other collections of jokes, and in 1739 published his work as "Joe Miller's Jests; or The Wit's Vade-mecum;" and thus Joe, the jestless, has been made the father of all jests, jokes and witticisms, past, present and to come—for whenever the parentage of any funny or humorous saying is now in doubt, people exclaim at once "That's an old Joe Miller."

This first edition of "Joe Miller" contains 247 jokes. A copy of the work may be seen in the British Museum. It is so scarce now that, at a book sale, the slim octavo has been sold for £2 10s., whilst a copy of the second edition has fetched £11 5s., because it had some manuscript additions. Before the year 1740 four editions had been printed, and eleven editions by 1747, such was the great demand for this work. As to the number of editions published at the present day, that is quite unknown, but in 1846 a new "Joe Miller" came out, containing 1,286 repartees and jokes—of course, all the offspring of honest Joe of immortal fame, who will always be held in remembrance as a facetious humorist, a merry companion, and an honest fellow.

THE PUBLIC DISPENSARY.

THE object of this Institution is to relieve the poor with medicine and medical advice. Those within the limits of the following parishes or places are attended at their own habitations when requisite: viz., St. Clement Danes, St. Mary-le-Strand, the Precinct of the Savoy, St. Giles-in-the-Fields, St. Martin-in-the-Fields, St. Paul, Covent Garden, St. George, Bloomsbury, St. George the Martyr, St. Andrew, Holborn, St. Sepulchre Within, St. Bride, Bridewell Precinct, Whitefriars, St. Dunstan-in-the-West, the Liberty of the Rolls, and any other places within the circuit named. The medical officers are:— J. WATERFIELD, M.D., D. HOOPER, M.D., C. EVANS, M.D., J. WOOD, Esq. and C. KELLY, M.D.

The total number of patients relieved from 1782 (the date of the institution of the Charity), is 294,488; of which number 58,319 have been attended at their own homes. The applicants for relief amount to between 4,000 and 5,000 annually.

R. TWINING, Esq., is the treasurer, and Mr. J. S. PHILLIPS, 5, Bishop's Court, the honorary secretary.

The Dispensary will shortly be removed from Carey St. to the new premises at the corner of Holles St. and Stanhope St., Clare Market.

Dispensaries were first established in 1770, when the Royal Dispensary was founded at Shaftesbury House, Aldersgate Street.

Authorities, &c., of St. Clement Danes.
1867-68.

At the present time the Parish is under the management of the following Authorities and Officers:—Rector, two Curates, two Churchwardens, four Overseers, ten Assistants, elected under an old Act of Parliament, and forming a Board for the purpose of assisting the Overseers in making the Rates; nine Guardians, two Clerks to ditto, two Relieving Officers, twenty-four Vestrymen, who meet in Open Vestry under the "Metropolis Local Management Act," for the purpose of adjusting the Rates, electing the Members of the Board of Works, and the Officers of the Vestry; five Auditors, fifteen Members of District Board of Works, two Clerks to ditto, two Surveyors, Medical Officer of Health, three Inspectors, and one Messenger; two Collectors of Rates and Taxes, Sexton, two Registrars, two Medical Officers, Beadle, Vestry-House Keeper, and two Turncocks. For the Holborn Estate Charity:—twelve Trustees, twenty-four Managers, Treasurer, Solicitor to the Trustees and Collector of Rents, Clerk to the Managers, and Surveyor and Architect.

BOARD OF WORKS FOR THE STRAND DISTRICT.

The offices are situated at 5, Tavistock Street, Covent Garden, and were erected by the Board shortly after the passing of the "Metropolis Local Management Act," in the year 1856.

The Board of Works consists of forty-nine members, elected from the following parishes:—St. Ann's, 18; St. Clement, 15; St. Mary-le-Strand, 3; St. Paul, Covent Garden, 9; The Liberty of the Rolls, 3; Precinct of the Savoy, 1.

Mr. T. M. JENKINS, Clerk to the Board; Dr. C. EVANS, Medical Officer of Health; Mr. G. F. FRY, Surveyor.

The total expenditure of the Board for twelve months ending March 1867, was £22,311 15s. 9d.

The amounts paid to the Board by the Parish of St. Clement Danes are:—for General Expenses, £4,547 19s. 8d.; Sewer Expenses, £1,745 16s. 8d.; Main Drainage Rate, 1,195 19s. 0d.; Incidental, £1 0s. 11d.—Total, £7,490 16s. 3d.

We extract the following from the Report issued by the Board:—

ST. CLEMENT DANES IMPROVEMENT BILL.

"A company promoted a Bill in Parliament, under the title of 'The St. Clement Danes Improvement Bill,' having for its object the removal of the blocks of houses on the north side of the Strand, between St. Clement Danes' Church and St. Mary-le-Strand Church, and the erection on the site of more valuable buildings. The promoters having agreed with the Board to insert a clause in the Bill, preserving, as a minimum, the existing assessment for the rates; and also giving up gratuitously to the public, in order to widen the thoroughfare in the Strand, a strip of ground, fifteen feet wide at the east end (near St. Clement's Church), and terminating in a point at the west end (near St. Mary's Church); and also to widen Wych Street; the Board arranged with the promoters not to oppose their Bill, and the same became law."

WIDENING OF CAREY STREET.

"A favourable opportunity having arisen, by the demolition of several old houses, of widening the narrow portion of Carey Street at its junction with Chancery Lane, and the Board having, after considerable negotiations, received promises of sundry contributions from the Government, the Metropolitan Board of Works, and others, towards the said improvement, to an extent of about £17,000, entered into a contract for the purchase of the necessary property for the sum of £17,000. The cost to the District will be from £1,200 to £1,500." The Board of Works contributed £5,000 and Her Majesty's Treasury £7,000 towards the expenses of widening Carey Street.

The paving, cleansing and lighting of the Parish was, until the passing of the "Metropolis Local Management Act," performed by a Board established by the 23rd George III., cap. 89.

The first Highway Rate was made in the reign of Edward III., and the first place repaired with the money so collected was the roadway between Temple Bar and St. Giles's Church,—Wych Street, Drury Lane, &c.

THE POOR OF ST. CLEMENT DANES.

This Parish joined the Strand Union at the time the Union was declared, February 22, 1836. The amount paid by the Overseers of St. Clement Danes to the Union for maintaining the poor of their parish for the year ending Lady-day, 1867, was £12,212 15s. 10d.—the average weekly cost per head of the poor being, for provisions, necessaries and clothing, at the Workhouse, 4s. 10¼d. ; at Edmonton, 3s. 9¾d. £370 1s. 6d. was the share of expense paid by the parish for collecting the rates.

THE WORKHOUSE DIETARY FOR ABLE-BODIED INMATES.

No. 1. The Ordinary House Diet for Men and Women.	BREAKFAST.			DINNER.							SUPPER.			
	Bread.	Gruel.	Tea.	Bread.	Meat.	Potatoes.	Soup.	Pudding.	Broth.	Milk.	Bread.	Cheese.	Broth.	Tea.
	oz.	pints	pints	oz.	oz.	oz.	pints	oz.	pints	pints	oz.	oz.	pints	pints
Sunday	6	1½	..	..	5	12	..	..	..	..	5	..	1½	..
Monday	6	1½	..	..	..	..	..	14	..	..	5	2	..	..
Tuesday	6	1½	..	..	5	12	..	..	..	..	5	..	1½	..
Wednesday	6	1½	..	4	..	..	1	..	..	..	5	2	..	..
Thursday	6	1½	..	..	5	12	..	..	..	..	5	..	1½	..
Friday	6	1½	..	..	..	..	..	14	..	..	5	2	..	..
Saturday	6	1½	..	4	..	..	1	..	..	..	5	2	..	..

DAILY DIETARIES for the SICK, as directed by the Medical Officer.

	Bread	Gruel	Tea	Bread	Meat	Potatoes	Soup	Pudding	Broth	Milk	Bread	Cheese	Broth	Tea
No. 2—Or, Meat, daily	6	..	1	..	5	8	..	..	..	..	5	..	..	1
No. 3—Meat and Broth	4	..	1	4	4	..	..	..	1	..	4	..	..	1
No. 4—Milk (fever diet)	4	..	1	4	..	..	..	..	..	1	4	..	..	1

To Nos. 2, 3, and 4, is added 5 oz. of Butter weekly. Suckling women are allowed, in addition to No. 1 Dietary, a pint of Beer daily, and Meat and Potatoes on Saturday in lieu of Soup. The Aged and Infirm have in addition to the able-bodied dietary, mutton broth, leg of beef soup, beef, bacon, and tea and butter every day. Children have milk, pudding, treacle, dripping, &c.

TABLE
SHEWING THE TOTAL EXPENDITURE OF MONEY LEVIED FOR POOR RATES
IN THE
PARISH OF ST. CLEMENT DANES.

DATE.	AMOUNT.	DATE.	AMOUNT.	DATE.	AMOUNT.	DATE.	AMOUNT.
1813	9,896	1827	8,847	1841	9,203	1855	13,786
1814	9,344	1828	9,022	1842	9,715	1856	12,533
1815	8,123	1829	9,472	1843	9,544	1857	14,351
1816	7,539	1830	9,353	1844	9,806	1858	12,635
1817	8,573	1831	11,684	1845	9,041	1859	12,400
1818	8,660	1832	11,008	1846	10,682	1860	12,053
1819	6,921	1833	10,057	1847	10,440	1861	12,253
1820	8,306	1834	10,806	1848	11,140	1862	13,098
1821	10,114	1835	12,855	1849	12,489	1863	12,502
1822	10,115	1836	11,471	1850	11,218	1864	12,673
1823	8,529	1837	9,217	1851	10,454	1865	12,799
1824	7,927	1838	10,646	1852	10,071	1866	13,524
1825	7,401	1839	8,730	1853	10,629	1867	15,275
1826	8,422	1840	8,940	1854	11,646		

The Strand Union is under the management of a Board of Guardians elected from the following parishes forming the Union:— St. Anne, 9; St. Clement Danes, 9; St. Mary-le-Strand, 3; St. Paul, Covent Garden, 5; the Liberty of the Rolls, 3; the Precinct of the Savoy, 1. Mr. JAMES KILNER is the Clerk to the Board. The total expenditure of the Union for twelve months ending Lady-day, 1867, was £36,187 15s. 8d. Arrangements are pending for this parish to amalgamate with the Holborn Union, who are about purchasing property in the Gray's Inn Road, adjoining the Holborn Union Workhouse, consisting of various plots of ground amounting to 37,013 superficial feet; this has been valued approximately by Mr. DENT at the sum of £42,329, to acquire complete possession.

The Old Poor-House of St. Clement Danes, which joined the Graveyard in Portugal Street, was purchased by the inhabitants in 1638.

A Survey of St. Clement Danes,

MADE BY THE COMPANY OF PARISH CLERKS
IN 1732.

"THE Old Church was built 730 years ago, and between 1608 and 1633 the repairs cost £1586; in 1721 the Churchyard was beautifully paved. It is situated on the north side of the Strand, a little westward of Temple Bar, in the Liberty of the Duchy of Lancaster, in the County of Middlesex. It is a rectory in the gift of the Earl of Exeter, the value near £600 per annum, but some say that not above £400 is collected: it is rated in the King's books at £52 7s. 1d. The Rector is the Rev. Mr. BLACKWELL, and the Lecturer the Rev. Mr. PETERS. The Vestry is select.

"THE PARISH OFFICERS ARE—	THE PEACE OFFICERS ARE—
6 Burgesses and their Deputies.	8 Constables. 8 Scavengers.
2 Churchwardens.	4 Surveyors of the H. W.
5 Overseers, of which 4 are Collectors.	24 Jurymen for the Duchy Liberty.
2 Surveyors for regulating the Paving of the Streets.	4 Ale-Conners.
	4 Flesh-Tasters.

"In the upper churchyard are three schools, one for seventy boys, who are taught reading, writing, and arithmetic by the master, who is allowed £40 per annum, and coals and candles. The boys are also instructed in the mathematics, and are taught to sing by masters who are paid for teaching them. In the second school are forty girls, under a mistress, who teaches them to read, sew, knit, &c., and she has £20 per annum, besides coals and candles. These girls have also a singing master to teach them; and both boys and girls are clothed in blue. The third school is the Horn-book school, where thirty children are taught by the mistress.

"In the upper churchyard there are also six Almshouses with six rooms, and twelve poor women in each house, who are allowed 2s. per week; and in the lower churchyard are five rooms for poor women, each of whom has 2s. 6d. per week; they have also coals at Christmas, if they can make interest to get them.

"This parish begins westward on the south side of the Strand at Cecil Street, including the east side of that street, and reaches to the house of Mr. Collins (exclusive) and begins again two doors westward from Strand Lane, and reaches to Temple Bar, taking in all the streets, courts, &c. in that compass to the River Thames. On the north side of the Strand it begins at Burleigh Street, and takes in the east side of that street, except the uppermost house, and extends to the house of Mr. Nicholson, the Pewterer, at the corner of Katherine Street, and comprehends part of that house and the courts within that compass. It begins again two doors westward of the Five Bells Tavern, and extends to Temple Bar, taking in Holywell Street, commonly called the Back of St. Clements, and Butcher Row. It takes in also the west side of Sheer Lane, all Carey Street, the greatest part of Searl's Square, commonly called Lincoln's Inn Great Square, Portugal Street, Searl Street, Clare Market, Vere Street, and therein Bear Yard; and from Vere Street it extends eastward on the south side of Duke Street to the Stable-yard, adjoining to the Ambassador's Chapel; it takes in all Stanhope Street, except two houses. In Drury Lane it begins over against the Play-house, on the east side, and extends to Wych Street, taking in all the north side of that street, and the south side of the same, from the back door of the Five Bells Tavern, inclusive, and all the streets, lanes, courts, &c. within that compass.

"This parish is divided into two Liberties, viz., the Upper and the Lower. The Upper, which is in the Liberty of Westminster, contains four Wards, viz., Temple Bar Ward, Sheer Lane Ward, Drury

Lane Ward, and Holywell Ward. The Lower Liberty is in the Duchy of Savoy and contains also four Wards, viz., Royal Ward, Church Ward, Middle Ward, and Savoy Ward.

"Streets, Lanes, Courts, Alleys, &c.

"*Temple Bar Ward takes in*

Part of Butcher-Row
    Peach Tree-court
    Star-court
    Newcastle-court
    Bear and Harrow-court
    Old Bosvile-court
Part of St. Clement's-lane

Plow Stables-alley
    Yeats's-court
Part of Clare-market
  ,, Vere-street
    Bear-yard
Part of Duke-street.

"*Sheer Lane Ward contains*

    Gilbert's-passage
    Carey-street
Part of Searl's-sq., commonly called Lincoln's Inn Gt. square
    Searl-street
    Portugal-street
    Cook's-court
    Grange-court
    New-court

    Boswell-court
Part of Sheer-lane
    Little Sheer-lane
    Crown-court
    Hemlock-court
    Peachy-court
    Ship-yard
    Cucumber-alley

"*In Drury Lane Ward are*

Part of Drury-lane
    Drum-alley
    Kings Head-court
    Bennets-court
    White Horse-yard
    Clare-court
    Blackmoor-street

    Craven-buildings
    Craven-passage
Part of Maypole-alley
    Stanhope-street
    Peter-street, properly Denzile-street
Part of Clare-street

"*In Holywell Ward are*

Part of Holywell-street, commonly called the Back of St. Clement's
    Kings Arms-court
    All Wych-street, except from Little Drury-lane end, to the back door of the 5 Bells Tavern
    Wych-alley

    Carpenters-court
Part of St. Clements-lane
  ,, Clare-market
  ,, Clare-street
    Holles-street
    Clements Inn-passage
    Houghton-street
    New Inn-passage
Part of Maypole-alley

A SURVEY OF ST. CLEMENT DANES IN 1732.

"Royal Ward has

Part of Temple-bar
Cross Keys-alley
Devereaux-court
Essex-street
Little Essex-street
Part of North side of the Strand
 " Milford-lane, and therein
Milford-stairs

Essex-stairs
Sadlers-court
Bakers-yard, & Tweezers-alley
Greyhound-court
Part of The south side of the Strand
The south side of Butcher-row
The north side of St Clements Church

"Church Ward comprehends

The north side of St Clements Church-yard
The west side of the same
The south side of Holy-well-street, commonly called the Back of St Clements

The west end of the same
The north side of the Strand from the New Church to St Clements Church
Pi—ing-alley

"Middle Ward takes in

Milford-lane
Water-street
Arundell-street, and therein
Pear Tree-hall
Norfolk-street

The Boarded Entry
Angel-court
Naked Boy-court
Surry-street
Strand-lane

"In the Savoy Ward are

Part of South side of the Strand
Dutchy-lane
Savoy
Savoy-alley
White Lyon-court
Green Arbour-court
Jesuits-ground
Fountain-court

Herberts-passage
Beaufort-buildings
Beaufort-street
Worcester-ground
Dirty-lane
Part of Cecil-street
 " Burleigh-street, and therein
Burleigh-court.

"No. of Houses, 1,750.   "ROBERT COX, Clerk."

In imitation of our Saviour's pattern of humility, the Kings of England formerly performed the annual ceremony, on Maundy Thursday, of washing the feet of as many poor men as they were years old. Cardinal Wolsey, at Peterborough Abbey in 1530, washed and kissed the feet of fifty-nine poor men, and afterwards gave to each twelve pence in money, three ells of good canvas to make them shirts, a pair of new shoes, a cast of red herrings, and three white herrings. Queen Elizabeth, when in her thirty-ninth year, performed this ceremony upon thirty-nine poor persons at her palace at Greenwich, after which, clothes, victuals, and money were distributed. This strange ceremonial, in which the highest was for a moment brought beneath the lowest, was last performed in its full extent by James II. King William left the washing to his almoner, and such was the arrangement for many years afterwards. The custom has been entirely given up for a considerable number of years, and since the beginning of the reign of Queen Victoria an additional sum of money has been given in lieu of provisions.

St. Clement Danes—Institutions, &c.

THE ROYAL COLLEGE OF SURGEONS, ENGLAND.

This Institution is situate on the south side of Lincoln's Inn Fields. It was erected from designs by Sir Charles Barry, R.A., in 1836, at a total cost of about £40,000. The exterior is remarkable for the great beauty of its portico, consisting of six lofty fluted columns of the Ionic order, selected* from the temple on the banks of the Ilyssus at Athens. Some of the cornice mouldings and the echinas of the architrave are carved—the entablature bearing the following inscription, from the classic pen of C. J. Blomfield, Bishop of London, then one of the Trustees of the Hunterian Collection:—

"Aedes Collegii Chirurgorum Londinensis Diplomate Regio Corporati. A.D. MDCCC."

On entering the hall an inner vestibule is seen, and directly in front the arms of the College, which formerly appeared on the portico (with Machaon and Podalirus as supporters). This heraldic device is now let into the wall, and surmounted with the College crest—an eagle holding the mace. On the right of the entrance-hall is a smaller vestibule, leading to the Museum, an account of which is appended. On the left are the Secretary's offices, where the names of students are received for examination and registration; and here, in October last, we find that as many as 1,125 gentlemen, including 355 freshmen, registered their attendances at the eleven metropolitan hospitals. In the rooms above, the students are examined, and during the collegiate year ending July, 1867, there were twenty-three

---
* From a previous design of the late Mr. Dance.

who passed for the Fellowship, and five rejected; for the Membership, the large number of 355 passed, and sixty-eight were referred to their hospital studies. For the Midwifery license forty-four passed, and seven were rejected. For the Dental license only ten offered themselves, all of whom passed to the satisfaction of the examiners. The annual receipts of the College, from Midsummer-day, 1866, to Midsummer-day, 1867, amounted to £12,409 3s. 11d., and the disbursements during the same period to £11,511 12s. 10d. The Council-room, in which the examinations take place, has some fine portraits, as that of John Hunter, the *chef d'œuvre* of Reynolds; Sir Cæsar Hawkins, by Hogarth; Sir Astley Cooper, by Lawrence; the original cartoon, by Holbein, representing Henry VIII. granting a charter to the "*Companie of Barber-Chirurgeons.*" There are also in this room numerous busts by Flaxman, Chantry, Weekes, Behnes, Turnerelli, Hollis, &c., and one has just been added of the veteran Lawrence, who died in July last, at the great age of eighty-five years. Adjoining the Council-room is the magnificent Library of the College, of which a short account is subjoined. Mr. J. CHATTO is the librarian.

The Council—the governing body of the College—consists of twenty-four members, three of whom, when no vacancy either by resignation or death has occurred during the year, go out in rotation annually in July, but are eligible for re-election by the Fellows of the College. The Court of Examiners consists of ten members, elected by the Council from the Fellows of the College. The gentleman who at present fills the President's chair is Mr. JOHN HILTON, F.R.S. Surgeon to Guy's Hospital: he has just deservedly been appointed Surgeon-Extraordinary to Her Majesty. The Secretary to the College is Mr. EDWARD TRIMMER, M.A. Cantab.

THE MUSEUM.

The Hunterian Collection, which forms the basis, and still a large proportion, of the contents of the present Museum of the College, was originally arranged in a building which its founder, John Hunter, erected for it in 1784, behind his house in Leicester Square.

John Hunter died October 16th, 1793, aged sixty-four. By his will he directed his museum to be offered in the first instance to the British Government, on such terms as might be considered reasonable, and in case of refusal, to be sold in one lot, either to some foreign state, or as his executors might think proper.

In the year 1799, Parliament voted the sum of £15,000 for the Museum, and an offer of it being made to the Corporation of Surgeons, it was accepted on the terms proposed by Government.

In 1806 the sum of £15,000 was voted by Parliament in aid of the erection of an edifice for the display and arrangement of the Hunterian Collection; a second grant of £12,500 was subsequently voted, and upwards of £21,000 having been supplied from the funds of the College, the building was completed in Lincoln's Inn Fields, in which the Museum was opened for the inspection of visitors in the year 1813.

In consequence of the large number of additions, this building became too small for the adequate display and arrangement of its contents; and more space being at the same time required for the rapidly increasing Library, the greater portion of the present building was erected, wholly at the expense of the College, in 1835, at a cost of about £40,000, and the Hunterian and Collegiate Collections were re-arranged in what are now termed the Western and Middle Museums, which were opened for the inspection of visitors in 1836.

Further enlargement of the building having become necessary by the continued increase of the collection, the College, in 1847, purchased the extensive premises of Mr. Alderman Copeland, in Portugal Street, for the sum of £16,000, and in 1852 proceeded to the erection of the Eastern Museum, at the expense of £25,000, Parliament granting £15,000 in aid thereof. The re-arrangement of the specimens was completed, and the additional portion of the building opened to visitors in 1855.

Among the contents are skeletons of O'Brien, the Irish giant; Freeman, the American giant; Caroline Crachami, the Sicilian dwarf;

Jonathan Wild, the notorious criminal; skeleton of "Chunee," the fine elephant, shot when in a paroxysm of madness, at Exeter Change, then a large menagerie in the Strand, where the great Hall now stands; some eggs of the Great Auk, which at recent sales have fetched upwards of £30 each; skeletons of the Gorilla, and the Whalebone Whale; portions of the bows of H.M.S. "Fawn," which had been pierced by the sword-fish, whose jaw had penetrated the copper sheathing, the felt, the deal and the hard oak timbers to the depth of fourteen inches, and nearly that extent of the sword had been broken off by the force of the blow, and retained in the wood; and the embalmed body of Mrs. Van Butchell.

There have been four conservators of the Museum since its establishment, viz., Mr. William Clift, the apprentice of John Hunter; Professor Owen, Professor Quekett, and the present worthy successor of those gentlemen, Mr. W. H. FLOWER, F.R.S.

The Museum is open on the first four days of the week, from twelve until five o'clock in summer, and until four o'clock in winter, to members and visitors introduced by them, personally or by orders.

A Synopsis for the unprofessional visitor is published for sixpence.

THE LIBRARY.

The formation of a regular Library may be said to have commenced in the year 1801, at which time and in succeeding years presentations and bequests of books, often in considerable numbers, were made to the College; the principal donors being Dr. Baillie, Sir Everard Home, Sir Charles Blicke, the widow of Mr. Sharp, Sir Ludford Harvey, Dr. Fleming, Mr. Cotton, and Mr. Long. The Court of Assistants also directed from time to time the expenditure of small sums of money for the purchase of books, and eventually voted a sum of £100 per annum for this purpose. Sir Charles Blicke, in the year 1816, invested the sum of £300, the proceeds of which were to be devoted to the same object. Some of the purchases thus made were considerable, as in the cases of the Libraries of Mr. Pitt, Mr. St. Andre, and Sir Anthony Carlisle. In this way a Library of considerable value was gradually accumulated, but it was only accessible to a limited number of persons. In 1827 active steps were taken to render it more generally useful, and with this object catalogues and extensive lists of desirable acquisitions were ordered to be prepared. Large sums of money were also expended during this and the ensuing two years, amounting in the aggregate to nearly £6,000. A Librarian was appointed, and in 1828 the Library, then containing 10,500 volumes, was thrown open to members of the College, and all other persons engaged in the pursuit of natural science were freely admitted. This large collection, thus opened, offered great facilities to the studious. It has no pretensions to be regarded as a *curious* or *antiquarian* collection. It contains few books that are either typographical curiosities or remarkable for their rarity. But, on the contrary, it is eminently *practical*, containing a very large proportion of the books which the student, whether in pursuit of the history, the science, or the practice of medicine, and the collateral sciences, desires to consult. Its collections of periodical works, transactions of learned and scientific societies and journals is very large and remarkably perfect; it has the transactions of almost every society of any note upon its shelves. The entire collection now contains 31,647 volumes, consisting of 13,220 works and 34,689 tracts, pamphlets, and theses. There have been three Librarians since the establishment of this valuable collection, viz., Dr. Robert Willis, Mr. T. M. Stone, and the present custodian—Mr. JOHN CHATTO.

The Library is open every day from eleven until five, except on Saturdays, when it is closed at one o'clock. It is also closed during the month of September, for the necessary dusting and rearrangement.

Having said thus much of the new building, some account of the old institution called " Surgeons' Hall " may, perhaps, interest the reader. We find that in 1461 the Barber Surgeons were incorporated; and in this year the office of Serjeant-Surgeon was instituted, when William Hobbys was appointed, with a salary of forty marks per annum.

These barbers practising surgery, having associated themselves, formed one of the guilds or companies in London; and in the first year of the reign of Edward IV. obtained a charter to legalise their corporate capacity, and to give them authority over the rest of their mystery in and about the metropolis; they kept little shops for cutting hair, shaving, bathing, and curing the wounded, particularly about the royal palaces and houses of the great, exhibiting the long bandaged pole which is still occasionally seen at their doors, as a symbol. In the year 1745 the surgeons applied for an Act of Parliament to be separated from the barbers, which they obtained; and, leaving the hall of the latter in Monkwell Street, built Surgeons' Hall in the Old Bailey, where, as Pennant states, "by a sort of second sight the Anatomical Theatre was built near the court of conviction and Newgate, the concluding stage of the lives forfeited to the justice of their country, several years before the fatal tree was removed from Tyburn to its present site. The hall was a handsome building, ornamented with Ionic pilasters, and with a double flight of steps to the first floor. Beneath was a door for the admission of the bodies of murderers and other felons, who, noxious in their lives, made a sort of reparation to their fellow-creatures by becoming useful after death."

When Earl Ferrers was executed at Tyburn, in 1760, the body was conveyed in his own landau and six to Surgeons' Hall, to undergo the remainder of the sentence, and was then publicly exposed to view. At this hall the Court of Assistants sat to examine candidates for the diploma, and as to their qualifications for admission into the medical service of the navy and army. Among others so examined the writer of this hurried notice discovered, in the books of the College of Surgeons, the following:—"James Bernard, mate to an hospital, and Oliver Goldsmith found not qualified for ditto." The hall was taken down in 1809. Down to a recent period, the bodies of all murderers executed at the Old Bailey were claimed by the College of Surgeons, and taken by Calcraft and his assistant to a house provided for that purpose in Hosier Lane (No. 33). Here, in the presence of the sheriff, a member of the Council, or more frequently Mr. Clift, the conservator of the Museum would make a slight examination, after which the body or bodies would be distributed to the anatomical schools in the metropolis. The last so received, it is believed, was that of a man named Smithers, who was executed for firing his house in Oxford Street to defraud an insurance company, "killing and slaying" two female lodgers.

ST. CLEMENT DANES' SAVINGS' BANK.

This Bank, in connection with Government, was established in 1830. There are eight Trustees, a Treasurer, thirty-three Managers, an Auditor and Actuary. The Offices are at 40, Norfolk Street. An Act of Parliament orders all money to be invested in the Banks of England and Ireland, and the Officers of the Bank engaged are compelled to give good security.

Dr. Amount of Liabilities.			Assets of the Institution. Cr.		
	£	s. d.		£	s. d.
To Total Amount due to all Depositors	80,761	19 3	By Balance invested on the General Account	80,538	0 1
,, Clear Surplus (after all demands)	318	4 11	,, Balance in the hands of the Treasurer	542	4 1
	£81,080	4 2		£81,080	4 2

Examined and found correct,
(Signed) · S. LOVELOCK,
Auditor appointed under the Act of 1863.
21st DECEMBER, 1866.

Certified by me,
RICHARD TWINING,
Treasurer.
T. P. SCRIVENER, *Actuary.*

In this Parish the principle of depositing small savings has been extended still further by the establishment of a Penny Bank, which, as the title implies, receives the pence of the poor, under conditions similar to those that govern savings' banks generally. See p. 20.

WHITTINGTON CLUB.

This Club was established in 1846, under the auspices of the late Douglas Jerrold, Esq., and many other gentlemen eminent in literature, science, and art. The object of the Club is to combine a Literary Society with a Club House, upon an economical scale, for the middle classes. The present Club House, which is situated at 37, Arundel Street, Strand, was erected in 1858, at an outlay of nearly £15,000, and is governed by a managing committee, elected half yearly by the members. Besides the purposes of the Club, lectures, meetings, and entertainments of a superior class are held in the great hall, which is capable of holding 800 persons; in it a weekly ball is held during the winter months; there are also reading, billiard, smoking, chess, dressing rooms and lavatories attached. Mr. S. HOLROYD is the Secretary. A member's contribution is two guineas annually. Newenham's celebrated picture of "Whittington listening to Bow Bells," which was presented to the Club by its founder, may be seen here.

CROWN AND ANCHOR TAVERN.

This once celebrated resort of the great in political and literary circles stood on the ground now occupied by the Whittington Club, having an entrance also in the Strand. Its great room measured 84 feet by 35. The sign was taken from the anchor of St. Clement. The Academy of Music was instituted here in 1710. The famous Crown and Anchor Association against so-called Republicans and Levellers, as the Reformers were styled by the Government party in 1792, owed its name to this tavern. In 1725 there was a great ferment in the parish of St. Clement's, in consequence of an order from Dr. Gibson, Bishop of London, to remove at once from the Church an expensive new altar-piece, supposed to contain portraits of the Pretender's wife and children, painted by Kent, who was originally a coach-painter in Yorkshire, but then patronized by the Queen, the Duke of Newcastle, and Lord Burlington. This picture, caricatured by Hogarth, was for some years one of the ornaments of the coffee-room of the Crown and Anchor, whence it was removed to the vestry-room of the church, over the old almshouses in the churchyard. After 1803 it was transported to the new vestry-room on the north side of the churchyard, where it remains at the present time. In 1798, upon the occasion of Fox's birthday, 2,000 persons were entertained at a banquet at this tavern. Here Dr. Johnson occasionally supped with Boswell; and Macintosh, Rogers, the Poetical Banker, and other eminent men were frequenters. It afterwards became celebrated for public and political meetings. Here, during the Westminster elections, the candidates on both sides have often addressed the electors. The recollection of the Crown and Anchor will long live amongst the people of England.

The King of Clubs was instituted here about 1801, by Mr. Robert (Bobus) Smith, brother of Sydney, a friend of Canning's, and Advocate-General of Calcutta. It sat every Saturday, the house at that time being famous for its dinners and wines, and a great resort for clubs. Politics were excluded. One of the chief members was Mr. Richard Sharpe, a partner in a West India house, and a Parliamentary speaker during Addington's and Percival's administrations. John Allen, and M. Dumont, an emigré and friend of the Abbé de Lisle, were also members. Erskine, too, often dropped in to spend an hour stolen from his immense and overflowing business. He there told his story of Lord Loughborough trying to persuade him not to take Tom Paine's brief. He once met Curran there. A member of the club speaks of the ape's face of the Irish orator, with the sunken and diminutive eyes that flashed lightning, as he compared poor wronged Ireland to " Niobe palsied with sorrow and despair over her freedom, and her prosperity struck dead before her."

From the platform of this tavern the silvery notes of Burdett, the stern sense of Cobbett, and the impassioned appeals of O'Connell to the people of England respecting the wrongs of Ireland, and other great questions, will long be remembered. Some scenes which now and then took place in this ancient Temple of Freedom are to be looked back upon now with regret.

It was at the Crown and Anchor that O'Connell first assailed that venerable champion of civil and religious liberty—Henry Brougham, the setting of whose sun is now watched by the people of England with pious and affectionate solicitude. It was here that Cobbett fell foul of Sir Francis Burdett, who at once angrily responded by stating that Cobbett owed him a thousand pounds; Cobbett acknowledged receiving the money, but stated that it was a gift, and consequently not a debt. But these giants of democracy have passed away, and the popular forum has become a club-house.

48TH MIDDLESEX ("HAVELOCK") RIFLE VOLUNTEERS.

THIS Corps, the head-quarters of which are at No. 6, Cook's Court, Carey Street, was first formed in Surrey, as the "24th Surrey," and originated by some young teetotallers inducing an ardent brother teetotaller, Mr. GEORGE CRUIKSHANK, the artist, to assist them in raising a temperance regiment, to consist *entirely* of total abstainers. LORD LOVELACE, the Lord-Lieutenant of the County, having given permission to form such a corps, Mr. Cruikshank was induced by his friends to take the command of the same, as Captain of the "24th Surrey." Upon going round to the different temperance societies, for the purpose of "recruiting," it was discovered that another party of teetotallers in the City had also been endeavouring to form a temperance corps, and had succeeded, all but being accepted by the Lieutenancy of the City, and as it was found, in recruiting, that these two bodies of Teetotal Volunteers clashed, it was thought by both parties that it would be best for them to amalgamate, and as men were fast joining the corps, Mr. GEORGE CRUIKSHANK informed LORD LOVELACE that there was a sufficient number of men to form a battalion; but, as a great many of these men resided in different parts of the metropolis, and as his Lordship would not accept any men who were not "domiciled" in Surrey, the Corps was dissolved in that county and re-formed in Middlesex, and accepted by the MARQUIS·OF SALISBURY, the Lord-Lieutenant of the county.

The number of men on "the Roll" being sufficient to form a battalion of eight companies, Mr. G. CRUIKSHANK became Lieutenant-Colonel. They have two bands, a "Brass Band" and a "Drum and Fife Band."

When first formed, this regiment was a *total* temperance corps, from the colonel down to the drummer-boy; but being opposed by many of the temperance people, particularly the Peace Society, it was found necessary, in order to keep up its numbers, to admit "all comers," and it is therefore no longer a *total* temperance corps.

The Corps is composed principally of clerks and artizans. The commissioned and non-commissioned officers appointed to the corps by the War Office authorities are Major HOCKLEY as Adjutant, who having seen twenty years' service, is an officer of considerable experience; and JOHN SPOONER, who having also seen twenty years' service, performs the duties of Sergeant-Major in a most satisfactory manner. There are also two Sergeant Drill Instructors, one formerly in the Foot Guards, and the other in the Rifle Brigade.

As Sir Henry Havelock was a total abstainer, and as Lady Havelock was one also, application was made to her Ladyship to allow the corps to bear their name; and her Ladyship kindly giving permission, the corps became honoured by the adoption of the name of "Havelock."

MANCHESTER UNITY INDEPENDENT ORDER OF ODD FELLOWS.

The "City's Pride" Lodge of this Society is held at the Wheat Sheaf Inn, Vere Street, Clare Market. It consists of 128 Members, who are entitled, when ill, to a payment of 12s. per week for twelve months, and 6s. per week afterwards, so long as the illness may continue. On the death of a Member, his widow or representative is entitled to a sum of £12, and, on the death of a Member's Wife, he is entitled to a payment of £6. At the present time the City's Pride Lodge has a capital of £1,228 7s. 2d. It was established in 1846. There is also a Widows' and Orphans' Fund in connection with this Society. On the death of a Member his Widow is entitled to a bonus of £15, or 8s. per calendar month, so long as she remains a Widow. Children under fourteen years of age are entitled to 2s. each per month. In the case of parentless children, the amount given is, in the discretion of the Committee, within 8s. per month.

The North London District, of which the above-named Lodge is a branch, consists of eighty-eight Lodges, and 11,621 Members, and has a capital of upwards of £92,000. In addition to this sum, the Widows' and Orphans' Fund has a capital of over £10,000.

The entire Unity, at the end of the year 1866, consisted of 405,255 Members. Its Lodges are spread nearly all over the civilised world. The receipts for 1866 are as follows :—

In Contributions	£380,617	19 0
,, Admission Fees	13,512	15 10
,, Interest	70,796	14 0
	£464,927	8 10
Expended for Sickness Benefits ... £235,689 7 0		
,, Funeral Benefits .. 75,803 5 2	311,492	12 2
Showing a gain on the year of	£153,434	16 8

The total Capital of the Society is £2,408,404 13s. 10d.

ST. CLEMENT DANES' MISSION HOUSE,
35, CAREY STREET.

President, Rev. R. HENRY KILLICK, M.A.; Treasurer, FREDERICK TWINING, Esq.; a Committee of Ladies and Gentlemen; the Parochial Clergy, *ex officio;* Lady Superintendent; Librarian, Miss SARAH HATTON; Matron, Miss BROWN; Bankers, Messrs. TWINING, 215, Strand; Secretary, Mr. CHARLES LIVETT; Collector, Mr. GEORGE CROSSLEY, 23, Newcastle Street, Strand.

Attached to this Institution is a Library of 600 volumes, for the use of the inhabitants. The late Archbishop Sumner presented all his works to the Rev. R. H. Killick; as also the American poetess, Mrs. Sigoursy. The Treasuser of the Inner Temple sent a large supply of Bibles and Prayer Books.

It is a House of Call for all the parish workers, and for the poor to come and state their troubles, which are entered in a book, and the cases are immediately visited. The sick are provided with beef-tea, mutton-chops, and wine during the year. In the winter the Soup Kitchen is in constant use.

The Mission House Shop is opened for the sale of articles at cost price, with the view of giving employment to poor women at their own homes. Lodgings are provided for eight young women out of place, at 2s. per week. On Thursday evenings there is a plain service for the poor; also regular Bible Classes. During the Winter a Night School is held. On Sundays there is a School for Children that have never attended any other school. The Dinners and Laundry are suspended for want of suitable premises. It will, perhaps, not be out of place here for us to say a few words about the

OLD MISSION HOUSE, CLEMENT'S LANE.

If there is any feeling more pure and sacred than another which lives in the human heart it is the desire to perpetuate the past. To this noble and God-like feeling we are indebted for those records which lend an undying interest to some of the lone spots of earth, and hold up as it were a perpetual light for the future guidance of unborn ages. The deeds of great men are not permitted to perish. Why should the deeds of the good be forgotten?—those who upon earth far more resemble their Heavenly Master. When we visit in distant lands the spots where heathen temples once stood and where now are found but silence and decay, it awakens strong emotions within us; but surely the spot once consecrated to Christian labours should awaken far holier feelings. In the vast improvements which our City, both for purposes of utility and of beauty, is now undergoing, there will be swept away from their present sites many institutions the memory of which we do not wish to die. Surely if the street in which Milton was born or Newton lived are still held in pious regard by a thoughtful nation, the spot upon which God-like charity was once dispensed and immortal souls saved for light and glory, should awake still holier emotions.

We have been led to these remarks by reflecting upon the countless Christian benefits conferred by the Mission House of St. Clement's Lane; nor are we willing that it should pass away from its present site without recording some of its many virtues. A great writer commences a great work by saying that "posterity may not be deceived;" but, although we cannot appeal to so awful a tribunal, still, perhaps, when we are gone some Christian young man or woman may pause and say, "Oh, here once stood the Mission House of St. Clement's Lane, and I have a little record of its good deeds in my pocket." It may not be presumptuous to think that in the eyes of gentle woman may come some hallowed tears, when she reflects how in the days gone by (for the present will then be the past) many of her sisters were saved from worldly degradation and eternal loss by the labours of the old Mission House of Clement's Lane. She will learn how in this unpretending yet noble institution, food, clothing, mental culture, healthful and practical employment, religious instruction, and Christian tuition, were all provided for the less fortunate children of earth, thus rescuing them with a strong and all-potent arm from the million wrecking lights of London. She will bring to mind the names of benefactors of the St. Clement's Lane Mission House, then enjoying, through God's help, the rewards of the just—who proved how easy it was in those days for benevolent beings to diffuse Christian light around them; to dig a fountain of perpetual delight in the midst of a wilderness; and make everything in their vicinity freshen into smiles and human comfort. We do not believe that, for its limited means and compass of action, any little institution rendered more practical and Christian benefits than our Mission House has. It sprang up in one of the most poverty-stricken and debased neighbourhoods of the great City, and still made its moral influence felt around.

Although the stately temples of justice in classic proportions arise upon the spot where once stood the Mission House, still be its holy labours ever unforgotten, and let the pomp of worldly knowledge succumb to the teaching of Him who permitted "little children to come unto Him."

QUEEN'S (WESTMINSTER) RIFLE VOLUNTEERS

Is formed of companies from each parish in the City of Westminster. St. Clement Danes sends one company, consisting of captain, lieutenant, ensign, and eighty men—the officers are Captain SCRIVENER, Lieut. BERRY, and Ensign FARLOW. Its armoury-house is at 22, Surrey Street, Strand, by the permission of the DUKE OF NORFOLK. The Lieut.-Colonel Commandant of the regiment is EARL GROSVENOR, M.P.; the Lieut.-Colonel being LORD GERALD FITZGERALD. The regiment musters 1,200—its Head-Quarters are in Belgrave Road, Pimlico. The company is very strongly supported by the parishioners, and the prize lists are large, being of the value last year of £70. There is also a Challenge Cup in the company, subscribed for by the parishioners, value £63, which is competed for half-yearly, and will become the property of any member winning it three times successively. Members can be enrolled on application to the officers. Hon. Sec. J. F. ISAACSON. Esq., 40, Norfolk Street, Strand.

Westminster Elections.

HE contests for the representation of the City of Westminster form some of the most important epochs in the political history of this country. From the days of Cecil, the wise and brilliant courtier, down to the oldest champion of civil and religious liberty—CHARLES JAMES FOX, and from his period to EVANS—the "bravest of the brave"—it has always been the most severely contested representation on the political map of England.

It was in this ancient city that the celebrated Duchess of Devonshire lavished her unrivalled charms to sustain the great Whig cause,* then frowned down upon by a King and shaken by the rapid and matchless conquests of Napoleon. She used to relate, towards the close of her life, that of all the compliments paid to her during a long reign of ascendancy, the drunken Irishman who asked to "light his pipe by the fire of her beautiful eyes," paid her the highest. Upon the hustings of Covent Garden were oft seen the massive form of Demosthenic FOX, and the eminently patrician form of Sir FRANCIS BURDETT.

The election at one time lasted for forty days; and in illustration of the slow mode of voting adopted, it is said that as the solitary voter presented himself, there arose from the multitude a cry of cheerful recognition—"Fox, here's another!"

---

* " Array'd in matchless beauty, Devon's fair
    In Fox's favour takes a zealous part;
  But, oh! where'er the pilferer comes—beware!
    She supplicates a vote, and steals a heart."

Written in consequence of Her Grace's Canvass in support of Mr. Fox.

FORTY DAYS' POLLING—FOX, HOOD & WRAY.

The following table, showing the numbers polled each day during the "Forty-days' poll" of 1784 (from April 1st to May 17th), will clearly illustrate the method of returning "a fit and proper person" to represent the ancient City of Westminster:—

DAYS OF POLLING.	THE NUMBER OF EACH DAY'S POLL.			DAYS OF POLLING.	THE NUMBER OF EACH DAY'S POLL.		
	Hood.	Fox.	Wray.		Hood.	Fox.	Wray.
First Day	264	302	238	Twenty-second	52	79	40
Second	970	941	866	Twenty-third	39	77	29
Third	951	680	871	Twenty-fourth	39	56	36
Fourth	1,077	945	1,010	Twenty-fifth	25	38	23
Fifth	674	545	637	Twenty-sixth	16	42	12
Sixth	522	414	495	Twenty-seventh	14	29	13
Seventh	339	299	303	Twenty-eighth	12	24	12
Eighth	80	75	69	Twenty-ninth	14	33	11
Ninth	341	271	299	Thirtieth	12	35	5
Tenth	246	205	207	Thirty-first	14	20	11
Eleventh	117	142	97	Thirty-second	10	9	8
Twelfth	151	186	116	Thirty-third	11	21	9
Thirteenth	143	143	113	Thirty-fourth	23	15	19
Fourteenth	96	82	79	Thirty-fifth	5	16	6
Fifteenth	81	75	65	Thirty-sixth	5	17	6
Sixteenth	68	65	68	Thirty-seventh	4	12	3
Seventeenth	54	73	41	Thirty-eighth	3	7	2
Eighteenth	65	76	49	Thirty-ninth	6	17	5
Nineteenth	35	51	27	Fortieth	13	16	11
Twentieth	52	45	49	Total	6,694	6,234	5,998
Twenty-first	51	56	38				

Nor was this contest untainted by blood—for, in one of the many skirmishes which took place between the various partizans, two men were killed and the accused tried at the Old Bailey. The trial was converted into political capital, but the accused left the dock amidst the tumultuous rejoicings of the people. But those were great days of earnestness, of political belief, and heartfelt politics. Then appeared upon the broad stage of life those pioneers of freedom through whose glorious exertions the long closed and ponderous gates of the constitution have been at length opened to all ranks of our countrymen.

In these struggles no portion of the ancient city played a more prominent part than the parish of St. Clement Danes. As we write the words, there arises before us the well-known form of the late

THOMAS PROUT, ESQ.,

for forty years a resident of that parish, and who went from amongst us on July 25th, 1859. He was the liberal supporter, and an eminently useful and practical member of that glorious league which brought the golden sheaf to England; and in supplying our own wants from the abundant resources of other nations, taught us that wise mutual dependence recorded in holy writ—

"The kings of Arabia and Sheba will bring gifts. Here shall be a handful of corn on the earth—on the top of the mountain."

Thomas Prout was a Member of the Ballot Society, which he deemed to be the necessary shield and protection of the English voter. Upon his death, that distinguished society paid the following tender and glowing tribute to his memory :—

"At a Meeting of the Executive Committee of the Ballot Society, held at their offices in Guildhall Chambers, on 2nd August, it was proposed by Major-General Thompson ; seconded by S. Harrison, Esq. ; supported by E. C. Whitehurst, Esq., and unanimously resolved :—That this Committee, on the occasion of its first meeting after the lamented decease of their colleague, Mr. Thomas Prout, desire to record on their minutes and to express to his family their sense of the irreparable loss which this Society and the cause of reform in general sustains by the decease of Mr. Prout. The Committee gratefully acknowledge his unwearied devotion, his self-denying exertions, and his generous liberality on all occasions to this Society, and they feel bound to acknowledge that in the earliest and most critical periods of the Society's existence its continuance depended on the sacrifices cheerfully made by their departed friend. The Committee further desire to record their sense of the disinterestedness evinced by Mr. Prout throughout his long political career, and they feel that they cannot better close this imperfect tribute to the memory and services of their colleague than by expressing the feeling that the best monument they can raise to his memory is to continue and increase every possible exertion until the ballot becomes the law of the land, when among those who contributed to the success of the cause of electoral purity and freedom the name of Thomas Prout will deservedly be placed in the highest rank."

THE LATE THOMAS PROUT, ESQ.

Mr. Prout was a warm and liberal supporter of the Westminster Liberal Registration Society throughout his long political career, believing that one of the best means to secure the interest of the Liberal cause was to properly and thoroughly revise the List of Voters; and further, by uniting the Liberal party in Westminster, the election of the best Liberal representatives would be secured. He also took a very active part at the following Westminster Elections:—

December, 1832.			July, 1841.		
Sir Fras. Burdett	...(L)	3248	Hon. Capt. H. J. Rous	..(C)	3338
Sir J. C. Hobhouse	...(L)	3214	John T. Leader	...(L)	3281
Col. De Lacy Evans	...(L)	1096	Sir De Lacy Evans	...(L)	3258
On Sir J. Hobhouse's acceptance of the C.H.			On Capt. Rous becoming a Lord of the Admiralty.		
May, 1833.			February, 1846.		
Col. De Lacy Evans	...(L)	2027	Sir De Lacy Evans	...(L)	3843
Sir J. C. Hobhouse	...(L)	1835	Hon. Capt. H. J. Rous	...(C)	2906
Bickham Escott	...(C)	738	August, 1847.		
January, 1835.			Sir De Lacy Evans	...(L)	3139
			Chas. Lushington	..(L)	2831
Sir Fras. Burdett	...(L)	2747	Chas Cochrane	...(L)	2810
Col. De Lacy Evans	...(L)	2588	Visct. Mandeville	...(C)	1985
Sir T. J. Cochrane	...(C)	1528	July, 1852.		
On Sir Fras. Burdett's acceptance of the C.H.			Sir J. Shelly, Bart.	...(L)	4199
			Sir De Lacy Evans	...(L)	3756
May, 1837.			Lord Maidstone	...(C)	3373
Sir Fras. Burdett	...(C)	3567	William Coningham	...(L)	1716
John T. Leader	...(L)	3052	March, 1857.		
			Sir De Lacy Evans	...(L)	
August, 1837.			Sir John Shelley, Bt.	..(L)	
John T. Leader	...(L)	3793	April, 1859.		
Col. De Lacy Evans	...(L)	3715	Sir De Lacy Evans	...(L)	
Sir Geo. Murray	...(C)	2620	Sir John Shelley, Bt.	...(L)	

(*The above facts and figures are extracted from "Acland's Poll-Book, 1832-64."*)

At the Annual Meeting of the members of the Westminster Liberal Registration Society, the following resolution was passed, and printed in the Report for 1858-9:—

"The cause of Reform in Westminster has, however, since the last Election, sustained an irreparable loss, by the death of one of its most valuable supporters; namely, the late Thomas Prout, Esq. To those who knew

Mr. Prout, the announcement of his death must have been received with reverence and respect; his unremitted and disinterested devotion to the Reform cause in Westminster, during the last fifty years, has been unsurpassed; the profound attention he bestowed on every subject affecting its political interest, gained for him the confidence and esteem of all earnest Reformers."

It has not pleased the Great Disposer of human events to spare our warm and generous-hearted friend, Mr. PROUT, to witness the glorious strides which the cause he lived and struggled for through life has made at the present hour. His well-trusted friend and fellow labourer in the vineyard, GILBERT POUNCY, is gone, too; likewise ALEXANDER WRIGHT, DAVID MALLOCK, R. ENGLEFIELD, and GEORGE HUGGETT, the well known Secretary of the Society for upwards of twenty years;* and of the illustrious band, the great chieftain

GENERAL SIR DE LACY EVANS

still remains, the gallant and illustrious survivor of many a well-fought field, the consistent and faithful representative of the people of Westminster for thirty-five years, during which time he neither made enemies in the House nor sought favours from any Government, and we feel it is only due to so great and just a man as General EVANS to record that a more honourable and independent Member never sat in the House of Commons; for we can speak from our own knowledge that it was entirely in consequence of the earnest desire and request of the leaders of the great Liberal party in Westminster, that he was induced to remain in the House so long.

---

* At a meeting of the Reformers of all shades of opinion in Westminster, called by the Westminster Liberal Registration Society, by adjournment of their annual meeting held at Caldwell's, July 4th, 1866, a Provisional Committee was appointed from that meeting, for the purpose of extending the objects of the Westminster Liberal Registration Society. Mr. THOMAS GILBERT, Jun., of 47, Charing Cross, was elected Secretary to the Society, at a meeting of the Committee held at Mr. Storr's, Covent Garden, July 10th, 1866. Messrs. JOHN PROUT, W. LANE, and S. SAINSBURY, of this parish, have for many years been active and liberal supporters of this Society.

WESTMINSTER ELECTIONS.

A Comparative Table of the Pollings at the Elections of 1837 and 1841.

Name and Date.	St. Anne.	St. Clement Mary & Savoy.	St. George Inward.	St. George Outward.	St. James.	St. John.	St. Margt.	St. Martin.	St. Paul.
Evans, 1837	235	317	561	512	759	315	320	549	149
Evans, 1841	254	239	409	499	619	329	322	449	138
Leader, 1837	248	316	572	529	780	324	331	566	147
Leader, 1841	265	248	381	517	601	364	320	455	140
Murray, 1837	123	322	651	267	472	177	176	365	86
Rous, 1841	135	326	867	348	544	265	294	470	109

The majority of Rous over Evans being 80, and over Leader 57. The plumpers for Sir De Lacy Evans were 59, and those for Mr. Leader 99. If the plumpers given for the Reform Candidates had been split between them they would have been successful.

The table hereunder shews that in 1846 Westminster again recovered the position which it maintained from 1807 to 1841, of being represented by Reformers.

	ROUS.				EVANS.			
NAME OF PARISH.	1841 Number voted.	1846 Number voted.	1846 Loss.	1846 Gain.	1841 Number voted.	1846 Number voted.	1846 Gain.	1846 Loss.
St. Anne	135	158	—	23	254	346	92	—
,, Clement's	290	227	63	—	202	296	94	—
,, George	1196	1015	181	—	908	1109	201	—
,, James'	543	480	63	—	619	595	—	24
,, John	265	208	57	—	329	426	97	—
,, Margaret	294	284	10	—	322	381	59	—
,, Martin	470	413	57	—	449	481	32	—
,, Mary	25	27	,,	2	31	38	7	—
,, Paul	109	86	23	—	138	153	15	—
The Savoy	11	8	3	—	6	18	12	—
	3338	2906	457	25	3258	3843	609	24

1846. Evans' gain over preceding Election, 609 ; Rous' loss, 457 ;—Difference in voting, 1,066. Deduct Rous' majority in 1841, 80 ; gain present Election, 25 ; Evans' loss, 24 ;—Difference in voting, 129. Majority declared by the High Bailiff, February 19th, 1846, 937.

Previous to the Election in 1847 General EVANS had obtained at four contests in Westminster the majorities of 937, 1,066, 1,095, and 1,132. Since that time, with one exception, he has been at the head of the poll at four elections.

From the following extracts from Minutes of the Annual Meeting of the members of the Westminster Liberal Registration Society, held at Caldwell's Rooms, Dean Street, Soho, March 13th, 1865, HENRY BIDGOOD, Esq., in the Chair, on the occasion of Sir DE LACY EVANS announcing his intended retirement from the representation of Westminster, we may form some opinion of the esteem in which the general was held by his constituents :—

"The CHAIRMAN, in calling attention to the retirement of General Sir De Lacy Evans, in very complimentary terms noticed the fact that his promotion had been owing to his great services, talents, and time, without the aid of any aristocratic friendship or relationship. (Hear, hear.) He had served the country faithfully, and hoped that his merits would be duly recognised and appreciated. (Hear, hear.) The Chairman further stated that the General had never sought a favour from the Government, and spoke of him in most glowing terms as their representative, and concluded by calling upon the Secretary to read Sir De Lacy Evans's address.

"The SECRETARY then read as follows :—

"TO THE CONSTITUENCY OF THE CITY OF WESTMINSTER.

"Gentlemen,—It is not without a feeling akin to sorrow that I have to acquaint you that at the next election I shall not be a candidate for your kind and generous suffrages. The fact is that whatever degree of energy I may have possessed is now exhausted, and I should no longer be capable of fulfilling the duties which would devolve upon me as your representative.

"The position of the City of Westminster has rendered you at all times peculiarly cognizant of the conduct of public men and the course of public affairs, and I have, therefore, felt additionally flattered by the favour and confidence you have so long and conspicuously shown me.

"Before I came into Parliament, now some thirty-five years back, I had expended some of the best years of my life as a soldier. A general peace was fortunately concluded. On becoming a member of the Legislature, I united myself heart and soul with the (then) Liberal party. This was not very advantageous to me as a professional man. From that period, however, followed a series of improvements in the laws and prosperity of this country, unequalled during any similar interval in the long course of our national history, or probably in the history of any other country. I allow myself to look back with, I trust, pardonable complacency to my honest, if not adroit, support of the great and salutary measures which led to those results.

"Knowing, as I had ample opportunities of doing, the pure and independent qualities by which you were actuated, I felt a pride in being associated with you personally and with your political interests. My career is now closing, and I shall only permit myself further to hope that you will continue to regard me as having been a faithful comrade in the often recurring contests for the promotion of the public welfare.

"Gentlemen and dear friends, I remain most sincerely yours,

"Feb. 4. "DE LACY EVANS, General.

"Mr. GEORGE said during thirty-five years the General had supported many useful reforms. Among other matters advocated by him were the following:—

"1. The vote by ballot.

"2. An extension of the suffrage to every householder in the kingdom; and that each constituency returning two members to Parliament ought to consist of at least 5,000 electors.

"3. The repeal of the 27th clause of the Reform Act, which makes the payment of rates and taxes (before a particular day) a condition of the franchise.

"4. Triennial Parliaments.

"5. A more extensive reform of municipal corporations, especially those of London and Ireland.

"6. A repeal of the window and corn taxes, so grievously pressing upon the industry of the country.

"7. The abolition of all pensions not merited by known public services.

"8. The removal of all taxes which impede the diffusion of knowledge amongst the people, but most especially the stamp duty upon newspapers.

"9. The reform of the Church Establishment.

"10. A proper application of the funds known to exist in the country for the purposes of education.

"Mr. GEORGE concluded by moving the appointment of a sub-committee to draw up an address to General Sir De Lacy Evans, which would be a faithful exposition of the views of the Reformers of Westminster.

"Mr. INGLEFIELD seconded the motion.

"Mr. MALLOCK spoke in highly eulogistic terms of the General's conduct.

"After some further remarks from the meeting, the Chairman put the proposition, which was carried unanimously.

"The following gentlemen were then elected to draw up an address to Sir De Lacy Evans, viz., Messrs. Bidgood, Nelson, George, and Mallock."

WILLIAM HENRY SMITH, ESQ.

When General EVANS took leave of Westminster, closing a life varied in all things, except in steadfast political honour and spotless chivalry, it was felt we took leave of one age and were embracing another. Nor did an unworthy representative of this new age appear. For the first time since the days of Elizabeth, the parish of St. Clement Danes sent forth one of its own sons, in the person of

WILLIAM HENRY SMITH, ESQ.,

of the eminent firm of W. H. SMITH and SON, of the Strand. Those who knew him best gave him the most fervent support, and in his own parish he received the support of 378 voters, being more than double the amount polled by either of the other candidates, as will be seen by the state of the poll at the last Election for Westminster, July 11th, 1865, and detailed in the table below. The total number of Registered Electors was 13,375.

DISTRICT OR PARISH.	GROSVENOR.	MILL.	SMITH.
St. Ann's	209	226	147
St. Clement's	159	170	378
St. Mary-le-Strand	23	26	35
Savoy	9	8	16
St. Paul's	78	92	104
St. George's Inwards	556	514	554
St. George's Outwards	1,217	1,202	921
St. James's	698	727	647
St. Margaret's Ward No. 1	140	133	99
St. Margaret's Wards 2 & 3	335	306	280
St. Peter's	3	8	5
St. John's	762	762	279
St. Martin's	345	356	359
Totals	4,534	4,525	3,824

A greater number of votes was recorded in his favour than for any other Conservative in Westminster, and we may confidently assert that the position he obtained at the last Election was not altogether because he is so much esteemed by his neighbours and the constituents of Westminster generally, for the great interest he takes in the welfare of our city, or because he is ever ready to support the cause of charity, but in consequence of his being a Liberal Conservative, and his great commercial knowledge and position; for by his own energy, added to that of his late honoured father, he has become so large a dispenser of the current literature of the day, that through his vast establishment there flows an unbroken stream of knowledge and hourly intelligence to all parts of the civilized world. The late

SIR JOHN VILLIERS SHELLEY, Bart.,

represented Westminster from 1852 to 1865, during which time he paid considerable attention to the Parliamentary and local business of the city. In his address to the Electors on his retirement, issued May 30th, 1862, he said:—" I am determined, however, to be no party to a course which must bring about the triumph of the political party to which I am opposed; and I have therefore decided on resigning any claims which I may have upon you in consequence of long and faithful service in your interest."

In consequence of the retirement of Sir JOHN V. SHELLEY and General EVANS, both seats became vacant at the same time, and again Westminster returned two Liberal representatives :

CAPTAIN THE HON. R. W. GROSVENOR, M.P.,

who belongs to a family intimately connected with Westminster, the members of which have ably and consistently occupied a foremost position in all the struggles for civil, religious and political freedom in this country for a considerable time; and

JOHN STUART MILL, Esq., M.P.,

the first political economist of the day, who declared that he would not pay anything for his seat, and also declined to give any pledges as to his votes, or to undertake much of what is called local business. Westminster accepted the terms of the great scholar and thinker, and few constituencies can boast so distinguished a representative.

[Westminster first returned members to Parliament 1st year of the reign of Edward VI., 1548.]

Theatres of St. Clement Danes.

LYCEUM.

This theatre is situated in New Wellington Street, Strand. The original premises, in 1675, were occupied by a Society of Artists. Afterwards GARRICK, who died 1799, bought the lease, to prevent them being turned into a theatre. From 1789 to 1794 the premises were let for various entertainments. In 1795 Dr. ARNOLD bought the lease, and built a theatre. The license being suspended, it was then let for musical and other entertainments. In 1809 the theatre was enlarged by Mr. S. A. ARNOLD, and opened as the Lyceum. WRENCH first appeared here, October 7th, 1809 : he died in Pickett Place in 1843. HARLEY first appeared at this theatre, 1815. It was rebuilt in 1816, and opened with an address spoken by Miss KELLY, who was twice shot at while acting. In 1818 the late Mr. MATHEWS gave his entertainment of the "Mail Coach Adventures," at this theatre, which ran forty nights. It was destroyed by fire February 16th, 1830 ; again rebuilt, and opened with English Opera, July 14th, 1834. The great object of Mr. Arnold being to divert public patronage from foreign performers and music to English histrionic and musical talent, the opera of the "Mountain Sylph" was produced, and attracted crowded houses. At first success appeared certain, but, subsequently, Mr. Arnold's losses became so great, that in the middle of the season of 1835 he shut up the house.

The English Opera Company, under the management of Mr. BALFE, opened in 1841. Equestrian performances were introduced,

January 16th, 1844: on April 8th, the same year, it opened under the management of Mrs. KEELEY. Madame VESTRIS and CHARLES MATHEWS held it from 1847 to 1856. Madame RISTORI appeared here in 1856. Opened by Mr. GYE, for forty nights, April 14th, 1857, and by PYNE and HARRISON, September 21st, 1857. Messrs. G. WEBSTER and E. FALCONER'S management commenced July, 1858, and closed April, 1859. Madame CELESTE held the theatre in 1859-60; and the Savage Club performances took place here during March, 1860; Italian Opera, from June 8th, 1861: followed by Mr. FECHTER, whose management commenced in 1862, and terminated at the end of 1866.

OLYMPIC.

IN 1803 PHILIP ASTLEY purchased the Old Craven House in Wych Street, and built the Olympic Pavilion, which he intended for Equestrian feats. It was first opened September 18th, 1806. In 1813 he sold the lease to ROBERT ELLISTON (born 1774, appeared first, 1797), who produced a piece called "Rochester," founded on the well-known anecdote of Henry V. It ran one hundred nights in succession, and attracted the fashion of the West end of the town to a theatre which had before been considered amongst the very lowest in London. He also produced "Giovanni in London," which met with most decided success. Afterwards Mr. Elliston became lessee of Drury Lane Theatre; and in 1822-3 Mr. EGERTON undertook the management of the Olympic, for some time with tolerable success.

The following celebrated actors and actresses have appeared at this theatre:—Elliston, Power, Edwin, Oxberry, Charles Kean, Fitzwilliam, Charles Mathews, Keeley (born in George Court, Carey Street, 1794), and G. V. Brooke (who was lost in the "London," January 11th, 1866). The first character he played at this house was "Othello," and with such success, that it was considered the theatrical event of 1848.

In 1832 Madame VESTRIS (who was born 1797, died August 8th, 1856), undertook the management of this theatre, and continued it till 1839. The versatile talents of this popular actress, together with the great favourite actor LISTON (whose first appearance in London was June, 1805, and last, May 31st, 1838), attracted the most fashionable audiences. He lived at 147, Strand, for some time. The profits are supposed to have been at least £4,000 per annum. Madame Vestris was first brought out as Prospero in a ballet founded on the "Tempest." Her appearance was most successful. It was about this time she was unfortunate enough to attract the notice of George IV., whose too rigid attentions annoyed her considerably. One night he seized hold of her under the piazza of His Majesty's Theatre, and tried to take her away in his carriage, but was prevented by her mother and attendant. She was engaged by the two rival houses, Covent Garden and Drury Lane, for three nights a week, at £100 from each.

In 1840, Mr. GEORGE WILD became the proprietor. He was born the 28th April, 1805, took to the stage in 1825, and with mingled success and misfortune was the proprietor of the West London, Tottenham Street, and other theatres.

About this time the house was under the management of Mrs. BROUGHAM; and Mr. DELAFIELD opened it with great splendour.

On November 11th, 1844, Miss DAVENPORT appeared; and Mr. WATTS became manager in 1848. It was burnt down March 29th, 1849; rebuilt, and opened by Watts on Boxing Night of the same year. Mr. FARREN became manager in 1850; Mr. A. WIGAN on October 17th, 1853, and continued till 1857.

The late Mr. F. ROBSON (who was born at Margate, 1821; played at the Grecian Saloon, as a comic actor and singer, from 1846 to 1849) joined Mr. FARREN (who was born 1787, and took farewell of the stage, 1855) in the early part of 1853, and in conjunction with Mr. EMBDEN, held the management from 1857 to 1863. Here he displayed his talents, and acquired a great reputation in various pieces, viz., "The Yellow Dwarf," "To Oblige Benson," "The Lottery Ticket," and "The Wandering Minstrel." After this Mr. WIGAN again became the lessee, producing the "Ticket of Leave Man," which had an enormous run, and in which Mr. H. NEVILLE's acting was so much admired. It is now under the management of Mr. B. WEBSTER, and is drawing fashionable and crowded houses by means of Mr. and Mrs. CHARLES MATHEWS.

STRAND.

THIS theatre was originally Barker's Panoramic Exhibition. It was first used for dramatic entertainments, and called Punch's Playhouse, in 1831, under the management of Mr. RAYNER and Mrs. WAYLETT, the singer; and there was introduced at this house, by Mr. HAMMOND (whose management commenced 1839), some of the best burlesques of the day. ATTWOOD (who died about this time), was a great favourite at this theatre. Mr. FARREN took the management in 1849; Mr. HOLCROFT in 1855. Some of Douglas Jerrold's earlier plays were produced here. GREGORY, the proprietor of "The Satirist," performed a round of Shakspearian characters with much ability. Some of Charles Dickens' Christmas pieces were dramatised and produced here with great success. Miss SWANBOROUGH, under whose management Miss MARIE WILTON appeared, and the late Mr. ROGERS, so celebrated in burlesque female characters, was manageress from 1858 to 1861; Mr. SWANBOROUGH, Sen., 1862; and Mr. W. H. SWANBOROUGH in 1863. Mrs. SWANBOROUGH is the present proprietress.*

ANCIENT DRAMA.

As two of the earliest English theatres were established in St. Clement Danes, it may prove not uninteresting to our readers if we give a brief account of the rise and progress of the drama.

---

* "Anson's Dramatic Almanack," and "Haydn's Dictionary of Dates."

ANCIENT DRAMA.

It would appear that Edward III., during his reign ordained by Act of Parliament "that a company of men called vagrants, who had made masquerades throughout the whole city, should be whipt out of London, because they represented scandalous things in the little alehouses and other places where the populace assembled." Thus it would seem that these amusements had existed for some time in London, but had received no check previously. Edward's absolute decree was the means of preventing the acting of any play that was not of a religious character, and thus through the representation of sacred pieces, which no doubt was patronized by the wealthy and noble, the theatre began to assume a tangible form.

In the year 1378 the clergy and scholars of St. Paul's School presented a petition to Richard II. praying His Majesty "to prohibit a company of unexpert people from representing the history of the Old Testament, to the great prejudice of the said clergy, who have been at great charge and expense in order to represent it publicly at Christmas."

From 1378 to 1520 there is no account of the performance in London of any farce or play otherwise than of a sacred character. In the latter year Hollingshed's Chronicles say, "The 7th day of May, 1520, the King caused a masquerade to be prepared, and ordered a stage to be raised in the Great Hall at Greenwich, &c. The King, Queen, and nobility came there to the representation of a good 'Comedy of Plautus,' being the first perfect one ever played."

The first perfect tragedy was played before Queen Elizabeth. It was termed "Forrex and Porrex," and performed by the gentlemen of the Inner Temple before Her Majesty on the 18th of January, 1565. The first royal licence was granted 1574. In the year 1590 there were professional comedians in London, but they had no established theatre and played no tragedies. About this time William Shakspeare having come to London and commenced as a player, wrote his rich and admirable comedy, the "Merry Wives of Windsor" at the request of Queen Elizabeth, who, to show her satisfaction, granted a patent to the comedians, declaring them her servants. They were then formed into a company, with proper appointments, and granted the use of a theatre, the prices for admission at which were: gallery, 2d.; lords' room, 1s. In the year 1596 Shakspeare,* at the age of thirty-three, produced his first tragedy, "Romeo and Juliet;" and in the following year "Richard the Second."

Upon James I.'s accession, he confirmed the privileges to the comedians granted by Elizabeth, and named nine new actors. The license recites, amongst other matter:—"And we permit them to perform the said plays, tragedies, interludes, moral pieces, pastorals, stage plays, and such like in public, and for their greater advantage (when the infection of the plague shall cease) as well in our house called the Globe, in our county of Surrey, as in the cities, halls, public places, or any other privileged place, and in any borough of our said kingdom."

Kynaston, the actor, played female characters in so very pleasing a manner, that, coupled with the fact of being exceedingly handsome, the ladies of quality prided themselves in taking him out for a ride in their coaches to Hyde Park in his theatrical costume, after the performance, which was at that time in the afternoon. An excuse made to the King for the actor's late appearance at the theatre on the occasion of a royal visit, was that "the barber had not arrived to shave the Queen!" and his Majesty accepted the excuse with a good laugh.

In 1639 Charles I. granted to Sir William Davenant a patent for theatrical representations, &c., after the manner of early kings. On the north side of Portugal Street, supposed to have been then called Portugal Row, was built one of the earliest theatres—called the "Duke's Theatre" from its great patron the Duke of York, and the "Opera" from its musical performances. It was previously a tennis-court, but was altered by Sir William Davenant, and opened in 1662, with his operatic "Siege of Rhodes," on which occasion appropriate scenery was first introduced upon the English stage. Here also, on March 1st, 1662, was

---

* Shakspeare died on his fifty-second birthday, April 23rd, 1616.

acted for the first time, Shakspeare's "Romeo and Juliet." Here also female characters were first sustained by women. The first play-bill was issued, April 8th, 1663. At this period theatrical costumiers were unknown, although the dresses worn on the stage were magnificent and costly, being the left-off clothes of royalty and the nobility—for instance, in 1671, in Lord Orrery's play of "Henry the Fifth" at this theatre, the actors Betterton, Harris, and Smith wore the coronation suits of King Charles, the Duke of York, and Lord Oxford. In this year the company removed to Dorset Gardens; and the King's company being burnt out from Drury Lane, played at the Duke's Theatre till 1673-4 when they left it, and it once more became a tennis-court. It was re-opened in 1695, when, for the first time, Congreve's comedy of "Love for Love" was produced. The great star of this theatre was Betterton, who acted Hamlet and Othello admirably, and created no less than 130 characters. He died in 1710. Steele says of him, "He was the jewel of the English stage." He was the friend of Dryden, Pope and Tillotson. The house was afterwards taken down and a new one built for Christopher Rich, and opened by John Rich in 1714, with Farquhar's comedy of the "Recruiting Officer." Rich introduced the first pantomime, playing harlequin himself. Here Quin sustained his best characters. The first English opera was introduced in 1717-8. From the circumstance of Quin's being on one occasion engaged in some disturbance, the serjeant's guard at the theatre royal was established. In 1727-8 the "Beggar's Opera" was produced, and played sixty-three successive nights. The success was so great that people were wont to say, "It made Gay rich and Rich gay."

At this theatre, Nell Gwynne having been abused by a spectator, a William Herbert took up her quarrel, when a sword fight took place between the two factions in the house.

This extraordinary woman is said to have been born in a cellar in Coal Yard, Drury Lane, and early in life obtained her living by selling oranges in the play-house.

Her first appearance on the stage appears to be in 1663, and she is supposed to have quitted it in 1672. Bishop Burnet speaks of her in these terms:—" Gwyn, the indiscreetest and wildest creature that ever was at Court, continued to the end of the King's life in great favour. The Duke of Buckingham told me that when she was first brought to the King she asked only £500 per year, which the King refused; but when he told me this four years ago, he said she had got of the King above sixty thousand pounds."

Pennant says she resided at her house in what then was called Pall Mall; it is the first good one on the left side of St. James's Square. One of the rooms was entirely of looking-glass; over the chimney was her picture. At this house she died in the year 1691, and was interred in the parish church of St. Martin's-in-the-Fields. Dr. Tenison preached her funeral sermon, believing that she died penitent. Charles loved her to the last—"Let not poor Nelly starve," were his dying words. She is most to be remembered for her exertions in behalf of Chelsea Hospital, which would never have existed but for her persevering and benevolent enthusiasm.

In 1732 Rich built a theatre in Covent Garden, and removed there, the "Duke's Theatre" being given over to Italian opera, in which some of the best singers from Italy appeared. Macklin, who died 1797, killed his brother actor Hallam by accident in a quarrel scene of an opera performing, May 10th, 1795. The last entertainments given here were oratorios, balls, concerts, exhibitions, &c. Betterton, Harris, Smith, a barrister of Gray's Inn, Sandford, Nokes, Quin, Eliz. Davenport, and many other celebrities appeared at this theatre.

Little Lincoln's Inn Theatre stood in Bear Yard, Vere Street, formerly Gibbon's tennis-court. Thomas Kelligrew turned it into a theatre in 1660. The poet Ogilby had a lottery of books here, June, 1668. Performances were continued until 1695. Betterton, of Drury Lane Theatre, appears to have been the last manager, for after he quitted it it was used as a carpenter's shop, slaughter house, &c., and destroyed by fire September 7th, 1849.

At an early period plays were acted on Sundays only. One piece composed the whole entertainment, which generally lasted about two hours. The audience, before the performance began, amused themselves with reading, playing at cards, drinking ale, smoking tobacco, &c. The critics sat on the stage, and were furnished with pipes and tobacco, the curtain being drawn back to each side instead of upwards, and the stage lighted with branches like those hung in churches. Changes of scene were at one time unknown. It is supposed that the names of places were written in large characters on the stage—stating, for instance, this is a wood, a garden, Thebes, Rome, or Alexandria, as the case might be. Such was the state of the stage at the commencement of the seventeenth century.

The butcher boys were the gods of the galleries, who puffed up or damned both plays and players, led the theatrical rows, were the great musicians at actors' weddings, and the chief mourners at players' funerals,—for most of the sons of Thespis were then interred in Portugal Street burying ground or the churchyard of St. Paul's, Covent Garden. Of such consequence, in those days, was the criticism of these men of grease, that many a strolling manager gave the bumpkins to understand, that his performances "had been highly approved of by the butchers of Clare Market!"

In 1624, Edward Alleyn, of Dulwich, in Surrey, founded a fair hospital for six poor women, six poor men, and twelve children belonging to the theatres of London. Sir Richard Baker, in his "Chronicle of England," says—" This man may be an example, who, having gotten his wealth by stage playing, converted it to this pious use, not without a kind of reputation to the society of stage players." In our own time, through the liberality and great exertions of B. Webster, J. Reddish, R. Churchill, G. B. Child, W. W. Dale, T. Williams, J. J. Stainton, W. R. Sams, and Nelson Lee, Esqs., efficiently aided by their indefatigable secretary, J. W. Anson, Esq., the benevolent example set by Edward Alleyn has been faithfully and nobly followed by the establishment of the Royal Dramatic College.

The Graves of St. Clement Danes.

CHURCHYARD AND VAULTS.

THE Churchyard contains 12,779 square feet, the ground behind the Vestry 3,219 square feet, and the vaults under the church 13,916 cubic feet. From the parish books it appears that during twenty-six years, ending 1848, the number of bodies buried in the churchyard amounted to 2,759; in the poor ground, 705, and in the vaults, 213. The burial fees received by the Churchwardens for fourteen years, previous to 1847, amounted to £2,237 12s. 0d. The charges for interments were:—In the vaults, £6 12s. 4d.; in the churchyard—for adults, £1 17s. 2d.; children, £1 10s. 2d.; non-parishioners, £2 15s. 10d. At the Portugal Street Ground, the following amounts were charged:—for adults, 14s. 10d.; children, 6s. 4d.; non-parishioners, £1 3s. 2d. for adults, and 12s. 4d. for children. (See page 17.)

GREEN GROUND, PORTUGAL STREET.

UPON that site where a noble hospital now rests (see page 31) once stood the pestiferous Church yard of Portugal Street; upon the spot where the stricken are now healed, and the sorely afflicted are tended with all the care which philanthropy and skill can command, there was once to be found perishing mortality, and the dismal process of the grave always going on. The imagination itself shrinks from its contemplation. A Committee, appointed by the parish, sitting upon this subject, in 1848, reported* that the ground contained 14,968 superficial feet, or rather more than one third of an acre; and that the number of bodies deposited in this space during the twenty-five years preceding 1848 were 5,518. The Committee also discovered that a bulk of coffins which would occupy one acre 5,510 feet if deposited together without any earth intervening, had by some unknown means been packed into a space of 14,968 feet or little more than one-third of an acre. The leading members of that Committee were G. A. Walker, Esq., M.R.C.S., Mr. W. Lane, Mr. T. Chapman, Mr. J. H. Dobby, the late Mr. Bateman, and the late Mr. George Huggett, who devoted much time and attention to the subject. The former gentleman, like many of the benefactors of mankind, has never yet received the public honour which his vast services have so well deserved; although the

---

* In consequence of that Report, and the agitation of the public mind on this subject, Parliament, in August, 1850, passed an Act prohibiting interments within the limits of the metropolis, and empowering the Government to "remedy the evils and guard against the dangers of burying the dead among the living." These powers were delegated by the Government to the Board of Health. The metropolis benefited greatly by the passing of this Act, but we very much question if a better state of things exists at the suburban cemeteries; for, according to Mr. Loudin's account, the graves in the London cemeteries are dug fifteen feet deep, in which ten bodies are deposited at a charge of £1 5s. each, which amounts to the enormous sum of £45,375 per acre. The Government reports show that it is the custom at all these cemeteries to place many bodies intermingled from various families in one grave; a custom repugnant to decency, and condemned and discontinued in all the other countries of Europe. Contrast this with the practice at the Woking Cemetery, where in all cases a separate grave is assigned for each interment, which is not afterwards opened, except at the desire of surviving friends for the reception of other members of their own family; and the charge for a separate grave, including the conveyance of the body from Westminster-road station, funeral service and interment, is only twenty shillings. The lowest charge at other cemeteries for a private grave is £5 5s.; the dimentions being, surface measurement, 6½ feet by 2½—area 16¼ square feet. The charge for a private grave at the London Necropolis is £2 10s.; and, by the provisions of the Company's Act, the space of land appropriated to such purposes, in each case, is, surface measurement, 9 feet by 4 feet—area 36 square feet. The Government inspectors, some years ago, reported that 9 feet by 4 feet were the smallest dimensions which ought to be allowed for the grave of a person over sixteen years of age; and this recommendation is sanctioned by the Burial Regulations of the Secretary of State for the Home Department. This cemetery consists of two thousand acres, and is of a firm sandy formation, covered with peat. It is therefore easily drained, or rather is self-draining; and graves 14 feet and more deep are dug without the aid of shoring, and when dug are perfectly dry. Owing to the great extent of the ground, this system of separate interment might be applied to the whole mortality of London for four centuries to come.

Committee of 1848, in their report of March 23rd in the same year, highly complimented that gentleman, and gracefully acknowledged that their labours had been greatly facilitated by the valuable information and assistance rendered by him.

If sorrow for the dead be the holiest of sorrows—the only grief which even if we could we would not be divorced from, the love which is the noblest attribute of the soul—then doubtless is he a never-to-be-forgotten benefactor who has, through his untiring exertions, made the graveyards of England a mournful ornament and a lasting beauty, in place of a foul and dishonouring national reproach. Mr. Walker is such a benefactor : his exertions were not merely confined to Portugal Street Church-yard, but he revealed the hideous and revolting mysteries of Enon Chapel. What loving child—what husband—what brother—what mother that saw her darling child perish like a flower nipped in the bud—nay, what lover whose passionate adoration the gloomy portals of the tomb could not crush—who amongst this sad and long line of mourners is not indebted to Mr. Walker? "We adorn their graves," says quaint old Evelyn, " with flowers and redolent plants, just emblems of the life of man, which has been compared in Holy Scripture to those fading beauties, whose roots being buried in dishonour, rise again in glory" Again, Bourne says—" We place flowers upon their graves to show that their course is finished with joy, and that they have become conquerors." It has been the custom of other nations by their laws and religion to separate the dead from the living, and the construction of tombs at a distance from cities was always kept in view. But until Mr. Walker arose, as far as this great metropolis was concerned, the grave was without honour or Christian remembrance. The decent and peaceful grave, which the thoughtful mind of an Englishman is ever desirous to give to those who have taken up their everlasting rest, was unknown in London.

---

* Note from "Medical Directory," of Mr. Walker's numerous and valuable contributions on this important subject.

ENON CHAPEL.

At the eastern entrance to Clement's Inn, through a gateway in the right hand corner of a narrow dingy court, once stood a building which, in 1823, was converted into a chapel for Dissenters, known by the name of Enon Chapel; and these pious people, looking very naturally to ways and means, turned the vaults beneath their meeting house into a burying-place, which soon became filled with coffins up to the very rafters, so that there was only the wooden flooring between living youth and the festering dead; for a Sunday school was held in the Chapel as well as the congregational meetings. This truly extraordinary state of things was allowed to continue till 1844, when a new sewer having to be made in the locality, and passing under the building, the Commissioners of Sewers discovered this loathsome charnel-house, and had the place closed, but left the bodies to lie there and rot, heedless of all consequences. The upper premises then became tenanted by a set of teetotallers who, among other uses, turned it into a dancing room—one of the sixpenny hops of the day—where the thoughtless and the giddy went to foot it away over the mouldering remains of sad mortality—part of the bygone generation then turning to dust beneath the dancers' feet.

This loathsome abomination ceased in 1847-8, when Mr. G. A. Walker, Surgeon, gained possession of the Chapel, with the intention of removing the remains to a more appropriate place. The work of exhumation was then commenced, and a pyramid of human bones was exposed to view, separated from piles of coffin wood in various stages of decay. This Golgotha was visited by about 6,000 persons previous to its removal; and some idea may be formed of the horrid appearance of this scene when it is stated that the quantity of remains comprised four upheaved van loads.

Application was made by Mr. Walker to the Board of Directors of the Abney Park Cemetery for sufficient space to inter these remains, but permission was refused by the chairman of the board, the Rev. Dr. Russell, except on payment of thirty pounds; the directors of the Norwood Cemetery, however, promptly gave Mr. Walker the required space, and he, at his own cost, had the whole, consisting of many thousand bodies, decently interred in this ground, while an enormous quantity of coffin-wood was consumed by fire at Sydenham.

In the passage leading into the Chapel adjoining this cellar (or as it was called by the undertakers, the " Dust-hole "), at that time was pointed out a copper, in which it was stated, and with good reason believed, that the linen, &c., in which the bodies therein deposited, but not buried, were clothed, was boiled previously to being disposed of in various ways by parties purchasing. It was abundantly proved by Mr. Walker that the bodies were rapidly disposed of by the use of quick-lime.

We cannot, in justice to Mr. G. A. Walker, leave the contemplation of this place without testifying, from our own personal knowledge, to the indomitable energy and perseverance with which that gentleman laboured, and the pecuniary and unrequited sacrifice made by him to suppress one of the then prevailing, most dangerous, and in very many cases most disgusting of the nuisances of the metropolis, viz., intramural interments.

It is hardly possible to conceive, but such is the fact, that within a few feet of the Strand no less than four burying grounds, viz., Green Ground, Enon Chapel, Poor Ground, and Churchyard and Vaults, were permitted so long to exist, and the living breathing on all sides an atmosphere so impregnated with the odour of the dead.

Enon Chapel, after having been turned into a concert-room, casino, prize-fighting ring, penny theatre, bath-room, &c., was about seven years since fitted up plainly but decently as a school during the day and for service. A careful arrangement and attention to details have given it a church-like look ; and it is now well known as Clare Market Chapel. (See page 19.)

Dr. Johnson in St. Clement Danes.

ON Sundays, as the bells of St. Clements were heard invitingly ringing, Dr. Johnson might be seen entering the church, as if anxious to escape all notice. The whole of the service was evidently with him a something real, for on one occasion we find him, after church, in the "good resolution" state of feeling, solemnly recording his determination to go to church every Sunday and read the Scriptures. Again, on Good Friday, 1773, Boswell tells us, he breakfasted with his tremendous friend (Dr. Levett making tea), and was then taken to church by him. "Dr. Johnson's behaviour," he says, "was solemnly devout." I never shall forget the tremulous earnestness with which he pronounced the awful petition in the Litany—'In the hour of death, and in the day of judgment, Good Lord deliver us.'" We also find he repaired to St. Clement Danes' Church on April 21st, in the last year of his life, at the age of seventy-five, to return "thanks to God" for his recovery from an illness which lasted one hundred and twenty-nine days.* (See page 14.)

Dr. Johnson has been often heard to say that, when he saw a worthy family in distress, it was his custom to collect charity amongst such of his friends as he knew to be in a state of affluence, and on those occasions he received more from Garrick than any other person.

At the Essex Head Tavern, the year before he died, Dr. Johnson established a club called "Sam's," from the landlord Samuel Greaves, who had been an old servant of his friend Thrale, the great brewer.

---

* Johnson's Dictionary was published 1755.

It was not so select as the Literary Club, but cheaper. Johnson, writing to Sir Joshua Reynolds asking him to join it, says—"The terms are lax, and the expenses light; we meet thrice a week and he who misses forfeits two-pence."*

Dr. Johnson used to sup at the Turk's Head coffee-house, No. 142, Strand, for the purpose, as he said, "to encourage the hostess, who was a good, civil woman, and had not too much business." Boswell mentions supping there with Dr. Johnson on July 28th, 1763.

Dr. Brocklesby, who was a very amiable and generous man, offered Dr. Johnson an annuity of one hundred pounds per year, to enable him to travel for his health, which Johnson gratefully declined.

It was at Clifton's eating-house, in Butchers' Row, in 1763, that Boswell with fear heard Dr. Johnson disputing with a petulant Irishman about the cause of negroes being black. "Why, sir," said Johnson, with judicial grandeur, "it has been accounted for in three ways—either by supposing that they were the posterity of Ham, who was cursed; or that God created two kinds of men, one black and the other white or that by the heat of the sun the skin is scorched and so acquired a sooty hue."

On the 2nd of March, 1737, the City of Lichfield had the honour of sending forth, on one day, the two greatest geniuses, in their respective paths, that the world has known,—Samuel Johnson and his pupil David Garrick,—who had previously exchanged sentiments, and resolved on an expedition to the metropolis, in order that they might enlarge their views.

In Exeter Street, Dr. Johnson, when he first came to London, lodged and dined for fourpence halfpenny a day, at a staymakers. He and Garrick were compelled to borrow five pounds on their joint note from Mr. Wilcox, the bookseller. Such was the position of two men, to whom perhaps this temporary pecuniary assistance was the means of displaying that genius which afterwards shone

---

* About 1763, Goldsmith, Burke, Gibbon, Jones, Garrick, Reynolds, Langton, Bennett, and other distinguished men joined the Johnson Club, of which the Doctor was president.

so brightly in their respective walks. At the Pine Apple, Dr. Johnson dined very well for 8*d.*—a cut of meat, 6*d.*, bread, 1*d.*, waiter, 1*d.*, observing that "the waiter who is forgotten, is apt to forget."*

In 1764 and 1765, Dr. Johnson was busily engaged with his edition of Shakspeare.

A gentleman being in the company of Dr. Johnson at the Crown and Anchor, in the Strand, while enforcing arguments for drinking added this—"You know, sir, drinking drives away care, and makes us forget whatever is disagreeable; would you not allow a man to drink for that reason?" To which Johnson replied,—" Yes, sir, if he sat next you."

Dr. Johnson was most particular in not permitting a lady to walk from his house to her carriage unattended by himself, and his appearance in Fleet Street always attracted a crowd, and afforded no small diversion. Johnson's fondness for tea is well known, but it is doubtful as to the number of cups he could drink. A lady once poured out for him seventeen cups—the cups were small China ones, and at that time the Bohea was 38s. a pound.

Dr. Johnson gives Earls Arlington and Ossory the credit of being the first to import tea into England. He says that they brought it from Holland in 1666, and that their ladies taught women of quality how to use it. Pepys, however, records having sent for a cup of tea, a China drink of which he had never drunk before. By an Act of Parliament of the year 1660, a duty of eightpence per gallon was levied on all sherbet, chocolate and tea made for sale. Coffee was first imported from Arabia in 1454.

Leaving Gough Square, where he lost his beloved wife, Letty, Dr. Johnson went to reside in Inner Temple Lane, from thence to No. 7, Johnson's Court, and finally, in 1766, to No. 8, Bolt Court, where he died on the 19th December, 1784, in his seventy-sixth year.

But, after all, the memory of the heroic, and much-enduring Hercules of the eighteenth century, Samuel Johnson, must ever remain most indelibly associated with this parish.

* Leigh Hunt's "Town," 1867.

Nobility of St. Clement Danes.

IN the earlier and later Stuart days, Boswell Court was the abode of the quality. Here dwelt, from 1622 till 1625, Lady Raleigh, widow of the martyred Sir Walter. Another distinguished resident was Sir Edward Lyttleton, successively Solicitor-General and Lord Chief Justice of England, in 1639.

From Boswell House, Gilbert Talbot wrote a letter of London gossip to his father, the celebrated Earl of Shrewsbury, of Elizabeth's reign, in 1589. This letter is printed in the second volume of Lodge's "Illustrations."

Among the eminent inhabitants of the court were Sir Richard and Lady Fanshawe. In the Memoirs of Lady Fanshawe, we find the following :—"In his absence, I, on the 16th, took a house in Boswell Court, near Temple Bar, for two years, immediately moving all my goods thereto."

Sir John Trevor, first cousin to the infamous Judge Jeffreys, a corrupt, though an able lawyer, who rose to be Solicitor-General, was twice Master of the Rolls, a Commissioner of the Great Seal, and twice Speaker of the House of Commons, was a parishioner. He, Sir John, had the courage to caution James II. against his arbitrary conduct, and to warn his cousin Jeffreys against his violent proceedings. But, through his own malpractices, he had the great mortification, as Speaker, of having to put the question to the House, "Whether he, Sir John, ought to be expelled for bribery?" The answer was, "Yes." He died at his residence in Clement's Lane, May 20th, 1717, and was buried in the Roll's Chapel, Chancery Lane. How true the mighty poet was when he wrote "Sermons in

NOBILITY OF ST. CLEMENT DANES.

Stones!" Never truer words came from the pen of man. Parliaments are said to have originated in the reign of Henry I.

Exeter House was founded by Walter Stapleton, Bishop of Exeter, who was Lord Treasurer of England in the reign of Edward II. It became the town residence of the bishops of that see, and is said to have been very magnificent. Lacy, Bishop of Exeter in the reign of Henry VI., added a great hall. The first Lord Paget laid violent hands on it in the grand period of plunder; improving it greatly, and calling it after his own name. The great Earl of Leicester resided here, and changed its name to Leicester House, leaving it by will* to his son-in-law, Robert, Earl of Essex, the unfortunate favourite of Elizabeth, who from thence made his frantic and imprudent sally, in the vain hope of exciting the City to arm in his behalf against its sovereign. The memory of Exeter House and these transactions is kept alive in the names of Essex Street, Essex Stairs, and Devereux Court.

Bath's Inn, inhabited by the Bishops of Bath and Wells, was wrested from them in the reign of Edward VI. by Lord Thomas Seymour, High Admiral, and received the name of Seymour Place. This house afterwards passed to Thomas Howard, Earl of Arundel, and was called Arundel Palace.† The Duc de Sully, who was lodged in it during his embassy to England on the accession of James I., says it was one of the finest and most commodious of any in London. The views from its extensive gardens up and down the river were exceedingly fine. Here was kept the magnificent collection of statues formed by the Earl. The palace was pulled down during the last century, but the names and titles of its illustrious occupants are retained in the names of the streets—Howard, Norfolk, Arundel, and Surrey—which rose on the site. After it came into possession of the Duke of Norfolk (the same who presented his library to the Royal Society) that learned body were permitted to hold their meetings

---

* Sydney Papers, 1—73.
† The Earl of Arundel introduced coaches into England, 1583.

in Arundel House; but on its being taken down, the meetings were removed to Gresham College.* The great family of the Drurys had a mansion in this vicinity, which was probably built by Sir William Drury, an able commander in the Irish wars.

Craven House, Wych Street, was in the possession of William, Earl Craven, in 1673, who rebuilt it. This nobleman was very indefatigable in preventing the ravages of fire in those days; and he and the Duke of Albemarle (the noted Monk) heroically stayed in town during the dreadful pestilence, and, at the hazard of their lives, preserved order.

Beneath a tomb with his figure expressed in brass, was buried, in Saint Clement Danes, John Arundel, Bishop of Exeter, who died in 1503, at Exeter House, the town residence of the bishops of that see.

In the old church of St. Clement's Sir Charles Sedley, the delightful song writer and oracle of the licentious wits of his day, was baptized. He was born in Shire Lane.

In the Register of Baptisms of St. Clement's Church, we find the name of the son of Lord Paget, of Clement's Lane.

Sir Arthur Atie Knight, secretary to the great Earl of Leicester, and attendant on the unfortunate Earl of Essex, lived in Shire Lane. He died 1604.

Oliver Cromwell once resided in Clement's Lane.

Peter the Great lived in Norfolk Street, Strand.

John Holles, the second Earl of Clare, resided in a splendid mansion, in magnificent style, on a site adjacent to Clare Market. His son Gilbert, the third Earl, died in 1689, and was succeeded by his son John Holles, created Marquis of Clare and Duke of Newcastle, May 14th, 1694. He died in 1711, when all his honours became extinct.

Between Arundel and Norfolk Streets, in the year 1698, lived Sir Thomas Lyttleton, Speaker of the House of Commons.

Salisbury and Cecil Streets were built by Sir Robert Cecil.

---

* Memoirs of the Howards, p. 94.

We cannot pass the name of Cecil without casting our eyes backwards upon the long line of glory with which it has been associated. Its great founder, Sir William Cecil, shared captivity in the Tower with the great Duke of Somerset, and he who was a prisoner in the brief and inglorious reign of the boy Edward, was destined in the fulness of time to be the wisest minister England ever had. As Secretary of State, while still Sir William Cecil, he signed the patent for the succession of Lady Jane Grey, thus casting aside the claims of Mary and Elizabeth, and recognizing the line of Suffolk. This was almost the solitary act of his great and wise career which he is said to have deplored, alleging that he signed the patent merely in the capacity of a witness, and not that of a minister.

On the accession of Elizabeth he was made Secretary of State, and the Church of England owes to him two great and transcendant services. When the unfortunate Mary Queen of Scots fled to England, Cecil advised his royal mistress to take active measures for the security for the Protestants of Scotland—a step which, although it might awake jealousy in the Court of France, would draw away the disaffected spirit from England. When, too, the Reformers returned from the Continent, armed with the purer spirit of Protestantism which they had acquired by the waters of Geneva, Cecil gave to them his best aid, and counteracted as far he could the still compromising spirit towards the ancient faith, which, like her father, Elizabeth carried with her to the grave.

When Mary Queen of Scots was impeached with the murder of her husband—a crime instigated by a desire to carry on her illicit amour with Bothwell—Cecil was appointed one of the Commissioners to investigate one of the most delicate and important accusations to be found in the pages of history. His vast sagacity, his knowledge of the human heart, his imperturbable wisdom, his calm and dignified bearing, won even the admiration of his enemies. He it was who afterwards was delegated with the important mission to the unhappy Mary, and who drew up the articles of agreement or treaty between the Scottish Queen and Elizabeth.

He had now achieved the zenith of his fame, and was created Lord Burleigh.

Nor can we take leave of this great man without submitting to our readers a priceless treasury of wisdom which he has left behind him. In an age like the present, when spurious and doubtful mental food is supplied for the young, we would fain bring them back to a healthier nutriment, and supply them with that which will lend vigour and buoyancy to their footsteps throughout the journey of life.

Lord Burleigh has left behind aphorisms to guide us in our daily intercourse, which affect daily ordinary life more than the wise suggestions of Bacon, and stand inferior but to the deathless wisdom of the suffering and inspired Psalmist. We invite both old and young to those undefiled fountains of wisdom, to slake their thirst with waters that do not poison, but invigorate.

"I. When it shall please God to bring thee to man's estate, use great providence and circumspection in chusing thy wife; for from thence will spring all thy future good or evil; and it is an action of life, like unto a stratagem of war; wherein a man can err but once. If thy estate be good, match near home and at leisure; if weak, far off and quickly. Enquire diligently of her disposition, and how her parents have been inclined in their youth; let her not be poor, how generous soever; for a man can buy nothing in the market with gentility; nor chuse a base and uncomely creature altogether for wealth; for it will cause contempt in others and loathing in thee; neither make choice of a dwarf or a fool; for by the one thou shalt beget a race of pigmies, the other will be thy continual disgrace, and it will yirke thee to hear her talk; for thou shalt find it, to thy great grief, that there is nothing more fulsome than a she-fool. And touching the guiding of thy house, let thy hospitality be moderate, and according to the means of thy estate, rather plentiful than sparing, but not costly; for I never knew any man grow poor by keeping an orderly table; but some consume themselves through secret vices, and their hospitality bears the blame; but banish swinish drunkards out of thine house, which is a vice impairing health, consuming much, and makes no show. I never heard praise ascribed to the drunkard, but for the well-bearing of his drink, which is better commendation for a brewer's horse or a drayman, than for either a gentleman or a serving-man. Beware thou spend not above three of four parts of thy revenues; nor above a third part of that in thine house; for the other two parts will do no more than defray thy extraordinaries, which always surmount the ordinary by much : otherwise thou shalt live like a rich beggar, in continual want : and the needy man can never live happily or contentedly, for every disaster makes him ready to mortgage or sell ; and that gentleman who sells an acre of land, sells an ounce of credit, for gentility is nothing else but ancient riches ; so that if the foundation shall at any time sink, the building must needs follow.—So much for the first precept.

"II. Bring thy children up in learning and obedience, yet without outward austerity. Praise them openly, reprehend them secretly. Give them good countenance and convenient maintenance according to thy ability, otherwise thy life will seem their bondage, and what portion thou shalt leave them at thy death, they will thank death for it, and not thee. And I am persuaded that the foolish cockering of some parents, and the overstern carriage of others, causeth more men and women to take ill courses, than their own vicious inclinations. Marry thy daughters in time, lest they marry themselves. And suffer not thy sons to pass the Alps, for they shall learn nothing there but pride, blasphemy, and atheism. And if by travel they get a few broken languages, that shall profit them nothing more than to have one meat served in divers dishes. Neither, by my consent, shalt thou train them up in wars ; for he that sets up his rest to live by that profession, can hardly be an honest man or a good Christian ; besides it is a science no longer in request than use : for soldiers in peace are like chimneys in summer.

"III. Live not in the country without corn and cattle about thee ; for he that putteth his hand to the purse for every expense of household, is like him that keepeth water in a sieve. And what provision thou shalt want, learn to buy it at the best hand ; for there is one penny saved in four, betwixt buying in thy need, and when the market and seasons serve fittest for it. Be not served with kinsmen, or friends, or men intreated to stay; for they expect much and do little ; nor with such as are amorous, for their heads are intoxicated. And keep rather too few, than one too many. Feed them well, and pay them with the most, and then thou mayest boldly require service at their hands.

"IV. Let thy kindred and allies be welcome to thy house and table ; grace them with thy countenance, and farther them in all honest actions ; for by this means, thou shalt so double the band of nature, as thou shalt find them so many advocates to plead an apology for thee behind thy back ; but shake off those glowworms, I mean parasites and sycophants, who will feed and fawn upon thee in the summer of prosperity, but in adverse storm, they will shelter thee no more than an arbour in winter.

"V. Beware of surety-ship for thy best friends; he that payeth another man's debts, seeketh his own decay; but if thou canst not otherwise chuse, rather lend thy money thyself upon good bonds although thou borrow it; so shalt thou secure thyself, and pleasure thy friend; neither borrow money of a neighbour or a friend, but of a stranger, where paying it thou shalt hear no more of it : otherwise thou shalt eclipse thy credit, lose thy freedom, and yet pay as dear as to another. But in borrowing of money be precious of thy word, for he that hath care of keeping days of payment, is lord of another man's purse.

"VI. Undertake no suit against a poor man without receiving much wrong ! for, besides that thou mayest make him thy compeer, it is a base conquest to triumph where there is small resistance; neither attempt law against any man before thou be fully resolved that thou hast right on thy side; and then spare not for either money or pains; for a cause or two so followed and obtained, will free thee from suits a great part of thy life.

"VII. Be sure to keep some great man thy friend, but trouble him not with trifles; compliment him often with many, yet small gifts, and of little charge; and if thou hast cause to bestow any great gratuity, let it be something which may be daily in sight; otherwise in this ambitious age, thou shalt remain like a hop without a pole, live in obscurity, and be made a football for every insulting companion to spurn at.

"VIII. Towards thy superiors be humble, yet generous; with thine equals familiar, yet respective; towards thine inferiors show much humanity, and some familiarity; as to bow the body, stretch forth the hand, and to uncover the head, with such like popular compliments. The first prepares thy way to advancement, the second makes thee known for a man well bred, the third gains a good report, which once got is easily kept; for right humanity takes such deep root in the minds of the multitude, as they are more easily gained by unprofitable courtesies, than by churlish benefits. Yet I advise thee not to affect or neglect popularity too much. Seek not to be Essex; shun to be Raleigh.

"IX. Trust not any man with thy life, credit, or estate; for it is mere folly for a man to enthral himself to his friend, as though, occasion being offered, he should not dare to become his enemy.

"X. Be not scurrilous in conversation, nor satirical in thy jests; the one will make thee unwelcome to all company, the other pull on quarrels, and get the hatred of thy best friends; for suspicious jests, when any of them savour of truth, leave a bitterness in the minds of those which are touched; and, albeit, I have already pointed at this inclusively, yet I think it necessary to leave it to thee as a special caution; because I have seen many so prone to quip and gird, as they would rather lose their friend than their jest; and if, perchance, their boiling brain will yield a quaint scoff; they will travail to be delivered of it as a woman with child. These nimble fancies are but the froth of wit."—(From the "Life of Lord Burleigh," published by Langley, High Street, Stamford.)*

This nobleman is endeared to the people of England as one of the wisest and best of her statesmen. But in the great house of Cecil, fame did not stand still, and genius became as hereditary as its territorial possessions. The second son of Lord Burleigh (Sir Robert Cecil) was made Secretary of State, and is still further renowned for his attachment to Raleigh, the most stricken and accomplished spirit which shines throughout the record of English history. He was also appointed Master of the Wards, an office long since passed away, but, at that time rendered remarkable because to gain it was the object of the ill-starred Essex, and the loss of it was the first sad indication that he was no longer the favoured child of fortune.

In Portugal Row (as the south side of the square used to be called) lived Sir Richard Fanshawe. He appears to have been a religious, faithful man, and good scholar, but born in unhappy times, and to an ill fate. Charles I. had, very justly, a great respect for him. He died in 1666.†

In this immediate neighbourhood stood the palace of the Earl of Lincoln. It took its name from that liberal nobleman—the site being presented by him to certain professors of the law. Part of the ground belonged formerly to the see of Chichester. The Bishop, however, in 1537, granted the inheritance to the Brothers Sulyard, students in the Inn, and the fee was ultimately sold to the Benchers for the modest sum of £520.

The living of St. Clement Danes is in the gift of Lord Exeter.

---

* Without anticipating too much, it may be remarked that both the sons of the Lord Treasurer had the dignity of an Earldom conferred upon them by James I. on the same day: Robert, the second son, being created Earl of Salisbury in the morning; and Thomas, the eldest, Earl of Exeter, in the afternoon; and from these two peers are respectively descended in a direct line the present noble houses of Salisbury and Exeter.

† Thornbury's "Haunted London."

Life in St. Clement Danes,
HIGH, LOW AND FAST.

LEMENT'S LANE, from being the polished abode of wit, genius, and fashion, was converted by the ruthless hand of Time into a huge overcrowded den, where blasphemy, rags, gin, hollow-eyed poverty, and stinted industry, were all fearfully huddled together.

Where noble dames once moved with costly and flowing trains, a short time since women in rags rocked to sleep the children of misery, to whom hunger gave a fearful vitality; and where courtiers used to exchange the polished bow of recognition, fearful and brutal collisions between man and man took place. Upon the once polished floor, now crusted in its filth, where stately revelry held its Court, human beings lay stretched, in that association which extreme misery only knows; and the once elegant boudoir of some dead duchess was inhabited by seven or eight wretched human beings; doors stood ajar with the gaping look of poverty and desolation, where the loud resounding knocks of some tall, gold-laced menial were once heard; and where the flaxen-haired children of wealth once sported, neglected children in filth and rags dozed out their wretched existence.

About the middle of Clement's Lane was an entrance to a large house, having also an entrance in Plough Court; at one time this was used as a poor house, but for many years past it has been a lodging-house, as many as eighteen families residing there.

The Irish in this dreary region lived, as they always do, apart and amongst themselves, carrying with them the many virtues and vices of their native land, and never becoming absorbed in the nation to which, for years, they may be attached. Swindlers, thieves and tramps may surround them, but do not in general affect them. Tom Malone still renews, upon English ground, his feuds with the O'Learys, commencing not within the memory of man ; and some Bridget O'Rafferty pays Ellen O'Connor for evidence given by her grandfather against the rebels of '98. It would be a curious investigation for the philosopher how far the interest and progress of this most gallant and interesting nation have been affected by what, in the absence of a better definition, we shall designate the absence of merging power. Nor is it less curious, that whilst the Irish preserve their national characteristics as steadfastly as do the Jews, that they have the quality of absorbing other nations, for we find that the English who settle in Ireland, not merely acquire the brogue, but become more Irish than the Irish themselves.

Ipsis Hibernis Hiberniores is as true now as it was in the days of the poet Spencer.

There are blackened vocalists called niggers, who delight the gaping crowds morning, noon and night, in and around the metropolis, who are in the habit of making themselves up with burnt cork, striped trousers and long-tailed coats, huge collars, woolly hair and other characteristics of the genuine Negro;—numbers of these interesting blacks might daily be seen emerging with lively steps and cheerful voices, dressed in their grotesque costumes, from under the tall archway leading into Pickett Street, on their way to amuse a generous public, and receive their coppery approbation. Rice, when he jumped "Jim Crow," thirty years since, little thought of being the progenitor of such a large family of colored melodists as appear necessary in the present day for providing al-fresco entertainments for laughter-loving crowds.

In Old Boswell Court stood an hostelry named the "Black Horse," which some thirty to forty years ago was one of the best frequented and most jovial of its kind in London, before the advent of music-halls; in fact it was "the" concert-room of that time. Considering the style of building and class of entertainment of the period, in many respects it is doubtful if our gorgeous and expensive music-halls are much of an improvement upon the Boswell Court concert-room, except in affording a greater scope and giving greater facilities for intrigue, and the exuberances of masculine and feminine "fast life."

Many of the public celebrities of thirty years ago were wont to gather round mine host of the "Black Horse," and assist, as the French say, at his nightly "sing-song;" to hear Dowson, Harry Perry, J. Bruton, Toplis, Mrs. Paul, and the celebrated Miss James in her favourite character of the Dashing White Sergeant; and such was the attraction of this fascinating vocalist, that she drew to this concert-room nightly a number of the fast men of the day. Although it was a mixed company, no doubt it was an advance upon the "Cock and Hen" sing-songs, there being a raised platform stage, &c. Occasionally the room would be visited by some sparkling, rollicking sporting men about town, upon whose entry additional devilry and life would be thrown into the scene. The singers might then be seen seated next a marquis or lord, who were never backward about the "one bottle more;" in fact potent liquors flowed freely amongst the whole company; gaiety and revelry was the order of the night, for the greater the glee and the heartier the spree when some of the jolly boisterers were made drunk early. These visits of the noble "bloods" were but the foretaste of future frolics, and but a slight sip at pleasure's fountain; for were there not in this neighbourhood deep and dangerous wells, overflowing with enticing charms, ever attended with beauteous but fallen nymphs, whose voluptuous attractions gathered around them the noble and wealthy, the poet and the painter, the swell and the rogue; and all fast London life here assembled to "make a night of it." We are writing of the days when the Elysium, Mother H.'s, "The Finish," Jessop's, &c., were in their zenith and glory. We are happy, however, to say that they have disappeared. Some yet living may remember the good-humoured though battered beef-steak looking face of "Deaf Burke," who frequented the room, and his "Mind yer, Mister, no flies," when calling for a pot of porter. To this celebrated pugilist is attributed the old story of the "flies in the gin-and-water," and hence the term "no flies" became prevalent. Burke in his youth was a humourist; he was enjoying a bottle one evening with a friend, and as a finish ordered some gin-and-water. "Hot and strong," shouted he of the undeveloped tympanum—"hot and strong, and a dash of lemon." The goblet was brought, steaming with a most inviting odour: young Burke raised the mortal nectar to his lips and beheld some dissipated flies lying at the bottom of the tumbler; he placed the glass on the table and deliberately removed the flies with the spoon, five or six in number, and laid them side by side before him, and then giving a hearty pull at the gin-and-water, he as deliberately replaced the flies within the rummer and passed it to his friend. His companion stared angrily: "Do you dare insult me, and in the presence of company?" said the irate vis-a-vis. "Pardon me," replied Burke, quietly handing the glass a second time—"tho' I don't drink flies myself, I didn't know but what others might." Hence "no flies" stuck to the old man to the end of his life.

Much as may be thought of the sensation comic singing of the present day, this much is certain, could a few of the comic vocalists of that time "re-visit the glimpses of the moon," they could give some of our "stars" a lesson in comic singing, and tell them what real comic songs are. Shades of Tom Hood and Tom Hudson, rest quiet, for sensation trash cannot last for ever!

Before taking leave of the "Black Horse," we have a word to say of a certain apartment on the basement of this house, or as it was styled in the flash cant, the "Patter fee Lumber"—lumber being a cant phrase for room. Herein used to meet some of the most notorious thieves, pickpockets, and cracksmen; in brief, all the "cross coves" of the district. Here they held a kind of club, established for the purpose of furnishing means to fee counsel to assist those who required "legal assistance." We may observe, that the "cross gents" of that day had got up a flash slang, understood only by themselves and some few of the great bloods of the day; and followers of fast life did not think themselves "fly, bang-up to the mark," unless they could "patter and tumble to the last bona dodges out, and were wide awake to every slum and fakement."

Painful is the remembrance of the too long tolerated existence of such a den of infamy as Newcastle Court was a few years ago. It was one of the lowest haunts of this parish, and consisted entirely of houses of ill-fame of the worst description, stored with the foulest moral pollution. There might be seen in the broad glare of day, sitting at the parlour windows of nearly every house, abandoned women, young and old, decked in tawdry finery, bloated with gin and debauchery, lavishing enticing smiles, and bandying obscene expressions to entrap the unwary passer by. The scenes enacted at night were of the most horrible description; and at last its abominable notoriety became so glaring, the parish authorities were compelled to indict the occupiers, which they did, and the vicious inhabitants were turned out; but only for some of them to resume their shocking mode of living in Wych Street. One of the frail sisterhood, whose magnitude of height and rotundity may be better conceived than described, when we state that her weight was above twenty stone, bore the cognomen of "The City Barge." This court then became the residence of hawkers, niggers, tramps, &c. In the Minutes of Evidence it is stated there were in this court two houses in which sixty persons slept. Fourpenny lodging-houses entertained thieves and vagabonds of the lowest class, and it need scarcely be remarked that this was the filthiest place in the parish, and contained more of the elements of disgrace to common humanity than any other place in London.

In New Boswell Court might be seen, until recently, a relic of the light of other days, in the shape of an ancient box (which used to be drawn up from the pavement during the day), fitted for the protection of those slow, antiquated, muffled-up guardians of the peace, covered with their many-caped drab coats, called Watchmen, who were instituted about 1253, who in their wooden house dozed away one-half the tedious night, and drawled out the hours during part of the other half, the dreary monotony of whose rounds would occasionally be relieved by some noisy brawlers returning from their drunken orgies, the cry of murder, or the rapid flight of the housebreaker or the foot-pad rushing away with his plunder, or fleeing from his half-butchered victim; but at length Charley got too slow, or the age got too fast, any longer to tolerate this worn-out piece of animated mechanism, and he found himself one fine morning superseded by that admirably constituted and well organized body, the new Police, as modelled by Sir Robert Peel, which appeared in the London streets for the first time, September 20th, 1829.*

These "Charlies," as the fast gallants and night rangers would call them, were especially marked out as a sport and butt by the nocturnal bloods to play off their spree and larks upon, their favourite game being to floor the "Charlies" in this way :—When they found a Charley snoozing in his box, to upset it, and cage him up, and leave him to kick and shout until relief arrived. Another favourite spree which the night birds indulged in, was to make poor "Charley," intoxicated, which was thus performed :—They would first offer him a drain to wake him up, which was seldom refused by Charley. Each of these drains was deeply drugged, and soon had the desired effect. A hand truck was then procured, and Charley and his box were then transferred to another locality. In these days there were no other officials to intercept the nocturnal transit, so that ultimately, when Charley awoke, he found himself and box ready for doing duty in another parish. This trick, according to the slang diction, was estimated to be a "multa bona fakement," a "ripping slum," and "nanty narking,"—a glorious lark, without interruption.

Bow Street officers were called by the fast men "Robin Redbreasts," on account of their wearing red vests; and though they

---

* In 1863 the Metropolitan police consisted of 6,116 men, who had charge of a district containing over 439,744 acres, had at that time to protect 3,110,654 persons, and to watch 461,845 houses. From a comparative statement it appears in eight years 1858-65, they apprehended 722,033 persons, 397,376 were convicted, 92,555 by indictment for various crimes, and 686,109 summarily convicted for lighter offences. There was 2,349 bad houses, 232 receivers of stolen goods, 2,961 known thieves, and 7,096 prostitutes, 1,356 attempted to commit suicide.—Scott's "Statistical Vindication").

were a set of brave and resolute men, they were too limited in numbers to be generally effective. Amongst the most vigilant and energetic we may mention Leadbitter, Ruthven, Keys, and Goddard. At night the only protection afforded was a tribe of guardians, who, though infinitely more in numbers, were far less useful in effect. These night guardians were generally aged and ineffective men; whose duty was to parade the streets; and the inhabitants, by rotation, had to sit up every night at the watch-house, in Portugal Street, to take the charges. A pleasant task, after a man had been attending to his business all day.

"Plough Tavern," Carey Street, was once kept by Gully, the prize-fighter, the conqueror of Cribb, and champion of England, afterwards M.P. for Pontefract.

Hemlock Court, had at last a dank and dreary aspect, as its name suggests; at one of the lodging houses in this court, it is stated in the Minutes of Evidence—"there are thirty persons who sleep there nightly; that is, they go there from night to night, and any person who could produce fourpence had a bed to himself."

In Plough Court, unhappily, drunkenness and immorality prevailed, where cleanliness and comfort should have existed : squalid misery, wretchedness and filth were rife—children roamed about dirty, ragged and neglected—and rows and fights were of frequent occurrence. Most of these horrors arose from one fruitful source, viz.—the misapplication of the hard gained earnings of the industrious poor, who too frequently leave the deserved fruits of their labour at the gin-palace, instead of applying them to the comforts of home. In and around the vicinity we are attempting to describe, resided a great many of that industrious and very useful class of people called costermongers, who make a great deal of money in a short time, and—much to their own misery—spend it in less.

The knight of the barrow—in the language of his fraternity—often boasts that if he "pulls up his boot" he can "make up his leg," by going to market early, and "knock in" his "ten or twelve hog afore breakfast," while the shopkeeper is in bed. What the horse is to the predatory Arab the donkey is to the costermonger—his all in all. The "coster" would sooner sell his wife in Smithfield, if the law would permit, than "swap" his "moke" at the cattle market. They often realise more profit on "fish" than on "green stuff;" with a little stock-money they can go to Billingsgate, buy up a lot of whitings or fresh herrings in the morning, and convert them into "dried Finnin haddocks," or "real Yarmouth bloaters," by dinner-time in a shed or cellar by a process only known to themselves. As a rule, the thrifty costermonger would sooner break into the Stock Exchange than break into his "stock-money." It is a mistake to suppose that he is addicted to gin drinking, his favourite beverage is a "pot o' four arf" or "drop o' cooper," between him and his Neddy, which the donkey is seldom "ass" enough to refuse.

There flourished, at one time, in Blackmoor Street, the celebrated "Hope Tavern Concert," whereat figured some of the professional vocal stars of the first magnitude. The noted Miss Toplis, and that scion of Comus, Bill Percy, here delighted auditors with their mirth-provoking, side-cracking comic duetts and humorous mimicry. Here Miss Frazier James, the fascinating Queen of Song, "poured forth her native wood notes wilde." Ladies of the first water might be seen here nightly, under the escort of some dashing scion of a noble house—some belted knight, or esquire of high degree—many of whom were wont to pass their midnight vigils at this famed chanting saloon. Here also did that versatile and facetious Bob Glindon open out his capacious comic budget, and rattle forth his "gibs," his "jibes," his "quidets," and his "qualits," and was "wont to keep the tables in a roar" by his never-ending and ever-varying funniments of fiction, chiefly all newly uttered coin from "Brain Mint," in conjunction with many other worthies of the same class, who bravely and dashingly kept up the fame and reputation of the Hope Saloon. Mine Host strictly adhered to the old motto of "No song, no supper." After the singing, the company repaired to the supper-room, and finished by chanting, "We won't go home till morning, till daylight does appear!" This was carried out to the letter; so that, after a riotous debauch in spinning out the night, they reeled "home with the milk in the morning."

The "Fountain," in Clare Street, is now conducted by Mr. Gaffer in a most respectable manner, but was, about forty years ago, a regular crack house for gamblers and sporting men, kept by Sy Nightingale. At this time it was used by "Duckey Fowler," the great cribbage player, "Goodey Levy," of the "Running Rein" notoriety, "Ben Warwick," and all the sporting and betting men of the parish, and in and about London. Another name we may mention was "Shock Jim," who played a man at this house for all he possessed, and won; he then played him for the hair of his head; he again won, and an eye witness assures us he saw "Shock Jim" gnawing it off.

It would appear that the last of the London stocks remained in Portugal Street until after 1820. We trust that our readers, from this circumstance, will not imagine that the inhabitants of this particular street were the worst in the metropolis, or more often required the use of these leg fasteners. It must, however, be admitted that they were certainly placed contiguous to a locality swarming with subjects eminently fitted for a few hours' repose—where they might rest their limbs, to the great benefit of the public.

It is not the most pleasant occupation to have to dwell upon sin and misery, but as faithful chroniclers it is our duty to describe the dark holes and corners of this parish, as well as its bright and illustrious spots, and one of the worst we now arrive at was Lower Serles Place, or Shire Lane, which has always been notorious for houses and taverns of bad repute, and of reputations too black to be repeated. The "Quarterly Review" No. 143, describes this place as a "vile squalid place, noisy and noxious, nearly inaccessible to either light or air, swarming with a population of the most disreputable character." This is applicable only to the lower portion of it, and Nos. 1, 2 and 3, Lower Serles Place, were houses of ill-fame, and it is said, many years ago, there existed a communication with the house, No. 242, Strand, through which the thieves used to escape after ill-using their victims. Nos. 13 and 14 were bad houses; Nos. 9, 10 and 11, where thieves used to meet, was known as "Cadgers' Hall;" and lately in one of the rooms of the middle house were found several bushels of bread placed there by the "distressed" beggars, not for a rainy day, but because they were, through the liberality of an indiscriminating, generous public, provided with better fare. No. 19 was a double house, called the "Retreat," where the thieves ran through, and down Crown Court, escaped into the Strand.* One of the dark deeds of Shire Lane is that in the days of the old parish watch a person was thrown downstairs, the body was carried away and placed against a neighbour's door, where it was found by the watch; no clue could be obtained as to the murderer at the time, but many years having elapsed, two desperate characters confined in the Queen's Bench were overheard during a quarrel to criminate each other respecting the murder. In this lane, at the "Angel and Crown Tavern," a Mr. Quarrington was murdered and robbed by Thomas Carr and Elizabeth Adams, who were hanged at Tyburn, January 18th, 1738. The "Temple Bar Stores" was formerly called the "Sun Tavern," being then a noted house for life in London. No. 13 in this lane was a large building used as printing offices, a portion of which was formerly the "Bible" public house, which about twenty years since was a house of call for printers, and where Jack Sheppard used to resort: there was a trap in the middle of a room, where it is said that Jack used to escape through a subterranean passage and make good his retreat into Bell Yard when being pursued.

The poet Sir John Denham, when a student in Lincoln's Inn in 1635, after a drunken frolic at the "Griffin," in this lane, went with a pot of ink and plasterer's brush, blotted out all signs between Temple Bar and Charing Cross, which cost Denham and his com-

---

* In 1328, the London thieves made their escape over the bridge into the village of Southwark, which, until then, was beyond the mayor's jurisdiction. Edward III. granted a charter assigning this village to the City for ever, and empowering the City magistrates to act in Southwark as in London.

rades some monies. An advertisement which appeared in the original edition of the "Spectator," No. 33, mentions the "Griffin," in Sheer Lane, Temple Bar, and begins thus—" Lost, yesterday, by a lady in a velvet furbelow scarf, a watch," &c.

A tavern named the "Antigallican" stood in this lane at the beginning of this century; it was kept by Harry Lee, of sporting notoriety, and father of Alexander Lee, the first and "original tiger" brought out by the noted Lord Barrymore. This public-house was much patronized by his lordship and others fond of low life, pugilism and brutal sports. The flash cognomens of the brothers Barrymore will afford a tolerably good idea of their amiable qualities: the eldest was called "Hellgate," the second "Cripplegate" (he was lame), and the third "Newgate," so styled because, although an honourable and a reverend, he had been in almost every goal in England except Newgate. This interesting family circle was completed by a sister called "Billingsgate," on account of the flowery and forcible language she made use of. The purification of this lane was a long and tedious process; for in the Minutes of Evidence, March 14th, 1865, one of the persons examined stated that only three weeks since a man in Shire Lane was prosecuted for robbery.

A retired sergeant of the F division of police, during the chartist agitation, was a member of a political society held in Shire Lane, and he tells us that on one occasion he attended a meeting, when a brother member announced to the chairman that they had a spy in the room, and made a proposition to throw him out of the window, but fortunately for our friend another member, displaying more humanity, made an amendment to the effect that the room-door be opened, and if the spy, whoever he might be, did not immediately depart, the original proposition should be enforced: the sergeant lost no time in making for the door, but had forgotten, in the excitement of the moment, of the arrangement made for the police at that particular time to occupy the lower part of the house and stairs for the purpose of arresting the members of the society, and his brother officers not recognising him in the disguise of a shoemaker, together with his eagerness to escape before he could make any explanation, knocked him down with their truncheons.

In Ship Yard the houses were built very high and close together, the upper part projecting over the lower, admitting very little air or light; some of them were of great age and highly detrimental to health: it was a very crowded part of the parish—few places in London having so many houses crowded into the same space—and was made up of narrow courts and alleys, without any roadway. This locality was at one time a colony of thieves; a very old inhabitant assures us that he remembers that when capital punishment was inflicted for robbery, an execution seldom took place without some one from this spot being amongst the number. Many cases of robbery and offences against the law which have taken place in this neighbourhood years back, might be related. Recently, however, although in this vicinity resided not only "unfortunates," but members of the swell mob and light-fingered gentry, respectable inhabitants and passers by were seldom molested. It appears to be pretty generally the characteristic of thieves to commit their depredations anywhere but near home.

At the back of this yard stood formerly a block of houses, from four to five stories in height, which were let out to vagrants, thieves, sharpers, smashers, and other abandoned characters. Throughout the vaults of this rookery there existed a continuous communication or passage, so that easy access could be obtained from one to the other, facilitating escape or concealment in the event of pursuit, which, from the nature of the nefarious traffic in practice, very often occurred. The end house of this block of buildings was selected for the manufactory of counterfeit coin, and passed by the name of the "Smashing Lumber." The ingenuity employed in the construction of the apartments may be mentioned. In the first place, every room had its secret trap or panel, that a free entrance or exit might be quickly effected from one place to the other; and from the upper storey, which was the workshop or factory, there was a shaft or well constructed, in direct communication with the cellar before noticed.

The whole of the coining apparatus and the employés could be conveyed away as by a touch of magic, by being lowered in a basket by means of a pulley. This secret mint had a prosperous run for many years, the master of which amassing a large sum, wisely disappeared; for not long after the formation of the new police and the appointment of detectives, this den was discovered and abolished.

On the north side of Temple Bar, a few years since, stood a small penthouse of lath and plaster, occupied for many years by the celebrated gambler Crockford, as a shell-fish shop. He made a large sum of money, with which he established a gambling club on the west side of St. James's Street; the decorations alone are said to have cost £94,000. Crockford became a millionaire; he retired in 1840. He never altered the shop in the Strand, but at his death the quaint penthouse and James I. gable were removed.

The "Three Horse Shoes," Milford Lane, was kept by M. F. Hawthorne, who died in 1843, better known as Jerry Hawthorne, and so called after the celebrated piece, by W. T. Moncrieff, Esq., of "Tom and Jerry; or, Life in London," which was produced in 1821 at the Adelphi Theatre and had an enormous run. It was acted to perfection by Messrs. Keeley, Wrench, Wilkinson, J. Reeves, Green, and Sanders, Mrs. Yates, and Miss Daly, the original caste.

Sir John Dean Paul, banker, of the Strand, and his unfortunate partners, were convicted October 27th, 1853, of disposing of £113,725 of their customers' securities. This was one of the oldest banking houses in London; it had suspended payment in 1679.

Notwithstanding sedan chairs and coaches, the Thames watermen, in their scarlet coats and badges, continued until the days of omnibuses and cabs gaily to "feather their oars with skill and dexterity" over the bosom of Old Father Thames.* Some of the smartest and jolliest of these young watermen plied their vocation at Strand Pier,

---

* The last we know of going by water to places of amusement on the banks of the Thames was the voyage of small boats to Vauxhall Gardens, at which the last entertainment took place July 25th, 1859. One night, in 1833, upwards of 20,000 persons paid for admission. It was a favourite place of amusement for upwards of 100 years. Sold by auction for £20,000.

but, alas! penny steamboats have engulphed them in a vortex, and the paddles have nearly given a finishing stroke to their occupation. Formerly there was in Strand Lane one of the most attractive and popular nautical resorts, viz., the Old Ferry House, known by the sign of "The Lightermen and Watermen's Arms." It was a snug, but not very capacious, hostelry. It was once kept by an old veteran of the Thames, one Jacob Tuller, who spared no pains to make it a snug "Cabin," or, as it was aptly styled, the "Craft," in allusion to a lighter; and Jacob, the Captain of the Craft, with the attention and assiduity he bestowed upon his guests, received a very profitable patronage, his place being the resort of the crack watermen of the day, all of whom had won their victories on the Thames ere they were wont to meet to pass the social hour and "fight their battles o'er again." The "Craft,"—"Lightermen and Watermen's Arms,"— was also attended by many of the amateur scullers of the day. Here they would arrange and get up sculling matches, mine host, old Jacob, acting as manager and referee. Not only was this the meeting-place of amateur and professional boatmen, but many of the leading bloods and sprigs of the nobility would get on board the Craft and become the frequent guests of old Jacob. Here, bets were freely given and taken, and a good spread and jollification invariably wound up the sports. Among the famous and successful professionals competitors for aquatic honours may be mentioned the renowned champion of the Thames, the inimitable unconquered Bob Coombes, Kelley, Tom Chambers, Dick Mortlake, and the celebrated time-honoured ex-champion of the day, Robert Castles. He not only defeated every one with whom he rowed, but he even contended with and conquered time, *apropos*, in a sculler's match, be it considered. Castles accomplished that trying task of rowing a thousand miles in a thousand consecutive hours. This gigantic labour was accomplished off Millwall. Castles was then made coxswain of the Royal Barge, afterwards appointed ferryman on the waters of St. James's Park, and died one of the most noted men that old Father Thames could boast of.

Having noticed thus much of the late "Lightermen and Watermen's Arms," we must not omit to mention the "Lion," at the corner of Newcastle Street, Strand, kept by the late Mr. Parish, the coxswain and trainer of the celebrated "Leander" Club, who by his gallant sculling won the championship of the Thames and many other laurels, was one of the crack sons of the river, and highly esteemed by all who knew him. He was a member of Watermen's Hall. The "Lion" is still under the management of his relict.

It is said that a waterman, who pretended to be deaf, once plied his oars on Father Thames and was extensively supported. Barristers desirous of drawing in eloquence and fresh air, and addressing an imaginary Court undisturbed, would eagerly employ this seemingly unconscious boatman. M.P.'s bursting with ideas which should electrify the House, would vent them in the silent waterman's boat. This artful sculler was always at a premium for lovers' trips. Must it not have been delightful to be gently ferried along the silvery bosom of the river on a bright summer evening by a deaf waterman! Then would be the time to pour into the willing listening ear the honied words of love, attachment, and constancy, without witness to the sweet and solemn declaration. This jolly waterman did well, kept his countenance and counsel, received his silver and was silent.

A well-known character called "Copper Holmes," lived with his wife and children somewhere along the shore in an ark he had framed from a West country vessel,* which cost him for copper and all about £150. An action was brought to compel him to remove the obstruction. He died in 1821, and was buried in the "Watermen's Churchyard," on the south side of St. Martin's Church.

Mr. Samuel Ireland, the father of Mr. T. Ireland, the celebrated literary impostor and forger of Shaksperian MSS. resided, in 1795, at No. 8, Norfolk Street. T. Ireland, then only eighteen, was articled to a solicitor in New Inn, where he practised Elizabethan writing, for the sake of deceiving credulous antiquarians. A forged deed exciting

---

* Another extraordinary craft was a butcher's tray, in which a man crossed the Thames in 1776. £14,000 depended upon the feat.

the admiration of his father, who was a collector of old tracts and a worshipper of Shakspeare, led him to continue his deceptions, and pretend to have discovered a hoard of Shakspearian manuscripts. A fellow clerk, discovering his forgeries, was made an accomplice. They then produced a Profession of Faith, signed by Shakspeare. He then tried original verse (a poem to Anne Hathaway and the play of "Voltigern.") Mr. Albany Wallis, of Norfolk Street, who had given to Garrick a mortgage deed bearing Shakspeare's signature, became the most ardent believer in the young clerk's deceptions. Ireland was to receive for the impudent forgery of "Voltigern" the sum of £300 down, and a division of the receipts, deducting charges for sixty nights. The spurious play, however, only lived one night, for which the Irelands received their half—£103. The final damnation of the play was secured by a rhapsody of Voltigern's—a patchwork thing from "Richard II." and "Henry IV.," the fatal line

"And when the solemn mockery is o'er,"

convulsing the house. Mr. W. H. Ireland, in later life, was editor of the "York Herald," and died in 1835.

In 1796 Mr. T. Ireland published a full confession of his forgeries, entirely relieving his father from all participation in his silly fraud, asking forgiveness for his deception, begun without intending to deceive—"I should never have gone so far, he says, but that the world praised the papers too much, and thereby flattered my vanity."

The "Coal Hole," in Fountain Court, Strand, was once celebrated for songs and suppers, and patronised by high, low, and fast men from all parts. After the theatres and other places of amusement were closed, this room became filled with the above named class. The entertainments were various, consisting of glees, which at one time were exceedingly well executed. We must not forget the comic songs and jokes of poor old Joe Wells, nor the extemporaneous songs of the well-known Charles Sloman, and the comic singing of Bruton, Bob Glindon, the noted Ross, with his "Sam Hall," and the renowned Tom Peneket, Sharpe and Cowell, nearly all of whom have passed away to a different scene. After this the late celebrated Baron Nicholson became the proprietor, and introduced his Judge and Jury entertainment, and although the sham trials were occasionally tainted with obscenity, they were frequently conducted with much wit and talent, and often pointed an excellent moral. "Poses plastiques" followed, and then the concert room became degenerated and lost its former lustre. Scenes of dissipation were enacted in those times till break of day. Society was not then blessed with an Act of Parliament restricting public-houses from being open after one o'clock.

Lyon's Inn degenerated into a haunt for all kinds of men about town—good and bad, clever and rascally, gamblers and swindlers. Mr. William Weare, who was murdered by Thurtell, October 24th, 1823, lived at No. 2, in this Inn. At the trial which took place at Hertford, January 5th, 1824, Thurtell pleaded Weare had robbed him of £300, with false cards at "blind hookey." Thurtell, who is supposed to have committed other murders, was hanged January 9th, 1824. His confederate Hunt, a public singer, turned king's evidence, and was transported for life. Probert, also his accomplice, was hanged June 20th, 1825, for horse stealing.

According to the statement of Thomas Winter, in his confession, it appears that the conspirators of the Gunpowder Plot of 1605 met in Clement's Lane, behind the church; for long prior to this period, and even before the Norman conquest, the ancient church was built, close to Clement's Lane. But we will quote Winter's own words:—"So we met behind St. Clement's, Mr. Catesby, Mr. Percy, Mr. Wright, Mr. Guy Fawkes, and myself, and having, upon a primer, given each other the oath of secrecy, in a chamber where no other body was, we went after into the next room, and heard mass, and received the blessed sacrament upon the same."

In the busy bustling of crowded Holywell Street, about fifty years since, in the midst of a dense population, was exhibited in two houses a collection of wild beasts, with attendant beefeaters, to attract— amongst those who honoured the menagerie with a visit was the late illustrious Duke of Wellington—the lovers of natural history. We are inclined to think the present inhabitants would not fancy being located so close to the denizens of the forest.

On the left side of Wych Street from the City scenes were often to be witnessed of the most disgraceful and infamous character. In a narrow dirty court in this street, Jack Sheppard, the robber and prison breaker, served his apprenticeship to Mr. Wood, the carpenter, and on a beam in the loft of this house Jack is said to have carved his name: he was born, 1701; hanged, 1724. At the east end of this street, from the window of an infamous house some years ago, a man was thrown and murdered.*

Nat Lee, the dramatic writer, going home from a carouse at the "Boar and Harrow," in Butcher Row, fell down in a fit in Clare Market, and was taken up dead. He was buried in the parish church of St. Clement Danes, at the age of thirty-five.

No. 30, Stanhope Street was, between twenty and thirty years since, known as the "Alphabet" public-house, and was much frequented by members of the theatrical profession.

Denzell Street, about fifty years since, was in such bad repute that respectable people would not pass through it; one of the houses being frequented by persons for an improper and immoral purpose, who were known as the "Denzell Street Gang."

---

* "London Low Life and London Dens." An octavo volume bearing the above title, purporting to be addressed to Mr. Hogarth, containing a description of London Low Life about a century ago, says:—"Link-boys who have been asking charity all the preceding day, and have just money sufficient to buy a torch, taking their stands at Temple Bar, London Bridge, Lincoln's Inn Fields, Smithfield, the City Gates, and other publick places, to light, knock down, and rob people who are walking about their business. Common beggars, gypsies, and strollers, who are quite destitute of friends and money, creeping into the farmers' grounds, about the suburbs of London, to find sleeping-places under haystacks." And subsequently, in the same chapter—"The gaming-tables at Charing Cross, Covent Garden, Holbourn, and the Strand, begin to fill with men of desperate fortunes, bullies, fools, and gamesters. Termagant women in back-yards, alleys, and courts, who have got drunk with Geneva at the adjacent publick-houses, are making their several neighbourhoods ring with the schrillness of their ungovernable tongues. Lumberers taking a survey of the streets and markets, and preparing to mount bulks instead of beds, to sleep away the remaining part of the night upon. . . . A great quantity of scandal published by people of the first quality, at their drums and routes. Merchants', drapers', and booksellers' apprentices begin to be merry at taverns and noted publick-houses, at the expense of their friends and mothers."
—*Notes and Queries.*

EXTRAORDINARY MEN.

The "Black Jack Tavern," Portsmouth Street,* is one of the most celebrated public-houses in London, not only for its Joe Miller and Jack Sheppard notoriety, but also for its having been the house in which the Cato Street conspirators held their meetings. Thistlewood, Brunt, Davidson, Ings and Tidd, the principals, were executed May 1st, 1820. It is also said that the great rebellion of '98 was planned in this house. Societies of a very different class meet here now, under the management of Mr. Smith, the worthy proprietor.

The "Craven Head Tavern," Drury Lane, was kept by Mr. Robert Hales, the Norfolk Giant, from 1851 to 1855. This extraordinary man stood seven feet six inches high. The Queen presented him with a gold watch and chain. He died November 22nd, 1863, at the age of forty-eight, much respected by a large number of friends.

In the reign of Queen Elizabeth, a gun was mounted on the top of St. Clement's Church, which was intended to be used against the mansion of the Earl of Essex; where was born that luckless son, whose infamous Countess was implicated in the poisoning of Sir Thomas Overbury.

On the 19th February, 1718, there died in Butcher Row a truly extraordinary man—Antony Motteux; he was a French Protestant, compelled to flee his country on the Revocation of the Edict of Nantes. He established himself as a merchant in Leadenhall Street; but on account of his extraordinary skill in languages, was appointed to a lucrative situation in the Post Office. He was such a master of the niceties of even our colloquial English, that he wrote, besides many songs, prologues and epilogues, no fewer than seventeen plays, many of which were highly popular. He is said to have met his death suddenly in one of those discreditable haunts which peculiarly characterised this locality from the time of Henry IV.— when, according to Shakspeare, the students of Clement's Inn "knew where the bona robas were,"—down to our own days.

---

* This house is not strictly within the parish of St. Clement Danes, being the next over the boundary.

Alderman Pickett in St. Clement Danes.

N the amusing, historical, topographical, and instructive "Trivia" of Gay are to be found these lines:—

> "Where the fair columns of Saint Clement stand,
> Whose straitened bounds encroach upon the Strand;
> Where the low penthouse bows the walker's head,
> And the rough pavement wounds the yielding tread;
> Where not a post protects the narrow space,
> And strung in twines; combs dangle in thy face;
> Summon at once thy courage, rouse thy care,
> Stand firm, look back, be resolute, beware!
> Forth issuing from steep lanes, the collier's steeds
> Drag the black load—another cart succeeds;
> Team follows team, crowds heaped on crowds appear,
> And wait impatient till the road grows clear."

Turning to a still older authority than Gay, we find that Stow thus describes a block of houses standing in the Strand in his time, and which continued to stand until the time of our grandfathers, but which, since 1810, has ceased to obstruct the view of the Church of St. Clement Danes from Temple Bar:—"On the north side, or right hand of the Strand, some small distance without Temple Bar, in the High Street, from a pair of stocks there standing, stretched one large middle row, or troop of small tenements, partly opening to the south, partly to the north, and up west to a stone cross (now headless) over against the Strand."

Fifty years ago there was a block of houses eastward of St. Clement Danes, of a character similar to that which is still interposed between St. Clement's and Saint Mary-le-Strand, bounded on the north by

Holywell Street, and on the south by the Strand; but with this difference—that the block demolished nearly sixty years ago was wider than that which, though doomed, still exists. The passage between the ancient block and the southern side of the Strand, immediately to the west of Temple Bar, was so narrow that the cant name of the place in Addison's time was "The Pass," or the "Straits of St. Clement." (See "Spectator," No. 498.) "The Pass, which is a military term, the brothers of the whip have given to St. Clement's Church." The southern front of this obtuse-triangle shaped block formed the northern side of the Strand, its northern front forming the south side of a narrow thoroughfare called Butcher Row, which led straight from Temple Bar towards Wych Street.

How Butcher Row came into existence, and gained its name, was after the following manner:—Edward I. granted a charter to Walter de Barbier to build houses in this locality for the residences of foreign butchers, as they were called, but who in fact, were simply country butchers, not of the exclusive City Guild, and they offered their meat for sale here, just beyond the bounds of the City jurisdiction. The creation of Butcher Row was indeed simply an act of free trade, and was extremely popular among consumers, the "foreign" butchers encouraging competition, and kept down prices. In Elizabeth's reign, the privileges of the "foreign" butchers were augmented by their street being formally constituted a regular market. In time, the locality attracted the vendors of fish and greengrocery. Just before Butcher Row was pulled down, its north side is represented by contemporary urban topographers as being devoted to the sale of flesh and other eatables; while its southern side comprised the shops of bakers, smiths, tinsmiths, &c. The houses were wooden, and contained many rooms. They had low ceilings, which were supported by heavy transverse beams, and furnished with ricketty casements.

It was almost entirely due to the energy of one man that the serious obstruction to the traffic of the metropolis which was caused by the block of buildings of which Butcher Row formed the northern frontier, was cleared away. Malcolm, in his "Anecdotes of London," published in the early part of the present century, says, "A stranger who had visited London in 1790 would, on his return in 1804, be astonished to find a spacious area (with the church nearly in the centre) on the site of Butcher Row, and some other passages undeserving of the name of streets, which were composed of those wretched fabrics, overhanging their foundations—the receptacles of dirt in every corner of their projecting stories—the bane of ancient London—where the plague, with all its attendant horrors, frowned destruction on the miserable inhabitants, reserving its forces for the attacks of each returning summer."

Alderman Pickett was the benefactor who effected this salutary change, and it was in honour of his memory that Pickett Street was so termed. This worthy civic dignitary deserves a passing notice at our hands. His life was praiseworthy, and in some respects pathetic. He carried on business as a silversmith, on Ludgate Hill and in Bond Street. He was made Alderman in 1783, Sheriff the year following,* and became Lord Mayor in 1789,† in which year he published a pamphlet advocating the changes afterwards carried out. His eldest daughter was burned to death before his eyes, in 1781, in her twenty-third year. His only son was killed by French pirates on board the "Triton," East Indiaman, in January, 1796. His wife died in October of the same year, and within a month he followed her to the grave. He lies buried in Abney Park Cemetery. Pickett several times unsuccessfully stood for the City. The grand public purpose of his life was the widening of the Strand eastwards and northwards of St. Clement's Church. He lived just long enough to see an Act passed (in 1795) for carrying out his project. But he had been long in his grave ere his purpose was effected. Although not within the City, the expenses of this alteration were defrayed from the civic chest; the Corporation being then, as ever, desirous of extending its

---

* Aldermen first elected in London, 1242. Sheriffs first in London, 1189.
† The first Mayor appointed 1189; made annual, 1214. Lord Mayor's Show—first 1453; last 1866.

jurisdiction and utility. The Act is 35 George III., cap. 126, and is entitled an "Act for Widening and Improving the Entrance into the City of London near Temple Bar; for making a more commodious street, or passage, at Snow Hill; and for raising on the credit of the Orphan's Fund, a sum of money for these purposes." Thus was London indebted to Pickett at once for Skinner Street, Snowhill, and the widening of the Strand.*

Perhaps the most *useful*, if not the greatest, man who was born in Butcher Row, was the late Rev. Andrew Reed, D.D., an independent minister in Eastern London, but best known as the founder of the Asylums for Fatherless Children at Clapton, and for Idiots at Earlswood. His father kept a watchmaker's shop, entitled Beaumont House, in the Row. It was so called because it had been (temp. James I.) the residence of M. de Beaumont, the French Ambassador, and in fact the very house in which the Duc de Sully had slept one night on account of the palace of Arundel not being ready for his reception. There is a woodcut of Beaumont House in the excellent biography of Dr. Reed, by his sons. It was not pulled down until 1813. It had a well-staircase from ground to roof, lighted by a skylight. Its exterior ornaments were roses, crowns, fleurs-de-lis, dragons, &c. It bore the date 1581.

Ben Jonson's more illustrious name also glorifies the locality. Aubrey says—"Long since, in King James's time, I have heard my uncle Danvers say, who knew him, that he (Jonson) lived without Temple Bar, at a comb-maker's shop, about the 'Elephant and Castle.'" In the next century Shenstone, at one period of his life, lived in the Row. His letters, about 1740, are dated from one Wintle's, who was a perfumer in the Row.

---

* The Westminster Paving Act was passed in 1762; before which, stalls, sign-posts, and projections of various kinds obstructed the streets, and each inhabitant paved before his own door, and in such a manner as his pride, poverty, or caprice suggested. Except in some of the principal thoroughfares, there were no footways; this Act ordered the names of streets to be affixed to the corners of each. Shop fronts were not enclosed and glazed till 1710, being open like butchers are. About the time of George I. the extension of buildings became visible in every direction and continues to the present time.

Temple of Justice in St. Clement's.

THE Parish of St. Clement Danes will become the most celebrated and important of all London, for its outer surface and extremities will be fringed and adorned by the new Courts of Law, forming one of the noblest buildings in the world. A large number of the population of this parish has drifted away, and before long their places will not be known, for a stately Palace of Justice will shortly rise triumphantly over fashion as well as human misery, and hold its solemn Court; the new Temple of Justice will rear its classic front amidst surrounding desolation, and the crumbling doorway will be supplanted by the well-turned and costly arch; where drunkenness and blasphemy were rife, learning and judgment will ere long preside, and the silver tongue of persuasion will succeed to the vile oath or passionate threat.

In ages yet to come, solemn covenants and great contracts will be interpreted here, and grand constitutional points will be illuminated by purity and learning; acquitted patriots will be met upon the threshold with the tears and applause of their fellow citizens, and mournful groups will speak in whispers, waiting for the verdict, for or against.

This parish will not only be renowned for the illustrious men in literature and in politics connected with it, for it will contain nearly all the seats of judicial learning in which most of our eminent lawyers and statesmen have acquired that legal knowledge and sense of justice which have been the means, combined with their worldly experience, of giving to England the most salutary and beneficent laws that ever governed a nation—for of all the classes that influence the destiny of this country, England is justly proud of the administrators of her laws.

Before they attained to seats upon the bench, very unjustly designated "the cushion of repose," they had "won their spurs" in many an intellectual struggle in the forum, the senate, and the platform of public life. Who does not recall the "chiefs" of our Courts of Law, —silver-tongued Mansfield, the prejudiced yet learned Ellenborough, the patriotic and pure Denman, who might sit for the statue of justice itself, and our present chief of the Court of Queen's Bench, Lord Chief Justice Cockburn, who immortalised the wrongs of Pacifico, and held the House of Commons captive from the close of one day to the dawn of another! If we turn our eyes from the brilliant stars who adorn our Courts of Law, to the great branch of equity "that cometh in," as Coke says, "to relieve the law," we shall find that it is adorned by men worthy of their exalted position.

What an illustrious line they form! What industry, application, untiring professional zeal marked their hopeful boyhood and vigorous manhood! What learning, wisdom, and wide experience gave honour and command to their old age! In that great and illustrious gallery we behold the form of the great Cardinal who sounded fortune in all its depths.

"I have touched the highest point of all my greatness, and from that full meridian of my glory, I haste now to my setting."

From Bacon, with his boundless wisdom and human infirmities, down to Thurlow, Eldon, Brougham, Lyndhurst, Westbury, and the present accomplished possessor of the great seals—Lord Chelmsford.

Thurlow was one of the greatest lights that ever adorned the judicial seat. Notwithstanding the violent political feelings he ever espoused, even in his extreme old age, his opinions were listened to with the utmost reverence; and his judgment upon the case of adultery committed with a wife's sister, awoke the wonder and amazement of the Lords. It was of him that the greatly gifted, yet unfortunate, Sheridan used to say—"That Thurlow was an impostor, because no man could be so wise as Thurlow* looked;" nor, in the mention of Chancellors, should the illustrious name of Lyndhurst be forgotten; although not possessing the universal powers of Lord Brougham, yet as a lawyer, and as an orator, he may be pronounced the most perfect and faultless of modern days. His satire was of the keenest order and his voice resembled the music of the spheres. It was a wonder, marvel, and delight, to see the old man upheld and placed upon his infirm legs by two peers, and then would mind show its triumph over bodily ills. His refined witticism addressed to the late Lord Campbell, when that learned peer published his "Lives of the Chancellors," is worthy of record. Meeting Lord Campbell, the venerable Chancellor said, "Oh! Campbell, you have added a fresh terror to death: you will write my life, if you outlive me."

Without taking a single note, every word in a debate was remembered and scrupulously dissected, and he summed up with the same lucidity which charmed the Parliament of another generation.

Few who had the good fortune to have been present, as we were, will forget his speech upon the Holywell Street nuisance; when he rioted in the full knowledge which he could so well command of all the great artists and painters, from the days of antiquity to the period in which he spoke.

Lord Eldon was an instance of how a marvellous grasp of mind both in equity and in law does not exercise the same prescience when connected with the larger field of politics. Notwithstanding the slowness in the delivery of his judgments, they stand as models of sound learning. He was the inveterate foe of that Ex-Chancellor who has now attained the patriarchal age of ninety, and who next to Cicero has exhibited the rarest powers of versatility in every department of knowledge.

Lord Brougham has but lately visited his own county—the earlier

---

* Lord Thurlow was not proud of his ancestry, for he says:—"There were two Thurlows in my county—Thurlow the secretary, and Thurlow the carrier. I am descended from the latter."

scenes of his mighty struggles against the great house of Lowther. What memories the well-known scenes must have awakened! What transitions the world has undergone since Henry Brougham walked over that varied purple-coloured heather, and ever worked on to the last in the cause he loved so well. He has transmitted to his countrymen a legacy against electoral corruption.

Ex-Chancellor Westbury enjoyed an immense practice at the Bar, and his elevation to the highest judicial seat met with public approval. We have unfortunately lost for the present one of the ablest and most accurate law reformers of any age.

The title of Chancellor originated with the Romans. It was adopted by the church, and became half an ecclesiastical and half a lay office. The Chancellor was intrusted with all public instruments which were authenticated; and when seals came into use, the custody of them was confided to that officer. The mere delivery of the king's great seal, or the taking it away, is all the ceremony that is used in creating or unmaking a Chancellor, the officer of the greatest weight and power existing in the kingdom. The first Chancellor in England was appointed in the reign of William the Conqueror, and, with only one exception, it was enjoyed by ecclesiastics until the time of Elizabeth, when such officers were called Keepers of the Great Seal. From the time of Sir Thomas More's appointment, which took place in the reign of Henry VIII., there is only one instance of a clergyman having been elevated to that office, namely, Dr. Williams, Dean of Westminster, in the time of James I. The Chancellor is a privy counsellor by office, and Speaker of the House of Lords by prescription. To him belongs the appointment of all justices of the peace throughout the kingdom. When the Chancellor was an ecclesiastic, he became keeper of the king's conscience, and remained so. He is also visitor of all hospitals and colleges of the king's foundation; patron of all livings under twenty pounds per annum in the king's book; the general guardian of all infants, idiots, and lunatics, and has the superintendence of all charitable institutions in the kingdom.

LORD CHANCELLORS.

A LIST OF SOME OF THE EARLY JUDGES IN EQUITY WILL BE FOUND BELOW, WITH THE DATE OF EACH APPOINTMENT AND THE TIME OF BOTH THE BIRTH AND DEATH OF EACH CHANCELLOR.

TITLES.	A BRIEF LIST OF LORD CHANCELLORS AND KEEPERS. Ld. K. means Lord Keeper, not Chancellor.	INN.	CREATED.	BORN.	DIED.
	Thomas a Becket, Archbishop of Canterbury.	—	1155	1119	1170
	William Longchamp, Bishop of Ely.	—	1189	—	1198
	Walter Hubert, Archbishop of Canterbury.	—	1199	—	1205
	Walter de Merton, Bishop of Rochester.	—	1261	—	1277
	Robert de Burnel, Bishop of Bath and Wells.	—	1274	—	1292
	John de Langton, Bishop of Chichester.	—	1292	—	—
	Robert de Baldock, Archdeacon of Middlesex.	—	1323	—	1326
	Sir John Knyvet, Serjeant at Law.	—	1372	—	1377
	Adam de Houghton, Bishop of St. David's.	—	1377	—	1389
	Richard le Scrope, a Cressy Warrior.	—	1378	1328	—
	Simon de Sudbury, Archbishop of Canterbury. [Killed by the Wat Tyler Mob].	—	1379	—	1380
1st titled C. named Earl of Suffolk	Michael de la Pole, Son of the Mayor of Kingston upon-Hull.	—	1383	—	1388
	William of Wickham, Bishop of Winchester.	—	1389	—	1404
	Henry Beaufort, Cardinal.	—	1403	—	1447
	George Neville, Bishop of Exeter.	—	1461	—	1476
	John Russell.	—	1483	—	1494
	John Alcock, Bishop of Worcester.	—	1485	—	1500
	William Warham, Archbishop of Canterbury.	—	1502	—	1532
	Thomas Wolsey, Cardinal.	—	1515	1471	1530
	Sir Thomas Moore.	L.I.	1529	1460	1535
Lord Audley.	Thomas Audley, Serjeant.	I.T.	1533	1488	1544
Ld. Wriothesley	Thomas Wriothesley.	—	1544	—	1550
Mrqs. of Wnchstr	William Paulet, Ld.K.	—	1547	1476	1572
Lord Rich.	Richard Rich.	M.T.	1547	—	1554
	Thomas Goodrich, Bishop of Ely.	—	1552	—	1554
	Stephen Gardiner, Bishop.	—	1553	1483	1555
	Nicholas Heath, Archbishop.	—	1556	—	1566
	Nicholas Bacon.	—	1558	1510	1579
	Sir Thomas Bromley.	I.T.	1579	1530	1588
	Sir Christopher Hatton.	I.T.	1587	1539	1591
	Sir John Puckering.	L.I.	1592	—	1596
Lord Ellesmere	Thomas Egerton.	L.I.	1596	1540	1617
Lord Verulam	Francis Bacon. [Fined £40,000 for accepting bribes]. "The wisest, brightest, meanest of mankind." POPE.	G.I.	1618	1561	1626
	John Williams, Ld.K.	—	1621	1582	1650
	Sir Thomas Coventry, Ld.K.	I.T.	1625	1578	1640
	Sir John Finch, Ld.K.	G.I.	1640	1584	1660
	Sir Edward Littleton, Ld.K.	I.T.	1641	1589	1645
	Sir Richard Lane, Ld.K.	—	1645	—	1646

From 1645 to 1660 is very barren of interest. Our second list will begin from the Restoration.

LORD AND VICE-CHANCELLORS.

SECOND BRIEF LIST OF LORD CHANCELLORS AND KEEPERS.
Ld. K. means Lord Keeper, not Chancellor.

TITLES.		INN.	CREATED.	BORN.	DIED.
Lord Clarendon.	Edward Hyde	M.T.	1660	1609	1674
	Sir Orlando Bridgman, Ld. K	I.T.	1667	—	1673
Ld. Shaftesbury.	Anthony A. Cooper	L.I.	1672	1621	1683
Ld. Nottingham.	Heneage Finch	—	1673	1621	1682
Lord Guildford.	Francis North, Ld. K.	M.T.	1682	1637	1685
Lord Jeffreys.	George Jeffreys, the Cruel	I.T.	1685	1648	1689
	In Commission, 1687.—Maynard, &c.				
	Ditto 1690.—Trevor, &c.				
Lord Somers.	John Somers	M.T.	1693	1650	1716
	Nathan Wright, Ld. K.	I.T.	1700	1653	1721
Lord Cowper.	William Cowper	M.T.	1705	1664	1723
Lord Harcourt.	Simon Harcourt	I.T.	1710	1660	1727
Erl. of Mcclesfld.	Thomas Parker	I.T.	1718	1666	1732
Lord King.	Peter King	M.T.	1725	1669	1734
Lord Talbot.	Charles Talbot	I.T.	1733	1684	1737
Erl. of Hardwicke	Philip Yorke	M.T.	1737	1690	1764
Erl. Northington	Robert Henley	I.T.	1760	1708	1772
Earl Camden.	Charles Pratt	I.T.	1766	1714	1794
	Charles Yorke	M.T.	1770	1723	1770
Lord Bathurst.	Henry Bathurst	L.I.	1771	1714	1794
Lord Thurlow.	Edward Thurlow	M.T.	1778	1732	1806
Ld. Louborough.	Alexander Wedderburn	I.T.	1793	1733	1805
Earl of Eldon.	John Scott; again 1807 and 1820	M.T.	1801	1751	1838
Lord Erskine.	Thomas Erskine.	L.I.	1806	1750	1823
Lord Lyndhurst.	John Singleton, Copley; again 1834	L.I.	1827	1772	1864
Lord Brougham.	Henry Brougham; and 1832	L.I.	1831	1778	—
Lord Cottenham.	Christopher Pepys; and 1847	I.I.	1837	1781	1851
Ld. St. Leonards	Edward B. Sugden; and 1853	L.I.	1845	1781	—
Lord Truro.	Thomas Wilde	G.I.	1851	1782	1855
Lord Cranworth.	Robert Monsey Rolfe; and 1865	L.I.	1854	1790	—
Lord Chelmsford	Frederic Thesiger; and 1866	I.T.	1859	1794	—
Lord Campbell.	John Campbell	L.I.	1860	1779	1861
Lord Westbury.	Richard Bethell	M.T.	1862	1800	—

For some of the dates in the above lists we have consulted Lord Campbell's "Lives of the Chancellors."

What a glorious galaxy of men the Chancellors of England form! Worthy to rank side by side with her undying poets, orators, historians, warriors and statesmen. Nor, in the homage paid to this brilliant constellation, should we omit the equally illustrious labourers in the vineyard, whose vast learning[*] and useful research, (although the world may be taking less note of them,) lighten the labours of the Great Seal, and supply it with many wise suggestions.

The clear perception of the late Lord Justice Turner, when he

---

[*] From Lord Bacon, whose legal acquirements formed a massive framework for those visions of future wisdom in which he half anticipated the discoveries of ages, down to the present time, the annals of the bar are rich in histories of men who have loved literature not only well but wisely.—*Law Magazine*.

filled the duties of Vice-Chancellor, the classic humour, vast learning, and fine judgment of Knight Bruce, and the truly equitable, upright and conscientious judgments of the eminent and distinguished men who now adorn our Courts of Equity, viz., Lord Cairns, Rolt, Stuart, Malins, and Page Wood, cannot fail to excite our highest admiration. We close this little notice of a few of the Chancellors and Vice-Chancellors of this country with the last-mentioned name, it being endeared to the people of England, not merely by the lucidity and clearness of his judgments, but by that holier and tenderer light which directs all the acts of a warm and truly Christian heart.

THE INNS OF COURT.

THERE are only four Inns of Court where gentlemen can be called to the bar, which have been oddly defined in the following doggrel lines :—

> "Inner Temple for the rich,
> Middle Temple for the poor,
> Lincoln's Inn for a gentleman,
> And Gray's Inn makes the four."

The learned Fortescue, who lived about the commencement of the 15th century, gives his opinion that the name Inns of Court arose from these places being the inns, hospitals, or hotels, where young men of family and other persons attached to the Court resided, and not from anything connected with law; for many persons of rank and opulence sent their sons here to study and improve their minds and manners without any thought of following the profession of the law.

These were formerly called the Inner Courts of Law, because the Inns of Law were once divided into three classes, viz., Inner, Utter or Outer, and Serjeants.

The Utter or Outer were designated Inns of Chancery, where the elements of law were acquired by students, prior to their entering the Inner Courts. Their number was eight, viz., Clifford's, 1345; Clement's, 1471; New, 1485; Lyon's, 1420; Thavie's, 1519; Barnard's, 1445; Staple, 1415; Furnival's, 1563. The dates denote when each of these Inns was founded, or perhaps more correctly speaking, is supposed to have been founded.

Serjeants' Inns once numbered three, but there is now only one left, which is situate in Chancery Lane. One of the other two was in Fleet Street, in a place which still retains its name, though no longer inhabited exclusively by Serjeants. The other was in Scroop's Court, Holborn, near St. Andrew's Church, but all its glories have passed away and its name too. From this, it is evident the number of Inns is thirteen, nine of which are within and four without the Liberties of the City, and all extra parochial till very lately, if not still so.

ROLLS COURT AND CHAPEL.

Serjeants' Inn seems to have belonged to the law as early as the reign of Richard II. In Henry IV.'s time it was called Faryndon Inne, and the Serjeants-at-law then resided here. The hall and chapel are worth seeing. The Society have taken a Stork as their arms.

Coke says the Order of Serjeants of Law is upwards of 1,100 years standing. They are mentioned in a statute during the reign of Edward I.

On the site of Rolls Court, Chancery Lane, once stood an hospital, or convent or monastery, built by Henry III. for the converted Jews, but the non-converted soon became money-clippers, and Edward I. caused about 280 of them, of both sexes, to be hanged for this crime; and about 1290 all the Jews in England were unjustly banished out of the realm.

In the year 1377, Edward III. granted these premises to the Keeper of the Rolls of the Chancery, and the first Master of the Rolls was then sworn in Westminster Hall, at the table of marble stone. These Masters were at first chosen from the Church, but in 1534, Thomas Cromwell, afterwards Earl of Essex, was appointed. This office follows in rank that of the Chief Justice of the Queen's Bench, and its duties are to assist the Lord Chancellor in the business of his Court, and to whom appeals may be made if the Master's decrees are thought to be wrong. The Master of the Rolls has the appointment of the six Clerks to the Court of Chancery, each of whom has fifteen assistants under him, called Clerks of Court.

The Rolls Chapel was first built in 1232, and rebuilt in 1617. It is thought to be the work of Inigo Jones. It is small, and has attached to it a peculiar air of gloom and solemnity. There is one monument here particularly deserving of attention: it is that of John Yonge, LL.D., Master of the Rolls during the early part of the reign of Henry VIII. The figure rests on a sarcophagus, and is habited in a long red gown and a deep square cap. It is the work of Pietro Forregiano, a very eminent Florentine, who, in his own country, was placed in competition with Michael Angelo, and there is little doubt that his talents must have been of the first order as a sculptor. The Master's house was erected about the year 1717.

Here it will be as well to mention a few of the Inns that have become defunct; and first, Chester Inn, which stood where Somerset House now stands ; a second was situate at Dowgate ; a third at Paternoster Row ; and a fourth near the Cathedral of St. Paul's, where each lawyer had his pillar, and during certain hours of the day, stood with pen and paper and book in hand, ready to receive instructions from clients. This practice was then so generally recognized, that when a new serjeant was made, the whole body of serjeants, dressed in their robes, walked to St. Paul's to invest their new brother with his particular pillar of business.

Even Lyon's Inn, in Newcastle Street, Strand, which once appertained to the Inner Temple, is now no more, having been alienated to a company and pulled down to form a grand hotel.

INNS OF COURT.

Barnard's Inn, Holborn, appears to appertain to none of the four principal inns of law, and very little is known about it. In its hall there is a portrait of Chief Justice Holt, who was a member of this society.

Thavie's Inn was dissolved in 1768.

The four principal Inns of Court are:—

I.—THE INNER TEMPLE.

THIS society was founded by the Knights Templars, about the year 1118. At the dissolution of this order, in 1312, though the members began so poor that two men riding on one horse was their great seal, yet so enormously rich had they become, that at their dispersion they were found to be possessed of 16,000 manors. Afterwards the Knights of St. John of Jerusalem had some interest in the Temple, through a grant to them from Edward III., which was entirely lost at the dissolution of the order, in 1539; for all monastic orders were wisely done away with between the years 1536 and 1540, at which time these religious houses held two-thirds of the lands within the City of London, and one in every five of the inhabitants belonged to these brotherhoods, which then separated the drones from the working bees. What a lamentable state of things! God forbid that England should ever see such idle and profligate times again. The friaries, priories, monasteries, nunneries, fraternities, &c., were too many to enumerate in a small work like this, but they all tended to impoverish the State, and to keep the kingdom from progressing, and the people in ignorance and laziness. This establishment first became one of the Inns of Court in the reign of Edward III., and was very early divided into two bodies,—the Inner and the Middle Temple.

The Flying Horse, or Pegasus, is taken as the Inner Temple arms. Did the society intend this emblem to show that fortune has wings, and that the law makes it fly in every direction? For it is certainly a most appropriate representation of wealth and fickle fortune.

The Inner Temple Gardens are very fine, and form a beautiful promenade on the banks of the Thames. At certain times in summer they are most courteously thrown open to the public. The society's autumnal show of dahlias, chrysanthemums, and pompons is truly magnificent.

INNS APPERTAINING TO THE INNER TEMPLE.

FIRST, Clement's Inn, the western boundary of the site of the intended New Courts of Law: its hall was built about the year 1715. This inn was the residence of the students of the law as early as the reign of Edward IV. Shakspeare has immortalised this place in the second part of his drama of Henry IV., in his facetious character of Master Shallow; and the black figure kneeling in the garden supporting a sun-dial is said to be of bronze, and turned by paint into a black-a-moor; it is considered to possess great merit. It was brought from Italy about the beginning of the eighteenth century, by the then Lord Clare, and presented by himself to this society. Lord Chief Justice Saunders, who succeeded Sir Francis Pemberton, Chief Justice in 1681, received the rudiments of his education in this Inn. He was originally, it is said, a strolling beggar about the streets, without known parents or relations; and, coming often to beg scraps at Clement's Inn, was taken notice of from his uncommon sprightliness; and, as he expressed a strong inclination to learn to write, one of the attorney's clerks taught him, and soon qualified him for a hackney writer. In this station he took all opportunities of improving himself by reading such books as he borrowed of his friends, and in the course of a few years became an able attorney, and a very eminent counsel. He was much employed by the king against the City of London, in the business of the *quo warranto*. Second, Clifford's Inn, so named from some of the ancient and noble families of De Clifford, lies behind St. Dunstan's Church, Fleet Street. It was transferred to students of the law during the reign of Edward III. It is supposed to be one of the oldest Inns of Chancery now extant.

II.—MIDDLE TEMPLE AND ITS NOBLE HALL.

This inn is but a part of the Inner Temple, as before stated. The hall is a fine specimen of the Elizabethan style of architecture, being built between the years 1562 and 1572; its length is about 100 feet, and its width about 40 feet. It only wants to be seen to be admired, which can always be done at term time, and at other times by an order from a bencher. In this hall is a portrait of Charles I., on horseback—said to be an original Vandyke; but many think it is only a copy by old Stone, who often tried to imitate Vandyke, but always failed, as his sombre and heavy tints prove, these being the distinguishing characters of all his pictures.

The Old Library, at the back of the hall in the Garden, was erected in 1625, but a new Library adjoining the garden, and on the banks of the Thames, was built a few years ago, and opened 31st October, 1861. The Middle Temple Gate was built in 1684, by Sir Christopher Wren, in the style of Inigo Jones.

In the Middle Temple Garden our immortal bard, Shakspeare, in his drama of Henry VI., part I., makes those unhappy badges of distinction, the White and Red Rose, to have originated in that fearful feud between the houses of York and Lancaster, saying—

"This brawl to-day,
Grown to this faction in the Temple Garden,
Shall send, between the Red Rose and the White,
A thousand souls to death and deadly night."

A lamb carrying a banner is taken as the arms of this society, showing that the members of the law protect their clients and preserve their property.

INNS APPERTAINING TO THE MIDDLE TEMPLE.

New Inn adjoins Clement's Inn in the Strand; it was once an inn or hostelry for travellers, and was known by the sign of the Blessed Virgin, and called Our Lady's Inn. In 1485 it became an Inn of Chancery. Students o the law settled here about the reign of Edward VI., and were removed from an old Inn of Chancery, situate in Seacoal Lane, a little south from St. Sepulchre's Church, called St. George's Inn, and was procured from Sir John Fineux, knight, some time Lord Chief Justice of the King's Bench, for the rent of £6 per annum, by the name of New Inn. This tradition is confirmed by Stow. The armorial bearings of this Society are: vert, a flower-pot argent. Sir Thomas More was one of its students in the reign of Henry VII. before he entered as a fellow of Lincoln's Inn. A "mootyng bout" took place at this Inn at the end of the last century. Such gesticulation and passion were shown by the gentleman wrangling that the passers by who heard and saw him thought he was beside himself. This mootyng means arguing points of law before the Benchers, and was done by men who had continued in the house five or six years. These law wranglers were called Utter Barristers, no doubt meaning outer, because not yet belonging to any one of the four superior Inns of Court.

THE TEMPLE CHURCH, CALLED ST. MARY'S.

This fine old edifice was built by the Knights Templars in the reign of Henry II. The plan of it was taken from the Temple near to the Holy Sepulchre at Jerusalem; it belongs to both the Inner and the Middle Temple Societies. The group of knights in stone in the entrance (formerly nine in number) is particularly striking. One of them lying cross-legged is said to have been William Marshall, first Earl of Pembroke, who died in 1219. Some think it is the effigy of Gilbert Marshall, third Earl of Pembroke, who was killed by a fall from his horse at a tournament near Ware, in Hertfordshire, June, 1241. Camden informs us, however, that William, and his sons William and Gilbert (all marshals of England and Earls of Pembroke) were buried and had statues in this Church; perhaps all their statues are amongst the group. Another represents Geoffrey de Mandeville, created Earl of Essex in 1148. The stone coffin amongst the figures is supposed to have contained the body of William Plantagenet, fifth son of Henry III. Plowden, Selden, and many other worthies were buried here, and in the churchyard lies that child of nature, the celebrated Oliver Goldsmith, who died in 1774, at the age of forty-six; his grave may still be seen, being marked out by a stone.

Dr. Johnson having resided in Inner Temple Lane, and Goldsmith in Brick Court, Middle Temple, their names have very properly been given to the new buildings leading from Fleet Street to the church and churchyard as a mark of respect for their great talents and erudition.

III.—LINCOLN'S INN.

LINCOLN'S INN, in its general and geographical sense, includes Old Buildings, New Square, Stone Buildings, and the site of the New Hall and Library, with the adjoining Gardens. It derives its name from Henry Lacy, Earl of Lincoln, who built a mansion here in the reign of Edward I. It is said that during his life he assigned his residence to the professors of the law. He was the confidential servant and friend of Edward I; he died in 1310, and was buried in St. Paul's Cathedral. During the Earl's life, extensive and productive gardens existed here. From documents now in the office of the Duchy of Lancaster, it appears that fruit of every description was grown here, sufficient not only to supply the Earl's table, but also to yield a profit by its sale.

Nearer towards Holborn was the "Coneygarth," so called from the number of rabbits found here; and by various ordinances of the society, in the reigns of Edward IV., Henry VII., and Henry VIII., penalties were imposed on the students hunting them with bows and arrows, or darts.

THE OLD HALL.

The Old Hall, situate in the first court opposite the gate entrance from Chancery Lane, is the oldest edifice of the Inn now remaining, having been erected in the 22nd of Henry VII. A.D. 1506. Over the gateway, it is said, Oliver Cromwell had chambers. The Hall has on each side three large windows of three lights each, the heads of which are arched and cusped, besides the two great oriels at the extremities.

The oriels have four lights each, transomed with arched heads and cusps. The walls are strengthened by buttresses, and the parapet is embattled. The entrance is under an archway at the southern extremity. The hall is about seventy-one feet in length and thirty-two feet in breadth; the height being equal to the breadth. Although extremely just in its proportions, and termed by old writers "a goodly hall," it certainly is not equal in stateliness to the Hall of the Middle Temple. At the southern end of the hall is a statue, by Westmacott, of Lord Erskine who was Lord Chancellor in 1806; it is one of the finest works of the sculptor, and cost 2,300 guineas, raised by subscription among barristers: there is also a painting of Paul before Felix, by Hogarth.

OLD BUILDINGS.

The Old Buildings are at the eastern part of the Inn, being about 500 feet in extent, in Chancery Lane: these buildings were erected at various times from Henry VII. to James I. The most noticeable of these buildings is the Gate House, which, excepting that at Lambeth Palace, St. James's Palace, and that of the Knights of St. John, Clerkenwell, is the only one of similar style and date now remaining in the metropolis.

THE CHAPEL.

Much criticism has been called forth on the origin and design of this building by various writers. There appears, however, to be but little doubt that it was built from a design of Inigo Jones, in 1620, by John Clarke (he being the mason employed) at a cost of £2,000. This opinion is confirmed by an entry in one of the Harleian MSS. No. 5,900, written about the year 1700. It is stated that Inigo Jones built the Chapel in Lincoln's Inn, "after the Gothick manner in imitation of that of St. Stephen's at Westminster." It was repaired by Wyatt, in 1791, at a cost of £7,000. Here Ben Jonson is said to have assisted with his trowel. The appearance of the chapel, on entering, is remarkably impressive, an effect produced by the chastened light transmitted by the beautiful stained glass in the very fine windows, the brilliant colours of which far surpass the generality of works in this style of art. The carved oaken seats merit attention, from their design and very superior execution, as specimens of taste in the reign of James I.; but the pulpit, of a later date, does not deserve the same commendation.

THE PREACHERS.

The first appointment of a preacher, or, as he was formerly called, divinity reader or lecturer, appears to have been in the year 1581, since which time many of the most distinguished and eloquent divines of the Church of England have filled the office of preacher to the society, amongst whom may be named Dr. Donne, Thomas Gataker, Archbishop Tillotson, Dr. Hurd, Bishop Warburton, and Bishop Heber.

The clergy were our only lawyers in early times; and when prohibited from pleading causes, in or about the thirteenth century, some priests, still continuing this lucrative employment, covered their tonsure, or bald place on the top of the head, with a piece of lawn called a coif, and the Serjeants-at-Law now wear a black patch in the middle of their wigs denoting their dignity.

Among the remarkable persons buried in the Cloister under the Chapel are John Thurloe, Secretary of State to Oliver Cromwell; and William Prynne, to whom English history is indebted for the preservation of many of the public records. On the ascent to the Chapel is a marble tablet to the memory of Eleanor Louisa, daughter of the Right Hon. Lord Brougham, with an inscription by the late Marquis Wellesley written in his 81st year.

NEW SQUARE.

The eleven houses forming three sides of the square were formerly called Serle's Court, having been built in 1682 by Henry Serle, one of the benchers of Lincoln's Inn; they are built of brick and are wholly occupied as chambers; many of the most eminent members of the bar and legal profession holding them. The open space was enclosed and planted with trees and shrubs in 1845.

STONE BUILDINGS.

So called from the material of which it is built, is at the north-eastern extremity of Lincoln's Inn; this is only part of a design in 1780 for rebuilding the whole Inn, which unfortunately was not carried out. The structure is commodious and imposing in appearance when viewed from the gardens, but is by no means in keeping with the other buildings in the Inn. The northern entrance is by handsome iron gates at the upper part of Chancery Lane.

THE GARDENS.

The Gardens of Lincoln's Inn were famous of old time, but have been greatly curtailed by the erection of the New Hall and Library, before which the venerable trees have fallen; and "the walks under the elms," celebrated by Ben Jonson, to which Isaac Bickerstaff delighted to resort and indulge in quiet meditations, have disappeared.

THE NEW HALL AND LIBRARY.

This magnificent edifice was built from the design of Mr. Hardwick, the eminent architect; the style is in accordance with the venerable associations belonging to the early history of the society and the character of the more ancient buildings of the Inn. The foundation stone was laid on the 20th of April, 1843, and the building completed within two years and a-half from that date. This noble building forms one of the chief ornaments of the metropolis. The magnificent dimensions of the Hall are of themselves sufficient to excite admiration, while in architectural beauty the room will bear comparison with the most admired examples. In size it exceeds the halls of the Middle Temple, Hampton Court, and Christ Church, Oxford.* The plot of ground known as Lincoln's Inn Fields was mapped out for a garden by Inigo Jones, who made the enclosure exactly of the dimensions of one of the Pyramids of Egypt at its base.

The original foundation of the Library of Lincoln's Inn is of anterior date to

---

* A comparison of the dimensions of some of the largest existing halls, copied from a work upon Lincoln's Inn, its ancient and modern buildings, with an account of the Library, by Mr. William Holden Spilsbury.

	Length feet	Width feet	Height feet		Length feet	Width feet	Height feet
Lincoln's Inn	120	45	62	Goldsmith's Hall	80	40	35
Westminster Hall	238	66	110	Euston Square Terminus	130	62	64
Guildhall, London	153	48	55	Christ Church, Oxford	115	40	50
Christ's Hospital	187	51	47	Hampton Court	106	40	45
Lambeth Palace	93	38	—	Eltham Palace	101	36	54
Middle Temple	100	42	47	New Hall, Boucham, Essex	90	40	—
St. Bartholomew's Hospital	90	35	30	St. George's Hall, Liverpool	170	74	82
Freemason's Hall	96	38	37	Town Hall, Birmingham	140	65	65
Crosby Hall	69	27	38				

that of any now existing in the metropolis. In the thirteenth year of the reign of Henry VII. (A.D. 1497), John Nethersale, late one of this Society, bequeathed forty marks towards the building of a library for the students of the law of England. The Library has been enriched at various times by donations from members of the Society, and now consists of stores of intellectual wealth from every clime and age. The present librarian is Mr. W. H. Spilsbury.

INNS APPERTAINING TO LINCOLN'S INN.

1st. Furnival's Inn, in Holborn, once belonged to the Lords Furnival, a family that became extinct in the male line as far back as the sixth of Richard II. The old building was erected during the reign of James I., but the present edifice was built at the beginning of the present century. This Inn first belonged to Lincoln's Inn in the early part of Edward VI.'s reign. Beneath this Inn there was formerly an ale or a cyder cellar, now unused.

2nd. Thavies' Inn, called Davy's from one John Tavie, to whom it once belonged, is situate near St. Andrew's Church, Holborn; it came into the possession of Lincoln's Inn in the reign of Edward VI. The students of the law resided there as far back as the time of Edward III. In 1768 this Inn was dissolved.

IV.—GRAY'S INN.

THIS Inn, situate near Holborn Bars, derives its name from the Lords Gray of Wilton, whose habitation it was from 1315;* it has two gateway entrances—one in Holborn, the other in Gray's Inn Lane. The hall, which was originally erected in the early part of the reign of Elizabeth, was rebuilt in 1687; it has very little to recommend it.

In the Chapel there is a most resplendent radie, issuing from a dove, well worthy the attention of the visitor. This chapel was originally called Portpool Chapel, and Gray's Inn Lane was anciently styled Portpool Lane.

This has been a law inn ever since the time of Henry VIII., though it is thought members of the profession resided here as early as Edward III.'s reign, 1357. A griffin is taken as the arms of Gray's Inn, evidently showing that this Society would not let any wrongs go unredressed.

INNS APPERTAINING TO GRAY'S INN.

1st. Staple Inn, situate between Holborn and Southampton Buildings, derives its name from dealers in wool meeting here, when it was called Staple Hall. The hall itself is considered to belong to the Elizabethan age. The woolsack is the arms of this Society. In this edifice are casts of the twelve Cæsars, brought

---

* Till the latter end of the reign of Henry VII.

from Italy; perhaps the style is rather too heavy, but still the workmanship is pretty good and the characters are well preserved. This Inn belonged to students in the law as early as the reign of Henry V.

In the hall may be seen a few portraits on stained glass of distinguished lawyers, as Lord Chancellor Camden, the Earl of Macclesfield, &c.

"In the earlier times the Inns of Court were filled with the sons of the aristocracy, who were sent thither not so much for the purpose of acquiring proficiency in the law as for the sake of mental discipline; and the expensive style of living in these legal seminaries was of itself sufficient to confine them exclusively to this class of students. At a later period also, there was an order made by King James I. in the first year of his reign, signed by Sir E. Coke, Lord Bacon, and other persons, that 'none be from thenceforth admitted into the society of any House of Court that is not a gentleman by descent.'

"In the reign of Henry VI. there were from eighteen hundred to two thousand students in the Inns of Court and Chancery—about one hundred in each of the Inns of Chancery, of which there were ten at that time, and two hundred in each of the Inns of Court. At present, the number of members of the four Inns of Court is upwards of four thousand.*

"There are three ranks or degrees among the members of the Inns of Court: Benchers, Barristers, and Students. The Benchers are the superiors of each house, to whom the government of its affairs is committed, and out of the number one annually fills the office of Treasurer. There was formerly a distinction between utter and inner barristers, and there seems to be some perplexity as to the meaning of the terms, which are variously explained by different writers. Blount, in his Law Dictionary, published in 1679, says: 'They are called Utter-Barristers, that is, Pleaders without the Bar, to distinguish them from Benchers, or those who have been Readers, who are sometimes admitted to plead within the bar, as the King's, Queen's, or Prince's counsel are.' This definition has been adopted in most of the Law Dictionaries, but the details of proceedings given by Dugdale, who does not allude to the etymology of the word, lead to the inference that it is derived from local arrangements in the halls of the Inns of Court. It seems that in the public mootings or exercises held in these halls, the benchers and readers occupying the dais, which was separated by a bar, some of the barristers who had attained a certain standing were called from the body of the hall to the bar (that is, to the first place outside the bar), for the purpose of arguing doubtful questions and cases, whence they probably derived the name of utter or outer barristers; or, in some cases,—for the forms and customs varied in the different Inns of Court—from sitting outermost on the benches."—*Spilsbury's Lincoln's Inn.*

* Barristers were first appointed by Edward I., about 1291, but there is earlier mention of professional advocates in England, they are of various ranks, as King's or Queen's Counsel, Serjeants, &c.—*Haydn.*

A few Words about Westminster.

THE City of Westminster is so called from its western situation in respect to the ancient city of London. The bounds of the latter city end where the former begin, viz., at Temple Bar. Westminster was formerly known as Thorney Island; it contains ten parishes, four of which were formed early in the last century, in consequence of the great increase of population at the west-end, and one since; two only of these parishes—St. Margaret's and St. John's—are considered to form the city of Westminster, the other eight being denominated the liberties of Westminster. The parish of St. Clement Danes being one of this number, we here insert its position and boundary in the city of Westminster.

ST. CLEMENT DANES.

AREA, 44 STATUTE ACRES, INCLUDING A PORTION OF THE RIVER THAMES.

Commencing at the south-eastern boundary, being the middle of the Thames nearly facing Essex Street, the line passes at the backs of the houses on the east side of Essex Street, the south sides of Devereux Court and Palsgrave and Thanet Places, as far as the back of No. 1, Fleet Street, being one house east of Temple Bar; it then crosses Fleet Street, and passes through the centre of Lower Serle's Place, and Serle's Place (formerly called Shire Lane) to Carey Street; thence it passes through to New Square, Lincoln's Inn, and includes the lesser portion of No. 5, and the southern and western sides as far as No. 11, through which it passes westward; crossing Serle Street at No. 3, it proceeds at the backs of the houses on the north side of Portugal Street, passing out into Portsmouth Street, which it crosses, up the centre of a court to the back of No. 7, Gilbert Street, and it then turns in a northerly direction, across Sheffield Street at Nos. 11 and 3; thence across Bear Yard at Nos. 19 and 5, it comes out at No. 31, on the southern side of Duke Street; thence it passes westerly in a direct line on the same side to No. 2, passing through to Stanhope Street, which it crosses at Nos. 38 and 35, passing at the backs of the houses on the southern side of

Princes Street to No. 121, Drury Lane; it then proceeds down the middle of Drury Lane and Wych Street, which latter it crosses at No. 54, and passes at the backs of the houses on the west side of Newcastle Street, crossing the Strand from Nos. 310 to 161, thence in a direct line to the middle of the Thames.

In addition to the above, there are two detached parts of the parish. The first is bounded on the eastern side by Wellington Street North; on the northern, by a line passing at the backs of the houses on the southern side of Exeter Street; on the western side by Burleigh Street; and on the southern side by the Strand. The other part is enclosed on the west, by a line drawn through the middle of Cecil Street; on the south, by the middle of the Thames; on the east, by a line drawn from the middle of the Thames parallel to Cecil Street to No. 106, Strand; and on the north, by the Strand from No. 106 to the corner of Cecil Street.

For many centuries London and Westminster were entirely distinct and separate.* Nourthouck says, the Strand, being the shore of the river, as its name implies, was a road to pass from one to the other. As the metropolis grew, the Strand, from Temple Bar to the Village of Charing, with its Cross,—erected by Edward I. in memory of the death of his beloved Queen Eleanor,—became studded with the mansions of the nobility and wealthy merchants, who had spacious and beautiful gardens, some running to the borders of the Thames, planted with trees and flowers: the northern part of this locality was composed of corn-fields, pastures, delightful meadows and pleasant streams. It is said that London and Westminster were one mile asunder so late as 1603, when the houses were thatched, and there were mud walls in the Strand.

Though the city of London may justly boast of its antiquity, commercial grandeur, splendid cathedral, royal exchange, banks, &c., the city of Westminster has also many glories of which it can boast, and which are not to be surpassed in the world. In Westminster are situated the royal palaces, the Houses of Parliament, the town mansions of nearly all the nobility and aristocracy, the law courts, splendid government offices, magnificent club-houses and hotels; the

---

* Westminster was erected by Henry VIII. into a Deanery in 1539, and into a Bishopric in 1541; but the latter lasted only nine years.

Westminster School, founded by Queen Elizabeth in 1560, which is the most celebrated amongst the many endowed schools in the metropolis; the Horse Guards; the two patent and eight other popular theatres; also the best concert-rooms, which receive the patronage of rank and wealth; Somerset House, once a royal palace; Exeter Hall, opened 1831; noble hospitals; Covent Garden, on which a convent once stood, and which is supplied with the finest fruits and the best vegetables grown, together with the most beautiful plants cultivated in all parts of the world. Two of the finest bridges in Europe connect Westminster with the county of Surrey, one of which—Waterloo Bridge—was commenced October 11th, 1811, and finished June 18th, 1817, on the anniversary of the battle of Waterloo, when the Prince Regent, the Duke of Wellington and other distinguished personages were present at the opening. Its length is 1,242 feet, its width 42 feet, the span of each arch, nine in number, is 120 feet: it cost £150,000. Westminster Bridge, as Haydn says,—"Is one of the most beautiful structures of the kind in the world?" one half was opened for use early in 1860, the whole on May 24th, 1862.

There was also built, and opened on May 1st, 1845, a suspension bridge connecting Hungerford Market with Lambeth; it was taken down July, 1862, to make way for the railway bridge. The site of Hungerford Market is now covered with a commodious station and the magnificent Charing Cross Hotel, in the front of which is a beautiful Cross erected to the memory of Queen Eleanor, nearly on the site of where one once stood erected by Edward I. A fluted Corinthian column, with a capital of cast metal, is erected in Trafalgar Square in honour of Nelson, who was killed at the battle of Trafalgar, October 21st, 1805; the column is 176 feet 6 inches high. Trafalgar Square is unquestionably the finest situation and most splendid site in the metropolis, and is surrounded by buildings worthy of notice. The National Gallery, which was erected in 1834-37, stands on the north-west side, facing Whitehall and Parliament Street; it has a front of 460 feet, with portico and dome in its centre, supported by Corinthian columns. The Duke of York's

Column is situated on the north side of St. James's Park, at the lower end of Waterloo Place, it was erected in 1833, and is 124 feet in height. Among the many fine churches in this city the most noteworthy, for its splendid portico and general architectural beauties, is St. Martin's-in-the-Fields, at the corner of St. Martin's Lane ; another we may mention, which adjoins St. Clement Danes, is St. Mary-le-Strand, at the west end of Holywell Street; it was one of the churches ordered to be built in the reign of Queen Anne ; the first stone was laid February 25th, 1714, and consecrated January 1st, 1723.

Westminster Abbey must not be forgotten, which, next to St. Paul's, is the noblest ecclesiastical edifice in London, and dates from the thirteenth century, though portions of the structure erected by Edward the Confessor may still form part of the building; great additions were made to it by Henry VII., who built the splendid chapel that still bears his name; it is 360 feet in length and 195 feet wide within its walls. Another most ancient relic of English architecture is Westminster Hall, first built by William Rufus in 1097, for a banquetting hall. The Hall became ruinous in 1397, and was repaired by Richard II. In 1236, on New-Year's Day, Henry III. caused 6,000 poor persons to be entertained in this hall and the other rooms of his palace, as a celebration of Queen Eleanor's coronation; and here Richard II. held his Christmas festival in 1397, when the number of guests each day the feast lasted was 10,000. Stow says the courts of law were established here by King John.

Westminster* is rendered healthy and beautiful by its splendid and extensive parks. It contains also some of the finest squares and streets in London, adorned with statues and rows of bright and glittering shops, stored with wealth and magnificence. In Westminster have lived many of the most illustrious statesmen, orators, divines, poets, and other distinguished individuals.

---

* "Westminster—a city constituted by Royal Charter and by many public privileges, but since swallowed up in the general vortex of modern London."—*Cunningham.*

Historical Sketch of St. Clement Danes.

s regards the Parish of St. Clement Danes taking the Anchor* as a crest, it is thought by antiquaries to have its origin with the Danish people, the early settlers in this locality, who, coming from abroad, and belonging to a seafaring race, must have cast anchor in the Thames, perhaps opposite the very Strand itself; and what so emblematical of a foreigner who invaded our island, and landed from a ship, as an anchor? A conjecture has been made that the Strand being the shore of a river, very possibly the anchor was first suggested through that circumstance; but we prefer the first idea as being most likely the real and only true cause of the crest being taken both by St. Clement's Inn and the Parish of St. Clement Danes.

It may be also fairly assumed that the word "Danes" was used to distinguish it particularly from other churches bearing the name of St. Clement—this church being built and frequented by the Danes especially; this portion of the town, as it would appear, having been set apart for their residence.

It is said by Stow, that St. Clement Danes, Strand, is so called "because Harold, a Danish king, and other Danes were buried there." Strype gives another reason—"That the few Danes left in the kingdom married English women, and compulsorily lived between Ludgate and Westminster, and there built a synagogue called 'Eccelesia Clementis Danorum.'"

---

* Anchors are of ancient use, and the invention belongs to the Tuscans.—*Pliny*. The second tooth or fluke was added by Anacharsis, the Scythian (592 B.C.)—*Strabo*. Anchors were first forged in England, A.D. 578. Those of a first-rate ship of war (four) will weigh 99 cwt. each, costing £450. —*Phillips*. The Admiralty anchor was introduced about 1841. Improved anchors were made 1831, 1846, 1848, 1853.—*Haydn*.

HISTORICAL SKETCH OF ST. CLEMENT DANES.

Fleetwood, the antiquarian, writing to Lord Burghley, who lived in this parish also, says—"When Alfred drove most of the Danes out of the kingdom in 886, those residing in London, who had married Englishwomen, were allowed to live between Westminster and Ludgate, and that they built a synagogue, which was afterwards consecrated and called by its present appellation, St. Clement Danes." Supposing Fleetwood's account to be correct, we have an explanation why Harold's body should be brought to St. Clement's, and why the Danes should fly thither for shelter in their extremity.

Pennant says—"Between Clement's Inn and the Strand is the church of St. Clement Danes, called so, either from being the place of interment of Harold the Harefoot, or of the massacre of certain Danes who had taken refuge there. It was one of the churches built on this tract before the conquest."

In the *Acta Sanctorum* (Tome VII, p. 694), we find the following notice of the patron saint of the Danes:—

"Natalis sancti Clementis episcopi, qui quartus à beato Petro Apostolo, Romanæ Ecclesiæ pontificatum tenuit, et sub persecutione Trajani in mare præcipitatus, martyrio coronatur."

And amongst other notes the following:—

Bruxellen. "Sic primam format Romæ, natale sancti Clementis Papæ et martyris, qui sub Trajani imperatoris persecutione, *anchora* ad collam ejus ligata, in mare præcipitatus, martyrio coronatur. Cujus corpus mari ad quatuor milia recedenti, in archa saxa, in templo marmoreo repertum, et ad Romani delatum est, ubi ejus nominis memoriam usque hodie extructa custodit ecclesia."

Which may be thus translated:—

"The anniversary of Saint Clement, bishop, (23 November) who, fourth in succession from St. Peter, held the pontificate of the Roman Church. Under the persecution of Trajan, he was precipitated into the sea, and crowned with martyrdom."

Bruxellen.—"At Rome the anniversary of St. Clement, Pope and martyr, who under the persecution of the Emperor Trajan, was precipitated into the sea with an *anchor* tied round his neck. On the reflux of the sea for four miles, his body was found, and was placed in a stone coffin in a marble temple and thence conveyed to Rome, where a church, built and dedicated to him, preserves his memory to this day."*

In a work of considerable research† we find the following remarks upon our Danish invaders and their connection with the foundation of the church of St. Clement Danes :—

"Approaching the city from the west end, through the great street called 'the Strand,' we see, close outside the old gate of Temple Bar, a church called St. Clement Danes, from which the surrounding parish derives its name. In the early part of the middle ages this church was called in Latin 'Ecclesia Sancti Clementis Danorum,' or the Danes' Church of St. Clement. It was here that the Danes in London formerly had their burial place, in which reposed the remains of Canute the Great's son and successor, Harold Harefoot. When, in 1040, Hardicanute ascended the throne after his brother Harold, he caused Harold's corpse to be disinterred from its tomb in Westminster Abbey and thrown into the Thames, where it was found by a fisherman, and afterwards buried, it is said, 'in the Danes' churchyard in London.' From the churchyard it was subsequently removed into a round tower which ornamented the church before it was rebuilt at the close of the seventeenth century.

---

* The old Crown and Anchor Tavern, Strand (see page 53 of this work). The association of the navy with the crown is natural; the union of these titles, as applied to other houses, appears appropriate enough, but this tavern being in the parish of St. Clement Danes, seems to have derived its second title from the legend of St. Clement, which states that he was cast into the sea with an anchor about his neck, and that on the first anniversary of his death the sea retired four miles from the shore, and discovered on the place where he suffered a superb temple of fine marble, in which was a monument of the saint, and that for several years the sea withdrew for seven days in succession. In allusion to this the device of the anchor may be seen on the boundary marks of the parish, and in various parts of the Church of St. Clement Danes, Strand. "St. Clement is stated to have been converted by St. Peter, and he was a zealous coadjutor of the Apostles. See Philip iv. 3.) Several works are attributed to him, but his Epistle to the Church of Corinth only is considered genuine. It is generally believed that this great and good man died a natural death about A.D. 100, at the commencement of the reign of the Emperor Trajan."—*Origin of Signs*; Cole, Newgate Street, 1825.

† "An Account of the Danes and Norwegians in England, Scotland, and Ireland." By J. J. A. Worsaae, For. F.S.A. London: Murray. 1852.

142 ST. CLEMENT CHURCH CALLED AFTER THE DANES.

"It has, indeed, been supposed by some that this church was called after the Danes (see page 18) only because so many Danes have been buried in it; but as it is situated close by the Thames, and must have originally lain outside the city walls, in the western suburbs, and consequently outside of London proper, it is certainly put beyond all doubt that the Danish merchants and mariners who, for the sake of trade, were at that time established in or near London, had there a place of their own in which they dwelt together as fellow-countrymen. Here it should also be remarked that this church, like others in commercial towns, as, for instance, at Aarhuns, in Jutland, at Trondhjen, in Norway, and even in the City of London (in Eastcheap) was consecrated to St. Clement, who was especially the seaman's patron saint. The Danes naturally preferred to bury their dead in this church, which was their proper parish church."

Walter Thornbury says "there have been great antiquarian discussions as to why the church is called St. Clement 'Danes.' Some think there was once a massacre of the Danes in this part of the road to Westminster. Some assert that the Danes, driven out of London by Alfred, were allowed to settle between Thorney Island (Westminster) and Ludgate, and built a church in the Strand."

Leigh Hunt says:—"It is not known why this church is called St. Clement Danes. Some think because there was a massacre of the Danes thereabouts; others because Harold Harefoot was buried there; and others because the Danes had this locality given them to live in when Alfred the Great drove them out of London, the monarch, at the same time, building the church in order to assist their conversion to Christianity. The name St. Clement has been derived with probability from the patron saint of Pope Clement III., a great friend of the Templars, to whom the church at one time belonged."

The hat makers have a tradition, that while St. Clement was fleeing from his persecutors his feet became blistered, and to afford him relief, he was compelled to put wool between his sandals and the soles of his feet. On continuing his journey, the wool, by the perspiration, motion, and pressure of the feet, assumed a uniformly compact substance, which has since been denominated felt. When he afterwards settled at Rome, it is said he improved the discovery; and from this circumstance has been dated the origin of felting. Hatters in Ireland and other Catholic countries still hold their festival on St. Clement's Day.

Before the Norman conquest, England was frequently being overrun by the Danes,* whose invasions were a scourge to England for nearly 300 years. It was divided into counties and hundreds in 886. In 995 an inglorious peace was made with the Danes, and it was agreed to pay them tribute annually, besides £16,000 in money, provided they retired and discontinued their invasions. In 1002, the Danes broke the agreement, committed horrid cruelties and devastations, and the timid Ethelred II. paid them no less than £24,000 for peace, which sum was levied by a tax on all the lands in England for Danegelt,† by which ignominious name this first land-tax was known and collected in England.

---

* The first descent of the Danes upon England was at Portland, 787; their second, in Northumberland, 794, when they were repelled, and perished by shipwreck; they landed on Sheppy Island, 832; again in Cornwall, and defeated by Egbert, 836; again at Charmouth, and defeated Ethelwolf, 840; landed at the mouth of the Thames, from 350 ships, and took Canterbury and London, 851; subdued by Ethelwolf, at Okely, in Surrey, 853; invaded Northumberland, and seized York, 867; defeated King Ethelred and his brother Alfred, at Basing and Merton, 871; surprised Warham Castle, and took Exeter, 876; took Chippenham, 877; 1205 of them killed by Odun, earl of Devonshire, 878; Alfred entered into treaty with them, 882; their fleet totally destroyed at Appledore by King Alfred, 894; invaded Anglesea, 900; submitted to Edward the Elder, 921; invaded Dorsetshire, 982; landed again in Essex, 991, and were bribed to depart the kingdom; their fleet defeated, 992; number of them massacred by order of Ethelred II. Nov. 12, 1003; made England tributary to them, 1007; under Canute, conquered England, 1017; continued their ravages, and defeated the English at Ipswich, 1010; took Canterbury, and put nine out of ten of the inhabitants to death, 1011; settled in Scotland, 1020; expelled England, 1041; landed again at Sandwich, 1047, and carried off much plunder to Flanders; joined the Northumbrians, burnt York, and slew 3,000 Normans, 1069; invaded England again, but were bribed by William to depart, 1074.—*Tablet of Memory.*

† Dane-Geld or Dangelt, a tribute paid to the Danes to stop their ravages in this kingdom; first raised by Ethelred II., in 991, and again in 1003, and levied after the expulsion of the Danes to pay fleets for clearing the seas of them. The tax was suppressed by Edward the Confessor in 1051, revived by William the Conqueror, 1068, and formed part of the revenue of the crown until abolished by Stephen, 1136. Every hide of land, *i. e.* as much as one plough could plough, or, as Bede says, maintain a family, was taxed, at first 1s., afterwards as much as 7s.—*Haydn.*

ST. CLEMENT'S INN.

In the spring of 1008, the Danes subdued great part of the kingdom: to stop their progress it was agreed to pay them £48,000 to quit the kingdom. In the space of twenty years they had £469,687 sterling. Soon after Swein entered the Humber, when Ethelred retired to the Isle of Wight, and sent his sons with their mother Emma into Normandy to her brother, and Swein took possession of the whole kingdom, 1013. Swein was proclaimed king of England in 1013. His first act of sovereignty was an insupportable tax, which he did not live to see collected. He died February 3rd, 1014, at Thetford, in Norfolk.

Between St. Clement's churchyard and Clare Market is Clement's Inn*—an appendage of the Inner Temple. It appears to have derived its name from the church near which it stands.† A house or Inn of Chancery for the education of the students of law was situated on this site in the time of King Edward IV. It is not known, however, whose inheritance it originally was. In the year 1486 (2 Hen. VII.) Sir John Cantlowe, Knight, by a lease bearing date the 20th December, in consideration of ninety marks fine, and £4 6s. 8d. yearly rent, demised it for eighty years to William Elyot and John Elyot, in trust, it may be presumed, for students of the law. About the year 1528 (20th Henry VIII.) Cantlowe's right and interest was passed to William Holles, citizen of London, afterwards Knight and Lord Mayor of that city, and ancestor of the Dukes of Newcastle, one of whom—John, Earl of Clare, son and successor of Sir John Holles, the first earl—demised it to the then principal and fellows.

---

* "There is no evidence," says Mr. Jesse, in his "London and its Celebrities," "of Clement's Inn having been a Court of Law previous to 1485." A writer in *Notes and Queries* comments thus on Mr. Jesse's remark :—"This Inn was neither a 'Court of Law' nor 'an Inn of Court, but an Inn of Chancery,'" according to the distinction drawn by Sir John Fortescue, in his *De Laudibus Legum Angliæ*, chap. xlix., written between 1460 and 1470. The evidence of its antiquity is traced back to an earlier date than 1486 ; for, according to Dugdale (Orig. p. 187), in a *Record of Michaelmas*, 19 Edward IV., 1479, it is spoken of as then, and *diu ante*, an Inn "*hominum consiliariorum ejusdem legis.*"

† "Because it standeth near to St. Clement Church; but nearer to the fair fountain called Clement's Well."—*Stow.*

THE CHURCH OF ST. CLEMENT DANES.

That St. Clement's Inn was once the property of the parish is evident from the following*:—

> "Clement's Inne was a messuage belonging to the parish of St. Clement Dane; the deuise whereof is an anchor without a stocke, with a capital C couchant upon it, and this is grauen in stone over the gate of Clement's Inne. It seemeth to be a hieroglyphike or rebus (as some conjecture) figuring herein. Saint Clement, who having bin Pope, and so reputed head of the Church (and the Church being resembled to a shippe), both his name and office are expressed in this deuise of the C and the anchor."—*Sir George Buc in Howes.*

The old church escaped the Great Fire, but being decayed and ruinous, was taken down in 1680, and rebuilt by Edward Pierce (who lived in Surrey Street) under the superintendence of Wren. "He (Edward Pierce) much assisted Sir Christopher Wren in many of his designs, and built the church of St. Clement under his direction."—*Walpole's Anecdotes*, (see page 13). Dr. Burrowes was the rector at the time Dr. Johnson attended this church (see page 85). Sir Robert Cecil, afterwards Earl of Salisbury, on June 6th, 1563, and the Earl of Shaftesbury (author of the "Characteristics") on March 7th, 1671, were baptized at St. Clement Danes' Church (see pages 16 and 90).

The marriage of Sir Thomas Grosvenor, Bart., and Mrs. Mary Davies, of Ebury, the great heiress who brought the Pimlico property to the Grosvenor family, was solemnized in this church, October 10th, 1676.

The first person buried at this church after it was rebuilt was Nicholas Byer, the painter; (for the last person buried, see page 17). There were also buried here the following eminent persons:— Sir John Roe, who died in Ben Jonson's arms, of the plague, January 17th, 1606; John Lowen, the player, one of the original and most eminent actors of Shakspeare's plays, August 24th, 1653; (see pages 17 and 90). The three stained-glass windows over the altar by Collins were erected March 23rd, 1844 (see page 13).

It was near the church that Sir Edmondsbury Godfrey was last

---

* For Clement's Inn as an Inn of Court, see page 127.

seen alive. Arundel, Drury, Essex, Burleigh, Salisbury, Boswell, and Beaufort Houses were all situate in this parish. The arms of the Dukes of Norfolk and the Earls of Arundel and Salisbury in the south gallery of the church of St. Clement Danes show that these noblemen were once inhabitants of the parish (see page 89). The lay-stall of the parish was in Long Acre till 1632, when the site was leased by Lord Cary and others to Mr. Loveing. A tablet with the following inscription has recently been erected in St. Clement Danes' Church :—

In Memory of
Mr. THOMAS PROUT,
Who departed this life July 25th, 1859,
Aged 74 years.
Such was the high estimation in which he was held, that for 30 years
He was the most influential elector of the great and patriotic City of Westminster.
This Tablet is erected by General Sir de Lacy Evans, G.C.B.,
In grateful recollection of his deceased friend.

(See pages 63 and 65.)

Feckett's Field, or Croft's, was the old name for Little Lincoln's Inn Fields, now New Square, Lincoln's Inn. A plot of ground of about ten acres, extending from what was the "Bell" (the site of Bell Yard, Temple Bar) to Portugal Street, lying in the parishes of St. Dunstan-in-the-West, and St. Clement Danes (but chiefly in the latter), including all that is now known as Carey Street and the courts behind, Old and New Boswell Court, Portugal Street, Cook's Court, Serle's Street, and part of Lincoln's Inn, New Square, down to the Chancery Lane end of Carey Street, formerly called Jackanape's Lane ;—this field, also called the Templar's Field, is described in the earliest grant extant as " Terram sive Campum pro, Saltationibus Turnamentis aliisque Exercitiis Equitum Militumque Regni, nostri Angliæ presertim vero Equitum Sancti Johannis Hierosolinitatis," and in the priory of St. John of Jerusalem it remained until the dissolution of the monasteries, when it was granted by Henry VIII. to Anthony Stringer, to hold *in capite*, under the description—" Totum ill' Campum, terram et pasturam vocat Feckett's Field, adjacens messuag vocat le Bell," &c. From Stringer it came to John Horneby, from whom it passed to his son Richard, who died about 1563,

HISTORICAL SKETCH OF THE STRAND.

leaving Alice his daughter and heiress, who married Edward Clifton, and had a son Horneby Clifton, by whom (in 3 Jac. I.) this field was conveyed to John Harborne, of Taskley Com., Oxon, Esquire. The description of this property on the decease of John Homeby is as follows:—

> "All that messuage and tenement called the Bell, with all its appurtenances, lying, and being in the parish of St. Dunstan, in Fleet Street, London, lately belonging to the Priory of Saint John of Jerusalem, &c., and a certain field and pasture called Feckett's Field, near, adjoining, together with ingress and egress, with horses and carriages, by two gates at the east end of the said field (that is to say), through one gate leading from the lane called Chancery Lane towards the aforesaid field, and through the other gate at the west end of the same way, abutting upon the aforesaid field."—*Cunningham.*

The Strand, with which are connected associations of the most lively and exciting description, is doubtless one of the most bustling, busy, gay and crowded thoroughfares in the metropolis, of which it forms a principal artery. The Strand, in 1245, was merely a long beach, open to the river, with scarcely a house upon it. Pennant says, "In the year 1353, that fine street, the Strand, was an open highway, with here and there a great man's house, with gardens to the water-side. In that year it was so impassable, that Edward III., by an ordinance, directed a tax to be raised upon wool, leather, wine, and all goods carried to the staple at Westminster from Temple Bar, to Westminster Abbey for the repair of the road; and that all owners of houses adjacent to the highway should repair as much as lay before their doors."

"In the year 1385, the 8th of Richard II., and in 1446, the 24th of Henry VI., tolls were granted for paving the Strand from Temple Bar to the Savoy Inn."

In 1532, the reign of Henry VIII., an act was passed for "sufficiently paving, at the charge of the owners of the lands, the street-way between Charing Cross and Strand Cross."

Van de Wyngerede's view, 1543, shows straggling houses on the south side; but on the north side it is all open to Covent Garden. There were three watercourses, crossed by bridges.

"The first ascertained inhabitant was Peter of Savoy, uncle of Henry III., to whom that King, in the thirtieth year of his reign (1245) granted all those houses upon the Thames which sometime pertained to Briane de Insula de Lisle without the walls of the city of London, in the way or street called the Strand. The Bishops were the next great dignitaries who had inns or houses in the Strand, connecting as it were the City with the King's Palace at Westminster."
—*Stow*.

"Anciently," says Selden in his "Table Talk," "the noblemen lay within the city for safety and security, but the bishops' houses were by the water-side, because they were held sacred persons nobody would hurt."

As many as nine bishops possessed inns or hostels on the south or water side of the present Strand at the period of the Reformation.

Pennant says:—"'There was no continued street here till about the year 1533; before that time it entirely cut off Westminster from London, and nothing intervened except a few scattered houses, and a village which afterwards gave name to the whole. St. Martin's stood literally in the fields; but about the year 1560 a street was formed loosely built, for all the houses on the south side had great gardens to the river, were called by their owners' names and in after-times gave name to several streets that succeeded them, pointing down to the Thames; each of them had stairs for the convenience of taking boat, of which many to this day bear the names of the houses. As the Court was for centuries either at Westminster or Whitehall, a boat was the customary conveyance of the great to the presence of their sovereign. The north side was a mere line of houses from Charing Cross to Temple Bar. All beyond was country. The gardens, which occupied part of the site of Covent Garden, were bounded by fields, and St. Giles's was a distant country village."

The Strand was divided from Fleet Street in 1670, and is three quarters of a mile long. From the above particulars an idea can be readily formed of the wonderful increase which has taken place in the size of our capital during the last three centuries.

Temple Bar consisted, at first, of posts, rails, and a chain. Afterwards, in 1079, a wooden edifice was built, which fell a sacrifice to the Great Fire of London, when Sir Christopher Wren, about the year 1672, erected the present building. It is now the only gate remaining at the extremity of the City Liberties.* Over this gateway, looking up Fleet Street, are the statues of Queen Elizabeth and James I., and on the side looking towards the Strand, are the statues of Charles I. and Charles II. in Roman habits. On the top of this gateway were exhibited the heads of the unfortunate men who embarked in the rebellion of 1745. About the same time the head of a barrister named Layer, which had been exhibited for upwards of thirty years, tumbled down, was taken into a public-house in the neighbourhood, and buried in the cellar; afterwards purchased by Dr. Rawlinson, and on his death buried in his right hand. The remains of some of these blanched, or rather blackened, skulls, were visible up to the end of the last century; but these ghastly specimens of frail mortality, and of barbarous times, have long since vanished, and it is to be hoped none will ever more be seen in England.

The owners of a forge in the parish of St. Clement (which formerly belonged to the City, and stood in the high-road from the Temple to Westminster, but which now no longer exists) used to be called forth to do suit and service at Westminster Hall, on the 9th of November yearly, when an officer of the Exchequer Court, in the presence of the Lord Mayor elect and party, produced six horse-shoes and hobnails, which were counted over in form by the newly-elected Lord Mayor before the cursitor baron, who, on this

---

* The other London gates were *Aldgate*, one of the four original gates of the Roman city, rebuilt 1606, finally taken down in 1762. *Bishopsgate*, built by Bishop Erkenwald in the seventh century—re-erected in 1731, and finally taken down in 1760. *Moorgate*, erected in 1415, and was one of the most magnificent. *Cripplegate*, pulled down in 1760. *Aldersgate*, one of the four original gates, rebuilt 1617, and repaired after the fire, 1670; pulled down in 1760. *Newgate*, rebuilt after the fire, and used as a prison; pulled down in 1760. *Ludgate*, one of the original four gates, pulled down in 1760, and *Posterngate*, on Tower Hill, erected soon after the Conquest.

particular occasion, was the immediate representative of the sovereign. The origin of this usage is a grant in 1235, from Henry III., to Walter de Bruin, a farrier, of the said piece of ground, whereon to erect a forge, he rendering annually to the exchequer, for the same, a quit-rent of six horse-shoes, with the nails belonging to them. In process of time the ground became vested in the City, and, though now lost to it, the City till very lately rendered the quit-rents.

STREETS AND PLACES OF ST. CLEMENT DANES.
(THOSE MARKED * ARE REQUIRED FOR THE NEW LAW COURTS.)

ARUNDEL STREET

Was built in 1678, on the site of Arundel House.* It derives its name from one of the titles of the Duke of Norfolk, whose palace stood on a part of this site. Mrs. Porter the actress, lived here. John Anstis the Garter-king-at-arms, resided here in 1715-16. Simon Harcourt, Esq., afterwards Lord Chancellor, 1727, also dwelt in this street in 1688. Rymer, whose Fœdora is our best historical monument, died at his house in this street in 1713, and was buried in the parish church of St. Clement Danes. Thomas Parr (Old Parr) was brought here from Shropshire by the Earl of Arundel, to be shewn to Charles I. His mode of living being changed—for here he fed high and drank wine—he was taken ill, and died

---

* "Arundel House was taken down, and the present Arundel Street, Surrey Street, Howard Street, and Norfolk Street erected in its stead."—*Cunningham.*
Thomas Howard, the son of Philip, was restored to the earldom of Arundel by James I., in whose time Arundel House became the repository of that noble collection of works of art, of which the very ruins are ornaments now to several principal cabinets. The collection contained, when entire, 37 statues, 128 busts, and 250 inscribed marbles, exclusive of sarcophagi, altars, gems, fragments, &c., which he had paid for, but could never obtain permission to remove from Rome. A view of the statue gallery forms the background to Vansomer's portrait of the Earl, and a view of the picture gallery to Vansomer's portrait of his Countess. Here Hollar was lodged, and here he engraved several views of the house, and drew his well-known view of London, as seen from the roof. Thomas, Earl of Arundel, died 1646, and at the restoration in 1660, his house and marbles were restored to his grandson, who, at the instigation of Evelyn, gave the library to the Royal Society, and the inscribed marbles, still known as the Arundelian Collection, to the University of Oxford. The donor of the marbles died in 1677.—*Walpole's Anecdotes.*

CLEMENT'S LANE, STRAND.

November 14th, 1635, at the age of 152 years and 9 months, having outlived nine sovereigns, and part of the reign of the tenth. He was dissected by Harvey, who attributed Parr's death to inflammation of the lungs, brought on by the impurity of a London atmosphere and sudden change of diet.

BEAUFORT BUILDINGS

Occupy a site which formerly sustained a palace belonging to the Bishops of Carlisle, and then called Carlisle House. It was exchanged by the Bishops with Henry VIII. for Rochester Place at Lambeth.

The king gave it to his favourite Bedford, who made it his residence. It then passed, by purchase, to the Marquis of Worcester, who wrote "The Century of Inventions:" it was then known as Worcester House, and thence came into the hands of the Marquis's eldest son, who was created Duke of Beaufort; its name was then changed to Beaufort House.* Lord Clarendon lived here whilst his house was being built at the West; and here, in 1660, was married Ann Hyde, the Chancellor's daughter, to the Duke of York, according to the Protestant rites. The mansion was taken down and a smaller one built, which being burnt down with some others† (Strype says "by the carelessness of a servant in one of the adjacent houses") in 1695, the present Beaufort Buildings were erected.

At the east corner, upon the site of 96, Strand, lived Charles Lillie, who sold snuffs, perfumes, &c., and took in letters for the "Tatler," "Spectator," &c., directed to him at the desire of Steele.

Aaron Hill was born in a house which stood on the site in 1685.

Rudolph Ackermann, the German printseller, who introduced lithography and annuals, resided at the corner.

---

* Now the Printing Establishment of Messrs. Whiting and Co.

† "On Saturday, in the evening, about five o'clock, a violent fire broke out in Beaufort Buildings, in the Strand, in the house of John Knight, Esq., treasurer of the Custom House, which, in less than two hours, burnt that house down to the ground, and also consumed the Duke of Beaufort's house and another."—*The Postman*, 1695, No. 80.

BOSWELL COURT, OLD,*
(SEE PAGE 38.)

Was at one time the abode of quality. It was so called from the house of a Mr. Boswell. There is a vulgar error that it received this designation after the biographer of Johnson, which the above fact sufficiently disproves, and to distinguish it from the New, the epithet Old was prefixed. New Boswell Court was planned and built at a period considerably posterior to the erection of the tenements which constituted the more ancient court. A considerable proportion of the small number of houses which constituted Old Boswell Court, comprised the premises of Messrs. Kelly & Co., publishers of the well-known "London Directory," one of the most extraordinary results of modern enterprise.

How great the contrast between the "London Directory" for 1677 and that for 1868. We have now before us a facsimile reprint of the former. On its fly-leaf is imprinted "Licensed October 11th.—Roger L'Estrange," and the following is a verbatim copy of its title page:—

> "A Collection of the names of the Merchants living in and about the City of London—very useful and necessary. Carefully collected for the benefit of all Dealers that shall have occasion with any of them. Directing them, at the first sight of their name, to the place of their abode. London: Printed by Sam Lee, and are to be had at his shop in Lombard Street, near Pope's Head Alley; and Dan Major, at the Flying Horse in Fleet Street, 1677."

This little Directory contained but between 1,300 and 1,400 entries. What a contrast, we repeat, between this and the Directory for 1868, probably the thickest and bulkiest book now published in England. It is reckoned that the capital kept locked-up in type for this work represents a sum of about £13,000.

This Court, as also Milford Lane and Ship Yard, at one time were notorious for the secret gambling dens they contained. There was a path or passage through St. Clement's Churchyard, leading across the Strand from Boswell Court, forming a near cut to Milford Lane. In this passage there is recorded an account of a most daring murder of a very startling and romantic character having been perpetrated by a celebrated character known as Fielding. At daybreak one morning the dead body of a man named Percival was discovered fearfully gashed and mangled; it would seem that a desperate struggle had taken place, from the hands of the deceased being much lacerated and his coat torn; not a vestige of writings, coin, watch or rings was found on the body; rewards were offered, and several persons of doubtful character arrested, but were discharged in default of evidence. Eventually, tempted by the reward, one of the gambling school—who, it seems, was present during the time the deceased was engaged at play at one of the houses in this Court—came forward, and the following evidence was adduced:—that the murdered man had been introduced into the gaming-room by the notorious gambler, Henry Fielding. It also transpired that Fielding, to entice his victim into deep play, had allowed him to win a very heavy stake, and afterwards wanted him to continue play; this he declined, which refusal sealed his doom: on leaving the gaming-room he was followed by Fielding, by whom it is presumed he was murdered and plundered. Fielding was never heard of in England afterwards. His hat was found near the scene of the murder, while that of the deceased was missing.

BOSWELL COURT, NEW,*
(SEE PAGE 100).

Was entered by a flight of steps from Old Boswell Court, and was described by Hatton, in 1708, as a pleasant place. Most of the houses in this court had been modernized—the heavy old eaves being taken away and replaced by parapets; some of them were of considerable height, having noble staircases, twisted ballusters, and other remains of departed grandeur. Barristers and solicitors were principally the occupiers of these houses, amongst whom we may mention Messrs. Nicholl, Burnett, and Newman, and Messrs. Harrison and Lewis, now Lewis, Munns, Nunn, and Longden, of the Old Jewry.

For the Nobility of Boswell Court (Old) see page 88, not 38 as inserted in error in previous page.

CAREY STREET*

Although possessing at the present moment a somewhat dull and sombre appearance and surrounded with an air of quiet business respectability, little doubt exists but that it was at one time the spot on which many a gay and lively scene was enacted. The "Grange Tavern," with its old picturesque inn yard, which stood in this street, was patronized by the theatricals of the Duke's Theatre, and others that formerly existed in this locality. The Grange was taken down in 1853 for the site of King's College Hospital.

> "Housekeeper: 'The poet has a special train behind him; though they look lean and empty, yet they seem very full of invention.'
> "Player: 'Let him enter and send his train to our house—Inn the Grange.'"—*Sir William Davenant*, "The Play-house to be Let."

The "Plough Tavern," (see page 102) also stood in this street, and would appear to have been a well-known and ancient hostelry of much repute, as the following extract from "Notes and Queries" will confirm:—

> "Willis, writing from 'Donstable, April 27, 1748, Wednesday Night' to 'John Duncombe, Esq., att His Seat at Barley End, near Ivinghoe, Buckingham County,' says, 'If you will send me any papers to London at the Plough Inne, Carey Street,' &c.
> "I quote from the autograph letter before me; the Plough Inne, Carey Street, however respectable it may be in its present way, must have been a very different place when Browne Willis, Esq., of Whaddon Hall, co. Bucks, thus hailed from it. "JAMES KNOWLES."

We are often amused with the unmeaning and laughable absurdities which tavern signs occasionally exhibit; they may, however, generally be traced to alterations made by persons ignorant of the true meaning of the original sign. In this street there were four taverns, respectively named "The Plough," "The Alma Stores," "The Law and Equity Stores," and "The Seven Stars." The two former are required for the New Law Courts. "The Seven Stars" we fear has been denuded by some vulgar person

---

* The south side only required for the New Law Courts.

of its leg or league. We remember reading in "The British Apollo," 1710:—

> "I'm amused at the signs as I pass through the town,
> To see the odd mixture—'A Magpie and Crown;'
> 'The Whale and the Crow,' 'The Razor and Hen,'
> 'The Leg and Seven Stars,' 'The Axe and the Bottle,'
> 'The Tun and the Lute,'
> 'The Eagle and Child,' 'The Shovel and Boot.'"

What interest a magpie could have in a crown, or on what terms of intimacy a whale could be with a crow, or what use a razor would be to a hen, it is as difficult to imagine as it would be to discover the corruption of the language which originated the absurdities.

The sign of the "Leg and Seven Stars" was merely an orthographical deviation from the "League and the Seven Stars" or "Seven United Provinces;" and the "Axe and Bottle" was doubtless a transposition of the "Battle Axe," a very emblematic sign in warlike times. The "Tun and Lute" seems to accord with the pleasures arising from the blending of wine and music. The "Eagle and Child" had some meaning, but no application; but we cannot come at any rational definition of what is meant by the "Shovel and Boot."

In the year 1807, an annotator on "Beloe's Anecdotes of Literature," says:—"I remember, many years ago, passing through a court in Rosemary Lane where I observed an ancient sign over the door of an alehouse, which was called the 'Four Alls.' There was the figure of a king, and on a label, 'I rule all;' the figure of a priest, motto—'I pray for all;' a soldier, 'I fight for all;' and a yeoman, 'I pay all.' About two years ago I passed through the same thoroughfare, and looking up for my curious sign, I was amazed to see a painted board occupy the place with these words inscribed "The Four Awls.'"

We have seen in the neighbourhood of Clare Market a house bearing the sign of the "Alphabet," (see page 113) which seems to have been originally "Alpha Beta," having probably a sacred allusion, like many of Commonwealth origin. This house had the whole of the letters—from A to little Z—over the door. In the seventh chapter of Ezra, the twenty-first verse contains all the letters of the alphabet. "The Bible," formerly a tavern in Shire Lane, Temple Bar, was a house of call for printers, and probably so named in consideration of the typographic art, without reference to the sanctity of the holy volume—books on theology being the first that gave employment to that class of artizans. The "Holy Rood Palace," in the Strand, pulled down for the New Law Courts, must have been taken from the Holy Rood, which was an image of Christ on the cross placed on what was called the rood-loft, built in churches over the passage that leads to the chancel. The most famous of these crucifixes was found at Bexley Abbey, in Kent. It was called the "Rood of grace," and by the aid of springs the eyes and lips were moved, and the head turned at the pleasure of its keeper. This identical image was exhibited at Paul's Cross in the year 1537, and after a sermon was delivered upon the relic, it was broken in pieces.

The "Lamb" an old sign in this parish, is a very common one, and certainly betokens more innocence than is usually found in alehouses, and seems more appropriate for the sign of a church or chapel. It had its origin, like many others, in the days of the pilgrimages; it was a noteworthy mark for a house of rest, and if the host and hostess were alike in temper, the sojourner might expect civil treatment and small charges.

It might have allusion more particularly to the wool trade; and the history of St. Agnes will apply to both. This saint, who suffered martyrdom when only fourteen years of age, in the year 306, is usually painted with a lamb at her side. It is reported that her parents, shortly after her execution, went to pray at her tomb, and continuing all night, they saw a glorious company of angels, among whom was their own daughter, with a snow-white lamb by her side. The Roman ladies still offer yearly two of the purest lambs at St. Agnes' altar, from whence they are taken, by the order of the Pope, and placed in a rich pasturage until the time of sheep-shearing, when they are shorn, and the wool is hallowed, and made into a fine white cloth, which is consecrated every year by the Pope, for the purpose of being sent to every archbishop, to be worn as a pall.

It is stated in a work entitled "Tavern Anecdotes, or the Origin of Signs," that, before 1766, many of these signs were large, finely gilt, and very absurd: golden perriwigs, saws, axes, razors, trees, lancets, knives, cheese, salmon, blacks' heads with gilt hair, half moons, and sugar-loaves, being repeated from Whitechapel to Piccadilly.

Perambulating the streets must have been rather unpleasant during a high wind, with hundreds of signs swinging on rusty hinges above threatening a descent, and pent-houses and spouts pouring cascades upon one's luckless head. In 1718 the sign and front of a house in Fleet Street, opposite Bride Lane, fell down and killed two young ladies, the king's jeweller and a cobbler. Many accidents having occurred by the falling of signs, the City at last compelled the shopkeepers to fix their signs against the walls.

Sir Wm. Blackstone, author of the celebrated "Commentaries on the Laws of England," lived in Carey Street, in 1761.

Mrs. Chapone, a lady well known for her "Letters on the Improvement of the Mind," and a disciple of Richardson, resided in this street until her husband's death.

Mr. Robert Keeley, the actor, was born in Grange Court, Carey Street, in 1794.

NEW COURT CHAPEL.*

On turning out of Carey Street into a court that doubtless was once "new," though latterly it did not retain a vestige that could bear such a designation, stood an ancient ecclesiastical building—a dark, heavy, brick elevation, relieved only by two large circular windows and two very plain doorways. During the last two or three years of its existence it had gone under thorough repair and considerable alterations and improvement. It was one of the oldest metropolitan meeting houses of the Congregational body; and at one time the worshippers were of a stately and influential order, for New Court Chapel gathered within its walls one of the most important congregations of Independents in the metropolis. The closing services of this old London chapel were appropriately conducted by the Rev. W. C. Younge—one of its own sons, the last of the old standards—who emphatically gave it out that the site being required for the erection of the New Law Courts, the Commissioners had, by virtue of powers granted to them, taken the building, making compensation for it to the amount of £6,500, which he stated had been lodged with the Commissioners in Chancery for the purchase of property, and held under the same trust.

"There are stirring memories that gather around these old walls. If they 'could speak' they could tell how, in 1709, four years after its erection, a mob, instigated by the celebrated Dr. Sacheverell, who was great in statecraft, broke into the chapel, tore down the pulpit and pews, and, dragging them into Lincoln's-inn-fields, there set them on fire. They could also bear witness to the zeal and manly force of one of the renowned ministers of that old meeting-house, the Rev. Thomas Bradbury, in stemming the torrent of Jacobite arrogancy, and in working out the religious liberties of our country. For this he did, not only by his writings, but in his sermons, after the manner of his times, when the pulpit had to do what is now generally committed to the platform and the press. During the latter part of the reign of Queen Anne, when Jacobinism and Popery were fast gaining the ascendant, this worthy minister did more, perhaps, than any other man in the British metropolis to oppose bigotry, and to guard his fellow citizens against the wiles of those who still clung to the fortunes of the Stuarts. These same walls might also be able to tell how within them the death of Queen Anne was first publicly announced, and the accession of George I. proclaimed, and of the comfort the event of a Protestant succession afforded to a congregation of Protestant Dissenters. This last circumstance is accounted for by the fact that Mr. Bradbury was intimately acquainted with Bishop Burnet, and that through the kindness of that prelate, messengers were dispatched to the Nonconformist pastor whilst he was conducting service, informing him of the demise of the Queen and the accession of the House of Hanover. There is a legend to the effect that by a preconcerted plan the messenger on entering the Chapel dropped or waved a white handkerchief as a sign to the preacher of the expected event, and that then and there the congregation gave thanks for the accession of the hoped-for Protestant rule in the land. It is indeed disputed by some whether this circumstance took place while Mr. Bradbury was pastor of New Court or of Fetter Lane Chapel; by the dates of Mr. Bradbury's pastorate at New Court it would seem to have taken place in that chapel. But, beside events like these, which savour of troublous times, the walls of this old sanctuary could tell of a change of ecclesiastical policy in the government of the church some forty-three years after the erection of the chapel— from English Presbyterian to Independent—a change not very considerable, perhaps, for that kind of Presbyterianism was very limited; and indeed several of our old Independent chapels have passed through a like change of government, and that without any change of congregation. But, above all, those old walls could tell of earnest and intelligent and faithful ministries exercised within them—by the first pastor, the Rev. Daniel Burgess, a man of great eccentricity but of great earnestness, who used to have an hour-glass by his side when preaching, and for whom the church was formed in the days of the second James, a year before the Revolution; by the Rev. James Wood, who was ordained by the Rev. Matthew Henry, and who afterwards became pastor of the Weigh-house; by the Rev. Henry Francis, a Welshman, who was friend and fellow-student at Tewkesbury with Mr. Thomas Secker, afterwards Archbishop of Canterbury, and the intimate friend of the immortal Dr. Watts; by the celebrated Thomas Bradbury, whom even the offer of a bishopric could not tempt from fidelity to conscience and to the liberties of his brethren; by the Rev. Richard Winter, a faithful and laborious minister of Christ, who was for fourteen years assisted by his son-in-law, the Rev. Frederick Hamilton, from both of whom one of the most accomplished and brilliant Independent preachers of the past generation gained both ancestry and name—Dr. Richard Winter Hamilton of Leeds; by the celebrated William Thorpe, who for five years before going to Bristol exercised his ministry here; by the faithful and much-venerated minister of Christ, Dr. Winter, who was nephew to the former pastor of that name, and grandson on the mother's side to the Rev. Thomas Bradbury, and no unworthy successor of both; and by several others who followed in the wake of their Nonconformist ancestors, each of whom, according to his several ability, excercised, we may believe faithfully, the trust committed to him. It is worthy of remark that, during the nearly one hundred and eighty years of this church's existence, it has not had more than ten pastors, and some five assistants to its pastors, and that all through its course, whilst many of the old Presbyterian congregations lapsed into the Arian heresy, no "uncertain sound" has ever been heard within the walls of the New Court Chapel. It is true that in more recent times one of its former pastors, the Rev. R. Ainslie, whom none would speak of but with respect, has embraced other views than those which he promulgated when occupying that sphere of labour; but this happened some years after his retirement from it."—*Christian World*, Sept. 28th, 1866.

CECIL STREET

Derives its name from Sir Robert Cecil, Lord High Treasurer to James I., who was created Earl of Salisbury in 1605. Salisbury House was erected by this nobleman; Queen Elizabeth being present at the house-warming. About 1678, a part was pulled down and Salisbury Street built. The other portion, next to Great Salisbury House and over the long gallery, was converted into shops and stalls, and called the Middle Exchange; which latter was taken down in 1696, with Great Salisbury House, and upon the site was erected Cecil Street, which Strype describes as "a fair street with very good houses fit for persons of repute." Many persons of note resided in this street: at the last house on the west side, in 1706, lived Lord Gray, and from 1721-24 the Archbishop of York lived at No. 24.

Dr. Wollaston was living at No. 18 in 1800. He discovered palladium and rhodium, two new metals, and made more than £30,000 by inventing a way to make platinum malleable. He carried on his experiments with the simplest instruments. Once, shortly after inspecting a grand galvanic battery, meeting a brother philosopher in the street, he led him by the button into a corner, took from his pocket a tailor's thimble, poured into it some liquid from a small phial, and instantly heated a platinum wire to a white heat.[*] In this street and at the "Globe," in Salisbury Street, lived Partridge, who was cobbler, astrologer and almanack maker. The almanack ("Merlinus Liberatus,") continued to be published, and in 1723 advertised Dr. Partridge's night drops, night pills, &c., as before by his widow at the "Blue Ball," in Salisbury Street.

CLARE MARKET
(SEE PAGES 79, 103.)

Was first named New Market, but afterwards called Clare Market, after the Earl of Clare,[†] who had a residence adjacent.[‡] The City

---

[*] The "Temple Anecdotes," p. 50.
[†] William Holles, created Baron Houghton, of Houghton, in the County of Nottingham 1616, and Earl of Clare, 1624.
[‡] According to the rate-books of St. Clement Danes, he was a parishioner in the year 1617.

THE COLONNADE, CLARE MARKET.

This long building consists of six houses used by a late Curate, as a Club for Working Men, Refuge for Boys, School, &c.

and Lord Clare had a long law suit concerning this estate; ultimately the City yielded, and from the success of the noble lord several charters have been obtained for the erection of other markets since the year 1660.

"Then is there, towards Drury Lane, a new market, called Clare Market; then is there a street and palace of the same name, built by the Earl of Clare, who lived there in a princely mansion, having a house, a street, and a market, both for flesh and fish, all bearing his name."—*Howell's Londinopolis*, 1657, p. 344.

"Clare Market, very considerable, and well served with provisions, both flesh and fish; for, besides the butchers in the shambles, it is much resorted unto by the country butchers and higglers. The market days are Wednesdays and Saturdays. The toll belongs to the Duke of Newcastle (Pelham Holles) as ground landlord thereof."—*Strype*, Ed. 1720, B. iv., p. 119.

"In 1538 it was enacted that butchers should sell their meat by weight, beef one halfpenny per pound, and mutton three farthings. Butchers sold pieces of beef, two-and-a-half pounds or three pounds, for a penny, and thirteen or fourteen such pieces for 12d.; mutton 8d. per quarter, and a cwt. of beef for 4s. 8d."—*Howe's Curious Black Letter Volume*.

"The Duke of Newcastle built a chapel at the corner of Lincoln's Inn Fields, near Clare Market, for the use of the butchers. There are about twenty-six butchers in and about Clare Market, who slaughter from 350 to 400 sheep weekly in the market stalls and cellars. There is one place only in which bullocks are slaughtered. The number killed is from fifty to sixty weekly, but considerably more in winter, amounting occasionally to 200. The number of calves is very uncertain. Near the market is a tripe-house in which they boil and clean the tripes, feet, heads, &c. In a yard distinct from the more public portion of the market, is the place where the Jews slaughter their cattle, according to a ceremony prescribed by the laws of their religion. Here great attention is paid to cleanliness."—*Old London Markets*.

The associations connected with this market are numerous and interesting; for here life of all kinds has been enacted—grave and gay, ludicrous and lamentable, tragedy and comedy.

John Henley, that disappointed demagogue who had set up his pulpit, called "The Gilt Tub," in Newport Market, in 1726, removed close to Clare Market in 1729, where he had an oratory or chapel. He preached in a tub covered with velvet and gold, the altar being inscribed "The primitive Eucharist." Here, "preacher at once and zany of the age," he lectured upon theology, "Skits of the Fashions," "the Beau Monde, from before Noah's Flood," and "Bobs at the Times;" but straying into sedition, he was cited before the Privy Council, who dismissed him as an impudent fellow. He lectured here for nearly twenty years: the admission was one shilling. He was talented, but a disappointed man as regards preferment in the Church. He became a violent satirist of the great and leading men of the day. Hogarth introduces this clever buffoon in two of his sketches: in one, he is christening a child; in the other, he is mounted on a scaffold, with a monkey by his side, and the motto "Amen." His vanity and ambition may be seen by his having the medals of admission to his lectures struck with a star rising to the meridian, with the words—

"Inveniam viam aut faciam."
"By all the powers that in me lay,
I will find or make a way."

He wrote a poem called "Esther," and was the editor of the "Hip Doctor," a periodical full of nonsense. In him there was much of the ludicrous: on one occasion he filled his oratory with shoemakers, by announcing to them he would teach a new and short way of making shoes, which was—by cutting off the tops of boots. Amongst some of the wild discourses of Henley we may mention his sermons on "The Tears of Magdalen," "St. Paul's Cloak," and "The last Wills of the Patriarchs." He left behind him 600 MSS. which he valued at one guinea a-piece, and 150 volumes of common places and other scholarly memoranda: they were sold for under £100. When Henley was once accused that he did all for lucre, he replied that "some do *nothing* for it." Henley, who at last, it is said, grew coarse, brutal and drunken, died October 14th, 1756. The "Gentleman's Magazine" announces his death thus:—" Rev. Orator Henley, aged 64."

A singular story appeared in most of the newspapers in 1845, setting forth that Mr. Smith, the proprietor of the "Hope Tavern," in Blackmoor Street, Clare Market, had in his possession the portraits, painted by Thornhill, of Jack Sheppard and his mother; and sold them, a few days since, to Mr. Merivale, of Gray's Inn, for ninety-seven guineas. In removing the portrait of Jack's progenitor from its frame, there was found, below the moulding, seven guineas, together with a number of copper coins of the period. Put thus accidentally upon the scent of some of Jack's secrets, it was an easy inference that it might be worth while to make a careful examination of the other frame, which besides was of a suspicious thickness, and it yielded up his treasures accordingly. Between the moulding and lining were found a number of papers and documents relating to the rising in 1745: some extremely curious, and all bearing the postmark of the time, besides furniture more characteristic, and which should have been left as appropriate frame-work to the portraiture of Jack. There was a portion of a note for £10 and a cheque for £17. It is Mr. Smith's intention that the British Museum shall be their repository. Among the papers also is a printed order for turning the Lincoln's Inn Theatre into a guard house, and suspending a performance announced on that occasion.

At the "Bull's Head" in this market, met the "Shepherd and his Flock Club." The "Artist's Club" used also to meet here, of which Hogarth was a member, and Dr. Ratcliffe a frequent visitor; and it was here that the latter was carousing when he received news of the loss of his £5,000 venture. The "Spiller's Head" was the sign of an inn in this market where one of the most famous tavern clubs was held. This meeting of artists, wits, humourists and actors originated with the performances at Lincoln's Inn about the year 1697. They counted many men of note amongst their members. Colley Cibber was one of the founders and its best president, not even excepting Tom d'Urfey. James Spiller, it should be stated, was a celebrated actor, who flourished in 1700. His greatest character was Mat o' the Mint, in the "Beggars' Opera." He was an immense favourite with the butchers of Clare Market (see page 79), one of whom was so charmed with his performances that he took down the sign of the "Bull and Butcher" and put up "Spiller's Head." At Spiller's death (Feb. 7, 1729), the following elegiac verse was made by one of the butchers of that locality :—

> "Down with your marrow bones and cleavers all,
> And on your marrow bones ye butchers fall ;
> For prayers from you who never prayed before,
> Perhaps Poor Jimmie may to life restore."

That eminent actress, Mrs. Bracegirdle, used to be in the habit (says Tony Aston) of frequently going into Clare Market and giving money to the poor unemployed basket women to such an extent, that she could not pass that neighbourhood without receiving the thanks and well wishes of all classes.

Bannister happening to meet a young gentleman in company who had taken more than he could well carry, and who had in consequence remarked upon his own folly in spending a fortune which his father, a tripe-seller in Clare Market, had left him, Charles inquired how he had spent the money, and was answered "that he had got rid of it by horse racing." "Never mind," says Charles, "you have lost that by gallopers which your father gained by trotters."

In a passage called White Horse Yard, leading from Stanhope Street into Drury Lane, lived, many years ago, a character who in all probability may yet be remembered by many inhabitants of this parish. We allude to an aged African negro who, despite every description of weather, might constantly be found at his post, or rather "shop," as he termed it, at the bottom of Ludgate Hill,— the Fleet Street corner—sweeping a clean path for foot passengers. By passers-by and those whom he termed his customers, he was called and known by the cognomens of "Tim-buc-too," and "Brutus Billy," which arose in all probability from the extraordinary figure he displayed: he was of short thick-set stature; his complexion of the jet African black, and his hair of a brilliant silver white, the forelock being carefully trained up to a topee, for he was in his way a follower of the fashions. It would appear that, from his civility and constant attendance to his crossing, he had earned the golden opinion of all kinds of persons, among whom was the daughter of the famed Alderman Waithman. This lady, whom it would seem possessed a remarkably charitable disposition, always relieved the poor African sweeper, and in addition to pecuniary gifts, usually provided him with a dinner on Sundays. Tim-buc-too was of most industrious and indefatigable habits, for after he had swept the mud back on his crossing, and "shut up his shop," he might be seen with his basket of nuts and fruit about the neighbouring places of public entertainment; thus he had been able to accumulate and fund a considerable sum of money, and at his death, to prove that he possessed a truly christian and grateful heart, he willed it to the person whom he considered his first and greatest benefactor, Miss Waithman. Poor Brutus Billy was replete with story and anecdote. He died in Chapel Court, 1854, in the eighty-seventh year of his age.

At the corner of Holles Street, Clare Market, is the Public Dispensary, removed from Carey Street, 1868; it was established in 1783, in Bishops Court, Lincoln's Inn, under the presidency of H.R.H. the Duke of Sussex and the Earl of Eldon (see page 37).

Among the many remarkable characters once resident in this parish we may mention George Honygold, of eccentric habits, who may be remembered by some of our readers. He was an artist of no inconsiderable talent, and possessed a large share of originality. The drawings of his celebrated theatrical characters were delineated with strict attention to the costumes they wore in the dramatic representations they were intended to represent, to which were added sketches of the scenery incidental to the pieces performed. From this arose the toy or model stage, which not only became a favourite with the juveniles, but also a great boon to the theatrical professors, insomuch that the celebrated Harley, the melodramatic actor, previous to rehearsing a piece, always had recourse to his model stage to arrange the position of his characters. This style of printing or drawing was adopted by many minor printsellers, and is still a thriving trade. Honygold was a very agreeable companion, having collected a rare and racy fund of anecdote; this led him much into company, and caused him to indulge too much in intemperate habits, which ended, we regret to say, in an untimely death. He constantly used the noted "No. 9," a gin-palace in Clare Market. He afterwards frequented the "Fountain," No. 4, Clare Market. In this house he imbibed his last drop; he had been indulging freely, and when the house was cleared, being deeply intoxicated, he fell down. He was taken to the Charing Cross Hospital, where he expired, at the age of sixty nine, in the year 1866.

In Clare Market was employed and lived Thomas Pett, the miser, a native of Warwickshire, who came to London at ten years of age with a solitary shilling in his pocket. An old woman who sold pies befriended him until he could procure himself a crust. He got apprenticed to a butcher in Southwark, and when out of his time he entered the service of a butcher as journeyman in Clare Market. For the first five years he was engaged at £25 per year, with meat and drink. The accumulation and keeping of money were the two sole objects of his thoughts. He made a rash vow one night when he was very thirsty, that as soon as he had saved a thousand pounds he would treat himself to a pint of porter every Saturday; this he was soon enabled to perform. He was never known, even in the depth of the coldest winter, to light a fire in his room, or go to bed by candle-light. For forty-two years he lived in Clare Market as journeyman butcher, and lodged thirty years in one gloomy apartment. He never treated man, woman, or child to a glass of any kind of liquor, never lent or borrowed a penny, never spoke ill or well of any one, and never ate a morsel at his own expense. He died on the 2nd June, 1803, and left £2,475 in the Three per Cents. to distant relations, not one of whom he had ever seen or corresponded with. About half-an-hour before he died he wanted to bargain for a coffin.

In former times in London, the burning of the effigy of Guy Fawkes on the 5th of November (see page 112) was a most important and exciting ceremony. The bonfire in Lincoln's Inn Fields was conducted on a very magnificent scale. Another tremendous pile was heaped up by the butchers in Clare Market, who, on the same evening, paraded through the streets in great force serenading the citizens with the famed marrow-bone-and-cleaver music, and the uproar throughout the town, from the shouts of the mob, the ringing of the church bells, and the confusion which prevailed, can be but faintly imagined by a person of the present time.

Close to the Tennis Court Playhouse, near Clare Market, stood a tavern where was held a club called the "Man-hunting Club." It was composed originally of a number of young rakes, of the offices of Law and Equity in Chancery Lane and its vicinity. The first who attended was entitled to the chair for the evening, and one of their whimsical pastimes was, that the chairman should nominate two or three couple of hair-brained puppies, at the hour of ten or eleven at night, who were immediately to sally forth like hounds, wolves, or tigers in search of prey, and return betimes to give a relation of their sport for the amusement of the club. These would lay upon the borders of the fields until they heard the tread of a single person going along the footpath, when they would start up, draw their swords, and give chase, bawling out—"That's he, that's he, that's he!" and after three or four such chases, they would return and entertain the company with an account of their sport.

Rich, the celebrated harlequin, returning one evening from the theatre in a hackney coach, gave orders to be driven to the "Sun Tavern," in Clare Market. On passing one of the windows which happened to be open, he sprung out of the coach into the room. The coachman on letting down the steps was surprised to find the coach empty, and after cursing his fare for a bilker, was about to drive off, when Rich, who in the meantime had jumped back again, ordered Jarvey to turn and set him down, with no pleasant idea of his customer, who upon getting out began to rail at the coachman for being so very stupid, and then offered his fare. This Jarvey declined, saying that his master had ordered him not to take any money that night. Rich said his master was a fool, and offered him a shilling for himself. He declined taking anything, and gained his box, saying "I know you well, notwithstanding your shoes; and so Mr. Devil you are out-witted for once."

CLEMENT'S LANE.

Was entered from Pickett Street, Strand, through a tall archway, when the traveller would find himself in a narrow, stale-looking, crooked thoroughfare, filthy and inconvenient, the atmosphere redolent with the exhalations arising from a densely packed population, the majority of whom were of the grimy, grovelling class, living from hand to mouth by uncertain daily labour. The houses in this lane consisted chiefly of the tumble-down ricketty kind, many being built with a framework of wood interlaid with brick and then plastered; the ancient casements were replaced by sash windows, the architectural adornments of cornice, mouldings and columns begrimed with dirt and filth, and nearly the whole looking ready to fall by a puff from a forge bellows. Notwithstanding their decayed and dilapidated appearance, however, many of these houses bore a palatial and noble aspect, and were evidently erected to shelter very different specimens of humanity from those by which they were lately occupied. Several of the houses were as old as the time of James and Elizabeth: one being noted as the scene of some of those royal intrigues and misdeeds which figure in the " Memoires pour Servir " of Charles II. and his court. Nearly all the houses were very remarkable for a quaint style of building. It was once the Bond Street of London. Here Steele showed his gaudy attire, Bollingbroke his stately and noble presence, and Pope that decrepid form which was yet the tabernacle of a noble and expansive soul. Here Swift, with down-cast head and scowling visage, used to growl to himself, as the mighty satirist made and unmade Cabinets; and the gentle Addison here turned some of those polished periods which have evoked the envy and emulation of after ages.

Houses have their histories, like individuals and nations, and undergo similar and tragic transitions. Where a great priest once lived, a hairdresser plies his trade; and the study and library of

ST. CLEMENT DANES' CHURCH.

PILLARS—CLEMENT'S LANE, STRAND.

of Newton, where the world was "circumferented," has heard the sound of the billiard balls; a stately mansion, where the squire once shed around him the solid and homely delights which England alone enjoys, is converted into a wayside inn, and becomes the abode of petty peculation and heartless civility. But we doubt if, in in all the mutable and sad history of stones, any place has undergone a greater change than Clement's Lane.*

Oh! potent time, how mighty are thy changes, and how insignificant is man with all his divine attributes in thy aged yet unwithered hand: past, present and future years are all the same to thee, for thy scythe will mow down the posterity to be as it has laid low the ancestry of bygone ages.

According to Moser, some have thought that near this spot an inn stood as far back as the time of King Ethelred, for the reception of penitents who came to St. Clement's Well; that a religious house was in process of time established, and that the church thence arose. The "Holy Lamb," (see page 156) an inn on the west side of the lane, afterwards received the guests, and the monastery was converted into an inn of the law.

DENZELL STREET

Was so called by Gilbert Holles, Earl of Clare, in 1682, in memory of his uncle Denzil, Lord Holles, who died about 1680. He was one of the five Members of Parliament whom Charles I. so despotically attempted to seize. An inscription on the south-west wall of the street, set up in 1682 and renewed in 1796, records the origin of the name. (See page 113.)

---

* In consequence of the Old Mission House and Laundry, Nos. 16, in this Lane, and 2, Clement's Court, being required, at the close of 1866, for the New Law Courts, and the inability at the time of procuring suitab premises, the work for a few months had to be relinquished. Early in 1867, however, the house, No. 35, Carey Street, though with inferior accommodation, and at a greatly increased rental, was procured, and a part of the former mission work recommenced; but owing to the want of space, the Laundry, which had proved so useful to the poor in this crowded neighbourhood, could not be re-opened. At length, however, the Committee have succeeded in obtaining a very convenient house, 24, Carey Street, admirably suited to the purposes of the Mission, having twenty-four beds for servants and young persons out of situation; a Registry Office, Mission Room, where the Clergy, Scripture Readers, Bible Women, District Visitors, and poor can meet.

DEVEREUX COURT

So called after Robert Devereux, Earl of Essex, the Parliamentary general: it anciently formed part of the Outer Temple or district of the chivalric and wealthy Knights Templars, and abuts on Essex Street. By the establishment of two coffee-houses, Devereux Court became the resort of the *literati* of the two last centuries. One of these houses was kept by a Greek from the Levant, and known as the "Grecian." In 1664-5 he advertised his Turkey coffee-berry, chocolate, sherbet and tea, good and cheap, and announced his readiness to give gratuitous instruction in the art of preparing the said liquors. Steele, in No. 1 of the "Tatler" (April, 1709), notifies that he shall date all learned articles from the "Grecian," all gallantry from White's, all poetry from Will's, all foreign and domestic news from St. James's. At the house of one Kedder, in this court, in 1678, died Marchmont Needham, an energetic newspaper writer, who thrice during the civil wars changed his political notions to save his neck. Pope addresses a letter to Fortesque his "counsel learned in the law," at Tom's coffee-house in this court. Dr. Birch, the antiquarian, frequented Tom's, and there Akenside spent his winter evenings. Addison, in No. 49 of the "Spectator" (April, 1711), describes the spleen and inward laughter with which he views, at the Grecian, the young Templars come in about eight a.m., either dressed for Westminster, and with the pre-occupied air of assumed business, or in gay cap, slippers, &c., rising early to publish their laziness. Dr. King relates that two hot-blooded young gentlemen quarrelled one evening at this coffee-house about the accent of a Greek word. Stepping out into Devereux Court, they fought, and one of them being run through the body, died on the spot. Ralph Thoresby, the Leeds topographer, describes retiring to the Grecian after the meeting of the Royal Society, of which he was a fellow, with the president, Sir Isaac Newton. In 1843 the Grecian was closed, and it has since been turned into chambers. Where was once the coffee-house patronised by Goldsmith, Addison and Steele, there is now a bust of Essex, and beneath—" This is Devereux Court, 1676."

ESSEX STREET.

Which was built in 1682, is the first coach turning in the Strand from Temple Bar on the left, running to the riverside, where is a pier for steam-boats. Part of the ground now occupied by this street and Devereux Court anciently formed a portion of the Outer Temple, which, after being possessed (Dugdale supposes) by the prior and canons of the Holy Sepulchre, was transferred by them in the time of Edward III. to the Bishops of Exeter, who occupied it until the reign of Henry VI. In 1326, Isabella landed from France to chase the Spencers from her husband's side, and advanced on London. The King (Edward II.) and his evil counsellors fled to the Welsh frontier, but Walter Stapleton, then occupier of Exeter House, stoutly held out for his King, and as custos of the city of London, demanded the keys of the Lord Mayor, Hammond Chickwell, to prevent the treachery of the disaffected city. The watchful populace, fearing the mayor's submission, and roused by Isabella's proclamation—which had been hung on the new cross in Cheapside—rose in arms, and took the keys. They ran to Exeter House, then newly-erected, fired the gates, and burnt all the plate, money, jewels, and goods. The Bishop rode to the north door of St. Paul's to take sanctuary. There the mob tore him from his horse, stripped him of his armour, and dragging him to Cheapside, proclaimed him a traitor and an enemy of their liberties, and lopping off his head, set it on a pole. After being occupied by several distinguished individuals, Exeter House (see page 89) at last came into the possession of the unfortunate favourite Earl of Essex, from whom the street derives its name.

In Essex House was born a less brilliant, but a happier and more prudent man, Robert Earl of Essex, afterwards the well-known parliamentary general.

In this street the Robin Hood Society was established in 1613, at the house of Sir Hugh Middleton; in 1747, it was removed to the Robin Hood in Butcher Row, when it was presided over by a baker.

Here Burke first displayed those oratorical powers which afterwards became so transcendent. When, becoming reconciled to the Pitt administration, he went over to the Tory benches, exclaiming, "I quit the camp," Sheridan instantly rose and observed, "As the honourable gentleman had quitted them as a deserter, he hoped he would not return as a spy;" and when the King settled a pension on Burke, Sheridan remarked "that it was no wonder that Mr. Burke should come to the House of Commons for his bread, when he formerly went to a baker for his eloquence"—meaning the Robin Hood Club. The unsophisticated Goldsmith was a member of this club.

"Samuel Patterson, the bookseller, auctioneer, and catalogue maker, lived in this street in 1775, in rooms formerly the residence of Orlando Bridgeman. In these rooms Charles Dibden* commenced his entertainments, and here his fine song of 'Poor Jack' became famous."—*Smith's Nollekens.*

"In this street lived George Fordyce, a celebrated epicurean doctor of the eighteenth century. During twenty years he dined daily at Dolly's Chop-house, and at his meat he always took a jug of strong ale, a quarter of a pint of brandy, and a bottle of port. Having imbibed these refreshing stimulants, he walked to his house and gave a lecture to his pupils."—*Jeafreson's Book about Doctors.*

Mrs., or, as she was commonly called, "Lady" Lewson, an eccen-

---

* Charles Dibden was born at a village called Dibden, Southampton, 1745. His death took place 1814, in the sixty-ninth year of his age. He was interred in the burial ground of St. James, Camden Town, where, in the midst of a clump of flowering shrubs, his "frail memorial" tells us, from his own beautiful song, that "Though his body's under hatches, his soul is gone aloft." During his life he wrote above 1,300 songs, and his sons nearly double that number. Garrick, Sheridan, Harris, Charles Bannister, Bickerstaff, and Dr. Arne were, among other warm patrons, great admirers of his talent. In the year 1788, tired of dramatic contingencies, he entertained an audience in his own theatre, commencing in Essex Street, then at Fisher's Auction Rooms, Covent Garden, at both of these places, in an entertainment under the title of "The Whim of the Moment; or, Nature in Little." The song of "Poor Jack" was alone sufficiently attractive to insure him a profitable season of some weeks; and this was the commencement of a series of similar fashionable and profitable entertainments of unaided genius, which were the annual delight of the town for many years at the before-mentioned rooms, at the Lyceum, at Scot's and Idle's premises in the Strand, and at his own theatre, which he built and opened as the Sans Souci, in Leicester Square. He also gave a series of musical entertainments in Beaufort Buildings, in this parish.

tric widow, who died in London in 1806, at the age of one hundred and six, was born in Essex Street, and married early, was left a rich widow at twenty-six. For the remainder of her days her chief companions were an old man-servant, two dogs, and a cat. In dress she was fanciful and particular, adhering steadfastly to the fashions of her youth, when George I. was king. But she was a decided foe to cleanliness. Her rooms were never washed, seldom swept; and to personal ablutions she was an utter stranger, "People who washed themselves," she said, "were always catching cold." She used to smear her face and neck with hog's lard, and to "top up," as regarded her cheeks, with rose pink. Her health was good to the last, and she cut two new teeth at the age of eighty-seven. She was buried at Bunhill-fields burying-ground.

FOUNTAIN COURT

Derived its name from an adjacent tavern. It was well paved and its houses were respectably inhabited. The "Fountain Tavern" was well known for its excellent accommodation, good cellars, "curious kitchen," and old wine. The Fountain Club, of which Pulteney was a member, held its meetings in this tavern to oppose Sir Robert Walpole (*Glover's Life*). Sir C. H. Williams, that admirable lampooner, thus mentions it:—

> "Then enlarge on his cunning and wit,
> Say how he harangued at the Fountain;
> Say how the old patriots were bit,
> And a mouse was produced by a mountain."

Dennis the critic mentions in his "Letters" dining here with Loggen the painter.

Charles Lillie, the perfumer, lived next door to the "Fountain Tavern." He was burnt out and went to the east corner of Beaufort Buildings in 1709 (see page 151). Christopher Catt removed from Shire Lane to the "Fountain;" with him also the Kit-Cat Club, which was instituted in 1700 and died away about the year 1720.

Dr. Johnson frequented the "Essex Head," in Essex Street (see page 85).

Edmund Kean, the celebrated actor and really great tragedian, used to pass some of his leisure hours and find relaxation from theatrical duties at the "Coal Hole Tavern" in Fountain Court (see page 111). It was at this house that "The Wolves" held their club, with Kean for their leader or patron. Towards the close of the year 1813, he obtained an engagement at Drury Lane, receiving only a trifling salary; but on Wednesday, the 26th January, 1814, he made his famous debut as "Shylock," and we are told how the actor who left home doubtful and anxious, returned overflowing with brilliant anticipations. "Now, Mary," said he to his wife, "you shall ride in your own carriage, and Charles* shall go to Eton," and the child was roused from sleep that the promise might be sealed with a kiss. Mr. Edmund Kean died May 15th, 1833, aged forty-six.

HOLYWELL STREET,

This name must, upon reflection, awaken in the mind thoughts both of religion and antiquity; but from it the invading hand of time has obliterated every vestige of the ancient and historically recorded relics of by-gone days.

Here lies buried that perennial spring that at one period was hallowed by its appropriation to pious uses. The Ascension of our Saviour was commemorated here on Holy Thursday, when the newly baptized converts appeared clad in the white robes they assumed from Easter to Pentecost.

Here the motley train of devotees on their pilgrimage to Canterbury used to halt, the holy brotherhood and the whole cavalcade encamping on this spot to refresh themselves and horses. The holywell was thus rendered sacred. It is said to have been one of the oldest springs, and the water is described by Fitz Stephen as "sweete, wholesome, and cleere, and much frequented by scholars and youths

---

* The late Mr. Charles Kean was born at Waterford, in Ireland, on the 18th January, 1811. He was educated at Eton. His first appearance on the stage was October 1st, 1827. He was married to Miss Ellen Tree on the 29th January, 1842, and died the 22nd January, 1868, aged 57 years and 4 days, and was buried on the 30th of the same month at Catherington Church, Horndean, Hampshire.

of the Citie in summer evenings, when they walk forth to 'take the aire.'" This street derives its name from the holy-well referred to. It is a narrow thoroughfare, running parallel with the Strand from St. Clement's Church to the New Church of St. Mary. It is still frequented by scholars—for here may be purchased every description of literature, and until lately, we regret to say, an abundance of a class totally unfitted to circulate amongst respectable people. (p. 121.)

There existed, until its destruction, an entrance into Lyon's Inn, and the passage opposite, sculptured with a lion's head, was formerly the inn entrance from the Strand. Holywell Street was, in Styrpe's time, inhabited by divers salesmen, piece-brokers and staymakers.*

HOWARD STREET,

A small street crossing Norfolk Street between Surrey Street and Arundel Street, is erected on part of the site which formed the palace and grounds of the Earls of Arundel. Many celebrated characters have resided here, amongst whom we may mention Congreve, the poet and dramatist, who was commissioner of hackney coach and wine licenses; he also held a place in the Pipe Office, a post in the Custom House, and was secretary in Jamaica. On becoming acquainted with the Duchess of Marlborough, he removed from Howard Street to Surrey Street, where he died January 19th, 1729. The body of Congreve lay in state and was afterwards interred with great solemnity in Henry VIII.'s Chapel.

Mrs. Bracegirdle, the fascinating actress and the belle and toast of London, lived in this street (see page 164). The young men of fashion adored her, wits praised her beauty in verse, and Congreve

---

* "The father of Miss Ray, the singer, and mistress of old Lord Sandwich, is said to have been a well-known staymaker in Holywell-street. His daughter was apprenticed in Clerkenwell, from whence the musical lord took her to load her with a splendid shame. On the day she went to sing at Covent Garden in 'Love in a Village,' Hackman, who had left the army for the Church, waited for her carriage at the Cannon Coffee House, Cockspur Street, Charing Cross. At the door of the theatre, directly opposite the Bedford Coffee House, Hackman rushed out, and as Miss Ray was being handed from her carriage he shot her through the head, and then attempted his own life. Hackman was hanged at Tyburn, and he died declaring that shooting Miss Ray was the result of a sudden burst of frenzy, for he had only planned suicide in her presence."—*Thornbury.*

says it was the fashion to avow a tenderness for her. Amongst those who worshipped her was a Captain Hill, a disreputable fast-living profligate, and a friend of the infamous duellist Lord Mohun. One of Mrs. Bracegirdle's favourite parts was Statira; the part of her lover, Alexander, being played by her neighbour, the eminent actor Mountfort. Captain Hill, upon witnessing the love scene, and acting upon the assumption of its being a display of real love, determined to be revenged upon Mountfort and to carry off the lady by force. Lord Mohun, ever ready to engage in any desperate action, agreed to assist him in his base design. At six o'clock on the night appointed they went to Drury Lane; but Mrs. Bracegirdle not acting that night, they proceeded to her lodgings in Howard Street. Finding that she was gone to the house of a Mr. Page, in Princes Street, Drury Lane, they went there and waited until she left. Mr. Page lighted her out, and Hill immediately seized her and attempted, with the assistance of some hired roughs, to drag her into the coach where Lord Mohun sat with a pistol in each hand; but her brother and Mr. Page rushing to the rescue, Hill was forced to let go his hold and fly. Mrs. Bracegirdle and her friends then proceeded to her lodgings, followed on foot by Lord Mohun and Captain Hill, who attempted to gain admission to the house, as they said, to beg Mrs. Bracegirdle's pardon, but were not allowed; they then sent for a bottle of wine which they drank in the street, and walked about with their swords drawn, saying they would be revenged upon Mountfort. Messengers were sent to warn him, but he could not be found. The watch were sent for, but being cautious fellows, they merely requested the gallants to put up their swords and then left. Unfortunately, Mountfort about this time passed down the street on his way home, and on coming up to the swordsmen, he was saluted by Lord Mohun, who said, "Mr. Mountfort, your humble servant; I am glad to see you."

"Who is this, Lord Mohun?" said Mountfort.

"Yes, it is."

"What brings your Lordship here at this time of night?"

Lord Mohun replied, "I suppose you were sent for, Mr. Mountfort?"

"No, indeed, I came by chance."

"Have you not heard of the business of Mrs. Bracegirdle?"

"Pray, my lord," said Hill, breaking in, "hold your tongue; this is not a convenient time to discuss this business!"

Hill pulled Lord Mohun to get him away; but Mountfort, taking no notice of Hill, continued to address Lord Mohun, saying he was sorry to see him assisting Captain Hill in such an evil action, and begging him to forbear.

Hill then gave the actor a box on the ear, and on Mountfort demanding what that was for, attacked him sword in hand, and ran him through before he had time to draw his weapon. Mountfort died next day of the wound, declaring with his last breath that Lord Mohun had offered him no violence.

Lord Mohun met a similar fate, for he afterwards fell in a duel with the Duke of Hamilton.

HOLLES STREET.

In 1642, Charles I. granted a license to Gervase Holles, Esq., to erect fifteen houses, a chapel, and several streets from thirty to forty feet wide. These streets retain the names and titles of their noble founder in Clare Street, Denzell Street, Holles Street, &c. Let into the wall of a house in this street there is a stone inscribed "Holles Street, 1647."

MILFORD LANE

Is named from a ford over the Thames at the extremity, and a windmill in the Strand near the site of St. Mary's Church. Sir Richard Baker, the Chronicler, lived in Milford Lane, 1632-9.

In 1641, according to the "Publick Newes:"

> "After intelligence was given to some joint confederates with the Rebels, that 18 were sent to New-Gate, they amongst themselves appointed a meeting in *Milford Lane*, where they consulted to set the *City of London* on *Fire*, in vindication of their friends; and taking an oath amongst themselves to confirm their resolution, credible information was given to divers constables, who summoned a strong watch, and apprehended 36 more of them, who are now committed to safe custody."

Among the names of these we find three Captains—Griffin, Hornway, and Spencer, and Lieut. Williams.

On the east side, near the Strand, stood some very picturesque buildings principally built of wood, with bay windows, which are described in a deed dated 1694; they were taken down in 1852. St. Clement Danes Infant Schools are in this lane (see page 25). The Chapel of the Holy Ghost also stood near this spot.

NEWCASTLE STREET

Was formerly known as Maypole Alley, but since named after the ground landlord, John Holles, Duke of Newcastle (1711). Here in 1713 stood a tall maypole, 100 feet high, a remnant of vile heathenism, round which people in holiday time used to dance, quite ignorant of its original intent and meaning; it was removed in 1718, and given to Sir Isaac Newton as a stand for his large telescope. Pope makes this the locality where the heroes of the "Dunciad" assemble.

> "Where the tall maypole o'erlooked the Strand,
> But now (so Anne and piety ordain)
> A church collects the saints of Drury Lane."

The following account of this maypole is from an old tract, entitled, "Citie's Loyalty Displayed," 4to., 1661:—

> "This maypole was 134 feet high, and was erected upon the cost of the parishioners there adjacent, and the gracious consent of his sacred Majesty, with the illustrious Prince the Duke of York. This tree was a most choice and remarkable piece; 'twas made below bridge, and brought in two parts up to Scotland Yard, near the King's Palace, and from thence it was conveyed, April 14th, 1661, to the Strand, to be erected. It was brought with a streamer flourishing before it, drums beating all the way, and other sorts of musick. It was supposed to be so long that landsmen could not possibly raise it; Prince James, Duke of York, Lord High Admiral of England, commanded twelve seamen off aboard ship to come and officiate the business; whereupon they came and brought their cables, pullies, and other tackling, and six great anchors; after these were brought three crowns, borne by three men bareheaded, and a streamer displaying all the way before them, drums beating, and other music playing, numerous multitudes of people thronging the streets with great shouts and acclamations all day long. The maypole then being joined together and hooped about with bands of iron, the crown and cane,

with the King's arms richly gilded, was placed on the head of it ; a large top like a balcony was about the middle of it. Then, amid sounds of trumpets and drums, the loud cheerings and the shouts of the people, the maypole 'far more glorious, bigger, and higher than ever any one that stood before it,' was raised upright, which highly did please the Merrie Monarch, and the illustrious Prince, Duke of York ; and little children did much rejoice, and antient people did clap their hands, saying, golden days began to appear."

Another writer subsequently refers to it :—

"Fairly we marched on, till our approach
Within the spacious passage of the Strand,
Objected to our sight a summer broach—
Yclep'd, a maypole, which, in all our land,
No city, town, nor street can parallel ;
Nor can the lofty spire of Clerkenwell—
Although he have the advantage of a rock—
Perch up more high his turning weather-cock."

Where the new church in the Strand is erected, a windmill stood in the reign of James I., and here was permitted the first stand for hackney coaches,* in 1634, which was abolished in 1853.

In Maypole Alley, near Drury Court, which leads from the new church, Strand, to Drury Lane,† Nan Clarges, Duchess of Albemarle,

---

* "1555. This year Walter Ripon made a coach for the Earle of Rutland, which (saith he) was the first coach ever made in Englande, and anno 1564 he made a hollow turning coach with pillars and arches for her Majestie. Also in 1584 a chariot throne with four pillars behind to bear a canopy, with a crowne imperiall on the toppe, and before two lower pillars, whereon stood a lion and a dragon, the supporters of the royal arms."—*From Howe's Curious Black Letter Volumes.*

† Drury Lane derived that appellation from the mansion of the Drury family, that stood on part of the site of the Olympic Theatre. "Young Sir Drue Drury, at a taverne, called for tobacco-pipes. The fellow, in laying them downe on the table, broke most of them ; presently Sir Drue swore a great oath, they were made of the same metal with the Commandments. 'Why so?' said one : he replied, ' Because they are so soon broken.'"—*Merry Passages and Jests.* Harl. MS. 6395. The diurnals of 1768 mention, "Yesterday [August 25th] the inhabitants of Drury Lane had orders to take down their signs, as the streets in that place and the neighbourhood will soon begin to be new paved."

In this street formerly stood Drury House, which came into the possession of Lord Craven, the hero of Creutznach, who rebuilt it in four stories, and was afterwards called Craven House, where the Earl died in 1697. This mansion was taken down in 1803, and the ground purchased by Philip Astley for the site of the Olympic Pavilion. In its latter time the Craven Mansion was a public-house, with the sign of the " Queen of Bohemia," which arose from its having been occupied by the daughter of James I., through whom the family of Brunswick succeeded to the throne of England, and who is suspected to have been secretly married to her heroic champion, Lord Craven and wife of General Monk, the promoter of the restoration of Charles II., was born. She was the daughter of a blacksmith, whose forge stood at the eastern corner of the place. Newcastle Street was then called Magpye Lane. In another account we find that Little Drury Lane also bore the cognomen of Maypole Alley, retained long after the maypole had vanished. The neighbourhood must have been densely populated. In October, 1781, a fire that began at the house of a hatter named Ballard, eastward of St. Mary-le-Strand, next door to the "Spotted Dog" tavern, notwithstanding every possible exertion to extinguish it, destroyed the old lath-and-plaster buildings with such rapidity that upwards of thirty houses were consumed; passing on to Holywell Street, consuming two houses in Horne Court, and through the "Five Bells" tavern, up to Wych Street. The iron railing on the north side of the new church was forced down by the falling of two of the houses. The site lay in ruins till leave was given by the House of Commons (May 17th, 1782) to bring in a bill to form a street from the Strand to Clare Market, the present Newcastle Street. Adjacent to this street, between Wych Street and Holywell Street, stood Lyon's Inn.* (see page 112). It was originally

---

The present "Craven Head" (see page 114) public-house was one of the offices of Craven House, and the adjoining stabling belonged to that mansion. Who would now suppose, in passing this spot, that it was once the abode of wit and elegance, of a lord and queen, and the scene of more than one romance of real life. At 14, White Horse Yard, in this lane, Francis Westland died, August 30, 1867, aged 100 years.

The first Drury Lane Theatre was built in 1617; rebuilt 1629; burnt down 1671; rebuilt 1674; enlarged by Garrick 1762; pulled down 1791; rebuilt and opened 1794; burnt down 1809; present theatre opened October 12, 1812.

* The entrance to Lyon's Inn was in Holywell Street, on the spot occupied by Mr. Berger, the publisher, lately deceased, and also through Horne Court, the entrance to which is now the private door of Mr. Parry's, the Optician, No. 24, in this street, next door to the famous "Old Dog" tavern, the coffee-room of which is supposed to have been immediately over the well which gave name to the street. The history of the "Old Dog," which, thirty years ago, was advertised as having been "established upwards of 200 years," is now, unfortunately, but a relic for the pages of a local work. Situated and being No. 23, Holywell Street, it provided till its death good fare for those who patronised the "antient hostelrie," and it was not till the gigantic scheme of the "Strand Hotel Company, Limited," sprang into existence that the "Old Dog" died— died through the visitation of a commercial speculation. On Tuesday, the 22nd of March, 1864, in about twenty lots (being the third "clearance sale" for the Hotel) was sold the building materials and fixtures of the famous tavern. We now say a word or two of the site, first noting

a hostelry with the sign of the Lion, and was converted to an inn of Chancery in the reign of Henry VIII. It was an appendage to the Inner Temple, and of considerable antiquity, entries having been made in the stewards' books in the reign of Henry V. The hall bears the date 1700. There was formerly a sun-dial and a few trees in this Inn. Sir Edward Coke was one of its readers in 1578.

The poor old Inn is, however, now swept from off the earth, and like that still more ancient relic, the "Holy well" adjacent, lost to view; but the latter sacred spot no hand can utterly destroy. Upon examination, we find there is no reason for supposing the Holy well was under the "Old Dog" tavern, there being much older wells near this spot. Some time since the Strand Hotel Company purchased the damp, decaying site, intending to erect a whole region of houses, offices, and

its dimensions, as given in a recent plan of the estate. To Holywell Street it had a frontage of 16 feet 6 inches; on the west, a depth of 69 feet 9 inches; on the east, 67 feet 9 inches; and on the north, 14 feet 4 inches. To the ordinary reader, these measurements may appear particularly frivolous; but when it is stated that the land was purchased nearly two centuries and a-half ago by the parish of St. Giles', Cripplegate, the reason will not appear so strange.

It appears that Richard Budd, by will dated 20th July, 1630, bequeathed £300 to the churchwardens of St. Giles', without Cripplegate, and their successors, to buy lands or houses, for the parish to pay out of the yearly profits threepence to each of such poor who should attend the early Friday morning prayers at St. Giles' Church; and John, Lord Bishop of Ely, by will dated 16th April, 1631, bequeathed £50 to the poor of the same parish, to be yearly distributed on Good Friday. The parishioners thereupon, by indenture dated 13th April, 1633, between Thomas Preston of the first part, and William Fuller, D.D., Vicar of St. Giles'; Robert Batt, John Wills, Nicholas Fawcett, and Edward Buckley, churchwardens; and William Wase (executor of Richard Budd) of the second part; and Roger Gardner, and twenty other parishioners of the third part, purchased of the said Thomas Preston "all that messuage or tenement being the sign of 'The Rose and Crown,' and all shops, buildings, gardens, &c., and appurtenances to the same belonging, situated in the parish of St. Clement's Danes in the County of Middlesex, abutting upon Lyon's Inn on the north, and upon the King's highway on the south?" Here, then, is the site of our "Old Dog" tavern known under another sign 235 years ago. No subsequent trust-deeds of the property have been found. In March, 1825, one Edward Sandwell took the house on lease, but becoming bankrupt, it was transferred to William Hardstaff for a term of thirty and a-half years from Christmas, 1825, at a yearly rent of £81, the tenant undertaking before the next March to thoroughly repair the building.—*History of the Charities of St. Giles', Cripplegate*, 1830, p. 79.

On the south side of Holywell Street, at the north-west corner of the passage leading into the Strand, and forming one of a row of the picturesque houses of Old London, is one which for many years has been the observed of all passers-by by reason of the curious gilt *sign of the half-moon* suspended over the door. When the house changed hands some time since, a friend of ours was offered this interesting relic for a few shillings, but rather than see the thoroughfare lose one of its curiosities, our friend begged that it might be retained in its old position, and we are pleased to chronicle that the favour was granted him.

squares ingeniously devised to economise the space of the metropolis. The company, however, came to grief, and the buildings, exposed to the elements, have commenced a course of decay: massive walls, lofty pillars reaching to the roof, across which are giant girders of mighty weight and size, are all mouldering to a state of ruin. The project has proved a failure, and the site of old Lyon's Inn is still the seat of desolation and dreariness.

At No. 16 existed for many years Varney's Eating House, and of which a valued friend speaks thus:—

> "Among the many remarkable characters who used to frequent this well-known eating-house was a Mr. Fallowfield, a retired gentleman, who used to walk some miles every day to dine at this house. I rather think I have been told that he had not missed one day for seventeen years, either summer or winter, be the weather what it would. His portrait used to hang in the room after his death; I have seen it frequently. Many other well-known persons dined there, and Varney's rice puddings were in great request."

NORFOLK STREET

Was built in 1682, on a portion of the site on which stood Arundel House and grounds. Many notabilities have resided in this street; amongst whom, at the south-west corner, lived William Penn, the Quaker, son of Cromwell's stout Bristol Admiral and the founder of Pennsylvania. In Penn's old house afterwards resided for thirty years that good and amiable man Dr. Richard Brocklesby, the physician, a great friend of Burke and Johnson, who gave to the former a thousand pounds. He was a most generous man: he attended the poor for nothing, and had many pensioners.

William Shoppen, M.P., also lived in this street. Of him Sir Robert Walpole remarked, "that he would not say who was corrupted, but he would say who was not corruptible—and that was Shoppen."

Mortimer, a rough picturesque painter, and who was called "the English Salvator Rosa," lived in this street. At No. 21, Albany Wallis resided, who was a friend and executor of Garrick. Sir Roger de Coverley, that lively old country gentleman, is said by Addison to have put up in this street before he went to Soho Square.

Dr. Birch, the historian of the Royal Society, lived in this street. He was the son of a Quaker tradesman, at Clerkenwell, but joining the Established Church became rector of St. Margaret Patten's, in Fenchurch Street. He left some books, manuscripts, and money to the British Museum. He was killed by a fall from his horse in 1766.

"On Monday night the Czar of Muscovy arrived from Holland and went directly to the house prepared for him in Norfolk Street, near the water side."—*The Postman*, Jan. 28th, 1698.

Peter the Great lived in this street.

Mr. Ireland's house, No. 8, in this street, was daily crowded to excess by persons of the highest rank, as well as by the most celebrated men of letters. He was the father of the manufacturer of the Shaksperian plays. (See page 110.) He died in 1802.

The houses in this street were afterwards occupied by merchants, bankers, lawyers, and persons of high rank, the street being one of the best in the now heart of London, and the River Thames, when not converted into a receptacle for house drainage, being "a pleasant thing to look upon." Fortunately the drainage is now to be effected by sewers, constructed at the cost of some millions of money, and Norfolk Street is about to become a main thoroughfare, in connection with the Thames Embankment and intended Metropolitan Railways. Of late, the houses have nearly all been used as private hotels, but the St. Clement Danes Savings Bank (see page 52) and the Royal Farmers' and General Insurance Company have now offices there, and no doubt other public companies will ere long seek to be in the same neighbourhood. The Royal Farmers' and General Insurance Company, established in 1840, had the prefix "Royal" added to its original title under the sanction of Her Majesty Queen Victoria in 1843, the Company having previously had the patronage of the late Prince Consort, who insured his farming stock in the office John Reddish, Esq., is the actuary and secretary to the company.

Sir Francis Ommaney, the Navy Agent, — Speeding, Esq, Solicitor to the Admiralty, lived in the street; the late R. Twining, Esq. resided for many years at No. 35; J. F. Isaacson, Esq., Solicitor and Clerk to the Vestry of this Parish, has resided in this street for many years.

Mr. Vincent Darling, for so many years editor of *Bell's Life in London*, resided in Norfolk Street.

At No. 33, in this street, are the offices of the Conservative Land Society, enrolled under 6 and 7 William IV. cap. 32, as the "Conservative Benefit Building Society and United Land Company, Limited, incorporated under the Companies' Acts of 1862 and 1867."

The formation of this Institution arose out of the Middlesex election of 1852, when the present Duke of Marlborough (then the Marquis of Blandford) was the Conservative candidate, and was defeated by Mr. Bernal Osborne. On the registry of votes being examined after the return, it was discovered that the narrow majority which lost the noble Marquis his seat for the County of Middlesex was entirely in one district, namely, Bethnal Green, and that a large number of votes had been registered in that eastern division of Middlesex through the instrumentality of the National Land Society, of which Messrs. Bright and Cobden were the leading members. Mr. Pownall, the chairman of the Marquis of Blandford's committee, and Mr. C. L. Gruneisen, for many years connected with the *Morning Post* at home and abroad, who was a member thereof, considering that for the protection of conservatism in the higher counties a Land Society should be formed similar in operation to the Radical Land Society, were preparing the organization of the new undertaking, but Mr. Charles Edward Lewis, a solicitor practising in Boswell Court, of the firm of Harrison and Lewis (now of the Old Jewry in the City) had anticipated the action of Mr. Pownall and Mr. Gruneisen by organising a scheme called "The Conservative Franchise Society." Messrs. Harrison and Lewis convened a meeting at St. George's Hotel, on the 9th of August, 1852, at which the Earl of Winchelsea (then Viscount Maidstone), Viscount Ranelagh, Lord Alfred Churchill, the late Sir William Codrington, Bart., Colonel Knox, Colonel Aldy, Colonel Dickson, Messrs. H. B. Ray, Pownall, R. Steven, W. Sangster, G. M. Miller, were present, and resolutions were passed to carry out the object of a Conservative Land Society, the title eventually adopted on the motion of Mr. Gruneisen, who was a member of the first executive committee. On the 7th of September, 1852, the society began its operations in Boswell Court, and was installed before the year had expired at No. 33, Norfolk Street, Strand — Mr. Gruneisen having been appointed Secretary, and Messrs. Harrison and Lewis, Solicitors to the Society. Public meetings were held in various parts of England with signal success, and the Society grew into importance rapidly; but as time went on, the valuable social and commercial advantages of the Society became much more apparent than its political purpose, although it succeeded completely in stopping the influx of faggot votes in counties, those who acquired the franchise through its instrumentality being *bonâ fide* investors in land through the assistance of the Friendly Societies' Acts. Such was the onward progress and prosperity of the Conservative Land Society, that in 1867 it was found necessary to enlarge the Norfolk Street premises by the acquisition of the adjoining premises, 11, Howard Street. Under the design and direction of Mr. James Wylson, the Architect and Surveyor to the Society, an imposing edifice has been erected, with frontages both in Norfolk Street and Howard Street. The Executive Committee of the Society include the names of Viscount Ranelagh, Viscount Ingestre, the Hon. and Rev. W. Talbot, the Hon. Robert Bourke, Colonel Knox, M.P., Colonel Meyrick, Colonel Jervis, M.P., J. C. Cobbold, Esq., M.P., J. Goodson, Esq., M.P., Sir Lawrance Palk, Bart., M.P., Messrs. Currie, T. H. Holmes, Newcomen and Winstanley, and the General Committee; a list of patrons included the names of nearly 100 noblemen and gentlemen, many of whom are members of the Legislature. Up to the annual meeting in December, 1867, the number of shares issued amounted to 27,783, representing a subscribed capital of £1,389,150. The withdrawals amounted to

£306,749, and the total sale of land to £537,051, and the reserve fund is £13,348. The Society has bought sixty-seven estates in twenty-seven counties. Under the premises in Norfolk Street and Howard Street are subterranean passages communicating between the Duke of Norfolk's mansion in Arundel Street and Strand Lane.

PALSGRAVE PLACE.

Near this place was the site of the "Palsgrave's Head" tavern, erected in compliment to the Palsgrave Frederick, afterwards King of Bohemia, who married the Princess Elizabeth, daughter of James I. in the old banqueting hall in Whitehall, on December 27th, 1612. Some of the taverns of the seventeenth century appear to have been established over the shops, for in 1679 a goldsmith named Crutch carried on business under this tavern. William Facthorne, an engraver of great merit, lived "at the sign of the Ship, next to the Drake, opposite to the Palsgrave's Head Tavern, without Temple Bar."

Near the "Palsgrave's Head" tavern was Heycock's ordinary, much frequented by Parliament men and gallants. Andrew Marvell usually dined at this ordinary, and here he administered a severe castigation to certain members of the House known to be in the pay of the Crown for ensuring the subserviency of their votes. Having ate heartily of boiled beef, with some roasted pigeons and asparagus, he drank his pint of port, and on the coming in of the reckoning, took a piece of money out of his pocket, held it between his finger and thumb, and addressing his venal associates, said, "Gentlemen, who would lett himself out for hire, while he can have such a dinner for half-a-crown?"

Here Prior and Montague make the country mouse and the City mouse bilk the hackney coachman.

> "But now at Piccadilly they arrive,
> And taking coach t'wards Temple Bar they drive,
> But at St. Clement's Church, cut out the back,
> And slipping through the Palsgrave, bilkt poor hack."

PICKETT STREET*

IN 1789, Alderman Pickett (see page 115) proposed a plan for making this street. The proposal was accepted; and between the years 1795 and 1811, Acts were obtained, and at an expense of over a quarter of a million of money, the houses were pulled down, the street widened, and the site let for long terms to contractors for the new buildings; but, unfortunately, as Leigh Hunt observes, "They turned out to be on too large a scale," the leaseholders being ruined fast, for they had soon expended £150,000 on the buildings, which, since 1802, had remained unlet. At last they hit upon a plan to relieve themselves. This was to obtain an Act of Parliament to enable them to dispose of their interest in this property, and also other property at Skinner Street, Snow Hill, and Fleet Market, by way of a lottery. To this end they printed and sent to the members of the Corporation an octavo volume of a very elaborate description—that is to say, although "The Representation of the Leaseholders and Contractors interested in the Houses and Buildings in Pickett Street, near Temple Bar, Skinner Street, Fleet Market, and Snow Hill, with the Scheme of the proposed Lottery," contained but an address in ten pages—the rest of the volume comprised no less than nine plans and elevations of the Pickett Street property, and sixteen of the other property at Snow Hill, &c. The address asked the assistance of the Corporation, by giving their sanction to dispose of the property by way of lottery. From the "Scheme," it appears the "First Division" consisted of five houses on the north side of the Strand, and numbered (from adjoining Temple Bar, westward) 1, 2, 3, 8, and 9, (all unoccupied), and seventeen houses of the Snow Hill property—the twenty-two houses being of the estimated value (agreeable to the surveyor's report, &c.) of £105,000, and "it being necessary in the event of the property being disposed of by way of chance, that each house should be insured in some one of the public insurance offices, the following amount is presumed equal to the risk, which will protect the public in case of accident, viz., £70,000." The "Second Division" consisted of five houses in Pickett Street, numbered 4, 5, 7, 10, and

11 (all unoccupied) and fifteen houses of the other property—total value, £100,000; insurance, £66,000." The "Third Division," comprised ten houses in Pickett Street, Nos. 6 and 12 to 20,* and seventeen houses of the other property — total value, £90,000; insurance, £60,000.

The capital prize in the "First Division" was the house No. 44, Skinner Street; in the "Second Division" No. 9, Skinner Street; in the "Third Division," No. 13, Pickett Street—"two houses situated east and west of the gateway leading to Clement's Inn. This property, consolidated, is intended to be offered to the public, as the capital prize in the third lottery."

The plan of the improvement was, further, to form a new street from the Strand to Lincoln's Inn Fields, of which Pickett Place was the commencement.

In due course the Court of Common Council debated on the matter, and, what was more, resolved to assist the applicants to obtain an Act, which was subsequently passed the 3rd of July, 1809. Parliamentary powers being once more obtained in respect to the property, the next step taken was by the Corporation conveying the fee simple and inheritance (subject to the leases and agreements for leases) to the then Lord Mayor (Sir James Shaw), Aldermen Anderson and Combe, Recorder Silvester, and Common-Serjeant Knollys and their heirs, as trustees for the purposes of the said Act and lottery.

In order that the buildings might be disposed of to the best advantage, three distinct lotteries were decided on, and the sum to be raised by each lottery was limited to £100,000; the number of tickets in each lottery not to exceed 20,000. No tickets to be sold for less than £5, and that all expenses, including insurance of buildings, were to be first paid out of moneys arising by the sale of tickets.

On the 14th of April, 1807, the first of the *Great City Lotteries*

---

* Nos. 6 and 12 were built, but not occupied; the others were in progress of building. No. 17 adjoined the Vestry and Court House on the west side.

was drawn at Guildhall, where, in order to prevent errors, the tickets, in the first place, were issued. An unexpected blow was felt by the promoters, however, in consequence of only £55,585 being the gross amount received instead of £100,000, from which sum all expenses had to be paid; and to make matters worse, the promoters having, through the non-sale of all the tickets, six prizes on hand, they sold these to Messrs. Walsh and Nisbett for £15,000, although valued by the surveyors at £25,200. To the same gentlemen they sold, or agreed to sell the other two lotteries, and, in order to carry out the Act of Parliament, paid into the Chamber of London the total amount specified.

But what was the surprise of every one to find these two gentlemen have a commission in bankruptcy issued against them about the 20th of September, 1808. Here, then, was another stop to the scheme, and, as troubles never come alone, the assignees refusing to take the third lottery, the time allowed for holding it expired, and as a wind-up, a fresh Act for extending the time, &c., had to be obtained.

The new year did not improve the state of affairs, for Mr. Walsh having obtained his certificate, made proposals to purchase the third lottery on his own account, took out of the Chamber and paid for 1,600 tickets, and then broke the contract, leaving the remaining 18,400 tickets in the promoters' hands. Of course, such a continuous flow of misfortune made the proprietors very down-hearted, especially when, after advertising the lottery and selling only 8,059 tickets (including the 1,600 paid for by Mr. Walsh) they found themselves after the lottery was drawn (March 23rd, 1811) with 11,941 tickets on hand, fifteen prizes worth £35,500, and a monetary loss of £24,205, which, with a loss of £29,415 on the first lottery, made a total of £53,620—without counting all the heavy expenses from first to last:—thus forming what may be termed, not inappropriately, one of the most gigantic explosive schemes of the nineteenth century. Briefly, the account stood thus:—

Three Lotteries at £100,000 each		£300,000
First Lottery Produced	£55,585	
Six prizes in hand	15,000	
Loss	29,415	
		£100,000
Second Lottery—Paid into Chamber		£100,000
Third ,, Produced	40,295	
Fifteen prizes in hand	35,500	
Loss	24,205	
		£100,000
		£300,000

The next step taken was to petition the Court of Common Council (15th July, 1811,) for some remuneration for the loss sustained, the petitioners arguing that the Corporation had all their demands settled, and therefore were no losers, but gainers. On a division (with a majority of 40 to 29) the petition was referred to the Temple Bar and Snow Hill Improvement Committee to examine and report, who (December 10th, 1811) reported that they had heard the case, and that counsel's opinion expressly stated the Corporation were legally not liable in the matter, and therefore the prayer of the petitioners could not be complied with.

But even this was not all, for another petitioner, one Lucy Blackburne, of Lynn-Regis, Norfolk, stated she had purchased a quarter-share of ticket No. 4,889 in the third lottery; that this number turned up the capital prize No. 13, Pickett Street (the two houses with the pillars and archway to St. Clement's Inn in the centre), valued by the London Lottery Office-keeper (Mr. W. Rolfe, of Skinner Street) at £20,000, and that on application she was told each of the other quarter-shares had been sold at Portsea, Chatham, and Edinburgh; that according to the conditions on the back of the ticket, the property would be put up to auction, but, as the Act of Parliament did not specify any particular date for this sale, he should take his own time in the matter; that ultimately, on August 16th, 1811, the auction took place, and that the premises were knocked down for £4,800; that on application to Mr. Rolfe he declared the premises were not sold, and that he was not liable for the £1,200 till realised.

The Common Council having referred this petition to the Committee, they reported (December 10th, 1811) that they had made due inquiries and found the property had been duly conveyed after the drawing to Mr. William Edmund Rolfe, the registered holder of the ticket, that the Act of Parliament or the Corporation never having sanctioned the division of the property into shares, they were powerless to act in the matter.

Thus it will be seen the Corporation were believed for a long time to possess the power to alleviate the distress and inconvenience attending the "Great City Lottery," whereas, in reality, they were only the trustees to see that the tickets were sold and money for them paid into the Chamber, and to see that the lotteries took place in due course. No less than six Acts of Parliament were obtained in this matter.

The first lottery in England, as far as is ascertained, began to be drawn on the 11th of January, 1569, at the west door of St. Paul's Cathedral, and continued day and night till the 6th of May. It consisted of 40,000 lots, at ten shillings each share. The last State lottery in England took place October 18th, 1826, at Coopers' Hall, Basinghall Street. The abolition of State lotteries deprived the Government of £300,000 per annum. Lotteries were not confined to money prizes, but embraced all kinds of articles; sometimes, as in the case of the Pickett Street scheme, they were turned to purposes of public utility. Thus, in 1736, an Act was passed for building a bridge at Westminster by lottery, consisting of 125,000 tickets at £5 each. London Bridge at that time was the only means of communication by permanent roadway between the City and Southwark. In 1774, the brothers Adam, builders, of the Adelphi Terrace, and surrounding streets in the Strand, disposed of these and other premises in a lottery, containing 110 prizes,—the first drawn ticket entitling the holder to a prize of the value of £5,000; the last drawn to one of £25,000. These lotteries created scenes of the greatest excitement during the time of drawing.

Pickett Street was formerly, and, as Brayley says in his "Londoniana," properly called Butchers' Row,* and originated in a flesh market. (See page 115).

The Vestry Hall of St. Clements was built at the time of the formation of this street. In it is a very valuable picture which was formerly the Altarpiece of the Church (see page 53). There is a peculiarity in connection with this Vestry Hall. The parish pays to the Duchy of Cornwall† as landlord, a rent of fourpence per annum. The rental is assessed at this mere nominal sum, in consideration of the right being conceded to the Council of holding meetings there when they choose. At certain intervals they do formally meet in the hall, in order that the right shall not lapse.

Luttrell says :—

"1708-9, March 24. The Duke of Newcastle and the Earl of Thanet having obtained a commission of the Lord Chancellor to inspect the Duchess Dowager of Albemarle and Montague for lunacy, met Sir John Bennet with the rest of the Commissioners at St. Clement's Vestry. They adjourned till Friday, April 5, and after examining several witnesses found her a lunatick."

Lord Ross, a rejected suitor, piqued at Lord Montague's success, addressed to him some trenchant verses on his marriage (for he married Elizabeth, the "Mad Duchess" of Albemarle, Sept. 13, 1692, and though sharing her wealth, he kept her close confined at Montague House, Clerkenwell, till compelled to produce her to the Court as explained above —for doubts were expressed as to her being alive). These verses ran :—

> "Insulting rival, never boast
> Thy conquest lately won;
> No wonder that her heart was lost—
> Her senses first were gone;
> For one that's under Bedlam's laws,
> What glory can be had?
> For love of thee was not the cause—
> It proves that she was mad."

---

* Peter Motteux, translator of "Don Quixote," died in 1718, at a bad house in Butchers' Row.
† The Duchy of Cornwall accounts for 1867, just published, show the receipt of £50,178 for rents, £6,284 for royalties and reservations from mines and quarries, £1,785 by dividends on stock, and £16,216 the payment from the public purse in lieu of the tin coinage duties. The payment made to the Prince of Wales in that year was £54,927, an increase of £1,524 over the payment in the previous year.

The Duchess died of old age (having survived her second husband thirty years) at Newcastle (formerly Montague) House, Aug. 28, 1734, aged ninety-six. She lay in state in the Jerusalem Chamber on the 11th of September, and at midnight was privately interred near the remains of her father-in-law (General Monk) in Henry VII.'s Chapel, Westminster.*

The yearly "Bill" made by the company of parish clerks of deaths between December 18th, 1623, and December 16th, 1624, gives the total of deaths in London and "out" parishes as 54,265, of which number 35,417 died of the plague. In St. Clement's the numbers were—buried, 1,284; 755 of whom died of the plague.

The following extract is from "An Account of the State of the Infant Parish Poor of London and Westminster," by Jonas Hanway, Esq., 1767:—

"Whereas the churchwardens and overseers of the poor of the parish of St. Clement Danes, in this county, have been summoned to attend this court, this present sessions, to shew how many poor children of the said parish they have put out to be apprentices, at the charge of the said parish, for the space of seven years last past, and their names; as also the names of the persons to whom they put them apprentices, and the places of their abode, and what money they gave with them, and what is now become of the said apprentices: and the said officers have attended this court, but have not given any satisfactory account to this court, in the premises, but desired time. It is, therefore, thought fit, and ordered by this court, that it be, and it is hereby recommended to Sir Thomas Rowe, Knight; John Phelips, Esq.; Thomas Done, Esq.; Simon Parry, Esq.; Richard Price, Esq.; and Peter Lugg, Esq.; his Majesty's justices of the peace of this county, or to any two or three of them, to cause the said churchwardens and overseers of the poor of the said parish, and such other persons as they think convenient, to come before them, and examine the said officers and persons concerning the disposal of the said parish children for seven years last past, and what is now become of them. And the said justices are hereby further desired to make a report to this court in writing, under their hands, how they shall find the true state of the premises, and how they shall find the muster-roll of the parish children, in the said parish, at the general sessions of the peace, to be held for this county next after Hillary term, now next ensuing.

---

* Wood's (Pinks) "History of Clerkenwell," page 100.

THE REPORT.

"Whereas, by an order made at last Christmas quarter sessions, it was desired, and referred to Sir Thomas Rowe, Knt.; John Phelips, Esq.; and several other his Majesty's justices for the said county, to examine what children the parish of St. Clement Danes have had under their care for seven years past, and how many of them have been put forth apprentices; and what charge the parish have been at with the said children, and how many of them now are in being,

"We the said justices do report as followeth:—

"'That we inspected the said books, and do find that in the year 1679 there were then at the charge of the parish 89 children, of which 16 were foundlings, all Clements. And we find that there hath been added to the charge of the parish 110 in the following six years, in all 199, of which 51 are Clements, children laid in the streets. We find that of these, 55 hath been put forth to apprentice, and that there are now in being 32 of the said 55 only. And we find that there now remains of children at the charge of the parish, of which 13 are Clements, 58; and the apprentices living, of which 3 are Clements, 32; in all, 90. We find that the officers have expended for nursing these children in seven years last past, £1,943 9s.; and for binding forth apprentices, £109 8s.; in all, £2,052 17s. And we further find that they have given away, on extraordinary charges at their pleasure, some of which are for the children, £2,708 16s. 5d.; all which we submit to this honourable court: Thomas Rowe, John Phelips, Peter Lucy, Simon Parry.'

"1. Note, that seven years ago the parish had 89 children, and there have been since added, 110, in all, 199; of these, (apprentices counted in) there is left but 90; so that there are lost and dead in the said seven years, or never were, though paid for in their books, 109.

"2. Note, that of 55 bound out apprentices in these seven years last past, which cost the parish £109 8s., there are only left 32; and how many of the 32 will stay to serve out their time is to be inquired further of.

"3. Note, that 51 of the 110 were foundlings, all Clements, laid in the parish in six years last, and so take the name of Clement from the parish, 51; were then there, 16; in all, 67.

"Now, only 3 are bound out apprentices, and 13 are left of the number 16; and the 51, all Clements, are all lost and dead. Now, the parish books have been searched how many were christened of these foundlings or Clements, or buried, and very few appear upon the register. It is questionable if they ever were all there, though paid for. It is much that 51 should die out of 67 in seven years. The particular money paid for nursing of these children is £1,943 9s. in seven years."

THE ANGEL INN

Presents a specimen of the Galleried Inn-yard, of which there are few remaining in the Metropolis, existed in this Parish not many years since.

PICKETT STREET.

The old "Angel Inn," which had its galleries and gable ends, and large court-yard, was of great antiquity. Bishop Harper, the venerated Martyr of the Reformation, upon his second committal to the Fleet Prison in 1553, refusing to recant his opinions, was condemned to be burnt in January, 1555. After his condemnation, he was aroused at four o'clock in the morning, and being committed to the care of six of Queen Mary's guard, they took him to the "Angel Inn," St. Clement's, then standing in the fields; thence he was taken to Gloucester, and there burnt on the 9th of February.

In the *Public Advertiser*, March 28th, 1769, appears the following advertisement :—

"To be sold, a Black Girl, the property of J. B——, eleven years of age, who is extremely handy, works at her needle tolerably, and speaks English perfectly well; is of an excellent temper and willing disposition. Inquire of Mr. Owen, at the Angel Inn, behind St. Clement's Church in the Strand."

The "Angel" was an old established travellers' inn. In the "Plumpton Correspondence" is a letter from York, dated February 6th, 1503, addressed "to Sir Richard Plompton, Knight, being lodged at the Angell, behind St. Clement Kirk, without the Temple Barr, at London." Seven or eight mail coaches* were nightly despatched from this inn. The freehold, the property of a family named Watson, was sold for £6,800, and closed as a public-house in the year 1853, by the late Mr. Walter Binstead, who afterwards became proprietor of the "Old George" tavern, 58, Stanhope Street, which house he conducted up to the time of his decease, January 10th, 1868. The "Angel" property was purchased by a builder, and the present St. Clement Chambers erected, the building of which commenced August, 1853.

---

* Mail coaches, at one time, passed in and out of London, to and from different parts of the kingdom every day, and both received and delivered letters at every post town or receiving house on the road excepting to London on Sunday morning, and from London on Sunday evening. On a general measurement of the whole kingdom in 1801, it consisted of about 58,335 square statute miles, and the number of acres at 37,343,400.—*Crosby's Gazetteer.*—The first mail coach for conveyance of letters, 1784; first sent by rail, 1838. A Bill was brought into Parliament to prevent the effeminacy of men riding in coaches, 1601; repealed, 1625. There was then only 20 coaches in London. In 1666, the number had so increased, that Charles II. forbade coaches blocking up the narrow streets.

Pennant says :—" I may venture to mention the great Bat Pidgeon who, in his advanced age, cut my boyish locks in the year 1740. He lived in the corner house of St. Clement's Church-yard next to the Strand, and was most eminent in his day amongst the very few who in that day practised the art."

On Monday, January 7th, 1867, a novel foot race came off for a stake of £10. The match was one in which a young medical student, named Hemmings, backed himself to run four times round the railings of St. Clement Danes Church, in the Strand, while the clock struck the hour of twelve and chimed the usual "Lass of Gowrie." The start was made at the first stroke of the clock bell, and a smart race was kept up. Each lap round is 170 yards, and the pedestrian having accomplished four circuits when the clock-hammer had twenty repeats to make, he walked in a winner. The clock occupies three minutes in striking the hour and chiming the subsequent tune.

In the sale catalogue of the carved works in wood by the well-known Mr. W. G. Rogers, sold by Mr. Phillips, at his rooms, New Bond Street, 19th March, 1868, were four lots worth a note :—

> Lot 29, Nineteen pieces of carving from the pulpit of G. Gibbons' parish church, St. Clement Danes.
> 30, Five panels, and a large quantity of Gibbon carving.
> 31, Six ditto; 22. six ditto.

1697, London, July 10.—"One Gowen Hardy, of St. Clement's Danes, in Middlesex, piece-broker, was at the sessions at the Old Bailey, indicted for felony upon a late Act of Parliament, for paying and putting off counterfeit milled money at a lower rate than the same was coined or counterfeited for, and was this day thereon tryed and convicted; who, craving the benefit of his clergy, it was allowed him, and he was burnt in the hand."

In 1708 the houses in the Parish and Duchy Wards were 1,729 in number, divided thus :—Royal Ward, 160; Middle Ward, 238; Savoy Ward, 162; Church Ward, 138; Hallowell Ward, 304; Drury Lane Ward, 253; Sheer Lane Ward, 254; Temple Bar Ward, 220.

Exeter House was originally the parsonage-house of St. Clement Danes, and falling to the Crown, remained as its property till Queen Elizabeth granted it to Sir William Cecil, Lord Treasurer, who enlarged and rebuilt it; after which it was called Cecil House and Burleigh House. Lord Burleigh (see page 92) died here, in 1598; being inhabited by his son Thomas, it was called Exeter House. After the Fire of London, it was occupied by the Doctors of Civil Law, till 1672—the lower part forming Exeter Change.*

Crown Court, leading from Pickett Place, took its name from the Crown Tavern situate near here, and Crown Place stood on the spot where the bishop's house and garden formerly stood.

CLEMENT'S INN.
(See pages 127, 144, 145.)

A large and rather handsome archway on the north side of this street, commencing Clement's Lane, leads to Clement's Inn. This Inn, like all other Inns of Court, is of great antiquity. Dugdale states it to have been an Inn of Chancery in the reign of Edward II. Upwards of six hundred years ago, St. Clement's Well, on the east of the Inn, is mentioned by Fitz-stephen.

The Clare family, who have left their name to Clare Market, appear to have occupied Clement's Inn during part of the reign of the Tudors. From their hands it reverted to the Law.

As to the liability of Clement's, Lyon's, and New Inn to the payment of poor rates, we are told that about a century since a cause was tried, and a decision arrived at, from which date these inns have been assessed, and the rates paid.†

---

* Thomas Clark, "the King of Exeter Change," took a cutler's stall here in 1765 with £100 lent him by a stranger. By trade and thrift he grew so rich that he once returned his income at £6,000 a year, and before his death in 1816 he rented the whole ground-floor of the Change. He left nearly half a million of money, and one of his daughters married Mr. Hamlet, the celebrated jeweller. Some of the old materials of Exeter House, including a pair of large Corinthian columns at the east end, were used in building the Change, which was the speculation of a Dr Barbon, in the reign of William and Mary.

† "Observations on the liability of places usually termed extra-parochial to the payment of poor rates, appended to the trial of an action for trespass between Clifford's Inn and Overseers of St. Dunstan's West." 1822, page 65.

A curious custom in this inn is thus described by a correspondent of "Notes and Queries":—

"I am an attorney; one of my predecessors in business was steward of Clement's Inn. He died, and his partner removed from the Inn to the City. I was articled to the partner, and I recollect that up to the time of his death, which occurred in 1837, he used to receive an annual visit from the minor officials of the Inn, beadle, porter, &c., who presented four oranges, and received in return half-a-guinea. I used generally to suck the oranges, but it never entered my head to enquire what was the origin of the custom."

Four houses in this Inn, with builder's yard* and porter's lodge, have just been purchased by the Commissioners for the New Law Courts at a cost of £11,942. 10s. 10d. for the freeholds, and about £1,450 compensation to the tenants, and £15,000 for Clement's Inn Chambers, Foregate. We will here also mention the cost of some of the property on the site; the largest amount paid to any one person is perhaps that to Miss Browning, who received for seventeen freehold houses in Boswell Court, comprising the whole of the court:—For the freehold, £36,500; leaseholders received £5,640; weekly tenants about £20; making a total of £42,160. Brazenose College received £2,250 for their interest in the houses in Yates' Court; one house in the Strand, together with two old houses in the rear (Ship Yard), cost £24,591; another (Mr. Holloway's) which fell down after it had been knocked down by Mr. Horne, the auctioneer, cost £15,500; this also had two small houses in the rear (Ship and Anchor Court); 18, Carey Street cost £10,300; 22-3, Carey Street, with stabling and two cottages in Plough Yard, about £10,000; for the freehold of seven houses in Plough Court, £6,200; three houses in Chair Court, £1,650; two houses in Crown Court, and two houses in Crown Place, £11,682; Dispensary in Carey Street, £3,450; the "Black Horse," in Boswell Court, £3,400; and the parish received £100 for the loss of the engine house in Clement's Inn Foregate.†

---

* Occupied by Mr. Williams, the builder, of Stanhope Street.

† In consequence of the titles to some of the property not being good, considerable difficulty and delay arises; also, from signatures being wanted from persons abroad at the present time.

PORTUGAL STREET

Was so named when Portugal Row, or the south side of Lincoln's Inn Fields, ceased to be known by that name. It runs parallel with the south side of Lincoln's Inn Fields. In Styrpe's time it was without a name; he proposed to call it Playhouse Street. Portugal Row was built 1657 by Sir William Cowper, Robert Henley, and James Cowper, and known as Portugal Row before the marriage of Charles II. to Catherine of Portugal.

In 1668 it was inhabited by the following persons:—

"The Lady Arden, William Pierpoint, Esq.; Sir Charles Waldegrave, the Lady Fitzharding, the Lady Diana Curzon, Serjeant Maynard, the Lord Cardigan, Mrs. Anne Heron, Lady Mordant, Richard Adams, Esq.; the Lady Wentworth, Lady Carr, Mr. Attorney Montague, the Lady Coventry, Judge Weld, the Lady Davenant."—*Rate Books of St. Clement Danes.*

Viewed in the present day, and judged by its gloomy dingy aspect and the quietude and oppressiveness which reigns, it would be difficult for a person to conjure up and realise the fact that this street was at one time a splendid rendezvous for the gay and gallant fashionables of the Court, or that it was the resort of brilliant wits, poets, painters, and actors, crowded with carriages and pedestrians, and alive with all the bustle and gaiety which arises from theatrical attractions; for be it remembered that a portion of the ground on which that noble institution the College of Surgeons (which was originally a Company incorporated in the thirty-second year of the reign of Henry VIII. by the title of "The Masters or Governors, or Commonalty of Barbers and Surgeons of the City of London," whence the Company obtained the name of Barber-Surgeons) (see page 46) now stands was formerly the site of the Duke's Theatre, (see page 76) where the best actors of the day entertained the public, but which, after 1733, was used for various purposes; the last tenant being Mr. Alderman Copeland, M.P., of whom the College purchased it in 1848. This gentleman and his partner, Mr. Spode, there carried on their well-known Staffordshire ware business.

The "Bell and Dragon," a noted theatrical house, stood opposite the Duke's Theatre; and next to Mc Nivens' coffee-house was the Parish watch-house, at which, in 1826, thirty-two men were employed as night watchmen to perambulate the parish, at an expense of £1,500; they were relieved every two hours, and resided in the parish. Their pay averaged in the winter months, 16s. 5d. per week, and in the summer, 13s. 3d. The time of service, according to the light, was from 7 to 7, 9 to 6, and 10 to 5 (see page 100.)

Will's Coffee-house, which stood at the north-east corner of this street, was in high repute, and frequented by celebrated members of the legal profession, and other distinguished characters. The house is now occupied by Messrs. Wodderspoon and Co., stationers.

We read that "opposite the theatre, in this street, is a very handsome house for the poor of St. Clements," which must have been on the ground where King's College Hospital now stands (see page 31), and which was formerly the burial ground for the parish (see page 80.) The following note must have reference to this ground, not the churchyard :—

"Thursday, July 10th, were deposited in St. Clement's Churchyard, in the same grave with her husband, the remains of Mrs. Miller, aged 83, relict of the celebrated Joe Miller." (See page 33.)—*London Chronicle*, July 12th, 1766.

Serjeant Maynard, the father of the infamous Countess of Shrewsbury, who will long be remembered for her memorable reply to William, third Lord Cardigan, lived in this street till his death in 16—. Lady Davenant, the widow of Sir William Davenant, to whose estate letters of administration were granted on May 6th, 1668, to "John Alway, principal creditor, the Lady Mary Davenant. having first renounced," was a resident. Wilmot, Earl of Rochester (died 1680), lived in the house next the Duke's Theatre. "If you write to me, you must direct to Lincoln's Inn Fields, the house next to the Duke Playhouse in Portugal Row, there lives your humble servant, Rochester." Davenant says in one of his epilogues—

"The prospect of the sea cannot be shown,
Therefore, be pleased to think that you are all
Behind the Row which men call Portugal."—*Wharton's Works*.

PORTUGAL STREET.

Although we have given an account of the Drama and Theatres in another part of our work (see page 71) Portugal Street being so famed for its dramatic theatre, we consider the following, for which we are indebted to Mr. Wood, the editor of the "History of Clerkenwell," will be interesting to our readers :—

"The drama flourished in early times in England; thus we find that from 1570 to 1629, when the playhouse in Whitefriars was finished, no less than seventeen playhouses had been built in London,* viz., St. Paul's Singing School; the Globe on the bank side, Southwark, which was destroyed by fire; the Swan; and the Hope there; the Fortune, a large round brick building between Whitecross Street and Golding (now Golden) Lane, which was the first playhouse erected in London,† and was burnt down in 1621; the Red Bull, in St. John's Street; the Cross Keys, in Gracechurch Street; Tuns; the Theatre; the Curtain, in Shoreditch, which had originally as its sign a striped curtain hung out; the Nursery, in Barbican; one in Blackfriars; one in Whitefriars; one in Salisbury Court; the Cockpit and the Phœnix, in Drury Lane. Prynne, in his 'Histrio Mastix,' published in 1633, mentions a playhouse in Bishopsgate Street, and another on Ludgate Hill called the Bell-Savage; the one in Bishopsgate Street was probably the Curtain, in Shoreditch. It has been said that the playhouse in Whitefriars was no other than that in Salisbury Court; that the Cockpit and the Phœnix were the same playhouse; and that which was called the Theatre was the playhouse in Blackfriars. Taylor, the water-poet, mentions another called the Rose.‡ Besides the theatre-actors, the children of the revels and of the chapel acted plays; there were likewise royal comedians; many noblemen kept companies of players; plays were also acted by the lawyers of the Inns of Court, by the students of the halls and colleges of the Universities, and by the London 'prentices; so that the old saying was almost literally true, '*Totus Mundus agit histrionem.*'

"Most of the old playhouses were only large rooms in noted ale-houses, or slight erections in places contiguous, or in gardens, the pits of which were unfloored, where the spectators either stood, or were badly accommodated with benches to sit on, and the music was mean and despicable.§ With regard to the old prices of admission, the playhouse called the Hope had five different priced seats, from sixpence to half-a-crown; some houses had penny benches; there was a twopenny gallery, and seats at threepence and a groat. The general price of what is now called the pit—probably from one of the playhouses having been a cockpit—seems to have been a shilling."

---

* Reed's "Preface to Dodsley's Collection of Old Plays."
† Maitland.
‡ True Use of the Waterman's Suit concerning Playhouses, 1613.
§ Sir John Hawkins's "History of Music.

1726. Visit of George I. to Lincoln's Inn Fields Theatre :—

"March 18.—Last night His Majesty went to the Theatre Royal in Lincoln's Inn Fields, to see the play of the *Country Wife* and the entertainment of *Apollo and Daphne*, in which was performed a particular flying on that occasion, of a cupid descending, and presenting His Majesty with a book of the entertainment, and then ascended—at which new piece of machinery the audience seemed much pleased."

Pepys tells us that on the 26th of March, 1668, coming from the theatre in Portugal Street, he and his party went to the "Blue Balls" tavern, where they met some of their friends, including Mrs. Knipp :—

"And after much difficulty in getting of musick, we to dancing and then to a supper of French dishes, which yet did not please me, and then to dance and sing, and mighty merry we were till about eleven or twelve at night, with mighty great content in all my company, and I did, *as I love to do*, enjoy myself. My wife extraordinary fine to-day, in her flower tabby suit, bought a year and more ago, before my mother's death put her into mourning, and so not worn till this day, and everybody in love with it, and, indeed, she is very fine and handsome in it. I having paid the reckoning, which came to almost £4, we parted."

We here introduce a few advertisements of the performances about this period; but, to one actress therein mentioned we must call particular attention, viz., Miss Lavinia Fenton, afterwards Duchess of Bolton, and whose portrait by Hogarth, the property of Brinsley Morley, Esq., was No. 240 in the second (1867) Exhibition of National Portraits at South Kensington. Rich tempted her from the Haymarket to Lincoln's Inn Fields in 1728, and gave her a salary of 15s. a week; but, on the success of the "Beggars' Opera," and in order to secure her then truly valuable services, this salary was raised to 30s. Such, however, was the rage of the town respecting her, that, night after night, a considerable party of her confidential friends had to guard her from the playhouse home. We give the two following advertisements relating to this celebrated lady as historical, and interesting to the reader generally :—

"Whereas my name has been the subject of several songs and pamphlets lately published: This is to inform the town that I never (before now) was privy or consenting to any one thing made publick ; but, being willing to entertain the town with something diverting, I have this day,* with the joint interest of another person who performs in the *Beggars' Opera*, published a pamphlet by the title of *Polly Peachum's* Opera, which contains a medley of new songs never before published, adapted to the several tunes I sing in the *Beggars' Opera*, with the song inserted in the 'Country Journal or Craftesman' of Saturday, April 13, 1728. To which is annexed a new ballad, inscribed to my father, my beloved Capt. Macheath, and the illustrious gang of highway robbers, to the tune of Green Sleeves *alias* Upon Tyburn Tree, which is from your humble servant, POLLY PEACHUM.

"N.B.—This treatise is dedicated to the facetious Sir R—— F——, and may be had at A. Dodd's, without Temple Bar ; E. Nutt's and A. Smith's at the Royal Exchange, and at the rest of the pamphlet shops in London and Westminster. Price sixpence."

"For the benefit of Polly. The forty-eighth night. By the company of Comedians. At the Theatre Royal in Lincoln's Inn Fields, on Saturday next, being the 4th day of May, will be presented *The Beggars' Opera*. Boxes 5s., Pit 3s., First Gallery 2s., Upper Gallery 1s.

"N.B.—For the accommodation of the ladies, Boxes are prepared on the stage, and servants will be admitted to keep places."†

"1729. By the Company of Comedians. At the Theatre Royal, in Lincoln's Inn Fields. To-morrow, being Friday, the 31st of January, will be presented the tragedy of *Macbeth*, written by Shakespeare. The part of Macbeth, by *Mr. Quin;* Macduff, Mr. Ryan; Banquo, Mr. Milward; Lenox, Mr. Walker; Malcolm, Mr. Chapman; Lady Macbeth, Mrs. Berriman; Lady Mackduff, Mrs. Buchanan; Hecate, Mr. Hall. The three Witches, *Mr. Bullock, Mr. Hippisley*, Mr. H. Bullock. With the musick both vocal and instrumental incidental to the play. The vocal parts to be performed by Mr. Legar, Mrs. Chambers, Mrs. Seedo, Mrs. Warren, and others. The dances performed by Mons. Salle, Mons. Dupre, Mr. Pelling, Mr. Newhouse, Mr. Lanyon, and Mons. Dupre jun., with the flyings, sinkings, and usual decorations."

"1729. Never acted before! By the Company of Comedians. At the Theatre Royal in Lincoln's Inn Fields, this present Monday, being the 10th of February, will be presented a new tragedy, call'd 'Themistocles: The Lover of his Country.' The principal parts to be performed by Mr. Walker, *Mr. Quin, Mr. Ryan*, Mr. Milward, Mr. Ogden, Mrs. Berryman, and Mrs. Buchanan. Boxes 5s., Pit 3s., Gallery 2s. All persons that should want places are desired to send to the stage door of the theatre, where attendance will be kept to prevent mistakes."

* 29th April, 1728.   † 4th May, 1728.

THE OLD INSOLVENT COURT IN PORTUGAL STREET.

A closed up temple of justice awakes many memories and summonses to view many bygone scenes. Where is the figure of the stately and solemn judge; into what deep silence have drifted the accents of the warm, impassioned advocate; where are the throbbing hearts and the moistened eyes of the still and listening audience? All gone for ever, many to a higher and more enduring tribunal, many to exile, aye, and cold indifference. We are now looking at an unpretending solid looking building, the old Insolvent Court in Portugal Street. Though it is now closed up and presents a dreary aspect, through its dingy portals passed the once brilliant leader of fashion; the man of genius and letters; the unfortunate speculator, the gambler, the faded wrecks of impoverished gentility, the swindler and the dreaming philosopher. In its latter days it used to be a rendezvous for amusement, when two Irish judges presided and threw over the sad records of disaster the gleam of their humour and boundless vivacity. The first we will mention is the late Mr. Commissioner Phillips, who was promoted from the Old Bailey to the judicial seat through the patronage of the Venerable Lord Brougham. He had achieved celebrity at the criminal bar by his remarkable power of cross-examination combined with considerable oratorical power, which partook of many of the beauties and all the blemishes peculiar to the oratory of his native land. His exaggerated figures of rhetoric wounded the disciplined mind of the scholar, while some of his appeals to the heart awoke the sympathy of the most callous. He possessed no wit like Curran, nor his withering sarcasm, nor did he have anything like the sustained power and lucid arrangement of Plunket, but his humour was racy of the Irish soil, to which his rich and harmonious brogue lent a dramatic power and an unrivalled effect. He achieved some celebrity as a man of letters, and his biography of John Philpot Curran is not a discreditable performance. He took an active part in the politics of his country when called to the Irish bar, but like many others of lesser note, had to recede before the majestic form of

O'Connell. The great agitator had not spoken to him for a series of years, but immediately before his dissolution, and to use Mr. Carlyle's idea "the great fact of death being upon him," he addressed Mr. Phillips in the Reform Club in the following quaint style, "Phillips, let us be friends—I am tired of not shaking hands with you." The most remarkable cases he was ever engaged in were the cases of Guthrie in Ireland, and Courvoisier, who was tried for the murder of Lord William Russell in June, 1840. The last case created extraordinary interest at the time, not merely from the exalted rank of the victim (uncle to present Earl Russell), but in consequence of a solemn asseveration made by Mr. Phillips in the progress of his speech as to the innocence of the accused. It is said that before the trial his client confessed to him his guilt, but Phillips, in his warmth of advocacy, invoked the Deity as to his belief in the innocence of the prisoner at the bar, and grave discussion arose for some years after in all the great organs of public opinion how far the Commissioner was to be condemned or vindicated in the conduct he pursued on this remarkable occasion. Barristers, judges, clergymen, and the public generally all entered into the arena of discussion, but the Commissioner's voice is now silent and his laughing auditory have withdrawn for ever.

Mr. Commissioner Murphy was a classical scholar of the highest order. He represented his native county of Cork in Parliament, but in the House of Commons he did not fulfil the anticipations held out in his earlier years. He was a great favourite, from his witticisms and his happy classical illustrations. He convulsed the House at one time by quotations from Mr. James Grant's descriptions of the House of Commons, and few will forget the portrait of the late Sir Robert Peel drawn with flunkey-like accuracy. Mr. Murphy read the following quotation in very solemn tones: "He," (Sir Robert Peel) said the author, "sacrifices much time to the graces, and every morning pays his constant devotion to the looking-glass." At this the House went into one of its most boyish fits of laughter, and none enjoyed the joke better than the great minister himself. Poor Murphy died comparatively young, and by industry and prudence he might have left a less perishable reputation behind him.

Mr. Commissioner Law (relative of the great Lord Ellenborough) was a consummate lawyer. The unfortunate insolvents trembled before him, and envied those whose lot it was to have their cases adjudicated upon by the other judges of the Court.

The late Mr. Cook enjoyed in those Courts an immense practice, and was finally promoted to a county Bankruptcy Court.

But the rain and the sunshine now fall upon the closed and worm-eaten doors; the law is dead which was long administered within its walls, and the grave has closed over its judges. It becomes a matter of deep consideration whether the law which has supplanted the old Insolvency Court of Portugal Street has not wounded the commercial integrity of this country, and made insolvency, not a stern and inexorable necessity as it used to be, but rather an open road for boundless extravagance and a fashionable epidemic.

COURTS OF JUSTICE CONCENTRATION COURT.

This was formerly the Insolvent Debtors Court, which was abolished by the Bankruptcy Act of 1861; it has jurisdiction in cases of compensation in regard to premises required for the contemplated New Courts of Justice. Next to this Court are the offices of Messrs. Field, Roscoe, Field and Francis, the eminent solicitors.

THE MIDDLESEX REGISTRY OFFICE OF DEEDS.

In this office all leases, assignments, conveyances, and mortgages of land or houses in the County of Middlesex should be registered, except leases for terms not exceeding twenty-one years. The office was formerly situated in Bell Yard, and the Act creating the Registry was passed in the year 1709. (7 Ann, cap. 20.)

These premises were previously occupied by Diprose Brothers, bookbinders, now of 5 and 6, Brydges Street, Strand, and formerly by Clarke, the well-known law bookseller.

At the western end of Portugal Street is Portsmouth Street, in which is the celebrated "Old Black Jack," the scene of many strange political and other meetings (see page 114), and among which the extraordinary "Pop-gun Plot" must not be overlooked. From various sources (including the printed account by the "Martyr" himself) we gather the following summary of this more than "Nine days' wonder":—

"This street was, at the close of the last century, the scene of the celebrated sensational, yet pretended, 'Pop Gun Plot,' a plot to kill the king with *a poisoned arrow!* It appears the unsettled state of the country caused a plan to be published in 1793, to bring about 'The British Convention of Delegates of the People, associated to obtain Universal Suffrage and Annual Parliaments,' in which plan the 'London Corresponding Society' and the 'Constitutional Society' were deeply interested. The 'Convention,' however, was never held—for, Thomas Hardy, the Secretary of the first named society, and eleven others were prosecuted for high treason. Of these, Hardy, John Horne Tooke, and John Thelwall were tried and acquitted, while Parliament, on the 23rd of May, 1794, passed an 'Act to empower His Majesty to secure and detain such persons as His Majesty shall suspect are conspiring against his person and Government.' It is not our purpose to enter fully into the well-known sensational character of those times suffice; it to say that one John Smith, of the 'Pop Gun,' Portsmouth Street, and George Higgins, were duly arrested on the charge of 'high treason,' examined repeatedly by the Privy Council, and ultimately discharged; but another member of the society, the unfortunate Paul Thomas Lemaitre, aged eighteen, appears to have suffered the worst. Arrested, while working as a gold watch case maker at his cousin's house, 13, Denmark Street, Soho, he was charged with 'treasonable practices,' as being a 'delegate' of the 'London Corresponding Society,' as being in connexion with Smith, to assassinate the king by means of a poisoned arrow! Arrested, Saturday evening, the 27th of September, 1794, he was for the next three days closely examined by the Privy Council, was, on the evidence of a *forged letter*, and one Thomas Upton (who had sworn to be revenged on him for seconding him, Upton, being turned out of the society), imprisoned, being the *first* person sent to the new prison at Cold Bath Fields; was kept confined within this 'British Bastille' as he called it, for thirty-two weeks (during which time his mother had died of grief), and finally liberated on the 9th of May, 1795, on giving bail for £50. Some months after, he was unnecessarily summoned before the Privy Council, and, after more delay, was, with John Smith, of the 'Pop Gun' (whom he knew 'as a member of the society, and one of whom I have frequently bought pamphlets, &c.") and George Higgins, tried at the Old Bailey, the 11th of May, 1796, and discharged. This, then, was the result of the 'plot,' but poor Lemaitre's case was for years before Parliament—various members endeavoured to get him redress, among whom Henry Warburton got a petition drawn up for him so lately as August, 1846, and Lord Dacre acknowledged in a letter to Warburton as having " for nearly half-a-century, with others of the early reformers, defended and assisted Mr. Lemaitre, and advocated his cause.' His history was indeed the history of a lifetime, yet, what a reflection to the government of the day."

Benjamin Franklin lived in Duke Street, near here, and worked as a journeyman printer in the neighbourhood. It is also supposed that he lived at 19, Carey Street.

SERLE'S STREET.

So called from a Mr. Henry Serle, whose arms are over the Carey Street gateway. He built Serle's Court (see page 131) now called New Square,* but formerly known as Little Lincoln's Inn Fields,

---

* This square, which is not a part of the Lincoln's Inn "property," was formerly open ground; and to go back for nearly three centuries, we must look into the last will and testament of "Bartholomewe Newsome, of the Parish of St. Marye, in the Strande, in the Countye of Middlesexe, clock maker," which, bearing date the 7th of January, 1586 (29th of Elizabeth), orders, among other things, that—

"All my right, title, interest and tearme of yeres, which I have or oughte to have anywaye of, in and to all those two gardens or garden plotts, lying and Leinge in Fir Ketts Field, in the Parish of St. Clemente's Danes without Temple Barr, in the County of Middlesex, being of the yerly rente of fyve-and-twentye shillinges, be soulde by my said wife within seaven yeares, as before is said."

This "Fir Ketts Field" formed the site of the present New Square, and was in Charles II.'s time known as Little Lincoln's Inn Fields. In the "Act for the Preventing of the Multiplicity of Buildings in and about the Suburbs of London," 1656, two proviso tell us—that there was an agreement made "between the Society of Lincoln's Inn and James Cooper and Robert Henley and other owners of ground in Lincoln's Inn Fields, for erecting, building, &c., on three sides of the said fields, and conveying the rest of the ground therein to the said Society, and for laying the same into walks for common use and benefit, so as to abate great nuisances customary there. Therefore, this Act is not to extend to any houses built by the said J. Cooper, R. Henley, and their heirs, before the 1st October, 1659, provided they pay the Lord Protector (&c.), within one month of the said erecting, one full year's value for every such house. Also provided that this Act is not to extend to any houses, &c., built before the 1st Oct., 1659, by Francis Finch, on his land in Lincoln's Inn Fields, if he pays within one month the value of the said houses, as aforesaid—the said houses not being built on the aforesaid ground belonging to J. Cooper and R. Henley." The New Square houses were completed in 1697, by Mr. Henry Serle, a bencher of Lincoln's Inn, who gave his name to the neighbouring Serle Street. The garden was railed and

and originally Feckett's Field. We also find he was engaged with a person named Clark, who had some claims upon the property which were settled by an agreement dated 34th year of Charles II. This fixed the property of the parties, and Mr. Serle was permitted to build on the field. He appears to have acquired much property in this neighbourhood, but ultimately became greatly involved, as the following extract from the "Autobiography of Sir John Bramston," will show :—

"In the beginning of the month of December this yeare, 1690, among the notes of the House of Commons printed, I found an engrossed bill sent down from the Lords for the transferring the estate of Mr. Henry Serle unto the Lord Chandos and Mr. Vincent, trustees for an infant, his heire, then out of England, for the payment of Mr. Serle by selling the lands. I was in this bill concerned thus :—There is a field by Lincoln's Inn called Ficket Field, or by most and vulgarly Little Lincoln's Inn Field. Sir John Birkenhead, —the same person that in the war against King Charles I. writ the 'Mercurius Aulicus,' and after the return of King Charles II. was Master of Requests to His Majesty ;—a man wittie and well learned, but he had some qualities not commendable,—he had purchased in fee some parts of a field called Ficket Field, and other parts he had a long lease of. He beinge indebted and haveing some kindred of his name, he demises by his will the said field to Randolph Birkenhead and to Rupert Birkenhead and their heires, to the intent that they should pay his debts and legacies, and if they did not pay his debts and legacies within six months after his decease or refuse to execute the trust, then he devised his lands to Sir Richard Mason and

---

planted in 1845 ; and in 1867 was erected, within the enclosure, the temporary building for the public exhibition of the New Law Court designs. (See page 7.)

Some years since a dispute took place as to whether New Square was "extra parochial"—part and parcel of the Lincoln's Inn property—or no. The case was carried before the Lord Chief Justice and a Jury at Westminster, 24th May, 1820, in an action for trespass—Nathaniel Clayton *v.* John Pope and George William Shury, Overseers of the Rolls Liberty. The case terminated in a verdict for the parish. The chambers, therefore, in New Square, Nos. 1 to 4, pay poor rates to St. Dunstan's in the West (the parish in which the Rolls is situated), and Nos. 5 to 10 pay, and have paid, the rates to St. Clements Danes for the past sixty years and more.

Frances Beamshon, Serjeant-at-Law, his executors and their heires. Within the time the Birkenheads and the executors sell all the estate of Mr. Henry Serle subject to Sir John's debts. He pays the debts and legacies. Soon after Mr. Serle died intestate much in debt and his lands all mortgaged."

Serle's Coffee-house, a contemporary of Squire's and the Grecian (see page 170), was much frequented by the notabilities of that day. Addison says, "I do not know that I meet in any of my walks objects which move both my spleen and laughter so effectually as those young fellows at the Grecian, Squire's, Serle's, and all other coffee-houses adjacent to the law, who rise early for no other purpose but to publish their laziness."—*The Spectator*, No. 49.

Addison seems to have visited Serle's Coffee-house to study from some quiet nook the humours of the young barristers.

There is a letter extant from Akenside, the poet, addressed to Jeremiah Dyson, that excellent friend and patron who defended him from the attacks of Warburton, at Serle's Coffee-house.

The second edition of "Barnaby's Journal" was printed in 1716 for one Illidge, under Serle's Gate, Lincoln's Inn New Square.

Formerly there was a passage leading from Serle's Street to New Square, which was closed in 1845. This was a near cut into Chancery Lane.*

Serle's Street leads from Carey Street into Lincoln's Inn Fields, which is allowed to be the largest and most beautiful square in London, if not in Europe. At one time it was a very dangerous place on account of robberies; though it seems to have been partially covered with buildings in 1580, when Queen Elizabeth issued a proclamation, forbidding the laying of foundations of houses about London. Within six years, however, a contrary mode of proceeding was adopted: the Government revoked its order; and in 1618, a commission

---

* The same street hath since been called Chancery Lane, by reason that King Edward III. annexed the House of Converts (between the Old Temple and the New) by Patent to the office of Custos Rotulorum, or Master of the Rolls."—*Stow*. "This Chancellor's Lane, now called Chancery Lane."—*Stype*.

from James I. was entrusted to the care of Lord Chancellor Bacon and other noblemen and gentry, for the better disposal of these grounds. The commission alleged that 'more public works near and about the City of London had been undertaken in the sixteen years of that reign than in ages heretofore; that Lincoln's Inn Fields was much planted round with dwellings and lodgings of noblemen and gentlemen of quality, but at the same time was so deformed by cottages, mean buildings, and encroachments on the fields, that the commissioners were directed to reform them, according to the plan of Inigo Jones, recited in the commission, and accordingly drawn up by way of map, &c. Thus authorized, it was the intention of the eminent architect to have built the whole in one style; but the taste of the projectors not according with his great genius and abilities, the work remained unaccomplished. A specimen of his design, however, is exhibited in the centre house on the west side—formerly inhabited by the Earls of Lindsey, and their descendants the Dukes of Ancaster, but now divided into two dwellings—and possesses that simple grandeur for which the works of Inigo Jones have been so celebrated. The four sides of the vast square were thus named:—the north, Newman's Row; the west, Arch' Row; the south, Portugal Row; and the east, Lincoln's Inn Wall.

Although the parish of St. Clement's occupies only a portion of Lincoln's Inn Fields, we believe that most of our readers will feel interested in a description of this locality in the year 1663, contained in a petition to the king, and which has been copied from the one in the Public Record Office:—

(Circa 1663-4)—Chas. II.
"To the King's Most Excellent Majesty.

The humble Petic'on of ye Inhabitants in Lincolnes Inne Feilds, in the Countie of Midds., whose names are subscribed—

Sheweth,

That your Maties. ffather of blessed memorie (att ye instance of his Royall Consort ye Queene) by his Lres. Pattents, dated ye 15th of December, in ye 15th of his raigne, and upon ye Petic'on of one Willm. Newton, Esqre. deceased, and the certificate of Edw. late Earle of Dorsett & others for ye

securitie of passengers & ornament of the said ffeilds, did graunt his Royall assent & lycence to ye said Newton & his heires for ye building of 14 new dwelling howses in the said feildes, in such manner as is therein expressed, notwithstanding any proclamac'on p'hibiting ye contrarie. That the said howses were built and enjoyed accordinglie. That by ye intent of the said lycence noe other howses were to bee built in the said feilds by the said Newton. That Tho. Newton sonn of ye said Wm. Newton and his assignees by color of the said lycence, and in abuse thereof hath lately erected severall wooden houses or shedds & digged gravell pitts in the middle of ye said feilds neere ye comon waies and passages there, & employed ye said houses for puppet-playes, dancing on ye ropes, mountebanks, & other like uses, whereby multitudes of loose & disorderlie people are daylie drawne together, and in darke evenings the said howses shedds and gravell pitts are Lurking places & receptacles for theives wch. doe great mischeifs to passengers in the night time, contrary to ye intent of ye said licence & p'clamac'ons, and to the great disquiet, and nusance of your people.
Wherefore,

Your Petitioners most humbly pray that your Matie. will be graciouslie pleased to give your Royall command and direc'on to the Commissioners for the high waies in & about the Cittie of London and lines of the late communicac'on or any three or more of them to cause ye said howses to be taken down, ye said abuses to bee reformed, and the like for the future p'vented, as to yor Matie in yor wisdome shall seeme meet for the safety and quiet of your Petic'oners & other your subjects.

And yor Petrs will praye :—

W. Howard	Cardigan	Middlesex
Ralfe Bovey	Belasyse	Geo. Cony
Hen. Arundell	Wm. Cony	J. Armyne
Robert Henley	C. Wyche	Richd. Cocks
Ran Egerton	Wm. Richardson	Tho. Gery
J. Hodges	Edward Ffarmer	Alexr. Davies
Tho. Phillpott	George Hill	Arthur Newman
Richard Wildraham	Richard Powell	E. Ffleetwood

"The accounts of the Right Honorable Richard Earl of Dorset and others nominated and appointed Commissioners for the repairing of the high waies and sewers in and about the Cities of London and Westminster for one year, ending 25th December, 1670 :—

"Pd. Mr. Wm. Middleton, for Councell for draweing the Writings for the Removeing of Temple Barr, &c. ... 100/

In another account from 25th March, 1672, to 25th March, 1673 :—

"Paid to James Buckland in full of his bill for setting upp Railes, and other worke done in Little Lincoln's Inn Fields as per bill appears 38/2

"Paid John Jolly for paving the Passage in Lincoln's Inn Fields, between Portugall Row and Lincoln's Inne Wall as per bill appears 18 11 8

Lincoln's Inn Fields witnessed the closing scenes of the patriotic lives of Lord William Russell and Algernon Sydney. The virtuous Russell lost his head in the middle of the square, on the 21st of July, 1683; Sydney was executed in the latter end of the same year.

Since the great families have deserted the square, some of the houses have been divided. The great one at the corner near Queen Street was called Powis House, having been built for the Marquis of Powis in 1686. It was the residence of Sir Nathan Wright, and that eminent statesman, Lord Chancellor Somers; after his decease it was inhabited by Thomas Pelham Holles, Duke of Newcastle, and is usually called Newcastle House. On this side were also the town houses of Sir Fletcher Norton, the Speaker of the House of Commons, the Sardinian Ambassador, &c. On the north side the houses form a goodly row of buildings in varied architecture. The south side has been distinguished by the residence of eminent legal characters, Lord Chancellors Camden, Loughborough; Lord Chief Justice Kenyon, Sir Henry Gould, Serjeant Adair, &c.

No. 13, is Soane's Museum, which is of great value for artistic study in architecture, painting, and sculpture. The contents of the museum cost Sir John Soane £50,000.

Judge Best lived in this square during the time of the riots; Newman Knowles lived at No. 48; Lord Erskine lived in Erskine Chambers; also Bell, a barrister, of Lincoln's Inn Hall, known as "Famous" Bell during Lord Eldon's chancellorship. George IV., when Prince Regent, asked Lord Eldon "Who was the cleverest man at the Chancery bar?" Lord Eldon replied—alluding to Bell— "That it was a man who could neither read, write, walk, nor talk." This answer was borne out by the facts that Bell had an impediment in his speech, by which he was prevented reading or talking distinctly; that he wrote so illegibly that none but his clerk could decipher his characters; and further, that he was unfortunately club-footed.

SERLE'S PLACE*
(See also pages 104 to 107.)

Divided into Upper, Lower, and Middle Serle's Place in 1845, was originally called Sheer, or Shire Lane, and in the reign of James I., Rogues' Lane. It was the boundary line between the City and Shire of Middlesex, and ran from Fleet Street, flush with Temple Bar, to Carey Street. Near this locality was a lane called Jackanapes Lane, eastward of Frickett's Field and Cup Fields, now called Lincoln's Inn Fields.

At all times this place has borne the very worst of reputations, and it was, if possible, to purge it of its foul and filthy associations that rather more than forty years ago the change of designation was made. It contained haunts of the lowest description (see page 104), in which not a few tragedies took place; portions, however, of this lane have of late years much improved in character, particularly the upper end, where Isaac Bickerstaff lived. Here stood the noted spunging-house where Theodore Hook was confined after his arrest in August, 1823, for the large defalcations of his treasurership of the Mauritius, amounting to £12,000. This incarceration in no way interfered either with his flow of spirits or his literary activity, for he not only conducted the *John Bull* quite unconcernedly while he remained a compulsory inmate of this tenement, but projected here not a few other literary ventures. Here he made the acquaintance of Dr. Maginn. He left Shire Lane in April, 1824, entertaining his friends ere his departure at a boisterous banquet.

But the lane had at once more interesting and less disreputable associations than these. In it the first Sir Charles Sedley lived, and his son, the dramatist, was born. Here, too, lived Elias Ashmole, and here Antony à Wood records that he dined with him. The latter writes thus, on May 1st, 1670:—"Dined with Mr. Ashmole at his house in Sheer Lane, near Temple Bar, and John Davis, of Kichnelly, was there. After dinner he conducted A. W. to his lodgings in the Middle Temple, where he showed us all his rarities—viz., ancient coins, medals, pictures, &c., which took them up near two hours' time." Ashmole was by turns an astrologer, alchemist, and antiquary. In 1658, he left the two former studies and devoted himself to antiquities. In 1660, he was called to the bar by the Middle Temple. His collection, including a fine library, 9,000 coins, a fine cabinet of seals, and charters of engraved portraits, was destroyed by fire in the Temple in 1679.

In the *Tatler*, No. 86, 27th Oct., 1709, Steele writes:—"In this order we marched down Sheer-lane, at the upper end of which I lodge. When we came to *Temple Bar*, Sir Harry and Sir Giles got over;* but a run of the coaches kept the rest of us on this side of the street. However, we all at last landed, and drew up in very good order before Ben Tooke's† shop, who favoured our rallying with great humanity; from whence we proceeded again until we came to Dick's Coffee-house, where I designed to carry them."

It was in Middle Serle's Place, which consisted of old houses, with their antique fantastic-looking gabled fronts overhanging each other as if for mutual safety, that the ancient fame and interest of this lane principally concentrated. Here stood the "Old Trumpet" tavern; there was a column on each side the doorway, and under the first-floor window was a small signboard of a trumpet. Many years since the sign was changed to the "Duke of York." This was, probably, one of the oldest licensed houses in the metropolis.‡ Andrew Marvell, who died in 1678, thus refers to the original sign by way of inuendo:—"Even then at the same time he sounds another trumpet than that in Sheer Lane; to horse and hem in the auditory." Its last host took great interest in the reputation of his house; he restored the sign-board (a modelled trumpet) to the house in its original place, and obtained the assent of

---
* That is, over the street.
† A celebrated bookseller of Fleet Street.
‡ The first licence for a public-house was granted in 1621.

the magistrates to the change. When the third coating of colour was removed in 1845 from the front of this house, the correct name was found to be Serle's Place, and not Lower Serle's Place, which commenced with the adjoining house. It was here that the club of what in modern conventional parlance we should term "old fogies" (so inimitably described by Steele in No. 132* of the *Tatler*) assembled nightly. Steele represents himself as lodging in the lane, and repairing to this quaint assemblage when his engagements permitted. His portraiture of the members has never been excelled in the style of quiet humorous description in which he is without a rival :—Sir Jeoffrey Notch, the broken-down country gentleman, whose talk is all of hounds and horses, and who "alone has the liberty of stirring the fire ;" Major Matchlock, the Commonwealth hero, who thinks no battle so renowned as Marston Moor ; honest old Dick Reptile, taciturn, but always ready to laugh at the jokes of the others; and the Temple bencher, who was a wild blade in his youth, and tells more than one suspicious tale in which a red petticoat figures.

But much of this may be ideal and the fruit of Steele's exuberant fancy. Not so the associations of the immortal Kit-Cat Club (which took its name from one Christopher Katt, a pastrycook who made delicious mutton pies, called "Kit Kats" from their savoury flavour), of which Steele, Addison, and, in a word, all the great Whigs—whether statesmen, wits, or men of fashion—of Queen Anne's time were members ; of which Jacob Tonson was secretary, and the features of whose members were transferred to enduring canvas by Sir Godfrey Kneller. (These portraits, we may remark parenthetically, are now in the possession of William Baker, Esq., of Bedfordbury, near Hertford, a lineal descendant of Jacob Tonson ; many of them were to be seen at the exhibition of pictures at Manchester in 1857.) The Kit-Cat Club was founded at the "Trumpet," and met there regularly until its removal to the "Fountain" in the Strand. "It is hard to believe," says a writer in the *National Review*, "as we pick our way along the narrow and filthy pathway of Shire Lane, that in this blind

---

* The first number was published by Mr. Steele, April 22, 1709.

alley, some hundred and fifty years ago, used to meet many of the finest gentlemen and choicest wits of the days of Queen Anne and the First George. Inside one of those low-ceiled rooms, Halifax has conversed, Addison mellowed over a bottle, Congreve flashed his wit, Vanbrugh let loose his easy humour, Garth talked and rhymed. The Dukes of Somerset, Richmond, Grafton, Devonshire, Marlborough, and Newcastle; the Earls of Dorset, Sunderland, Manchester, Wharton, Kingston [this is an error, the title of Evelyn Pierpoint was *Duke* of Kingston], Sir Robert Walpole, Granville, Mainwaring, Stepney, Arthur Attie, and Walsh, all belonged to the Kit-Cat." Anecdotes and associations of the Kit-Cat crowd upon us as we write. We can find space but for one. The club was famous for its toasting-glasses, on which were engraved verses in praise of certain ladies, most of them members of Whig families, and all of them beauties, or wits, or both. Among the "toasts" were the four beauteous daughters of the Duke of Marlborough, Lady Godolphin, and Mrs. Barton, the charming niece of Sir Isaac Newton. Of the " toasts" we take the following, from the pen of Lord Halifax, as a specimen:—

"THE LADY MARY CHURCHILL.
Fairest and latest of the beauteons race,
Blest with your parent's wit, and her first blooming face;
Born with our liberties in William's reign,
Your eyes alone that liberty restrain."

One day, at the regular meeting of the club to choose toasts for the year, a whim seized the Duke of Kingston to nominate his daughter Mary, then a child eight years old, afterwards Lady Mary Wortley Montague, who introduced innoculation into England. He alleged that she was far prettier than any lady in the room. To this his fellow-members merrily demurred, appealing to the rule which stipulated that no lady should be proposed who had not been seen by all the members. "That," said his Grace, "could be easily managed;" and he at once sent for his daughter, with orders that she should be attired in her best. The little wondering beauty came in due time, and was received with the utmost acclaim. She was passed from the lap of poet to patriot, from peer to man of fashion, and was caressed and admired by all. She was unanimously elected. "Pleasure," she said, "was too poor a word to express my sensations; they amounted to ecstacy; never again, throughout her whole future life, did she pass so happy a day."

Sarah Malcolm, a Temple laundress, aged twenty-two, who, for the murder of three women, was hung in Fleet Street, over against Fetter Lane, March 7th, 1733, is the subject of the rarest of Hogarth's engraved portraits; her printed confession was sold with such rapidity, that as much as twenty guineas is said to have been offered for a single copy.

SHIP YARD*

Was made up of narrow courts and alleys, and had almost lost its picturesqueness; some of the houses were, however, very lofty. It was formerly the site of the "Ship Inn" mentioned in a grant to Sir Christopher Hatton* in 1751, and which was standing in 1756. A token exists of "The Ship without Temple Bar," a tavern of the time, with the date upon it, of 1649. We read in "Chambers's Book of Days"—"Ship Yard denotes the sign of the Ship, a house established in honour of Sir Francis Drake, and taking for its sign the bark in which he circumnavigated the world." Leading from Ship Yard was

CHAIR COURT,*

Which derived its name either from chairmakers being located there, or because it was formerly a stand for sedan chairs.

The (Central) Ragged School Shoeblack Society's premises stood in Ship Yard. They are now situated at 12, Mac's Place, Greystoke Place, Fetter Lane. Since the commencement of this useful society, in 1851, (the first established) much good has been effected. There were last year, 1867, employed in connection with the Central Ragged School (red uniform) 69 boys, whose earnings

---

* "In 1571 an Inn near Temple Bar called the 'Ship,' lands in Yorkshire and Dorsetshire, and the wardship of a minor, were granted to him."—*Sir Christopher Hatton. Life and Times, by Nicholas.*

SHIP YARD—TEMPLE BAR.
South-west view of an Ancient Structure, supposed to have been the residence of ELIAS ASHMOLE, Esq the Celebrated Antiquary.

were £2,079, out of which sum the boys were paid as wages, £1,025. Paid into boy's banks to their credit, £546; the society retaining £508 for expenses. There are seven societies in the metropolis, in connection with fifteen Ragged Schools, from which boys are taken upon the recommendation of the superintendents of the schools. The total number of boys employed in the year 1866-67 was 329, and their gross earnings were £7,501. The treasurer to the Central Shoeblack Society is J. R. Fowler, Esq., of 1, Mitre Buildings, Temple; the honorary secretary is M. Ware, junr., Esq., 25, Old Square, Lincoln's Inn.

"In 1851, some gentlemen* connected with the Ragged Schools determined to revive the brotherhood of boot-cleaners for the convenience of foreign visitors to the Exhibition, and commenced the experiment by sending out five boys in the now well-known red uniform. The scheme succeeded beyond expectation; the boys were patronised by natives as well as aliens, and the Shoeblack Society and its brigade were regularly organised. During the Exhibition season, about twenty-five boys were kept constantly employed, and cleaned no less than 101,000 pairs of boots. The receipts of the brigade during its first year amounted to £656. Since that time, thanks to a wise combination of discipline and liberality, the Shoeblack Society has gone on and prospered, and proved the parent of other societies. Every district in London now has its corps of shoeblacks in every variety of uniform, and while the number of boys has increased from tens to hundreds, their earnings have increased from hundreds to thousands. Numbers of London waifs and strays have been rescued from idleness and crime, and metropolitan pedestrians deprived of any excuse for being dirtily shod."—*Chambers's Book of Days.*

STANHOPE STREET.

In a work entitled "The Present State of the Charity Schools in and about London and Westminster," published in 1714, we find the following as the results of the first fourteen years of the St. Clement's Danes Charity Schools, which are situate in this street:—

"There were two schools, which clothed twenty boys and forty girls, and were supported by voluntary subscriptions, amounting to about £114 per annum; collections at charity sermons about £44 per annum. The gifts to each school from the foundation were £928 16s. Ninety-one boys and thirty-nine girls had been apprenticed." (See page 31.)

---

* Principally members of Lincoln's Inn and the Temple.

The Statistical Society, in 1837, reported that St. Clement Danes had thirty-four schools, from two of which no report could be obtained. Of the remainder, thirty-one are day schools and one Sunday school, for a population of 11,758, according to the census of this parish in 1831.

A pleasing incident, and one which we cannot refrain from recording, came to our knowledge in connection with these schools. We allude to a circumstance that occurred on the marriage of Miss Stilwell, last year, to the Rev. Mr. Coxhead. The father of the young lady, J. G. Stilwell, Esq., of Arundel Street, presented a half-crown piece to each of the girls belonging to the charity schools. Mr. Samuel Brown, of 228, Strand, the churchwarden at the time, suggested that it should be placed to their account in St. Clement's Danes Savings' Bank, which was accordingly done, and we are exceedingly happy to find, upon reference to the books, that a great number of additions have been made to these first deposits. We mention this simple fact to show how much good may be done by rendering a little assistance, and setting an example to induce provident habits. This is but one of the smaller of the numerous acts of thoughtful kindness and well-directed charity which are daily being showered upon the necessitous residents of this parish, by the various members of this much-respected family.

THE CHARITY CHILDREN IN THE STRAND, 1713.—A very old and interesting engraving, by George Vertue, represents the view of the Charity Children in the Strand on the 7th of July, 1713, being the day appointed by Queen Anne for a public thanksgiving for the Peace, when both Houses of Parliament made a solemn procession to the Cathedral of St. Paul. This engraving represents a view of the Strand between the Maypole and Exeter Change; in the foreground is seen nine of the state equipages, and in the background the tiers of seats containing the children. The entrance to Catherine Street appears to have been the only break in the long line of heads. The gabled houses of the Strand and the venerable Maypole (now the site of St. Mary's Church) completes a very curious picture.

To arrive at a correct account of the numbers, &c., of the children present, we must refer to the minute book of the Society for Promoting Christian Knowledge, also to a memoir of Mr. Robert Nelson,* a worthy member of the society at that time.

Robert Nelson joined the society in 1699, and till his death, which took place on the 16th January, 1714-15, was ever thinking and working for its good. His name repeatedly occurs in the records relating to the charity schools of the period. It was he who laboured so successfully to carry out the annual meetings of the charity schools which now once a year adorn the interior of our noble cathedral, and to his organization was due the plan for the seating of the children in the Strand. The minute books of the Society tell us that on the 16th of April, 1713, Mr. Nelson reported "that the trustees of the charity schools had resolved to find out a way to place the children in view of the Queen, as she passes to St. Paul's Cathedral on the Thanksgiving-day; and that in order to levy money to defray the expense of it, they had agreed to advance sixpence for each child." 1713.—July 16.— "Mr. Nelson reported that upon the Thanksgiving-day for Peace, on the 7th current, 3,925 charity children, boys and girls, new clothed, with their masters and mistresses, were placed upon a machine, or gallery, in the Strand, which was in length above 600 feet, and had in breadth eight ranges of seats, one above another, whereby they were put in the full view of both Houses of Parliament in their procession to St. Paul's upon that occasion. That it was designed as a piece of respect to the Queen, although Her Majesty was *not* present. The charge was defrayed by the trustees of the several charity schools which appeared that day."

---

* "An Account of the Society for Promoting Christian Knowledge," &c.—By Rev. T. B, Murray: 1848. p. 63.

Charities and Charity Schools.—These are very numerous in this great country. The Charity Commission reported to Parliament that the endowed charities alone of Great Britain amounted to £1,500,000 annually in 1840, *Parl. Rep.* Charity Schools were instituted in London to prevent the seduction of the infant poor into Roman Catholic seminaries, 3 James II., 1687.—*Rapin.* See education, Mr. Low's "Charities of London," (2nd ed., 1862.)

In the "Act for the Preventing of the Multiplicity of Buildings in and about the Suburbs of London," 1656,* we find a special proviso, "That Edward Hall, John Hall, John Kizlingbury, Henry Sherborn, Roger Adey, Richard Tippin, John Phillips, and Mary Thomson, widow, having taken leases for forty-one years of ground in *Stanhope Street*, along a dead wall from the end of Blackmoor Street to Maypole Lane in St. Clement's parish, containing in frontage to said street 206 feet and a depth of 60 feet, who in the said leases are bound to build on the said ground substantial strong-built houses, removing any nuisances, and making the said place more secure for passengers, &c.; and having already disbursed great sums, this Act shall not extend to any houses built before October 1, 1658, by them, their executors, &c., so long as they do pay within one month after this Act one full year's value of all and every of the said houses to the Lord Protector," &c.

* One of the provisoes in this Act states—That John, Earl of Clare, having erected several new buildings, and improved the property in Clement's Inn Fields, in the parish of St. Clement Danes, for a *new* and *free market*, "That from henceforth for ever hereafter, on every Tuesday, Thursday, and Saturday, in every week, there shall be a common, open, and free *market*, held in *Clement's Inn Fields* aforesaid, where the said buildings useful for a market are erected, and in the places near unto adjoining, and to enjoy all liberties, customs, and emoluments incident, usually, and of right belonging and appertaining to markets." Half a century later, we read in "A Pacquet from Wells," 1701, that there was brought to Miles' Music House (afterwards and subsequently known as Sadler's Wells Theatre) at Islington, "a strange sort of monster, that does everything like a monkey, mimics man like a jackanapes, but is not a jackanapes; jumps upon tables and into windows, on all fours, like a cat, but is not a cat; does all things like a beast, but is not a beast; does nothing like a man, but is a man! He has given such wonderful content to the *butchers of Clare Market*, that the house is every day as full as the Bear Gardens, and draws the City wives and 'prentices out of London much more than a man hanged in chains." This extract proves that more than a century and a half ago the butchers of this market were of no insignificance, but rather the arbitrators in the fortunes of a house of entertainment. (See page 79.) Of residents in this district, we have records that many noted characters made the neighbourhood of this market their home. Of the number was one "Timothy Buck, of Clare Market, master of the noble science of self defence," who, in 1712, challenged to combat another "master," one Sergeant James Miller (lately from the frontiers of Portugal). And we read in the *Spectator*, No. 436, that the encounter came off at Hockley-in-the-Hole; and that Timothy Buck, having laid his opponent low, having cut him about the forehead, and a cut on the left leg, our Clare Market Butcher (!) was declared the champion. Sir Richard Steele, who was an eye-witness to the fray, concludes his account of it by stating, "The wound was exposed to the view of all who could delight in it, and sewed up on the stage. There is something in nature very unaccountable on such occasions, when we see people take a certain painful gratification in beholding these encounters. Is it cruelty that administers this sort of delight? or is it the pleasure which is taken in the exercise of pity?"

In Stanhope Street, on the 18th December, 1778, was born the ever memorable Joe Grimaldi, in whose shoes many a later clown would like to have stood, so far as popularity and originality make a hero and a nine days' wonder. Grimaldi's mother was Rebecca Brooker, who had been from her infancy a dancer at Drury Lane, and subsequently at Sadler's Wells played "Old woman," and made herself generally useful. Grimaldi himself made his first appearance at the "Wells," in 1781, in the character of a monkey; became part proprietor of the house in 1818; took his farewell benefit there, March 17th, 1828; and quitted it finally in 1832, the same year that the late T. P. Cooke played there for the first time in "Black-eyed Susan" as William. Grimaldi died suddenly at his house, 33, Southampton Street, Pentonville Road, the 31st of May, 1837, and on the following Monday was borne to his last resting-place in the burial ground adjoining St. James's Chapel, Pentonville, next to the grave of his friend Charles Dibdin.* (See page 172.)

The following epitaph on Spiller was written, under the nom-de-plume of the Poetic Butcher of Clare Market, by one of the wags of the Artists Club, which was held at the Bull's Head. (See page 163.)

> "The butchers wives fall in hysteric fits,
> For sure as they 're alive, poor Spiller's dead;
> But thanks to Jack Lagnerre, we've got his head.
> Down with your ready cole, ye jovial tribe,
> And for a mezzotinto cut subscribe;
> The markets traverse, and surround the mint;
> It shall go hard, but he shall be in print.
>   For
> He was an inoffensive, merry fellow;
> When sober hipp'd, blythe as a bird when mellow."

The neighbourhood of the Spiller's Head was then very respectable. "The houses round the market were recently erected by Lord Clare; and even Drury Lane must have been once of good repute, for Mr. Evelyn tells us in his 'Diary,' 'That he went to his niece's marriage with the eldest son of Mr. Attorney Montague, celebrated at Southampton Chapel.' He talks of *magnificent entertainment*, and the *bride* being *bedded* at his *sister's lodgings* in *Drury Lane!"—Wine and Walnuts*, 1823, vol. iii. p. 149.

---

* See the very interesting account of Grimaldi and Sadler's Wells Theatre, in "Pinks' History of Clerkenwell," edited by E. J. Wood, 1865.

STRAND.

Having previously given an account of the Strand (see page 147) we shall now merely allude to the most noted houses and matters of interest within the parish of St. Clement Danes. The great open space occasioned by the clearance of houses* from Temple Bar to Clement's Lane for the building of the New Law Courts reminds us of the title of a paper contributed by Mr. T. C. Noble to the pages of *Notes and Queries,* (3rd series, p. 81,) entitled "The Ruins of the Strand." From the *Daily News* of April 8th, 1868, we extract the following interesting account of the demolitions for the New Law Courts:—

> "For some time past every one who has had occasion to drive or walk between the City and Charing Cross has been subjected to the inconveniences inseparable from a "pulling down" upon a large scale; and gradually but steadily the houses† have been disappearing from the space which the legislature has appropriated to the reception of the new building. Most of the courts and lanes on the site have already disappeared; about three-fourths of the houses have been pulled down; and only a quarter, some hundred or so in number, now remain in position, surrounded by heaps of broken bricks and shattered timber, which mark the places where imposing but more or less decayed edifices stood a few weeks or months ago. The work of demolition has already occupied about sixteen months; but the first sale of old building materials, the natural and almost inevitable prelude to the process of destruction, did not take place until about the month of October, 1866. From that time the sales have gone on pretty regularly, keeping pace with the rate at which the property came into the hands of the representatives of the Government, and being regulated so as not to entirely flood the market with old building materials, and thus unduly depreciate the value, small enough at the best, of the bricks and timber that have to be sold. Even at present some "eligible lots" of most uninviting looking structures are announced for sale; but, if we are not misinformed, some legal difficulties which have only recently been discovered, threaten to interfere with the immediate clearing of the

---

* On Friday, April 17th, 1868, Messrs. Glasier and Sons, auctioneers, sold the old building materials of nine houses in Carey Street and Plough Court for £200, consisting of "The Plough" public house, yard, and stables, the grocer's next door, and seven houses in Plough Court.

† The door and carving over the doorway of the house, at the corner of Boswell Court, Carey Street, which was lately occupied by Messrs. Nicoll, Burnett, and Newman, being exceedingly handsome, has been saved from the general ruin, by order of the Commissioners, for the purpose of being transferred to the South Kensington Museum.

ground. Some property which has for a long period been always treated as freehold has, it is said, been found to be only leasehold, held upon unexpired leases of 300 years, and the legal advisers of the Government have not in all cases been able to trace the individuals who are the real freeholders, and whose interests must be considered before the land is taken possession of by the Crown. The district which has thus been, or is being, laid waste was one which, considering its position, possessed few objects of interest to attract the antiquary or interest the student. Nevertheless, there were included within its boundaries more than one street or alley, allusions to which are to be found in English classical literature, and not a few houses which have been the dwelling-places or the resorts of eminent public characters, real or imaginary. To begin from the eastward. Bell Yard, below the latitude of the highly-respectable law publishers at its northern end, is to the minds of most persons associated only with a curious combination of more or less dingy shops, in which greengrocers, silversmiths, well-known fishing-tackle makers, tailors, furniture dealers, and others, until recently plied their various callings. But Bell Yard had come down in the world. It was not always a mere lane of shops. A century and a quarter ago it appears to have been tenanted by persons of good position and station. Among them was Fortescue, the friend of Pope, who occupied a house at the upper end of the yard, "near unto Lincoln's Inn;" and although the irritable little poet described it as that "filthy old place, Bell Yard," perhaps this was only true of it from the Twickenham point of view; and making all allowance for its being in the heart of London, it may have been a very eligible and convenient residence for a professional man. Temple Bar, which has, indeed, no claims either architectural or historical to preservation, will, if it does not fall of its own accord, be swept away in these general demolitions; but as some persons regard it with a sort of sentimental reverence it is difficult to account for, it will probably be re-erected at no great distance—let us hope in some position in which it will offer no obstruction to traffic, and will be exposed to as little observation as possible. The bar itself, as most people know, was erected as late as 1670 from designs by Sir C. Wren. Although it has on several occasions seen at its gates a sovereign waiting to receive the welcome and submission of the Lord Mayor, it has never served any useful purpose. The iron spikes upon which the heads or quarters of traitors used to be exposed have disappeared with the lapse of years, but the sockets into which they fitted are still to be perceived in the stonework. The houses in the immediate vicinity of the north side of the old bar were neither remarkable in appearance, nor historical in character. Close against the northern buttress was, and still remains, a barber's shop, one door of which is in the city of London, while the other opens upon the borough of

Westminster. Grave questions have at various times been raised as to what would have been the consequence if a sovereign, annoyed at the closing of the gates, or anxious to avoid the clumsy homage of municipal dignitaries, had alighted from his vehicle, and passing through the premises of this humble tonsor, had entered the City without the permission of the Lord Mayor. But it is fair to assume that on all occasions that bellicose-looking person the City Marshal, the Sword-bearer, or some proper official to whom the duty belonged, took all due precautions to prevent such an evasion of the sufferings which sovereigns are bound to accept, and made it certain that not at a less sacrifice than going round by Holborn Hill should the King or Queen escape the ceremonies by submission to which they purchased the right to drive down Fleet Street."

In giving an account of the Strand Improvements, we consider the Thames Embankment should not be omitted, occupying as it does a very large portion of the parish on the south side of the Strand; and which will in the course of time form a very important item in the general history of the parish; we therefore append the following brief account of the

THAMES EMBANKMENT.

The embankment of the Thames is no new project; it dates from the period when the Romans occupied our island, who, according to Tacitus, pressed the Britons into the work. The maintenance and repair of these embankments has been traced to the reign of Edward I.; but the encroachments of wharfs and other buildings have materially contracted the water way immediately through the centre of the metropolis, so that the only relic of the old line is to be seen adjoining Waterloo Bridge (Timbs). In an old print the distance of the river front from Westminster Hall is 100 feet; it is now 300 feet. The plans for embanking the Thames have been extremely numerous and as various in design:—arcades, railways, promenades, terraces, and even as a gigantic sewer, to which purpose, and as a railway, it is now being put. Already several portions of the river have been embanked previous to our present great work, such as at the Custom House, Somerset House, the Adelphi, New Houses of Parliament, Milbank, &c. But for the past two centuries a more extensive scheme has been continually before the public, viz.: the entire embankment between Westminster and London Bridge. Even Sir Christopher Wren, the rebuilder of the city after the Great Fire of 1666, designed "a commodious quay on the whole bank of the river from Blackfriars to the Tower." Sir F. Trench may be considered as the first engineer who presented a definite plan for the embankment; and in 1845, John Martin, the painter, designed a railway along both sides of the

Thames, with an open walk from Hungerford to the Tower, and from Vauxhall to Deptford; also, another portion from Vauxhall to Battersea Bridge. Both these plans, which were brought forward at a time when the Thames was considered to be specially designed for the *cloaca maxima* of London, were abandoned, chiefly from the opposition of the wharfingers, as they were mere extensions of the river bank for the construction of a roadway, and involved, therefore, the destruction of the then existing wharfage. In 1843 a Royal Commission was appointed to consider the subject of metropolitan improvements. Of plans submitted for the Thames Embankment three were selected—those of Mr. Page, Mr. Walker, and Sir Charles Barry. These were referred to a number of scientific men, but the scheme never got beyond the walls of Parliament. Even at this time an intercepting sewer was not proposed, probably not thought of; yet, what did the Commission report?—"That though a general embankment between Vauxhall and London Bridges appears to be highly expedient, yet that it is most urgently required on that portion of the Middlesex or left bank of the river which lies between Westminster and Blackfriars Bridges." And "urgent" as the work was reported to be, full twenty years were allowed to pass by before the great reform was actually commenced. Of plans and propositions we may briefly note a few of the designs of the past:—Mr. Page proposed an embankment and terrace (from Westminster to Blackfriars) fifty feet wide, varying from three feet six inches to ten feet high, with brick walls and granite facings, to cost £366,409. Mr. Edward B. Walmsley proposed a Thames isolated embankment, with side canal and marginal low level intercepting sewer, the embankment to afford a double tramway, a wide carriage road, a footpath with two commodious quays—one at the river, the other at the canal side—both the extent of the embankment's length, with a grand crystal arcade surmounting the embankment on columns, at a level with the roadways of the bridge. Mr. Lionel Gisborne, C.E., in 1853, proposed his "Thames Improvement"—self-supporting, without pecuniary aid from Government or the Corporation—to confine the water-way of the river to a width of not less than 700 feet by means of quay walls built on both shores; a street forty feet wide, lying between two rows of buildings; the esplanade covered with a Paxton roof of glass; a railway also along the line; the estimated cost being £1,500,000, to be returned by annual ground-rents of shops, warehouses, wharves, &c., amounting to £100,000. Mr. W. H. Smith, in 1851, proposed an embankment both sides of the river, from Westminster Bridge to the Thames Tunnel on the north, and from Lambeth Palace to the tunnel on the south; to deepen and narrow the river; to form an esplanade and terraced highway; to form terraces and crescents thereon, along and around the natural curves of the river, with docks for ships at intervals within; to divert all sewers and convey them at a constant low level within this embankment, and out of London, by railway in air-tight tanks, for agricultural purposes; to form a railway tunnel within the embankment, and the total cost of this seven-and-a-half miles of embankment would be £1,500,000. We may add, this was the only plan, out of about one hundred, which the Commissioners of Sewers engraved for their report at the time. Having thus briefly recorded the various important plans for embanking the Thames of the past, we will now briefly note the scheme as now actually in progress. In 1858, Parliament authorised the Metropolitan Board of Works to proceed to the formation of the main drainage works, "through, along, over, or under the bed and soil and banks and shores of the River Thames;" and in 1860, the Embankment Select Committee recommended "that the construction of the embankment be also confided to them." On the 22nd July, 1861, the Royal Commission (William Cubitt, then Lord Mayor, being chairman) issued their report, which states :—" The main features of the majority of the plans are an embanked roadway on the north side of the river, and the formation of docks, with the view to retain all the existing wharves; in others, railways, in addition to the roadways and docks, have been proposed; whilst in a few a solid embankment and roadway, without either docks or railways, have been suggested." Among the latter, the Commissioners particularly notice that by Mr. Shields. They then recommend—" A spacious thoroughfare between Westminster Bridge and Blackfriars Bridge, by means of an embankment and roadway; and that the new thoroughfare thus created should be continued on eastward from Blackfriars Bridge by a new street, according to the line formerly laid down by Mr. Bunning, the City Architect, from the west end of Earl Street across Cannon Street to the Mansion House. Without such a street, no relief whatever would be given to the crowded thoroughfares of Ludgate Hill, St. Paul's Churchyard, and Cheapside. The line of embankment at Westminster would coincide with the terrace of the Houses of Parliament, and from thence to Blackfriars Bridge would nearly follow the line laid down for the Corporation of London in 1841, by Mr. Walker, Captain Bullock, Mr. Saunders, and Mr. Leach. The general level of the embankment and road would be four feet above Trinity high water." The recommendation in this report has been carried out, and the plan will very shortly be completed. Several Acts of Parliament have been obtained; the first being "An Act to continue the duties levied on coal and wine by the Corporation of London," 24 and 25 Vict., cap. 42, passed 22nd July, 1861, which provides moneys towards the fund for constructing this embankment. The north side, Thames Embankment, comprises the formation of a solid embankment from the Middlesex side of Westminster Bridge, to the eastern boundary of the Inner Temple, and from thence on a viaduct to the western side of Blackfriars Bridge. The works have been let in three contracts. The first contract comprises the formation of a granite-faced river wall, about 3,740 feet in length, with a portion of the Low Level Sewer and subway in connection therewith; the extension of several of the main outlets to discharge into that sewer; the construction of about 3,200 feet of brick sewer (four feet by two feet eight) for the interception of the smaller sewers and drains hitherto discharging on the foreshore, and the formation of new and commodious steamboat piers and landing-places, in lieu of those interfered with by the embankment. The contract for this length was let to Mr. George Furness for the sum of £520,000. The second contract embraces the formation of 1,970 feet of granite-faced river wall, with a portion of the Low Level Sewer and subway, in continuation of the works included in the first contract; the construction of 2,440 feet of brick sewer; a new steamboat pier and landing stairs in lieu of the old Temple Pier. This contract was let to Mr. A. W. Riston for the sum of £229,000. We have no return for the contract for the third and remaining length of about 900 feet; the delay being occasioned through the long dispute between the City Gas Company, the Board of Works, and the Metropolitan District (Inner Circle) Railway. The Railway Act of 1864 proposed the construction of a line along the entire length of the embankment (a *minimum* sum of £200,000 being paid to the Board of Works as compensation) at such a level as would require a solid embankment in front of the City Gas Company's premises, for the protection of the railway works, and to authorise the Board to continue the roadway on the embankment from the Temple Gardens to Blackfriars Bridge of a width of one hundred feet, instead of seventy feet, as provided by the Act of 1862. The total length of the embankment therefore, is nearly 7,000 feet, completely divided by Charing Cross and Waterloo Bridges. At Westminster Bridge the roadway rises at an inclination of 1 in 80 to the level of the bridge, is set back 30 or 40 feet from the face of the embankment wall, the intervening space being a promenade and steamboat pier, having access from the bridge by an imposing flight of steps opposite the Parliament Houses. Between Westminster and Charing Cross Bridges will be introduced the beautiful water-gate, so long seen at the end of Buckingham Street, Strand, and between Waterloo and Blackfriars Bridges the Temple Pier will be in line with Arundel Street. In addition to the ordinary embankment works, will be a series of street "approaches" from the Strand on to the esplanade, while the New Mansion House Street will be a handsome approach from the heart of the City to Blackfriars Bridge. On the south side of the river, the embankment (for which the first Act was obtained 26 and 27 Vict. c. 75, passed 28th July, 1863), is from Westminster Bridge to Gun House Alley, near Vauxhall Bridge, a line which occasioned the demolition of numerous haunts of very disreputable characters.

It comprises a roadway of an average width of 60 feet between Gun House Alley and Lambeth Bridge, and thence to Westminster Bridge. 20 feet wide, improvements of the adjacent roads and streets; landing stairs next Westminster Bridge; and a river wall about 4,300 feet in length. Mr. W. Webster took the contract for £309,000. In the rear of the roadway will be the magnificent pile of buildings, St. Thomas's Hospital, now in course of erection. In the *Illustrated London News*, June 22, 1867, will be found a full page engraving, showing a section of the embankment at Charing Cross Bridge, exhibiting Subway, Low Level Sewer, the Metropolitan Railway, and the Pneumatic (or Whitehall) Railway, which proposes to carry passengers in a tube under the River Thames between Charing Cross and the South Western Railway, Waterloo Road. It only remains for us to add, that these important works are being carried out by J. W. Bazalgette, Esq., engineer to the Board of Works, and that to Mr. T. C. Noble we are greatly indebted for many interesting notes relative to the history of the Thames Embankment.

The present Strand STEAMBOAT PIER is situate at the bottom of Essex Street, and as Timbs says in his " Walks and Talks about London," "What a change is here, from the water-gates and gaily-decorated barges of prelates and nobles, to the steamboat pier and its cheap steamboats, for the convenience and recreation of the million." And the *Builder*, in 1861, informed us that "in a view of the Thames, showing the frost fair, in the reign of King Charles II., the King, Queen, and Court are seen coming down the Temple Garden Stairs to witness the sports on the ice; and in part of the background is the archway; and beyond the archway are the gables and other parts of Essex House. A garden, with terraces, is between the arch and the river." Timbs further informs us, that the water-gate of Essex House remains, built into the modern houses at the bottom of Essex Street: it is a lofty arch, flanked by two Corinthian pilasters. Mark Lemon says, "a pair of fine large pillars, perhaps belonging to the water-gate, are all that now remains of Essex House."

THE THAMES POLICE SHIP

Is situate in this parish and moored off the above pier. It is the Thames Police Station for the West-end part of the river. In the seventeenth century, the "Folly on the Thames," or Floating Coffee-house, was one of the most noted lounges for the idle pleasure-seekers of the Second Charles' period. It was called "The Royal Diversion" on account of the Queen of William III. having once visited it, and the "'Folly,'" says Hatton, "perhaps from the foolish things there sometimes acted." Moored in the river between the Savoy and Somerset House, its career, through becoming "a scene of folly, madness, and debauchery," ultimately came to an end. Close to where this vessel floated in the past, there floats at the present time another vessel of a far different description: the one to a certain extent, encouraged crime; the other is for the more modern purpose of its prevention. To those who pass up and down the once "silent highway," now turned into a busy thoroughfare, the Police Ship must have often caught the eye; and, as the commerce of London demanded the establishment of a police force, so the roguery on the Thames in the last century caused the establishment of the River Police and the Police Ship.*

---

* Previous to the year 1798, when the Thames Police was established, the pillage on the River Thames was immense, especially in the West India trade, for it was estimated that the plunder reached in value £461,000 for that year, ending the 5th of January. The remedy for this great evil appears to have originated with two energetic gentlemen, John Harriott and P. Colquhoun—both so well known subsequently in connection with the Thames Police, and each of whom have left memoirs of their work entitled the "Struggles through Life, exemplified in the various Travels and Adventures in Europe, Asia, Africa, and America, of Lieut. John Harriott," 2 vols., 8vo., 1808. Mr. T. C. Noble has a presentation copy, with Mr. Harriott's portrait and autograph, to which work we are indebted for several facts; and a "Treatise, &c., on the River Police," by P. Colquhoun, 1800, 8vo. The earliest notice of the scheme appears to have emanated from Mr. Harriott, for he tells us that having had frequent conversations with a worthy near relative (Mr. Staples), a police magistrate, he sketched an outline of his plan, waited on the Lord Mayor, who, being unable to take action in the matter, caused him on the 30th October 1797 to lay his scheme before the Duke of Portland, principal Secretary of State. Subsequently, on the 30th of January, a committee of West India merchants resolved to inquire further on the subject, and they found the river trade had increased very rapidly, thus:—

Year.	Imports.			Exports.		
	£	s.	d.	£	s.	d.
1710	2,894,737	7	6	4,622,370	12	2
1750	5,540,565	4	8	8,415,218	2	5
1790	12,275,546	14	6	10,716,548	14	1
1795	15,384,777	14	5	16,523,001	6	8
1798	30,957,421	7	4	29,640,568	4	6

We also learn that in the year ending the 5th of January, 1798, there were 13,444 ships employed in the foreign and British trades, to which we must add 88 barges employed in the local trade on the Thames. The total value of property "floating" on the river annually was estimated at

Camden says, "The London Thames is the richest river in the world, and that it has been erroneously said its name is Isis till it arrives at Dorchester, when, being joined by the Thame, or Tame, it assumes the name of Thames. What was the origin of this vulgar error cannot now be traced; poetical fiction, however, had perpetuated the error, and invested it with a kind of classical sanctity. It was called Tames, or Tems, before it came near the Thames."

£70,032,989 11s. 10d. It was, therefore, no small loss to have £461,000 plundered, besides £45,000 for loss in tackle, apparel, &c.; total, £506,000 per annum. Several meetings were held, and Mr. P. Colquhoun's assistance obtained, when the scheme was thoroughly gone into. "My original plan," says Mr. Harriott, "was on a larger scale than the one adopted; the estimate I calculated at £14,000 a year, the present is but £8,000." He then writes:—"I do most candidly allow, and firmly believe, that but for the superior knowledge and clearer instinct into the management of obtaining attention to things of this kind, which I had the good fortune to experience some months afterwards when introduced to Mr. Colquhoun, the plan for the River Police would have died in embryo." On the 27th of March, 1798, the Secretary of State approved of the measure; on the 8th of June, the West India merchants resolved immediately to get officials; on the 15th of June, Mr. Harriott was recommended and appointed resident magistrate; and, on the 2nd of July—within nine months from the date of the first publishing of the scheme—a commodious police-office was opened at No. 259, Wapping New Stairs. The system adopted was—A general watch over the river and the vessels arriving or departing, and for the prevention of the wholesale plunder by the "Heavy Horsemen," or those that were employed to load and unload ships by day, and the "Light Horsemen" who acted in concert with the receivers, mates, and revenue officers by night. Many of these men cleared five guineas a night, and an apprentice to a "game waterman" often kept his country house and a saddle-horse. The office was where the prisoners were tried, and the officials consisted of a superintendent magistrate, a resident justice, clerk, chief constable, and fifty petty constables. The opposition to the working of the scheme was very great, as may be imagined, and we are told that in October, two months after the opening, some hundreds of the coal-heavers, receivers, "Horsemen," and others, marched to the office, broke the windows, and would have done more serious damage had not Mr. Harriott ordered the six or seven officers within to fire on those without. Mr. Colquhoun read the Riot Act, but one rioter was shot and two of the officers were seriously injured (one subsequently died) before the disturbance was quelled. One of the principal ringleaders was subsequently condemned. Soon, however, the new scheme obtained a footing, for," at the commencement there were thousands of plunderers and hundreds of receivers; the former, I believe, are reduced to less than hundreds, and the latter, to tens: in fact, the first year of its existence, the West India merchants computed they saved £100,000; at all events, 2,200 culprits were convicted of misdemeanours on the river during that period. Mr. Harriott was for several years a magistrate for Essex, and when appointed to the Thames Police, was put on the Commission for the Peace for Middlesex, Surrey, and Kent. His family has been traced back to the reign of William Rufus as residents at Brigstock, in Northamptonshire. Among the curious notes of his life is the fact of his *reclaiming for a time* an island by the sea, near Rochford, in Essex, overflowed in spring tides seven feet deep. He built a wall nearly three miles in circumference, enclosed it, built a farm-house, &c. In 1808 he patented a portable fire-escape, which is engraved in his memoirs.

STRAND VIEW OF TEMPLE BAR

TEMPLE BAR,
(See pages 149 *and* 225.*)*

Which we will briefly notice, takes its name from the Temple, and separates the freedom of the City of London from the liberty of the City of Westminster; or, as Hatton states, "The Bar opens not immediately into the City itself (which terminated at Ludgate), but into the liberty or *freedom* thereof." The late Mr. Gilbert a'Beckett used to say that he could not see the effectiveness of Temple Bar against keeping out an an invading army: "Because the army might bolt through the barber's." These gates were formerly closed at night, and on occasions of tumults or royal visits to the City. Elizabeth had to ask for admission when on her way to St. Paul's after the defeat of the Spanish Armada. So had Fairfax and Cromwell when on their way to dine in the City; and Queen Anne had to send in her card after Marlborough's victory. Upon the accessions of George IV., William IV., and Queen Victoria, admission was formally demanded by a herald and trumpeters, when the gates were opened and the procession admitted. On her Majesty's visit in 1837, the City sword was surrendered to the Queen and re-delivered to the Mayor, but at the royal visit in 1851 the ceremony was entirely dispensed with. In 1852 the City refused to spend £1,500 to restore the Bar* as in Wren's time (see page 149). The old bar never looked so gay as on that memorable Saturday when the people of this country welcomed the Princess Alexandra to her English home, the whole structure (under the superintendance of Mr. Fenton, the City Decorator) being most tastefully enveloped in boldly arrayed draperies and fringes, and studded with medallion portraits of the happy Prince and Princess, and beautifully-executed allegorical statues, the latter by Brucciani, who also eminently displayed his skill in the execution of the sculptures which adorned London Bridge and its triumphal arch on that eventful day. A visit to this artist's Galleria della Belle Arti, in Russell Street, is worthy a pilgrimage.

---

* We have been favoured with a sight of the MSS. of the "Memorials of Temple Bar," from the pen of Mr. T. C. Noble, whose great knowledge of the history and antiquities of London justifies us in calling it a faithful record of this weather-beaten fabric.

ST. CLEMENT DANES CHURCH.

(See pages 13 to 18, and 139 to 145.)

Looking at the map of Old London as it appeared in 1560, it would seem that the old Saint Clement* Church stood just through Temple Bar or gate, on the north side of the Strand. We extract the following interesting and important document from the works of the Rev. Joseph Mendham :—

| "The Arms of the Medici Family surmounted with the Tiara. The Keys in Saltier. | Pope Clement with a Cross in his right hand, his left resting on an Anchor. | The Arms of France and England, quarterly, supported by Two Angels kneeling, |

"These be the Indulgences and Pardons graunted unto the Bredren & Systren of Saynt Clement, without Temple Barre of London.

"Imprimis, the most reverende Fader in God Laurece Campege, Cardynall of our Holy Mother ye church of Rome and legate de latere : sent by our holy fader ye pope to ye moost myghttyest prynce Henry ye VIII. Kynge of Englande. Considerynge that the lyght and goodnes of Almyghty God dothe illumynate the worlde with his moost ineffable clearnesse ; than moost especyally doth gracyously here ye meke petycyons of crysten people trustynge of his moost infinite mercy. Whan holy Sayntes by theyr merytes doth make meane & intercessyon for the sayd petycyons of chryste people. And in as moch as Almyghty God hath gyven an habytacle in the See to the Holy Martyr Saynt Clement sometyme Pope of Rome, prepared by angelles handes in the maner & forme of a temple of marble, so yt certeyne tymes of the yere chrysten people may have recourse to the sayd habytacle in the departynge of the see : that they may goe and tell the great myracles of Almyghty God. Therefore that the paresshe church of Saynt Clement fouded without Temple Barre of London : may be repayned, coserved, & well maynteyned : and also cumly replenyssed with bokes, chalyces, lyghtes, & other ornaments ecclesyasticall necessary for devyne Servyce : and that chrysten people more gladlyer for cause of devocyon shall come or sende & with due honour worshyp the sayd Saynt Clement and Churche before sayd : and puttynge theyr helpynge handes to the reparacyons and other thynges aforesayd in asmoche they shal se themselfe moost plentyfully to be refreshed with gyftes of hevenly grace.

---

* Clement was a Roman by birth, and one of the first bishops of that city. This See he held from 64 or 65 till about the year 81. He was, for his religion, condemned to work in the mines, and afterwards, having an anchor tied about his neck, was thrown into the sea ; hence the anchor has been chosen as the emblem of this saint. A large anchor forms the vane of St. Clement's Church, Strand, London. St. Clement is the patron saint of blacksmiths.—*E. J. Wood.*

The foresayd moost reverend fader to all chrysten people truely penytent & confessed vysytynge or sendynge to the sayd churche of Saynt Clement upon Christmas day, Eester day, Ascencyon day, in the feest of al the Sayntes & the decolacyon of Saynt John Baptyst, from the fyrst evensong untyll the later evensonge inclusyve or the sayde feestes and puttynge to theyr helpynge handes to the premysses he hath graunted for every daye aforesayde in the whiche they shall do [it] XL. dayes of pardon : his grauntes to endure for ever. Farther he doth exhort all chryste people to study and prepare theselfe wyth all the affeccyon of theyr myndes to take upon them these indulgences and pardon yt through ye merytes of our Savyor Jesu Chryst & the blessed Vyrgyn owre Lady, Saynte Peter and Paule, Saynt Clement, and all the Sayntes, they may be defended from [the] gynes of our ghostly enemy the devyll, & afterwarde to entre the place of everlastynge joye.

"Item, the moost reverende fader Rycharde cardynall of our mother the holy church of Rome. To all chrysten people truely [penytent and confessed] vysytynge or sendynge yerely to the Churche of Saynt Clement in the feest of Saynt Johan Baptyst, in ye . . . . in ye feest of Saynt Katheryne, and in the feest of the dedycacyon of the sayde churche . . . evensonges inclusyve, and puttynge to theyr charytable and helpynge handes to . . . . an Ave for the bretherne and systers of the fraternyte erected in the sayd church . . . . graunted as often as they shall do it C. dayes of pardon, his graunt to endure for ever.

"Item, for lyke consyderacyons, V. other cardynalles of Rome : to all chryste people vysytynge or sendynge yerely to ye sayd paresshe chyrche of Saynt Clement, upon Monday in Eester Weke, upon Trinite Sonday, upon Saynt Clementes day, upon the annuncyacyon of our Lady, and upon the dedycacyon day of the said paresshe church of Saynt Clement, from ye fyrst evensong to the later evensong inclusyve, and puttynge to theyr charytable and helpynge handes as is aforesaid, hath graunted, as oftentymes as they shall do it, for every feest aforesayd, every of them C. dayes of pardon, theyr grauntes to endure for ever.

"Item, for lyke consyderacyons, other XII. cardynalles of the Apostolyke See of Rome. To all chrysten people truely penytent & confessed, vysytynge or sendynge yerely to the foresayd paresshe church, on Saynt Clementes day, in the octaves of Eester, in the octaves of Penthecost, upon Saynt James day the Apostle, & in the dedycacyon day of the sayd paresshe churche whych is celebrate in the feest of the decolacyon of Saynt Johan Baptyst [Aug. 29th], from the fyrst evensonge untyll the later evensonge inclusyve, and puttynge to theyr charytable and helpynge handes as is aforesayd, hath graunted, as often as they shall do it in every dayes aforesayd, every of them C. dayes of pardon, theyr grauntes to endure for ever.

"Item, our holy fader Pope Leo the X. that now is, of his specyall grace to all chrysten people truely penytent & confessed, vysytynge or sendynge to the sayd paresshe church of Saynt Clemetes & the chapel of Saynt John within ye same, upon Eester daye, Saynt James day, Saynt Clemens day, & in the decolacyon of Saynt Johan Baptyst, & in the feest of Saynt Anne, and by the octave of the sayd feestes, And also on the Wednesday in the seconde weke of Lent, from the fyrst evensonge untyl the sonne be set of the sayd feestes and the octaves and of the Wednesday aforesayd: and puttynge to theyr charytable and helpynge handes to ye reparacyon, conservacyon, and maynteynynge of the premysses, hath granted iiii. yeres and as many Lentes of pardo: his graunte to endure for ever, as doth apere by his bull under leed. Dated.

"Also, our holy fader Leo the X. beforesayd, now beynge Pope, hath by another bull under leed dated at Rome the xiiii. daye of July, the yere of our Lorde God M.CCCCC.XX., enlarged his graunt before rehersed in suche maner that in lyke wyse as . . . . persones vysytynge or sendynge to the sayd churche & chapell, at any of ye feestes, octaves, and Wednesday before rehersed: shall receyve the pardon of foure yeres and so many Lentes. So in lyke maner all suche as wolde vysyte the sayde churche & chapell and for any cause can not so do: the whiche wyll gyve byqueth or sende any parte of theyr goodes unto the reparacyons of ye sayde church and chapell as is beforesayd, shall have and obtayne lyke and as great pardon as thoughe they dyd vysette personally the sayd churche and chapell in the feestes, octaves, and Wednesday before rehersed: this also his graut & decree to endure for ever. The hole indulgence and pardon graunted by our holy fader Pope Leo that now is and XIX. Cardynalles: to the church of Saynt Clement and the chapell of Saynt John within the same church, is ix. M.CCCCC. yeres and iiii. Lentes of pardon."

The rev. gentleman informs us in his work that the above document "came to me with some other MSS. belonging to the late John Bayley, keeper of the Records of the Tower, &c., through Mr. Russel Smith, and purports to be copied from a broadside of Richard Pynson, in the Chapter Library in Exeter Cathedral; he regrets, that, on application to a very competent friend on the spot, to ascertain its existence there, the result extended to no further information than that articles of such a description were so liable to be misplaced and even lost, that its non-appearance could be no reasonable matter of surprise, and had accordingly taken place. There does not, perhaps, exist a duplicate."

Dr. John Donne, Lecturer at St. Clement's, lost his wife the 15th August, 1617, on the seventh day after the birth of her twelfth child; she was buried in St. Clement's Church. Her tomb on the north side of the chancel became decayed and was rebuilt. In Nicholas Stone's Pocket Book we read, "A tomb of Dr. Donne's wife in St. Clement's Danes for the which I had fifteen pieces." The first sermon he preached after his loss was in this church, and he took his text from the Prophet Jeremiah's Lamentations, iii., 1, "Lo, I am the man that have seen affliction."—*Walton's Life of Dr. Donne.*

As regards the present church, we learn from the Order Book of the Society of New Inn, that—

"On November 24th, 1681, Mr. William Barnes, the then treasurer, and thirty-four members of New Inn contributed £46 14s. 6d. 'towards building the church of St. Clement Danes;' and on the 26th November, 1719, a further sum of twenty guineas 'towards building the steeple of St. Clement's Church,' which was erected by Gibbs in the last-mentioned year."

It would seem that the pulpit in this church was changed to its present position about the year 1697, as we find the following order in the old order-book in question, under date 10th February, 1697:—

"Dean Hascard's request being considered, it is ordered that he, giving an acknowledgment under his hand that he has no title for any duty or tythe out of the house, and acknowledging also that the passage to the pulpit in the church through the pew of this house is on sufferance, and by permission of the house only, and not of right, that five guineas be given him by the treasurer of this house as a free gift of this house."

The following entries are from the journal of the Rev. Rowland Davies, Dean of Ross :—

"1689, 2 June.—'I went to St. Clement's Church, when I heard Dr. Hascard preach in the morning, and Dr. Horden in the evening.' *Memo:* Gregory Hascard, S. T. P. Dean of Windsor 1684 was instituted to the rectory of St. Clement Danes, on the presentation of Sir Vere Fane, K.B. Sep. 18, 1678. He died in 1708. John Horden, M.A., was instituted to the rectory of St. Michael, Queenhithe (then resigned by the above Dr. Hascard) May 5, 1671, and to the vicarage of Isleworth, Midx., April 16, 1681. He died holding both those livings in 1690. 1689, 5 June.—'Being a public fast, I heard Dr. Hascard preach at St. Clement's Church.' 9th.—'I heard Dr. Hascard preach in the morning at St. Clement's, and in the afternoon I preached myself, on Luke xvi. 25.' 1689, 27 Oct.—'At St. Clement's Church in the morning I heard Dr. Hascard.' 3rd Nov.—'In the morning I heard Dr. Hascard at St.Clement's.' 23rd Feb. 1690.—Similar entry, 12 Mar.—Same (being fast day).''

THE NEWSPAPER PRESS IN ST. CLEMENT DANES.

"DAILY TELEGRAPH."—(No. 253, Strand, required for the New Law Courts.)—On Friday, June 29th, 1855, the first number of the now well-known *Daily Telegraph* was issued, price 2*d*., by a company consisting of four gentlemen connected with the army, with Colonel Sleigh as manager. About six months afterwards the price was reduced to 1*d*.,* when Colonel Sleigh became sole proprietor, and so continued until February or March, 1857. The present circulation is from 150,000 to 200,000 daily, varying according to events; on the occasion of the entry of the Princess of Wales into London the sale amounted to 260,000. The advertisements occupy from 180 to 190 columns a week; the whole edition of the paper is printed within eight hours, by four Hoe's machines, one ten-feeder and three eight-feeders, from four sets of stereotype casts. The *Daily Telegraph*† is now printed and published in Fleet Street.

"ILLUSTRATED LONDON NEWS"—(No. 198, Strand)—was established by the late Mr. Herbert Ingram, and the first number was issued on the 14th May, 1842. Although it has had many imitators in this and other countries, it is still the chief, as it was the first, of illustrated newspapers, and has done much for the advancement and diffusion of art. Mark Lemon and Dr. Mackay wrote leaders. Mr. Peter

---

* "A century and a quarter ago, we had halfpenny and farthing newspapers sold about the streets without stamps, in defiance both of the law and the penalty. They were said to be got up by 'poor low wretches' living in obscure parts of the town, or in the Rules of the Fleet, and they were suspected to be supported by persons in power against the opposition papers and publishers. The *Farthing Post* circulated during the years 1740-43 ;—a boy is reading this cheap newspaper in the fourth plate of Hogarth's 'Rake's Progress.' Another of these journals was entitled *All Alive and Merry*. It was a small folio half-sheet, having three columns of letterpress on each side. Several specimens may be seen in Dr. Burney's collection of newspapers in the British Museum, vol. iii. 1741."—*Timbs*.

† A newspaper was published in 1848, entitled the *London Telegraph*, price 3*d*., but was soon brought to a close by the proprietor being thwarted in his printing arrangement. The first four numbers of the *Illustrated Times* met with a similar fate. It was originally published at 113, Fleet Street, and the first number appeared December 17th, 1853. Price 3*d*.

Cunningham and Thomas Miller, the basket-maker poet, were also on the staff. Some of the volumes of this pictorial record of the age in which we live are before us, and it is interesting to trace the improvements in the wood-engravings from its early numbers to the present time. In turning over the pages of these volumes we learned the curious fact—unparalleled, perhaps, in the annals of the newspaper press—that many of the numbers, owing to the extraordinary demand for them, have to be reprinted. Nearly all those in our copy of volume I., for example, bear on their first and last pages the word "reprint," and one number has on it "sixth reprint." This struck us as a fact worth chronicling. Mr. Ingram obtained a seat in Parliament for Boston. He was unfortunately drowned in Lake Michigan, the steamer in which he sailed being run down by another vessel.

The "News of the World" was the first successful attempt to establish a cheap weekly newspaper of high character and merit. The newspaper stamp duty* existed at the time, and the price of the *News of the World* (stamp included) was threepence. There was a paper published at twopence halfpenny, but that such price could not be sustained, was proved when, after the success of the *News of the World*, it was raised to threepence also. The principles of the *News of the World* are Independent Liberal; it is attached to no party, but proceeds upon the maxim that "Party is the madness of the many for the gain of the few." The *News of the World* was originally published at 299, Strand, but the office was removed in the year 1852 to the new establishment in Exeter Street, built for the late Mr. John Brown Bell. When the paper duty of three-halfpence per pound was abolished, it was found that so small a fraction of that sum applied to a single sheet that the price could have been reduced only by reducing the quality of the literature and news; the proprietor, therefore, preferred to throw the advantage

---

* The reduction of newspaper duty from fourpence to one penny took effect September 15th, 1836, and totally abolished (except for postal purposes) in 1855. Newspapers were first stamped in 1713; the *Public Intelligencer* was the first newspaper published in England, in 1663.

into the quality of the paper, so that the *News of the World* at twopence should be equal in all respects to the wants of the public. When the stamp duty existed, and the actual circulation of newspapers could be tested by official return, it was shown that the *News of the World* had a very large circulation. For the last six months of the official return the number was 2,885,000.

"OBSERVER."—(No. 170, Strand.)—This is a first-class weekly paper, which was established in 1791. It was purchased by Mr. W. T. Clements in 1825. It is published at five o'clock on Sunday mornings, in time for the early mails.

"BELL'S LIFE IN LONDON."—(No. 170, Strand.)—This, the first sporting journal in the country, was established in 1821, by Messrs. Pinnock and Maunders, two well-known booksellers. Mr. W. T. Clements purchased the property in 1825, when the circulation soon rose from 3,000 to 30,000.

"MARK LANE EXPRESS."—(late No. 246, Strand.)—The premises of Messrs. Rogerson and Tuxford being required for the New Law Courts, they have removed their printing and publishing business to No. 265, where this journal is now published. It was established in 1830, and is essentially an agricultural journal. In it special reports are given of every agricultural meeting of importance in the three kingdoms.

"THE TABLET" was established in 1840, and is published every Friday and Saturday, at 21, Newcastle Street, Strand. It is the advocate of the interests of the Catholic body; has always maintained the expediency of the union of all Catholics in a strong and independent line of policy, and is opposed to keeping the rights of Catholics as British subjects in abeyance, to suit the views of those political parties who were supposed to be less hostile to the concession of these rights than others.

"THE ENGINEER."—(No. 163, Strand.)—The first number of this paper was published on Friday, January 4th, 1856. It is the leading journal of the engineering profession. Published every Friday, by Mr. G. T. Riche.

"THE ATLAS," a weekly journal of politics, literature, and news (office, 45, Essex Street, Strand) was established May 21, 1826, having been previously registered May 9th of the same year, by Henry Edward Swift and James Whiting, proprietors, the latter being also printer and publisher, and from whose office Beaufort House, Beaufort Buildings, it continued from the first to be issued for a long series of years. It was printed on the largest sheet ever issued from the press, and created quite a *furore* in the town at its first appearance, as it was at that time quite a marvel. Its price was one shilling, which included the compulsory fourpenny stamp. On December 24, 1846, John William Kaye, of Well Hall, Eltham, appears as the registered sole proprietor; and in the last entry, made January 22, 1868, Daniel Bruton is given as the sole proprietor. William Hazlitt, Leigh Hunt, George Henry Lewes, and numberless others, of great literary and journalistic renown, have been intimately connected with *The Atlas;* the lately deceased Mr. Robert Bell, who was for many years editor of it, defended himself in a political libel case of great importance, and came off victorious, although he had to contend against the Lord Chancellor Lyndhurst. Louis Kossuth, the ex-dictator of Hungary, strayed into the press world as a writer in this journal about 1849. The late Sir David Brewster, D.C.L., F.R.S., and Hermann Merivale, George Prynne, and John Wilson, Esquires, were at one time closely associated with it. In politics *The Atlas* supports all measures which are based on constitutional principles, and are conducive to the progress of intelligence, liberty, and order. In literature, it is a complete journal of *Belles Lettres*, and the news is digested and succinctly and historically narrated. Its present price, unstamped (first lowered to this in 1858) is exactly one-sixth of what it originally cost.

"THE COSMOPOLITAN."—291, Strand, was, until recently, the office of this paper. It is now published in Northumberland Street, Strand, and in Paris. In 1862, *The Index* newspaper, the origin of the Confederate Notes, was removed to these premises, and was published there until it expired in 1866, on the downfall of the Confederacy. Many periodicals have been issued from these premises.

"THE BALLOT" was published some years since at 49, Essex Street. It was a weekly newspaper of advanced Liberal opinions, the property of Mr. Wakley, and its first editor was Mr. Douglas Jerrold. We believe we are right in stating that *The Ballot* was the first newspaper edited by Mr. Jerrold.* It is scarcely necessary to say that it was conducted with great spirit and ability.

"THE MAGNET," established March, 1837, at 299, Strand, is now published in Exeter Street; it is entirely devoted to agricultural interests.

---

* In 1852 he became editor of *Lloyd's Weekly Newspaper*, and his literary labours did much for its reputation and circulation. He occupied the editorial chair till his death in 1857, when he was succeeded by his son, Blanchard Jerrold, who still ably occupies his father's position. *Lloyd's Newspaper* is a striking instance of what can be done when intellect and capital are combined, for the sale is over half a million weekly, consuming above 1,000 reams of paper. This may be said to be not only one of the most remarkable features of modern enterprise, but the greatest success of its class. Mr. Lloyd formerly lived and carried on business in this parish, and gained much experience as regards the reading wants of the working and middle classes of society, in the conduct of several cheap literary miscellanies, of which he sold a large number. *Lloyd's Weekly Newspaper* when established in 1842 was threepence, but upon the repeal of the Stamp Act, Mr. Lloyd astonished the world, by announcing that in future his newspaper would be published for *One Penny*. Besides being his own printer and publisher, Mr. Lloyd is his own paper-maker. From his business tact and conversation he is evidently a man who has a strong reluctance to depend upon any other resources than his own; so in order not to be checked by a failure of the raw material for the manufacture of paper, and at the same time have under his own control, the supply of every necessary for the production of his newspaper, he turned his thoughts towards Africa, in which distant land he now occupies 200,000 acres of Algeria's soil in the cultivation of a stiffish sort of grass, called "esparto," which grows to a height of from twelve to twenty-eight inches. This grass is brought over to England in large quantities by ships chartered by Mr. Lloyd expressly for the service, which are unloaded near Blackwall, from whence the grass is brought up the Lea river in barges to Mr. Lloyd's Paper-mill wharf at Bow, and there stored in huge stacks resembling a ten-storey warehouse. The paper mills here are on the most extensive scale, and are fitted up with all the most approved modern machinery, at enormous cost, covering six acres of ground. An inspection of these works reveals the process of paper making from its earliest stage to the finish, where each paper machine turns out 100 feet run, or 600 square feet of paper per minute. So completely has Mr. Lloyd everything necessary for the development of his own business on his own premises, that he unships the raw material on to his wharf in the shape of grass, and in a short time turns it out to the world at large, as the manufactured article—*Lloyd's Weekly Newspaper!* This grass is also used for various other articles, such as carpets, of which are made very handsome specimens: mats of every description, and patterns are also made from it; it is also extensively used by moire antique manufacturers, and is very capable of being interwoven in silken goods, as when well combed out and dressed, it can hardly be distinguished from that material. A *Lloyd's Gazette* was published for three years one hundred and fifty years since.

"THE INQUIRER," (178, Strand,) was the organ of the Unitarians, and established July 9th, 1842.

"THE SPORTING TIMES" (282, Strand,) is a review of racing and sports of all descriptions, literature, art, and the drama. Edited by Dr. Shorthouse, and published weekly (price twopence) by Mr. Farrah.

"BRITISH LION," (282, Strand.)—A weekly penny Conservative newspaper* for the working classes. It is the organ of the Conservative and constitutional associations in the United Kingdom, and uses all efforts to "resist the progress of democracy."

"THE TOMAHAWK," (199, Strand), established May 11th, 1867, is a Saturday journal of satire and amusement. The illustrations are excellent, and it is full of wit. The *Illustrated News of the World* was published here about seven years since, and contained some very fine portraits of eminent persons.

"THE WEEKLY CHRONICLE AND REGISTER," (282, Strand,) represents the interests of Fire and Life Insurance Companies, &c.

"THE SOLICITOR'S JOURNAL," (59, Carey Street,) established 1857, contains reports of cases in both Law and Equity Courts.

"THE WEEKLY REPORTER," (59, Carey Street,) established 1852.

"THE LAW REPORTS," (51, Carey Street.) (including an authorised edition of the public statutes of the session,) in three series. I. The Appellate Series. II. The Common Law Series. III. The Equity Series. Yearly subscription, £5. 5s. for the entire series.

"THE WEEKLY NOTES," (51, Carey Street.)—The *Weekly Notes* are published every Saturday. They consist of statements of current decisions, and are intended for the information of practitioners, but not for citation or authority.

The following newspapers have been published in this parish, but have become extinct :—*The Day*, first number appeared March, 19th, 1867. *The Penny Newsman*, published in 1860, on which a large amount of money was expended in endeavouring to establish

---

* The *Standard* is the daily penny Conservative newspaper, and was established June 29th, 1857. It devotes its columns more to general news than some papers, and is consequently a great favourite amongst all classes, and the circulation is very large indeed.

but failed in consequence of *Lloyd's Newspaper* being reduced to one penny. *The Weekly Advertiser** was published at No. 6, Essex Street.

"BRITISH MEDICAL JOURNAL."—Established (new series) January 1853, was originally published in Essex Street, and now by R. Hardwicke, 192, Piccadilly. In its earlier form it was called the *Provincial Medical Journal*, and was then edited by Dr. Peter Hennis Green, and subsequently by Dr. Rose Cormack. The journal was afterwards edited by Dr. W. O. Markham, who was selected as Commissioner on the Royal Commission as to Remuneration of Naval Medical Officers from the ability with which he advocated their claims in the journal, and shortly afterwards was appointed Metropolitan Medical Inspector of the Poor-law under Mr. Hardy's Act. Dr. Markham was succeeded as editor by Mr. Ernest Hart in January, 1867. Since that date, the journal has attained a very leading position and extensive circulation, and upwards of 1,000 new members have joined the association, which is now the most numerous and influential professional association in Great Britain. It aims at the discussion of all social, sanitary, and professional questions in which the medical profession are interested, and it has a powerful organisation for influencing Parliamentary and local opinion.

"THE LANCET."—At No. 49, Essex Street, *The Lancet* was published for many years. This journal, which has exercised so important an influence on the medical profession, was established by the late Mr. Wakley in 1823. It was originally published by the late Mr. Onwyn, of Catherine Street, and printed at Mile's office, in Bolt Court. At this office, also, *Cobbett's Register* was printed, and this circumstance gave rise to a friendship between Mr. Wakley and Mr. Cobbett, which terminated only with the death of the latter. *The Lancet* was instituted at a time when the most glaring abuses existed in the medical corporations and the hospitals of the metropolis. To correct these abuses, and to initiate a better order of things, the

---

* The *Morning Advertiser*, established 1794, by the body of licensed victuallers, through whose exertions, together with that of the present editor, £10,000 is distributed annually for the support of children of decayed or deceased members; also the unfortunate and aged belonging to the Society. The *Weekly Advertiser* affected to serve similar interests.

efforts of Mr. Wakley were mainly directed; at great personal sacrifice, at great loss, and after years of unremitting toil, he gained his object. It must be admitted, that the medical profession and the public have derived great benefit from the exertions of this journal. *The Lancet* is now edited by Dr. J. G. Wakley, the youngest son of the late Mr. Wakley. One of his lieutenants, Mr. J. F. Clarke, has been connected with the journal for nearly forty years.

"THE MEDICAL TIMES."—The history of this journal is interesting, and shows what a medical student with ordinary application can do if he tries. It is now about thirty years ago that a young gentleman called on the writer of this short notice, and expressed an earnest desire to become a qualified medical practitioner; he had read, and "got up the bones," but had not the means wherewith to pay his hospital fees. He thought of starting a medical journal, and another young friend—one Albert Smith—offered to assist him by writing for it and receiving such remuneration as could be afforded. Others without money, but with pens of the ready writer, came forward, and the *Medical Times* made its appearance on the 28th of September, 1839, under the editorship of its proprietor, Frederick Knight Hunt, who was soon able to pay his "great gun," Albert Smith, *half-a-crown per column* for his very amusing "Confessions of Jasper Buddle, the Dissecting-room Porter." The journal succeeded, and Hunt was able to pay all hospital fees, and in due course wrote the much-desired M.R.C.S. after his name. He started in practice, but, disliking the drudgery of it, relinquished physic for printer's ink, became editor and proprietor of *Hunt's London Journal*, editor of the *Pictorial Times*, and died, at the early age of forty-two, chief editor of the *Daily News*.[*] The *Medical Times* again and again changed hands, until John Churchill became the publisher, and the journal is now a great and increasing property. The old-established *London Medical Gazette* felt the influence by a decreasing circulation, when the above indefatigable publisher became the proprietor and grafted it on his

---

[*] The *Daily News*, established January 21st, 1846, was first edited by Charles Dickens; reduced to one penny, June 8th, 1868.

own journal in January, 1852, which henceforth became the *Medical Times and Gazette*. We can judge of the influence of this highly scientific journal by the frequent extracts from its pages in the *Times* and other daily newspapers. Among the contributors are some of the most distinguished metropolitan and provincial physicians and surgeons of the day. For many years the journal was published in Essex Street, where also appeared offshoots of it under the title of the *Pharmaceutical Repertory*, from 1844 to 1846, and the *Pharmaceutical Times* from the latter date until 1848.

"NATIONAL MAGAZINE."—The first number of this work was published in 1857 at 25, Essex Street. It was edited by Mr. John Saunders and Mr. Westland Marston; 60,000 copies of the first number were sold. Mr. Stansfield, M.P., was connected with this publication.

"YOUNG'S NIGHT THOUGHTS," and "FALCONER'S SHIPWRECK."—In 1767 "A. Millar and T. Cadell," published "neatly bound in twelves, price bound 3s., the fifth volume, which completes the works of the author of the Night Thoughts," or the five volumes in 12mo. with cuts price 15s.; and in 1776 "T. Cadell, successor to Mr. Millar, in the Strand," issued "An Universal Dictionary of the Marine; or a copious Explanation of the Technical Terms and Phrases employed in the Construction, Equipment, Furniture, Machinery, Movements and Military Operations of a Ship;" by William Falconer, author of the "Shipwreck;" price one guinea in boards, or £1 4s. bound.

The Strand* and Fleet Street have been the cradle of printing, almost from its first introduction: Wynkyn de Worde (assistant of Caxton), at the Golden Sun, Swan, and Falcon, the latter in Falcon-court; the imprint to the *Demaundes Joyous* is as follows:—

"Emprynted at London in Fletestre
te at the signe of the Swane by
me Wynkyn de Worde
In the yere of our
lorde A M
c c c c c
and XI
.'.

---

* We read the following imprint to the title of a book more than a century and a half ago:— "London: Printed for Nich. Cox, at the Golden Bible, the corner of Palsgrave Court, without Temple Bar, 1703."

Having given some account of the newspaper press in St. Clement Danes, which may fairly be considered to occupy no mean position, we now briefly notice the largest newspaper depot in the world, viz.:

W. H. SMITH AND SON'S
Newspaper and Book Establishment, (No. 186, Strand.)—Perhaps the most extraordinary house of business in London, not alone from the marvellous dexterity of its operations, although they are most surprising, but the facility and certainty with which business is transacted to such an enormous extent in so short a space of time is really wonderful. The premises consist of a very extensive and handsome building, which is complete in every department; the ground floor comprises one noble and spacious hall, forming almost the extent of the entire premises, and is surrounded by two galleries. The bustle is at its height at about five o'clock in the morning and is quite indescribable; and to witness perfect order emerge from such a scene of apparently utter confusion seems altogether incredible. In the hall and galleries men and boys are employed making up packages for all parts of the world. Vehicles are engaged for fetching the *Times* and other newspapers from the different offices; they no sooner arrive at the Strand Office but are seemingly almost by magic folded up into oblong bundles, wrapped in brown paper covers already addressed, and deposited in the light flying red carts waiting for their several literary cargoes; and thus, by the skilful and excellent arrangements of this establishment, by eight o'clock in the morning country residents are perusing the events of the day and news of the world. Thousands of newspapers are transmitted to their destination in the course of the week from this establishment. Clerks are engaged in posting up orders received and goods forwarded. In addition to this extensive wholesale newspaper trade, Messrs. Smith and Son have instituted a circulating library upon a most extensive scale, from which subscribers can borrow and return at any of their establishments and agents all the best and leading books of the day. Advertising, printing, and bookbinding form important items in connection with this gigantic establishment,

in which upwards of one thousand persons are employed, and so admirable are the arrangements that each department is complete in itself, and conducted as a separate business, and yet united into one vast and great commercial undertaking. The late Mr. W. H. Smith, the father of the present proprietor, and founder of this gigantic establishment, was born July 7th, 1792, and at a very early age undertook the management of a newspaper business at the west end of the town, removing in a few years to the site of the present premises. He resided for upwards of forty years in this parish, and during that time was a most useful and energetic member of the vestry, and greatly helped to promote the welfare of the poor of the district. At the early part of this century, newspapers required two days to go to Manchester, Liverpool, and other great towns far distant from London, for they were only conveyed by the night coaches, which took from twenty to thirty hours to reach their various destinations, so that Monday's newspapers could not be received before Wednesday morning. To obviate this inconvenient delay, Mr. Smith started express carts and saddle-horses so as to overtake the early morning coaches, and thus the day's paper was delivered by the morrow, making a saving of twenty-four hours in the transmission. For some time this admirable project scarcely paid its way and it seemed almost a failure, but the perseverance of its projector was such that he boldly pursued his course under all its difficulties, and eventually won his way and acquired the largest newspaper agency trade in London, to which he then devoted himself wholly and solely, giving up entirely the stationery business with which he had previously incorporated it. As time changes all things, so coach travelling was superseded by railway locomotion, and Mr. Smith was not slow in adapting the conduct of his business to suit this wonderful alteration. In 1852 severe illness, unfortunately, came upon this gentleman, doubtless arising from the great strain his mind had undergone in his varied and arduous business transactions, and in 1857 his health became so impaired that he found it advisable to transfer the control of this gigantic establishment to his son, the present enterprising proprietor. Mr. Smith now retired into private life, and for above six years he resided at Bournemouth, in Dorsetshire, where his health became greatly improved; he exerted himself to do all the good he could in his new neighbourhood, for his activity was such that he could not be idle. He was in every sense of the word, a utilitarian. He died 1865.—*The Bookseller.*

NOTED HOUSES IN THE STRAND.

TWINING'S BANK, (No. 215, Strand).—This is one of the best private banks in London, having been established a long time before joint-stock banks, and has always enjoyed the confidence and patronage of the parishioners and the general public.

LONDON AND WESTMINSTER BANK.*—(No. 217, Strand).—The Temple Bar Branch, established June, 1855. Manager, Mr. G. R. Hemmerde. The confidence that exists respecting the stability of this joint-stock bank, which was established March, 1834, is undoubtedly unsurpassed by any other in the world. The capital of the Bank is £5,000,000 sterling, in 50,000 shares of £100. The sum of £20 has been paid on each share, so that the paid-up capital is £1,000,000. The new capital is £5,000,000, paid up £1,000,000. Thus, after the 1st of January, 1869, the paid-up capital of the Bank will be £2,000,000, and they have also a reserve fund £1,000,000. Secretary to the bank, Tressillian P. Shipp, Esq.

* Formerly the Bank of Strahan, Paul, and Bates, originally Snow and Walton. It was one of the oldest banking-houses in London, second only to Child's. At the period of the Commonwealth, Snow and Co. carried on the business of pawnbrokers, under the sign of the "Golden Anchor." The firm suspended payment about 1679 (as did many other banks), owing to the tyranny of Charles II. Strahan (the partner at the time of the last failure) had changed his name from Snow; his uncle, named Strahan (Queen's printer?) having left him £180,000, making change of name a condition. It is curious that on examining Strahan and Co.'s books, it was found by those of 1672 that a decimal system had been then employed. Strahan was known to all religious people. Bates had for many years been managing clerk. The firm had also a navy agency in Norfolk-street. They had encumbered themselves with the Mostyn Collieries to the amount of £139,940, and backed up Gandells, contractors, who were making railways in France and Italy and draining Lake Capestang, lending £300,000 or £400,000. They finally pledged securities (£22,000) to the Rev. Dr. Griffiths, Prebendary of Rochester. Sir John Dean Paul got into a second-class carriage at Reigate, the functionaries trying to get in after him; the porters pulled them back, the train being in motion! Paul went to London alone, and in spite of telegraph got off, but at eight o'clock next night surrendered.—(See page 108.)—*Thornbury.*

"TWINING'S TEA WAREHOUSE.—(No. 216, Strand.)—The front of which, surmounted with its stone figures of Chinese, has an elegant appearance in the Strand. We notice the house, not only on this account, but because the family have to boast of a very accomplished scholar, the translator of the "Poetics" of Aristotle. Mr. Twining was contemporary with Gray and Mason at Cambridge; and besides his acquirements as a linguist (for, in addition to his knowledge of Greek and Latin, he wrote French and Italian with idiomatic accuracy), was a musician so accomplished as to lead the concerts and oratorios that were performed during term-time, when Bate played the organ or harpsichord. He was also a lively companion, full of wit and playfulness, yet so able to content himself with country privacy, and so exemplary a clergyman, that for the last forty years of his life he scarcely allowed himself to be absent from his parishioners more than a fortnight in the year.

"CROWN AND ANCHOR."—(See pages 53 to 55, and 141.)—One of the most noted houses bearing this sign was in the Strand, and was famous for the meetings of Reformers. Among the many characters who have occasionally held forth here for the public good, none were more distinguished for manly independence and general consistency than Sir Francis Burdett. He was the idol of the people in the reign of George III., which was evinced by the extraordinary excitement displayed by the populace on the occasion of his being ordered to the Tower for a libel on the House of Commons, April, 1810. He died January 23rd, 1844, aged seventy-four, having only survived Lady Burdett thirteen days. They were buried side by side, in the same vault, at the same hour, on the same day, in the Church of Ramsbury, Wilts. The following epigrammatic lines were written on the duel which the baronet fought with a person named Paul, and on his being supposed to have pensioned the noisy demagogue, Peter F——.

"Knights of the past of old strove all,
By robbing Peter to pay Paul,
Sir Francis Burdett nicks it neater,
He pistols Paul and pensions Peter."

On Monday, November 3rd, 1806, a considerable number of the friends of Mr. Sheridan dined together at the "Crown and Anchor" tavern. Lord Barrymore was called to the chair. A good deal of anxiety at first prevailed among the friends of Mr. Sheridan, as a report was prevalent that he had been basely assaulted in coming from the hustings, by a person carrying a marrow-bone and cleaver. Mr. Sheridan, however, soon arrived, so that it was clear he had sustained no serious harm; though, in fact, it appeared that an attempt had been made to do him a personal injury. After dinner, several loyal and patriotic toasts were drunk, and the "Immortal memory of Mr. Fox" was not forgotten; also, that patriot's favourite toast, "The cause of liberty all over the world." These were interspersed by some excellent glees, sung by Lord Barrymore, Mr. Barry, Mr. Leeke.

BEN JONSON, to be near the "Devil" tavern,* lived in the Strand (see page 118). It was here he brought the "Wits" from the "Mermaid" at Cheapside, and founded the renowned Apollo Club, writing his admirable "social rules" for its guidance, in his favourite Latin. The "Devil" tavern was the favourite haunt of the wits and lawyers, and the latter placarded their chamber doors with the extraordinary announcement, "Gone to the Devil." Well might Ben Jonson exclaim :—

>"It puts Apollo
>To all his strength to follow
>The flights, and to divine
>What's meant by every sign."

ADVERTISING EXTRAORDINARY.—(No. 244, Strand.) — These premises, until required by the Commissioners for the Building of the New Law Courts (see page 198), were in the occupation of Professor Thomas Holloway, whose pills and ointment are so well known all over the world. The interior of this shop—

---

* This tavern was kept by Simon Wadloe, and taken down in 1788, when Child's Place was built in its stead. Child's Bank, which is the oldest banking house in London, is situated here; it is mentioned in the earliest directory, 1677. The room over Temple Bar is held of the City by this ancient firm, in which they store the books and records of the bank, and many of them are of a very interesting character and great value.

described so faithfully by Dickens in *All the Year Round*—was fitted up without regard to cost, and wherever you turned when inside, polished oak caught your eye. His present premises, however (533, New Oxford Street) far surpass those in the Strand. In fact, a person upon entering might well suppose he was passing into a City banking establishment. Mr. Holloway commenced advertising in 1837. As a proof of the difficult task he had to encounter, we may mention that after having expended £100 in one week, he only sold two small pots of ointment. This circumstance did not daunt his energy, for he continued to practice the most rigid economy and to work most assiduously, as he tells us that he made up his mind to be content with nothing less than girdling the globe with depots for his remedies. In the year 1842 his advertising cost £5,000; in 1845 he increased it to £10,000; and at the time of the Great Exhibition in London in 1851, his expenditure was £20,000 per annum; in 1855 the cost of publicity had risen to £30,000; in 1864 it reached £40,000; and since that time it has exceeded £50,000 per annum. His advertisments and directions have been translated into nearly every known tongue, and among his correspondents are kings, princes, and distinguished foreigners of all nations. He advertises in 5,300 newspapers, &c., which, as a matter of course, leads to a large sale of his medicines. But, independent of the Professor, the public seem to swallow pills pretty freely, for we find the Government making £60,000 in ten years by the sale of "Morrison's Pills." There is also an enormous sale for Blair's, Parr's, and Cockle's pills.

THE FIRST SHOP IN LONDON LIGHTED WITH GAS.—(No. 96, Strand.)—About 1810, before any company had been established, Mr. Ackerman's shop at this number in the Strand was regularly lighted with gas. It is said that a lady calling there one evening, was so delighted with the beautiful white jets she saw on the counter, that she offered any money for permission to carry them home to light her drawing-room. The first street illuminated with gas was Pall Mall, in 1807. Sir Walter Scott wrote from London that there was a *madman* proposing to light London with—What do you think?—why, with smoke! Even the liberal mind of Sir Humphry Davy failed to take in the idea that gas was applicable to purposes of street or house lighting. In 1810, a company was formed (the shareholders, of course, being pitied as idiots); and the system was put in practice for the first time on Westminster Bridge on the last night of the year 1812; it then gradually found its way into the various districts of London, other cities, and, finally, into other countries. While Dr. Johnson lived in Bolt Court, he is said to have had this prevision of gas-lighting: one evening, from the window of his house, he observed the parish lamplighter ascend a ladder to light one of the glimmering oil-lamps; he had scarcely descended the ladder half-way, when the flame expired; quickly returning, he lifted the cover partially, and, thrusting the end of his torch beneath it, the flame was instantly communicated to the wick by the thick vapour which issued from it. "Ah!" exclaimed the Doctor; "one of these days the streets of London will be *lighted by smoke*."

EXHIBITIONS AND ENTERTAINMENTS.

STRAND THEATRE,* (No. 169, Strand) originally Barker's Panorama, till it was altered in 1831, for Rayner, the low comedian, and Mrs. Waylett, the singer. The old "Panorama" removed to Leicester Square, and comprised a substantial brick building 90 feet in diameter, about 70 feet high, with an offset of ground 23 feet 7 inches at the north end, and staircase to upper gallery. The many years it was so noted must be our plea for inserting these details, otherwise foreign to our subject. We may mention here that Henry Aston Barker (who resided at Bilton, Gloucester) died in July, 1856, and Mr. Robert Burford, the artist and late proprietor of the panorama, expired at Camden Road Villas, on the 30th of January, 1861, aged seventy. (See page 74.)

---

* This Theatre was first called Punch's Playhouse, and is situate directly opposite the well-known "Spotted Dog" public-house.

CALVERT'S MUSEUM (No. 189, Strand).—This was the site of the old "Crown and Anchor," on which, about seventeen years ago, was erected a capacious house, now in the occupation of Mr. Fisher. Mr. Calvert informs us that in 1853 he arrived in England, after accomplishing vast explorations, (extending nearly all over the world), and removed here an almost endless variety of packages, and that during his peregrinations he traversed new and hitherto untrodden regions, and pursued his venturous course over trackless wastes. A portion of the interesting collection thus culled, at a considerable expenditure of time and labour and no trifling pecuniary cost, Mr. Calvert then arranged in a methodical form, and issued invitations for a conversazione on a most liberal scale, as the best means of exhibiting his horde of antique, literary, and mineral wealth. His extensive apartments were now thrown open for the space of two months, and excited considerable attention and interest. Amongst the many distinguished visitors was the late lamented Prince Consort, who was pleased to express his high appreciation of what he had inspected. Among the articles exhibited were a magnificent store of early MSS. embracing treatises on ancient oriental chemistry written on leaves of papyrus, Japanese metallurgical dissertations, manifestly printed on cloth about 2,000 years ago, and Egyptian cylinders, of extraordinary interest in their relation to the past ages of the world. A portion of the Museum still continues in the parish, having been removed to No. 172, Strand, at the corner of Surrey Street, whilst the greater bulk is located in one of the oldest houses left standing in the parish, being No. 164, Strand, which, from the circumstance of three Kings holding a conference under its roof, established for many years the sign of the "Three Kings." A further interest is attached to this now venerable house, from Julian Notary having printed there some of his rarest pieces, and it having since his time been in the occupation of a succession of authors, artists, and printers, many of whom have shed a lustre upon the annals of literature.

The following singular advertisement of an extraordinary exhibition in the Strand is dated 1725:—

"Removed from Stocks Market, to the Hole in the Wall in the Butcher Row, near St. Clement's Church, in the Strand, is to be seen a miracle in Nature, being a woman that has a Horn growing on the back Part of her Head, full ten Inches long, curled and twisted very beautifully, resembling a Sheep's Horn, and grows out of a Bunch like a Wen; she has likewise several of the like Bunches on her Head, which is thought will produce the like Horns. She has been viewed by Sir Hans Sloane and the Royal Society, who allow her to be the greatest Rarity they ever saw.

Also the greatest Piece of Art that ever the World produc'd, being a Spring Musical Clock; or, a curious Piece of Machinery, that performs an extraordinary Entertainment of Musick upon Variety of Instruments; and what is still more wonderful, this curious Piece of Work gives an Entertainment of an Aviary of Birds, where the Notes of the most choice Song Birds are so well imitated, that Life itself hardly exceeds it, the like never expos'd to publick View before. To be seen every Day from nine in the Morning, till nine at Night, without loss of Time. N.B. The Clock is to be sold."

The following is a copy of an advertisement in *Daily Advertiser*, July 5, 1770:—

"ENTERTAINMENT IN THE STRAND.—The Sieur *Boaz*, this and every evening at half an hour after seven o'clock, in the great room, at the *Ship and Dolphin Tavern*, ten doors *without Temple Bar*, will exhibit the many wonderful operations, as shown by the late Sieur Comus, and which so long gained the attention of the public in this metropolis; to which he will add many curious and uncommon magical deceptions, entirely the product of his own invention, and never attempted by any but himself. His amusements are chiefly calculated for the genius of the British nation, being more apt to improve the mind than affect the senses, and are of so singular a nature as to be past all human conception. Admittance in the front seats 2s. each person; back seats 1s., though a price quite inferior to such extraordinary performances."

ESSEX BUILDINGS.* "On Thursday next the 22nd of this instant, November, at the Musick school in Essex Buildings; over against St. Clements Church in the Strand, will be continued a Concert of Vocal and Instrumental Musick, beginning at five of the clock every evening. Composed by Mr. Banister.—*London Gazette, Nov.* 18, 1678."

---

* This famous "Musick Room" was afterwards Paterson's auction room."—*Pennant.* It is now known as Essex Street Chapel. (See page 19.)

PAGEANT IN THE STRAND, 1603.—"The Citie of Westminster and Dutchey of Lancster perceiving what a preparation their Neighbor Citie made to entertain her Soveraigne though in greatness they could not match her in greatness of Love and ductie, they gave testimonie, that both were equall. And in token they were so, hands and hearts went together; and in the *Strand* erected up a Monument of their affection. The Invention was a Rayne bow, the Moone, Sunne and Seaven Statres called the *Pleiades* being advanced betweene two *pyramides, Electra* (one of those seven hanging in the aire, in figure of a comet) was the Speaker, her wordes carrying this effect, that as his Majestic had left the Citie of London, happy by delivering it fro' the Noyse of tumult so he would crowne this place with the like joye ; which being done, shee reckons up a number of blessings that will follow vpon it. The worke of this [pageant] was thought upon, begun and made perfect in xij daies."—From '*The Magnificent Entertainment given to King James, Queene Anne his Wife, and Henry Frederick the Prince, upon the day of his Majesties Tryumphant passage (from the Tower) through his honorable Citie (and chamber of London) being the* 15 *of March* 1603,' *&c.* By Thomas Dekker, 4to, 1664.

NOTEWORTHY THINGS ABOUT THE STRAND.

THE STRAND FISHMONGERS.—"For divers yeares of late, certain fishmongers have erected and set up fish-stalls in the middle of the street in the Strand, almost over against Denmark House, all of which were broken down by special commission, this moneth of May, 1630, least in short space they might grow from stalls to shedds and then to dwelling houses, as the like was in former time in Olde Fish Street and in St. Nicholas Shambles and in other places."—*Howe's ed*, 1631, p. 1045. Mark Lemon tells us :—On our right stood, until very lately, the last of the bulk of shops of the Strand, and forming part of Butcher's Row (see page 116). In this house had resided generations of fishmongers, the last being Crockford—or Old Crockey—the notorious gambling-house keeper. We were told by one who knew him that it was his custom to risk the loss only of a certain sum ; when that was gone, he would leave the table and go home. If he won a certain amount, he would retire from the play, go home, drop his winnings down his own area, and then return to see what more Fortune had in store for him. When he became rich, he would not allow the old shop to be altered, possibly that it might remind him of the days of his innocency, when he sold other fish than "flat" fish. He established a gambling club in St. James's Street, which was shut up at his death, which took place in 1844, and is now the Naval and Military Club. In Dr. Reinhold Pauli's "Pictures of Old England," translated by E. C. Otte, we find that fish at one time was very generally used among the Londoners, owing to the many fast days, and in consequence of the intrinsic goodness and cheapness both of sea and fresh-water fish. The Stocks Market,* which stood nearly upon the ground occupied in the present day by the Mansion House, and where, on definite days, a market was held alternately for the sale of meat and fish, formed, as it were, the central point for this important article of diet.

HALF MOON PASSAGE, nearly opposite Surrey Street, leads into Holywell Street (see pages 112, 121, 174). The Half Moon which is suspended over a tobacconist's shop, at the corner of the passage in this street, was formerly the sign of a tradesman, who was staymaker to George III. (See page 175.) This passage was originally part of a great thoroughfare, for in olden days it continued across Holywell Street, and skirting New Inn, terminated at Great Wild Street. Many years ago a house situated on the north side of Holywell street, near this passage, was in the occupation of a diamond merchant. A thief walked into the shop one day, requesting to be shewn some diamonds, and whilst apparently examining them, he suddenly threw a handful of snuff into the face and eyes of the merchant, and was enabled to get clear off with a large number. The present occupier of these premises tells us that he has the deeds relating to this house in his possession, dated as far back as Queen Mary. The house is still in a very sound condition. Chambers described this street as a good and almost unique specimen of those which once were the usual style of London; it has a few lofty, gabled, and bayed dwellings, but nothing to remind us of Fitzstephen's

---

* So-called from the stocks that stood there.

account of it. Messrs. George and Henry Vickers, the well-known news agents and publishers, carried on business in this street for a great number of years.

In the Strand, between Arundel and Norfolk Streets, in the year 1698, lived Sir Thomas Lyttleton, Speaker of the House of Commons, and father of Pope's friend, the author of the "History of Henry the Second," a ponderous and pompous work. Next door to him lived the father of Bishop Burnet, a remarkable person, born at Edinburgh, in 1643. A bookseller of the same name, a collateral descendant of the fussy bishop, whom Swift hated cordially, afterwards occupied the house.

PILLORY IN THE STRAND.—Even so late as the year 1721, we read:—

"At the sessions, which ended March 24th, William Saunders, an attorney-at-law, being convicted of forging an affidavit, was fined £40, to stand in the pillory without Temple Bar, and suffer twelve months' imprisonment."

NORFOLK STREET.—In this street, John Hamilton Mortimer, the painter, one of the choicest spirits of the day, a pupil of Hudson, the portrait painter, lived and died. He was the delight of all his friends, and had he but the perseverance of Sir Joshua Reynolds (a fellow pupil with him at Hudson's) he would have been as equally great. He, however, was too careless of his constitution, and departed this life before he was forty years of age, on the 4th of February, 1779. "Supper at Mortimer's," forms the subject of a chapter in those chatty volumes called "Wine and Walnuts," published in 1823. On the 19th March, 1724, the royal assent was given to "An Act to enable Thomas, Duke of Norfolk, to make leases for 60 years of the houses and ground in Arundel Street, Norfolk Street, Howard Street, Surrey Street, and other his tenements and estate in the parish of St. Clement Danes, in the county of Middlesex." (See pages 182 to 186.)

An account of a singular marriage which took place in St. Clement Danes Church, appeared in a paper called *Lloyd's Gazette* in 1720. It seems that a gentleman, determined upon marrying a certain young lady, declared that he would have her divested of all worldly possessions, and bare of everything. The consequence was, that on the morning of the marriage, the bridegroom waited in the porch of the church and was there joined by the bride, who was in a house adjacent, in almost a state of nudity. Thus was the marriage solemnized.

John Weale, of Cornwall, who lost both his eyes in an engagement in the Straights, taught fencing at the Angel Inn, back side of St. Clement's, was commanded, August 17th, 1670, to give lessons before his Majesty at Whitehall, which was done to his great admiration.

The following advertisement appeared in a journal in 1664 :—

"At the 'Angel and Sun' in the Strand, near Strand Bridge, is to be sold, every day, fresh Epsum Water, Barnet Water, Epsum Ale and Spruce Beer."

Neele, the poet and lawyer, was born in the Strand, 1798, died by his own hands, 1828. Liston resided at 147. C. Mathews, born 1776, dwelt at No. 18. Howard Payne wrote "Brutus" and "Charles the Second" in the third-floor back of No. 227; R. Brough wrote "Medea" in the same room. Nat Gee was born here, 1655. Wrench died here in 1843.

SHIRE LANE.*
(See also pages 104 to 107, and 214 to 218.)

The "Trumpet" Tavern, in this lane, an ancient hostelry now doomed to destruction to make way for the centralised Law Courts, claims especial recognition to itself in this work from its immortal and classic associations. There are few places in this "world of London" that can claim a greater or an equal degree of veneration and respect. It is situated on the left hand, midway, going up Shire Lane (called since July, 1845, Serle's Place) from Fleet Street, close by Temple Bar, to Carey Street, and could be approached from the Strand by a back entrance from Ship Yard. At the time of writing, the house still stands, but the approaches are stopped up, and in course of demolition.

Shire Lane must have been scarcely habitable during the "weeks of burning" of the Great Fire of London in 1666; the devastating element approached within a stone's throw, and the smoke and heat from acres and acres of burning ruins must have been intense. But the historians and chroniclers of London have given us a picture of the place anterior to the date named above by 140 years, and thousands living in the town *to-day* can testify in a presumptive sense to the

accuracy of Stowe's and of Styrpe's description. Here it is, and very like:—
" Then hard by the Bar is another lane, called Shire Lane, because it divides the City from the Shire ;" " the upper part hath good old buildings but the lower part is narrow and more ordinary." Though it is only 150 or 160 years ago since Steele was in his prime, the world has moved with wonderful rapidity since then, and it is not easy, without taking some trouble to gather sufficient information, to be able to throw ourselves back into times with which we have so little in common. A modern writer (Leigh Hunt,) who as much as any man of our day, has illumined the fog and smoke of London with a genial halo of glory, and peopled the streets and buildings with the life of past generations, expressed a hope that Shire Lane, however altered and improved, might have no change of name "For here," says he, "is described as residing old Isaac Bickerstaff, the more venerable but not the more delightful double of Richard Steele, the founder of English periodical literature. The public-house called the "Trumpet," now known as the "Duke of York," at which the "Tatler" met his club, is still remaining. At his house in this lane he dates a great number of his papers and received many interesting visitors ; and here it was that he led down into Fleet Street that immortal deputation of "twaddlers" from the country, who hardly seem to have settled their question of precedence to this hour. The name was changed, however, as before-mentioned, but no alteration of the street or improvement was consequent upon it ; the numbering of the houses even was not rectified, and in this respect they were, in the lower part, in inextricable confusion. The name of the street was differently spelt at one end to what it was at the other, and the original line of demarcation of Serle's Place, and Lower Serle's Place, had become lost until accidentally discovered by the removal of coats of colouring in 1865 from the front of the "Trumpet," but the original old name of Shire Lane was more generally received and known to the last even by those living there than by the other.

In appearance the "Trumpet" was unpretentious, substantially built of red brick. In front, the first and second floors had each a row of four equal and well sized windows, with thick heavy oak sashes, and the third or attic floor was lighted by two dormer windows within and rising above the parapet. With the exception of the ground floor, or shop front, but little alteration had ever evidently been made. There is a curious old woodcut of the house extant, in which the above description closely tallies, and which shows the sign of the trumpet above the facia line, and below and between the window sills of the first floor ; higher up in the centre of the pier between the windows is the figure of Bacchus astride a barrel, and to the next pier between the windows southward is fixed the lamp-iron and inverted bell-shaped lamp of the fashion anterior to the discovery of gas. The ground floor shows the door to have been at the end adjoining the south party-wall, and three windows in unison with those above, but supplied outside with flap shutters with pierced holes. The cellar-flap is shown, but is in a different place to the one now existing: the truth of the print is borne out, however, by very patent evidence, which shows it to have been bricked up and a wider and larger one made in another place; the arches of the three windows are covered by the modern facia-board.

Steele's frequent mention of it and of Sheer Lane* would alone have rendered it famous, and indeed it must be admitted that his quaint and exquisitely humourous paper No. 132 *Tatler*, wherein he says—"The truth of it is, I should think myself unjust to posterity as well as to the Society at the *Trumpet*, of which I am a member, did I not in some part of my writings give an account of the persons among whom I have passed almost a sixth part of my time for these last forty years,"—give to the popular mind at least some elements of interest. To point out the further definitive literary associations of this home of the Muses in connection with Bickerstaff and his coadjutors who brought their powers of wit and humour and reason to bear so successfully on the entertainment, instruction, and improvement of their age, and which have been of incalculable benefit in moulding the taste, and imparting a tone to the mind of successive generations, one of the most exquisite and beautiful allegories in the language is in the first *Tatler*, dated from Sheer Lane;—it is a Vision of Justice, and forms the first of a series Steele calls his "Court of Judicature."† There is another and longer series in the same work more intimately woven into memories of the place and time now discoursed, which he calls "The Court of Honour."‡

But the true, immortal, and classic association which binds together the names of Steele and his compeers with Shire Lane and the "Trumpet," an immortality as great as that enjoyed by the "Boar's Head," the "Mermaid," or the "Mitre," remains yet to be recorded.

The "Trumpet" was the natal spot—the first meeting place of the most illustrious tavern club that ever existed, the renowned Kit-Kat—

"I sing the assembly's rise, increase, and fame,
That condescends to honour *Kit-Kat's* name;
Whose pride like thine, O Rome, from small beginnning's came!"‡

At the "Trumpet" in Shire Lane, in 1688, if not earlier, met a small coterie of men of some influence, to concert measures having reference to the times in general, and to the trial of the seven bishops in particular. These, however, formed the Society, out of which the most illustrious and noble "Order of the Toast," or Kit-Kat Club first grew. The "Knights of the Toast" introduced a custom of drinking ladies' healths, which custom, in a broader sense, with more or less variation of fashion, has extended and come down to our days, and is little likely to become obsolete. Malone (in his edition of Dryden's Prose Works,)

---

* Steele, although an excellent scholar, fell in with the common carelessness of his day in this instance, and accepted a phonetic spelling.
† See *Tatler*, Nos. 100, 102, 103, 107, 110, 113, 116, &c.
‡ See *Tatler*, Nos. 250, 253, 256, 259, 262, 265, &c.

says—"The word *toast* so applied, is not to be found in any dictionary printed before the Restoration." In the same work, in a *note* he further gives an ingenious and highly laudatory encomium of this Society: it is addressed by Elkanah Settle, "To the most renowned the President [probably, either Lord Dorset or Mr. Montague] and the rest of the Knights of the most noble "Order of the Toast," and appears to have been written in 1699—

> "Why should the noble Windsor Garters boast
> Their fame, above the Knighthood of the Toast?
> Is't on their first original they build?
> Their high prized knighthood these to you must yield.
> A lady dropped a garter at a ball;
> A toy for their foundation—was that all?
> Suppose the nymph that lost it was divine;
> The garter's but a relic from the shrine;
> The toast includes the deity—not one star,
> But the whole constellation of the fair."

This custom of drinking toasts is referred to by the *Tatler* thus:—"Though this Institution had so trivial a beginning, it is now elevated into a formal order, and that happy virgin, who is received and drank to at their meetings, has no more to do in this life but to judge and accept of the first good offer. The manner of her inauguration is much like that of the choice of a Doge of Venice—it is performed by ballot, and when she is so chosen, she reigns indisputably for that ensuing year, but must be elected anew to prolong her reign a minute beyond it. When she is regularly chosen her name is written with a diamond on one of the drinking glasses."

Epigrams (forty-two in number) written by most of the literary members are preserved, including those by Lords Lansdowne, Dorset, Wharton, Carbury, and Halifax; Addison, Congreve, Maynwaring, and Sir Samuel Garth.

Upon Addison's return to England in the latter part of the year 1703, or early in 1704, he was admitted into the Kit-Kat, and found his friend Steele already established therein. It appears likely that Steele proposed Addison for admission, if we may judge at all by the special mention of the honour with which they were both received at the "Trumpet."

Addison makes an allusion to the society by its early and true name in a letter to his friend Abraham Stanyan in February, 1699, and Steele mentions in a letter to his wife his attendance at one of its meetings in March, 1717, the Duke of Newcastle being in the chair on that occasion. The club is supposed to have existed for some years after that, but having accomplished the object it had in view, it gradually died away, most probably losing its cohesion on the death of its secretary, Jacob Tonson.

The bibliography of the Kit-Kat, its members, and their protogees would form an interesting article, but our space prevents its being entered upon. Suffice to say, the facetious Tom D'Urfey wrote a comic opera entitled, *The Wonders in the*

Sun; or, the Kingdom of the Birds, and dedicated it to the club; many of the most distinguished wits of that celebrated body having assisted their old favourite in writing the songs in it. Nearly all the members of the club whose names have come down to us contributed in a greater or lesser degree to the fields of literature, and indeed many of those beauties the "toasts" of the club also contributed their quota.

The curious *sobriquet* of Kit-Kat was derived from the host, Mr. Christopher Katt, who appears to have been quite competent to the task of catering successfully and to the satisfaction of his distinguished customers. His pies (somebody has wrote them down *mutton pies*, and everybody goes on quoting *mutton* pies eternally) acquired a notoriety and a name, and found their way into the plays and poems of the period; and, we may suppose, into everybody's mouth, at least into all who could afford to pay for them, the same as a Watling or a Melton Mowbray of our day. The Kit-Kat Club was something far beyond a mere coterie of wits, men of rank, followers and patrons of the arts; they were all thorough lovers of liberty, sticklers for the very letter of the Revolution Settlement, and when the time came, staunch supporters of the Hanoverian succession. Walpole styled them the Patriots that really saved Britain; ostensibly, however, their aim was to promote conviviality and advance the interests of literature and the arts. In 1709 the members subscribed four hundred guineas for the encouragement of good comedies; the subscription paper was all in the handwriting of no less a person than Lord Halifax.

Mr. Katt afterwards took the "Fountain," in the Strand, and the Club moved thither. We can understand the principal noblemen and gentlemen who had been instrumental in bringing about the Revolution, and who afterwards watched over the interests of the Protestant succession in the House of Hanover, growing more easy as their work became consolidated, and, having a taste for conviviality, making summer excursions to the "Upper Flask," on Hampstead Heath, a gay resort, with its races, raffles, and private marriages. Jacob Tonson, the eminent bookseller, being secretary to the Club, came in for a large share of vituperation from the opposite Tory party. In a poem by William Shippen, entitled "Faction Displayed," some very rancourous and bitter invectives find a place; and in another by John Lacy, Esq., with about as fulsome a dedication to R—— G——, and otherwise as egotistic a production as it is likely can be found in printed English, entitled "The Steelids; or the Tryal of Wit," a poem in three cantos, 1714. It supplies however a reading at once intelligible, that might not otherwise have been so to any but an ingenious reader of Blackmore's "*Kit-Cat;*" it is this—"*Bocai* is no more Hebrew than Jacob;" in other words Tonson is referred to throughout the poem by spelling his

---

* The "Kit-Cat," a poem by Sir Richard Blackmore, Knt., 1708, but written some years before.

christian name backwards. The Duke of Somerset is said to have first presented Tonson with his portrait in his capacity of secretary, and this was formed into a precedent for all the members; the portraits were executed by Kneller, on canvas, somewhat larger than a quarter and less than a half length; a size that has ever since been denominated a Kit-Kat as a term of art. The room where these portraits were originally intended to be hung (in which the Club often dined) not being sufficiently lofty for half-length portraits, is said to have been the occasion of a shorter canvas being used, but sufficiently long to admit a hand, the exact dimension being thirty-six inches by twenty-eight. Tonson had a residence at Barnes Elms, where he built a magnificent gallery for the reception of the Club portraits, and where he used to entertain the members. Engravings of the portraits, by Faber, were published by Tonson, in 1735. The volume was dedicated to the Duke of Somerset, "to whose liberality the collection of prints owed its very being, in setting the example to the other members of the Kit-Kat by honoring Mr. Tonson with these portraits, and who was ever eminently distinguished for that noble principle for the support of which that association was known to have been formed—the love of their country and its constitutional liberties." It appears from the will of the younger Jacob Tonson, the nephew of the first, which was proved in December, 1735, that he was then, by the grant and assignment of his uncle, entitled to this collection after his uncle's death, and that the testator had not long before erected a new room at Barnes Elms in which the Kit-Kat portraits were then hung. The third bookseller of the same name afterwards inherited them from him, afterwards passing to his brother Richard Tonson, sometime M.P. for Windsor, and who resided at Water Oakley, where he built a room lighted by a dome, and an ante-chamber for the reception of them. On the death of Richard Tonson, the portraits became the property of William Baker, Esq., of Hertingfordbury, near Hertford, and one of the Members of Parliament for the county. He was the son of Sir William Baker, Alderman of Bassishaw Ward, husband of the second daughter of the second Jacob Tonson, and brother-in-law of the third Jacob and of Richard Tonson. They remain at Hertingfordbury in the possession of the Baker family, by the present representative of which several of them were forwarded to the Fine Arts Exhibition at Manchester in 1857, and to the National Portraits Exhibition at South Kensington in 1866-7.

The following is a complete list of the known members of the Club:—Sir Godfrey Kneller; Charles Seymour, Duke of Somerset; Charles Lennox, Duke of Richmond; Charles Fitzroy, Duke of Grafton; William Cavendish, Duke of Devonshire; John Churchill, Duke of Marlborough; John Montague, Duke of Montague; Eveleyn Pierpoint, Duke of Kingston; Thomas Holles Pelham, Duke of Newcastle; Henry Clinton, Earl of Lincoln; Charles Montague, Duke of Manchester; Lionel Cranfield Sackville, Duke of Dorset; Thomas Wharton, Marquis of Wharton; Theophilus Hastings, Earl of Huntingdon; Charles Sackville, Earl of Dorset; Algernon Capel, Earl of Essex; Charles Howard, Earl of Carlisle; Richard Boyle, Earl of Burlington; James Berkeley, Earl of Berkeley; Richard Lumley, Earl of Scarborough; Francis Godolphin, Earl of Godolphin; Charles Montague, Earl of Halifax; James Stanhope, Earl Stanhope; Spencer Compton, Earl of Wilmington; Richard Temple, Viscount Cobham; Charles, Lord Mohun; Richard Cornwallis, Lord Cornwallis; John Vaughan, Earl of Carbery; John Somers, Baron of Evesham; Richard Boyle, Viscount Shannon; Robert Walpole, Earl of Oxford; William Pulteney, Earl of Bath; Sir Joseph Addison; Sir Richard Steele; Sir John Vanburgh; Sir Samuel Garth; John Tidcomb; George Stepney; Abraham Stanyan; John Dormer; Edmund Dunch; William Walsh; William Congreve; Charles Dartequenave; Thomas Hopkins; Edward Hopkins; Arthur Maynwaring, and Jacob Tonson.

Matthew Prior had been a member of this club, but was expelled for his Toryism.

STRAND LANE,

WHICH faces Newcastle Street, is unquestionably of great antiquity. Stow mentions the locality as a lane or way passing under a bridge down to the landing place on the banks of the Thames, which was a landing pier for wherries, (see page 108) and called Strand-bridge.* Addison describes landing here on a summer morning, arriving with ten sail of apricot boats, after having touched at Nine Elms for melons consigned to Covent Garden. It is the site of the Inn of the Bishops of Llandaff. Here is one of the curiosities of St. Clement's parish—the old Roman Spring Bath: this curious specimen of ancient workmanship Timbs describes as "Roman; the walls being layers of brick and thin layers of stucco, and the pavement of similar brick covered with stucco and resting upon a mass of stucco and rubble; the bricks are nine inches and a half long, four inches and a half broad, and one inch and three-quarters thick, and resemble the bricks in the City wall. The property can be

---

* Strand-bridge was at one time a common name for the beautiful bridge, by Rennie, now universally known as Waterloo Bridge. It was previously applied to a small landing-pier at the foot of Strand Lane.—*Cunningham.*

Then had ye in the High Street a fair bridge called Strand Bridge, and under it a lane or way down to the landing place on the bank of the Thames.—*Stow*, p. 165.

Strand Lane, in the Strand near Somerset House, led in the olden time to Strand-bridge (or pier) in the same way that Ivy Lane in the Strand led to Ivy-bridge or pier.—*Cunningham.*

traced to the Danvers (or D'Anvers) family, of Swithland Hall, Leicestershire, whose mansion stood upon the spot."[*] A much more elaborate description is given by Saunders,[†] who having surveyed the bath tells us it is "about thirteen feet long, six broad, and four feet six inches deep. The spring is said to be connected with the neighbouring Holy-well which gives name to Holywell Street, and their respective position makes the statement probable . . . . At the farther end of the Bath is a small projecting strip or ledge of white marble, and beneath it a hollow in the wall standing towards one corner; these are the undoubted remains of a flight of steps leading down into the water. Immediately opposite the steps, we learn from the authority of a gentleman who is connected with the management of the estate, was a door which communicated with a vaulted passage still existing below, and towards the back of, three houses in Surrey Street, and continuing from thence upwards in the direction of the Strand. These vaults have some remarkable features; among others there is a low arch of a very peculiar form, the rounded top projecting gradually forwards beyond the line of its sides in the house immediately behind the bath . . . . . . Although the existence of the bath was evidently unknown to Stow, Maitland, Pennant, and Malcolm, or the later historians of London, from the absence of any mention of it in their pages, yet, from time immemorial in the neighbourhood, the fact of its being a Roman bath has been received with implicit credence; and, lastly, that a kind of dim tradition seems to exist, that it had been closed up for some long period, and then re-discovered . . . . . The proprietors, we are happy to say, rightly estimate its value, and have long ago caused another bath to be built and supplied from it; and it is in the latter alone that persons are allowed to bathe." Now, although our London historians have not mentioned this interesting remnant of the Romans' occupation of Britain; yet, Pinkerton[‡] tells us—"In the cellar of a house in Norfolk Street, in the Strand, is a fine antique bath, formerly belonging to

---

[*] "Curiosities of London," p. 651.   [†] "Knight's London," vol. II, p. 165.
[‡] "Essay on Medals, 1719," vol. I, p. 10.

this Earl of Arundel, whose house and gardens were adjacent. It is a pity it is not more known and taken care of." Here, then, surely, is some evidence of the existence of an "Antique Bath" hereabouts, a century and a-half ago; whether the same one is meant is another thing, though Dr. Rimbault* has no doubt about it. We cannot close this brief description of such an interesting specimen of antiquity, without expressing our regret at the loss sustained a short time since, through the death of its old proprietor. We read in the Obituary:—"On the 22nd January, 1868, died at Albert Street, Stevenage, Herts, Charles Scott, Esq., twenty-eight years proprietor of the old Roman bath, Strand Lane, opposite Newcastle Street, Strand."

SURREY STREET

Is one that rose on the site of Arundel House and gardens. Styrpe describes this street as replenished with good buildings, especially Nevison Fox's Esq.; also that occupied by the Honorable Charles Howard, Esq., the eminent chemist who discovered the sugar refining process, brother to Henry, Duke of Norfolk. William Congreve, the dramatist, was living in this street when visited by Voltaire; he died January 29th, 1728-9. In 1736 died here George Sale, the translator of the "Koran." Sale published his "Koran" in 1734, and in the year of his death joined Paul Whitehead, Dr. Birch, and Mr. Strutt, in founding a society for the encouragement of learning. He wrote for the "Universal History."

VERE STREET

Is the second turning on the right hand side of Clare Market. Sir Thomas Lyttleton lived in this street, 1688. Here stood Gibbons' Tennis Court, which was so called after Charles Gibbons' its owner or keeper, who died 1668. It was converted into a theatre† by

---

* "Notes and Queries," 3rd Ser., II, 519.
† "Before the erection of established theatres, and long afterwards, plays were also acted in the yards of certain inns, such as the Belle Sauvage, on Ludgate Hill; the Cross Keys, in Gracechurch Street; and the Bull, in Bishopsgate Street. With respect to the regular theatres, we are not intimately acquainted with the details of its structure, but the interior economy appears to have resembled that of the old inn yards, and it was evidently provided with different accommodations

Killigrew (see page 78) and opened by the King's company on Thursday, 8th November, 1660, with the play of King Henry IV.* " The scattered remnant of several of the playhouses upon King Charles's Restoration formed a company, who acted again at the (Red) Bull (in St. John's Street), and built them a new house in Gibbons' Tennis Court in Clare Market, in which two places they

to suit different classes of visitors. There were tiers of galleries or scaffolds, and small rooms beneath, answering to the modern boxes. There was the pit, as it was called in the private theatres, or yard as it was named at the public ones. In the former, spectators were provided with seats ; in the latter, they were obliged to stand throughout the performance. The critics, wits, and gallants, were allowed stools upon the stage, for which the price was sixpence or a shilling each, according to the eligibility of the situation, and they were attended by pages, who supplied them with pipes and tobacco ; smoking, drinking ale, playing cards, and eating nuts and apples, always forming a portion of the entertainment at our early theatres. The stage appliances were extremely simple. At the back of the stage there was a permanent balcony, about eight feet from the platform, in which scenes supposed to take place on towers or upper chambers were represented. Suspended in front of it were curtains, and these were opened or closed as the performance required. The sides and back of the stage, with the exception of that part occupied by the balcony, were hung with arras tapestry, and sometimes pictures, and the internal roof with blue drapery, except on the performance of tragedy, when the sides, back, and roof of the stage were covered with black. The stage was commonly strewed with rushes, though on particular occasions it was matted over. The performance commenced at three o'clock in the public theatres, the signal for beginning being the third sounding or flourish of trumpets. It was customary for the actor who spoke the prologue to be dressed in a long velvet cloak. In the early part of Shakespeare's theatrical career the want of scenery appears to have been supplied by the primative expedient of hanging out a board, on which was written the place where the action was to be understood as taking place. Sometimes, when a change of scene was requisite, the audience were left to imagine that the actors, who still remained on the stage, had removed to the spot mentioned. During the performance, the clown would frequently indulge in extemporaneous buffoonery. There was always music between the acts, and sometimes singing and dancing. And at the end of the play, after a prayer for the reigning monarch, offered by the actors on their knees, the clown would entertain the audience by descanting on any theme which the spectators might supply, or by performing what was called a jig, a farcical doggrel improvisation, accompanied by dancing and singing.—*Howard Staunton's Life of Shakespeare*. Prefixed to his edition of "The Plays of Shakespeare."

"At the inferior playhouses the admission was as low as a penny for "the groundlings" who stood in the roofless pit, which still retained the name of "the yard"—evidently from the old custom of playing in the yards of inns. In the higher theatres a "room " or box, varied from sixpence to two shillings and sixpence. They played in daylight, and rose from their dinner to the playhouse. It was one of the City regulations, that " no playing be in the dark, so that the auditory may return home before sunset."—*Disraeli's Amenities of Literature.*

* The following are the names of the principal actors in Gibbons' Tennis Court, and in the order in which they were rated in the poor books of St. Clement Danes for 1663, and in the rank in which they were no doubt held, either for their shares or standing in the company :— Theophilus Bird, Michael Mohun, Charles Hart, Robert Shatterel, William Cartwright, William Mutershall, Nicholas Burt, Walter Clun, John Allington, John Lacy.

continued acting all 1660, 1661, 1622, and part of 1663." In his
"Diary," Pepys says:—"November 20th, 1660.—To the new
playhouse near Lincoln's Inn Fields (which was formerly Gibbons'
Tennis Court) where the play of 'Beggar's Bush' was newly begun,
and so we went in and saw it well acted; and here I saw the first
time one Moone (Mohun) who is said to be the best actor in the
world, lately come over with the King, and indeed it is the finest
playhouse, I believe, that ever was in England." Again, "January 3,
1660.—To the theatre (in Gibbons' Tennis Court) where was
acted 'Beggar's Bush,' it being very well done; and here the first
time that I ever saw women come upon the stage."—"Engag'd! No; faith let's make a match at tennis to-day. I was
invited to dine by two or three lords, but if you will let me have pen,
ink, and paper, I'll send my despatches and disengage myself. How
will that gentleman and you play with Stanmore, and I keep his back
hand at Gibbon's?"—*A True Widow*, by T. Shadwell, 4to, 1679.
At the theatre in this street, Pepys says, was an actress, whose
name is not ascertained, but who attained an unfortunate celebrity
in the part of Roxana in the "Siege of Rhodes." She was seduced
by Aubery de Vere, the last Earl of Oxford of that name, under the
guise of a private marriage—a species of villany which has made a great
figure in works of fiction up to a late period. The story is "got up"
in detail by Madame Dunnois, in her "History of the Court of
Charles II.; but it is told with more brevity in Grammont; and
the latter, though apocryphal enough, pretends to say nothing on the
subject in which he is not borne out by other writers.

> "The Earl of Oxford," says one of his heroines, "fell in love with a
> handsome, graceful actress, belonging to the Duke's Theatre, who performed
> to perfection, particularly the part of Roxana in a very fashionable new play;
> insomuch that she ever after retained that name. This creature being both
> very virtuous and very modest, or, if you please, wonderfully obstinate,
> proudly rejected the presents and addresses of the Earl of Oxford. The
> resistance inflamed his passion; he had recourse to invectives and even spells;
> but all in vain. This disappointment had such an effect upon him that he
> could neither eat nor drink; this did not signify to him, but his passion at

length became so violent that he could neither play nor smoke. In this extremity Love had recourse to Hymen; the Earl of Oxford, one of the first peers of the realm, is, you know, a very handsome man; he is of the Order of the Garter, which greatly adds to an air naturally noble. In short, from his outward appearance, you would suppose he was really possessed of some sense; but as soon as ever you hear him speak, you are perfectly convinced to the contrary. This passionate lover presented her with a promise of marriage, in due form, signed with his own hand; she would not, however, rely upon this; but the next day she thought there could be no danger, when the Earl himself came to her lodgings attended by a clergyman, and another man for a witness; the marriage was accordingly solemnized with all due ceremonies, in the presence of one of her fellow-players, who attended as a witness on her part. You will suppose, perhaps, that the new countess had nothing to do but to appear at court according to her rank, and to display the Earl's arms upon her carriage. This was far from being the case. When examination was made concerning the marriage, it was found to be a mere deception: it appeared that the pretended priest was one of my lord's trumpeters, and the witness his kettle-drummer. The parson and his companion never appeared after the ceremony was over; and as for the other witness, he endeavoured to persuade her that the Sultana Roxana might have supposed, in some part or other of a play, that she was really married. It was all to no purpose that the poor creature claimed the protection of the laws of God and man, both which were violated and abused, as well as herself, by this infamous imposition: in vain did she throw herself at the King's feet to demand justice; she had only to rise up again without redress; and happy might she think herself to receive an annuity of one thousand crowns, and to resume the name of Roxana, instead of Countess of Oxford."

Ogilby drew a lottery of books at the theatre in this street. He described the books in his advertisement as "all of his own designment and composure." Bear Yard is probably what was called Rein Deer Yard, and Gibbons' Bowling Alley, at the coming out of Lincoln's Inn Fields, towards Portugal Street.

The Gordon Riots, 1780.—"At the close of the evening June 5th, a large party assembled before the house of Mr. Rainsforth, a tallow chandler, near Clare Market, who had fallen under their displeasure, for giving evidence against some of the rioters on their examination before Sir John Fielding. After demolishing the windows, they entered the house, the inside of which they destroyed, and then brought out the fat and candles with whatever else was combustible, into the street, where they set them on fire, floating the kennels with particles of the melted tallow. On the first account of their being assembled, some soldiers, both horse and foot, attended; but neither in sufficient number, nor were they seemingly much disposed to impede the proceedings of the mob. Thirty boxes of candles, besides fat and tallow, were destroyed on this occasion."—*London Magazine*, 1780.

CLARE MARKET RAGGED SCHOOLS (6, Denzell Street, Vere Street, formerly of the Colonnade, Clare Market), were established in 1847, for the purpose of giving a free education to the children of the destitute poor. The influence and work of the schools have been largely extended since their establishment, and the operations now include Day, Night, and Sunday Schools; Mother's Meetings, Lending Library, Penny Bank, Clothing Fund, Children's Dinners, Relief Society, and Penny Readings during the winter months. The schools are wholly unendowed, and dependent for support upon voluntary subscriptions. Mr. John Palmer is the Honorary Secretary. On May 24th there was an interesting meeting of old scholars connected with this institution, about 4,000 having passed through since its establishment, chiefly through the instrumentality of Miss Turnery, twenty years ago. Mr. Ingham, Q.C., M.P, addressed the old scholars after tea, stating that he remembered many of their faces in years gone by, and was glad to hear that they were all occupying respectable positions in life. Mr. Stilwell, then, on the part of the old scholars, presented a handsome timepiece to Mr. J. Palmer, the director of the schools.

WELLINGTON STREET.

IN this street is situated the Lyceum Theatre (see pages 71, 72). In March, 1846, "Tom Thumb," the king of modern dwarfs, made one of his earliest appearances on a London stage at this theatre.* At this theatre has been held for many years a Beef-

---

* A very interesting account of the "little man" is to be found in Mr. Wood's work on giants and dwarfs, published by Bentley.

steak Club. From "Chetwood's History of the Stage," p. 141, it appears that a club bearing this designation was first established in the reign of Queen Anne (before 1709). The *Spectator* also mentions them in 1710-11. There were several clubs or societies bearing this title. It seems to have been an old custom at theatres to have a Beefsteak Club that met every Saturday, and to which authors and wits were invited. One met at a house in Ivy Lane, afterwards occupied by a bookseller as a warehouse. Smollett, Johnson, and many of their friends were members of it, as was the absent and eccentric Rev. G. Harvest. In 1735 a Beefsteak Society was founded by John Rich, the great harlequin and manager of Covent Garden Theatre, and George Lambert, the scene painter. This club was held for many years at Covent Garden Theatre, and afterwards for a considerable time at the "Shakspeare Tavern," and at the "Bedford." Mr. Sheridan, when manager of a theatre at Dublin, in 1749, founded a club of this kind, which was joined by fifty or sixty members, chiefly noblemen and members of Parliament, and no performer was admitted but witty Peg Woffington, who wore a man's dress and was president for a whole season.* It was customary at these Clubs not to partake of any dish but beefsteaks. Their provider was their president, and wore their badge, which was a small gold gridiron, hung round the neck by a green silk riband†. A Beefsteak Club is still in existence. A number of noblemen and gentlemen, each of whom may bring a friend, partake of a five o'clock dinner of steaks in a room of their own behind the scenes of the Lyceum Theatre every Saturday from November till June. The room in which they dine is rendered emblematical of the nature of the feast by being decorated with gridirons. The original gridiron of the society (the survivor of two extensive fires) is rendered prominent by being placed in the centre of the ceiling. This club is doubtless the offspring of those established by Wilkes, and Rich, and Lambert. Dr. King says, in his "Art of Cookery, humbly inscribed to the Beefsteak Club," 1709 :—

---

* Ward's "Secret History of Clubs," ed. 1709.   † *Spectator*, No. 468.

> "He that of honour, wit, and mirth partakes
> May be a fit companion o'er beefsteaks:
> His name may be to future times enrolled
> In Estcourt's book, whose gridiron's framed of gold."

Among some of the illustrious names who belonged to these clubs may be mentioned the Prince of Wales, afterwards George IV., the Duke of Clarence, the Duke of Norfolk (who ate at least three steaks at each meeting), the Duke of Leinster, Lord Brougham, Sir John Hippisley, Lord Sandwich, Garrick, Wilkes, Churchill, John Kemble; "Captain" Morris (author of some pleasant songs), who was a celebrity at this club until his seventy-eighth year; Estcourt, many years president; Beard, the singer; and numerous noblemen, members of Parliament, authors, actors, wits, and a whole host of distinguished characters.

WYCH STREET,
(See page 113.)

LEADING from Pickett Street to Drury Lane. The houses on the south side of this ancient, yet narrow thoroughfare, call to our mind the reflection that the houses of Old London, however picturesque as street architecture now, must then have been extraordinarily inconvenient, although at one time tenanted by people of fashion and quality. This street preserves a part of its ancient designation, for it originally formed a portion of the "Via de Aldwych," which was the old name of the way or lane that extended from the north side of the Strand to Broad Street, Bloomsbury. By the side of No. 16, on the same side, is White Lion Passage, in which was the temporary chapel of the Baptist congregation meeting in Elm Place, Fetter Lane. In 1788, the Fetter Lane place of worship was destroyed by fire, and from that date till the erection of the new edifice in 1790 the worshippers met in the Wych Street "house," the pastor of which church, the Rev. A. Austin, presided over it from 1785 till the day of his death in July 1816. This passage is now known as White Lion Court, in which was the celebrated White Lion Inn, the rendezvous of the notorious Jack Sheppard. On the north side of this street is the entrance to New Inn, which leads into Clare Market. Pennant in his "London," 1805, says :—"New Inn, where the students of the Strand Inn nestled after they were routed from thence by the Duke of Somerset; and Clement's Inn, mentioned in the time of Edward IV. I must not omit that in New Inn the great Sir Thomas More had the early part of his education before he removed to Lincoln's Inn." (See page 129.) Immediately opposite New Inn is a portion of the unfinished buildings of the "Strand Hotel Company." This company secured the site of Lyon's Inn (see page 93), and other ground upon a lease of ninety-nine years (with power to purchase the freehold) subject to an annual payment of £7. 13s. 4d. to the Honorable Society of the Inner Temple for the Lyon's Inn portion, formerly the property of Timothy Tyrrell, Esq.* Some idea may be formed of the magnitude of this scheme by mentioning that the capital was to be £100,000. The hotel was to have contained nearly 300 rooms, and a grand hall 145 feet long, 67 feet wide, and 36 feet high; this hall would have exceeded any building of a similar character in London. The company by degrees erected some buildings and finished the shops in Holywell Street and Wych Street for letting, but were compelled to put the property up for sale on the 14th March, 1867: it, however, did not sell and remains unsold. The estate has a frontage of 68 feet in the Strand, 53 feet 5 inches in Newcastle Street, and 68 feet 10 inches in Holywell Street, being the southern portion, as divided by the last named street. The northern or principal portion has frontages of 191 feet 6 inches to Wych Street, 180 feet to Holywell Street, and 13 feet 2 inches in Newcastle Street. The estimated rental to be derived from the shop property was—Strand, £78. 4s.; Holywell Street, £700, and Wych Street, £600. (See pages 181-2.) It is now decided to build a theatre upon this site (by Mr. Sefton Parry) to be called the "Royal Globe Theatre," which will open some time in October, with a new five-act comedy, by Mr. Henry J. Byron, and a strong company, comprising many actors new to London. The house will be of the second or third size.

* See the Inns of Court Commissioners' Report, 1855, p. 824.

On the present site of the three houses known as New Inn Buildings, Wych Street, there stood, in 1775, a house and premises, which was then lately burnt down. The present three houses were in the year 1775 built by a Mr. Mapa for a sum of £500. At their meeting in New Inn Hall, on the grand day, 9th February, 1774, the Treasurer and antients ordered the following, among other gratuities, to be paid for services rendered in putting out the fire :—" Mr. Samuel Lyon, clerk to Mr. Lucas, one of the Members of this Inn, being very active and of great service in assisting to extinguish the fire that lately happened near this Inn, and thereby neglected his own property, which was either stole or lost ; we do therefore in consideration of his services and great loss, desire his acceptance of eight guineas from this Society, and direct Mr. Richard to pay him the same. William Wilson, the butler, having informed us he lost great part of his clothes at the late fire, we do, in consideration of his care and assistance there, direct Mr. Richards to pay him two guineas and a-half for his loss." The name of our great and glorious dramatist is adopted for the sign of a public-house which stands on the north side of this street, " The Shakspeare's Head," which was until lately managed by a lady, who was the fourth wife of Mr. Adams, the former worthy landlord. This lady recently died, as did also her third husband, and they were buried within a few days of each other.

OLD SIGNS AND TOKENS OF ST. CLEMENT DANES.
From " Beaufoy's London Trades' Tokens."

RICHARD CARTER—A bell, in the field.
Rev. IN BUTCHER ROW—In the field, R. I. C.

Storer's engraving of "Temple bar, from Butcher Row, 1796," presents the best graphic illustration of this vicinity, of which a portion of the inconvenient building, with projecting stories, are yet extant on the south side, at the east end of Wyche street.

AT THE SHIP. WITHOVT—A ship, in the field.
Rev. TEMPLE BAR. 1649—In the field, W. M. S.

The Ship inn near Temple bar, the site now denoted by Ship yard, is mentioned among other grants to Sir Christopher Hatton in 1571. The token bearing date 1649 is evidence that the inner tavern of that sign was then extant. Walpole, in his memoir of Faithorne based on

Vertue's notes (*Catalogue of Engravers*, Dallaway's edition, 1828, 8vo. p. 132), states, apparently in error, that about 1650 Faithorne returned to England, married, and set up in a new shop at the sign of the Ship next the Drake, opposite to the Palsgrave Head tavern, without Temple bar. The contrary appears; as after the affair at Basing house in October, 1645, where Sir Robert Peake the printseller, Faithorne, and other artists and players, as royalist soldiers, were taken prisoners by the Parliamentarian forces, Faithorne, by leave or otherwise, went to Paris; and there in his need sold to the Abbe de Marolles the stock he then possessed of proofs, many now unique, of his own engravings, the whole of which enrich the royal collection at Paris. The year of his return, as stated by Walpole, is too early. That he was in London in 1653, but not before, seems corroborated by the fact that the portrait of Noah Bridges, prefixed to his *Vulgar Arithmetic* published in that year, is certainly by Faithorne, but is wholly without his W. F., or other marks. The portrait of the physician, Dr. Robert Bayfield, with his name, is dated 1654, when possibly as a royalist he had ceased to be inimical to the Commonwealth authorities. That Faithorne adopted the sign of the Ship is nowhere indicated. On the title of his *Art of 'Graving and Etching* is stated, "Published by William Faithorne, and sold at his shop next to ye signe of the Drake, without Temple barr, 1662," sm. 8vo.

John Reynolds, a cook, issued a token, the device of a fox stealing a goose, in Ship yard, in 1666. "The Ship tavern, in the Butcher Row near Temple bar," is noticed in an advertisement so late as June, 1756.

  IOHN LAWTON WTH OVT—St. John's head in a charger.
   Rev. TEMPLE BARR—In the field, I. I. L.

The sign of the Baptist's Head appears to have been one of much prevalency in the time of papal domination. The subject seems to have been very generally adopted by Guido and other eminent painters. In the Ellesmere gallery is a fine picture by Domenico Feti, of St. John's head in a charger, precisely as depicted on the tavern signs of old.

  IOHN BROMLEY IN Y$_E$ STRAND—A barber's soap-box.
   Rev. NEAR THE BRIDGE. 1666—HIS HALF PENY.

Lord Thurlow, in his speech, on July 17th, 1797, for postponing the further reading of the Surgeon's Incorporation Bill, stated that, "by a statute still in force, barbers and surgeons were each to use a pole, as a sign."

  AT THE CANARY HOVSE—CANARY, in monogram.
   Rev. IN THE STRAND. 1665—I? amid vine leaves.

Ben Jonson, in his *Every Man out of his Humour*, eulogises the liquor—"Canary, the very essence and spirit of wine."

In "A note of some disbursements for my brother, J. Thornton, of Brockhall, 1637," in the writer's possession, occurs, "Item, for a dozen of stone bottles of sacke, 14*s*. 6*d*." A bottle of sack, inscribed "New Canary, put in to see long keep good, April, 1659, Ri. Combe," was found by some labourers in August, 1735, while draining a fish-pond at Hempstead, Hertfordshire, embedded in mud, at least three feet deep. The mouth of the bottle was waxed over, and the wine perfectly good when tasted; but decay had nearly destroyed the cork.

The Canary House in the Strand was long distinguished as a place of public resort by persons of high character. Here, in March, 1655, Sir Theodore Mayerne, who had been physician of the household to King Henry the Fourth of France, and subsequently in the same capacity to King Charles the First, and was also the friend of Rubens and Vandyck, assisting them in the chemical composition of colours, became ill from the effect of drinking some bad wine, that, to a person of his advanced age, being then in his eighty-third year, operated as a deadly poison. He foretold, to the friends with whom he was drinking, the time of his death, and it happened according to his prediction. He was buried on the 29th, in the old church of St. Martin's in the Fields; and, in the vaults of the present church, the writer some years since, while on a fruitless search for some memorial of Nell Gwynne, saw, among other fine monuments unknown to archæologists, a superb memento to this distinguished worthy.

The Canary House was possibly Carey house, noticed as "near the Savoy in the Strand." Pepys, in his Diary, November 30th, 1667, mentions his proceeding from Arundel House "to Cary House, a house now of entertainment, next my lady Ashley's, where I have heretofore heard common prayer in the time of Dr. Mossum." Loveby, in Dryden's *Wild Gallant*, 1669, observes —"I think upon the sack at Cary house with the apricot flavour."

In the advertisement for the sale of some paintings in 1689, "at three o'clock in the afternoon," the Canary house in the Strand is described as being "between the Feathers tavern and Long's coffee-house, on the east side of Exeter Change."

DANIEL CLARKE AT THE—A griffin in the field.
Rev. NEAR THE NEW EXCHANGE—HIS HALF PENY.

The new Exchange erected by Robert Cecil, earl of Salisbury, lord treasurer in 1608, was, as Sir Richard Baker observes, "a stately building on the north side of Durham house, where stood an old long stable." The plan appears to have been similar to Gresham's Burse; cellars below, the ground-floor level with the street, a public walk, and on the upper story stalls or shops for the sale of wares of all descriptions. "On Tuesday, April 10th, 1609, it was begun to be richly furnished with wares, and the next day after, King James, the Queen, and Prince Henry, with many great lords and ladies, came to see it, and then the king gave it the name of Britain's Burse." In 1632, the building is thus described: "We went to see the new Exchange, in the great street called the Strand. The building has a facade of stone, built after the Gothic style, that has lost its colour from age, and is become blackish. It contains two long and double galleries, one above the other, in which are distributed, in several rows, great numbers of drapers and mercers very rich shops, filled with goods of every kind, and with manufactures of the most beautiful description. These are for the most part under the care of well-dressed women, who are busily employed in work, although many are served by young men called apprentices."

EXTRACTS FROM THE CALENDAR OF STATE PAPERS RELATING TO THE PARISH OF ST. CLEMENT DANES.

1555. "December 27.—John Bedell, Chr. Ashton, has been in London, and left a nag at the Checkers without Temple Bar. Understands that Mr. Dudley is gone, and that Sir Anth. Kingston is at liberty." (Vol. 1547-80, p. 73.)

1585. "March 24.—Examinations of such butchers within the liberties of the 'Dutchy' without Temple Bar, as kill and sell fish in Lent." (Vol. 1581-90, p. 232.)

1603. "August.—Warrant for a grant to Charles, Earl of Nottingham and his heirs, of Arundel House, Strand, part of the land of Philip, late Earl of Arundel attainted."

"August 10.—Grant to the same of Arundel House and other lands in the parish of St. Clement Danes." (Vol. 1603-10, p. 31.)

1607. "December 23.—Grant to the Earl of Arundel and Robert Cannefield, in fee simple, of Arundel House, St. Clement Danes, without Temple Bar, lately conveyed to the King by the Earl of Nottingham [docquet.]" (Vol. 1603-10, p. 890.)

1608. "July 27.—Certificate of acquittal of Humphrey Gifford, of St. Clement Danes, for Recusancy, a proof that he has attended church recently." (Vol. 1603-40, p. 449.)

1605. "January 8.—Anonymous to ——. The Earl of Salisbury is as violent as ever against Catholics; some of the best sort should request the mediation of the Spanish Ambassador; if that fail, they must 'ferire,' or 'perire.' His son might get a place in Salisbury's service, 'and see have an open way to doe what they list.' 'If Hector were gone the Troians would be quieter.' Signed—'You know me;' Indorsed—'Copy of a writing found in the street at one Lee's dore over against St. Clement's Church the 8th of January, 1605." (G. Plot Bk., No. 162.) (Vol. 1603-10, p. 278.)

1605. "Copy of the letter to Lord Monteagle, warning him to be absent from Parliament:—'Nov. 7. Salisbury House. T. Johnson to Mr. Percivall. Informs him of divers houses of recusants, in St. John's Street, amongst them Sir Henry James's and Thomas Sleeps. Johnson (Faukes) was often at Sleep's house. There is a wonderful resort there since his apprehension.' Nov. 7. Information that Faukes lodged two months ago with Mrs. Herbert, now Mrs. Wodehouse at the back of St. Clement's Church. Percy, the two Wrights, Winter, Catesby, and others had secret correspondence with him there. She disliked it, suspecting him to be a priest; he was tall, with brown hair and auburn beard, and had plenty of money." (Vol. 1603-10, p. 244.)

1605. "Nov. 9.—Tower. Declaration of Guy Faukes (made to Salisbury.) Further details of the Plot. It was communicated to Hugh Owen the Jesuit in Flanders. The Conspirators met at the back of St. Clement's Inn. Gerard the Jesuit gave them the sacrament to confirm their oath of secrecy, but knew not their purpose. They also met at Walley's (Garnet's) lodgings near Enfield. [On the 10th this declaration was acknowledged before the Lords Commissioners and is signed in a tremulous hand 'Guido.' The signature is supposed to have been extorted by the rack, and the prisoner to have fainted before completing it.]" (G. Plot Bk., No. 54.) (Vol. 1603-10, p. 247.)

1609. "June 15.—Commissioners for the Aid County Middlesex, to the council. Complain of the smallness of the composition offered by Sir John Hollis for his lands, &c. in St. Clement Danes, and of his disrespectful language. Inclose: Sir John Hollis to the Commissioners for the Aid Co., Middlesex. Remonstrates against their exacting £17 for his tenements in St. Clement Parish. Tenders a voluntary composition." (Vol. 1603-10, p. 519.)

1621. "March 6.—Certificate of the butchers who are licensed to kill flesh this Lent in London, being eighteen in number, with list of seventy-two who kill without license, and note that twenty others are suppressed. Peter Sweeper of St. Clements and Rich. Carpenter being in the liberty of the Duchy of Lancaster, plead exemption from the jurisdiction of the council: the former professes to have a license from the Chancellor of the Duchy.—(Vol. 1619-23, p. 232.)

1617. "Dec. 17.—License from Sir John Duckombe (Duchy House, Strand), for John Adams, Butcher, of St. Clement's Danes, in the liberties of the Duchy, to kill flesh during Lent; with confirmation thereof by Sir Edward Moseley, (Attorney of the Duchy), Feb. 24, 1618." (Vol. 1611-18, p. 502). [Temp, James I.] "License to Jane Foulkes, of the parish of St. Clement Danes to sell flesh privately during Lent." (Vol. 1623-25, p. 512.)

1628. "June 20.—Release (Westminster) to Henry Raleigh, late of St. Clement Danes, gentleman of penalties, accused, by three several judgments against him, for recusancy." (Vol. 1628-29, p. 170.)

1631. "June 1.—Justices of the Peace for Middlesex (Church-house St. Clement Danes) to the Council. Certificate of sums received, and those still owing, for levies upon publicans for defective measures in St. Clement Danes and the Duchy Liberty. [This certificate seems to have been personally presented to the Council. It would have been presented before, but Dr. Robert Bates had been obliged to retire with his family to Twickenham, the Plague being next door to him in Milford Lane. When ultimately presented, Laurence Whitaker excused his absence, having been commanded by His Majesty to take charge of Lord Reay.]" (Vol. 1631-33, p. 66.)

1632 (?).—"Petition of William Earl of Exeter to the King. Petitioner is seized in his demesne as of fee of the advowson of St. Clement Danes, Co. Middlesex, and Dr. Bates, the last incumbent, is lately deceased. For prevention of all controversies, prays the King to confer upon him all His Majesties right and title to the said presentation. (¾ of a page)." (Vol. 1631-33, p. 229.)

1634. "Dec. 6.—Assessment (in nine pages) made by Robert Parkhurst (Lord Mayor), Sheriff, Bailiffs of Westminster and St. Katherine's, and the Portreeve of Gravesend and Milton, by virtue of the King's writ, for providing a ship of 500 tons burden for H. M. service at a cost of £4,085. 18s. 7d. Westminster, consisting of St. Margaret's, St. Martin's, St. Mary-le-Savoy, and St. Clement Danes without the Duchy of Lancaster, provided £1,610. 17s. 10d. of this amount, and the Duchy of Lancaster in the Strand £264. 1s. 1d." (Vol. 1634-35, p. 345.)

1635. "April 16.—Frances Viscountess Purbeck, prisoner in the Gate-house, ordered to appear under the custody of the Keeper of the Gate-house to receive sentence, but appeared not, the Keeper saying that the Viscountess was unwilling to come thither, for that she wanted clothes fitting for her to come abroad in. Sentence was read against her, whereby she stands convicted of adultery with Sir Robert Howard, for which the Court ordered her to be brought to the Church of St. Clement Danes, without Temple Bar, on Sunday next come sen'night, according as shall be prescribed; and Dr. Rives was ordered to put in new articles against her for adultery with Sir Robert since the sentence of this Court." [Acts of the Court of High Commission, vol, 261, fo. 191.] (Vol. 1635, p. 181.)

1635. "July 14.—Returns of the Constables for the Westminster Liberty in St. Clement's Danes 'of all strangers born, resident therein':—Eight in number, including Vincent Gregory, D. D. (Italian); Gedion Lennie (Frenchmen), and two Dutchmen, Gracchianus Hannamor and Cornelius Blewe (⅓ page). In the Savoy, nine gentlemen and ten tradesmen." (Vol. 1635, p. 275.) "October.—A Certificate of the Justices of all strangers born who dwell, lodge, or trade in Westminster (on 10 pages); the number 279 includes, 'In St. Clement's, John Baptiste Ferine, Her Majesty's Perfumer" (a Dutchman), householder." (Vol. 1635, p. 457.)

1635. "Dec. 23.—The Council to Edward Lord Newburgh, Chancellor of the Duchy of Lancaster. The streets between Temple Bar and Westminster are very noisome by reason of the dirt and rubbish wherewith the same are pestered, and thereby the passengers are not only much annoyed, but the nastiness thereof is like to breed an infection. So far as concerns his precinct and liberties, he is to take order that the streets be cleansed and kept clean (draft ⅔ page)." (Vol. 1635, p, 590.)

1635. "Dec. 23.—Sir Henry Spiller and Lawrence Whittaker to the Council. Certify 22 cases of all new buildings upon new foundations erected since Feb. 2, including 8 in St. Martin's (mostly in and near Long Acre), 4 in St. Giles, and the rest scattered about the town. In St. Clement's— Richard Stocke hath a shed, George Thorowgood a shed, Henry Stocke a shed, and Peter Johnson a shed—which is called Mouse Hall, alias Littleworth Parish, near Lonch's Buildings, in Lincoln's Inn Fields—all of boards covered with pantiles. These have been set up about four or five years since, but are a general offence to the neighbours and passengers that way, and a public nuisance." (Vol. 1635, p. 595.)

1636. "September 1.—Petition of Richard Lea and Dorothy his wife, prisoners in the Gate-House, to the Council. That an order was made by the Council that the butchers that had their slaughter-houses near St. Clement's Well, should not kill any beasts until All Saints' Day, to prevent increase of the sickness: Petitioners killed not above three beasts to relieve themselves and their family, and were sent to the Gate-House, where they live miserably, and with their children likely to starve. They therefore crave that Mr. Rea, the Bailiff of Westminster, may take such bail as Petitioners are able to be tender for their forbearing to offend." (On one page.) (Vol. 1636-7, p. 110.)

1636. "December 10.—H. Jessey to William Howard. The party from whom he thought he received the book denies it; knows not from whom he had it. Begs advice for his enlargement from the Inn he is at, viz. the 'Lamb,' St. Clements, where 'the noises disturb his rest.'" (Vol. 1661-2, p. 175.)

1662. "February 5th.—Privy Council (Whitehall), Licenses: Michael Kees, Butcher, of St. Clement Danes, to kill and sell meat during Lent." (Vol. 1661-2, p. 266.)

1662. "March.—Grant to John, Earl of Clare, and his heirs of a Market to be held three times a week, in St. Clement's Inn Fields, parish of St. Clement Danes, Middlesex (Docquet). Reasons why the Earl of Clare should have the nomination of the Clerk of his Market, although Mr. Howard has a grant of the putting of Clerks into all Markets, viz.,—that Mr. Howard's grant should only extend to Clerks already established, and that the Clerkship of this Market will not be profitable, but rather an expense to the Earl of Clare." (Vol. 1661-2, p. 326.)

1664. "December 3rd.—Statement by Thomas Clarke, that Robert Nicholas, of Seend. co. Wilts, one of the Barons [of Exchequer] to the late ursurper, boasted that he drew up the charge against the late King, and would do it again if needful, for His Majesty is of the Norman race and unfit to reign. Desires a warrant against him, with the depositions of John Stokes that the words were spoken in May last, behind St. Clements, in the Strand. Sworn before John Coel, Master in Chancery. Endorsed with a note that Stokes lived at Seend, Wiltshire, near Devizes." [Copy also of the former part of the above, dated Nov. 20th.] (Vol. 1663-4, p. 101.)

1666. "November 15th.—H. Muddman (Whitehall) to George Powell (Pembroke), in which he relates that Mr. Marquis, one of the King's Life Guards, and Mr. Philpott were committed to the Marshalsea of the King's Bench, for beating and wounding the Constable of St. Clement Danes. The Lord Chief Justice declared he would acquaint the Lord General, that Marquis might be turned out of the Guards; that the Lord Chamberlain and Lord Crofts said, they would acquaint the King himself, 'the matter appearing very foul.'" (Vol. 1666-7, p. 263.)

Old newspaper advertisement, July, 1678:—"A servant boy about 20 years old, tall of stature, pale of complexion, with a dark perriwig, fair spoken, in a light coloured stuff frock, and a gray Hat, Run away from Mr. Thomas Potter, a Perriwig Maker at the Maidenhead near St. Clement's Church, the 9th instant. Whoever can secure or bring the said servant to his master aforesaid, shall be liberally rewarded."

Advertisement, 1694.—"Lost or mislay'd, the 27th inst., two Notes under the Hand of Thomas Farmer, for Mr. Robert Fowle, and Mr. Thomas Wotton, one of £260 payable to Thomas Marriot, esq., or bearer, on which £60 is indorsed; the other of £30 payable to Mr. John Coggs or Bearer, both dated the 27th inst. Whoever gives notice of them to Mr. Coggs goldsmith over against St. Clement's Church in the Strand, shall have 3 Guineas Reward."

Advertisement, Feb, 9, 1717.—"Matth. West, Goldsmith, at the 7 Stars in Clare St. Clare Market gives notice that the Dutch Lottery is done drawing, and all the numbers come over. Any persons concerned may have an exact account or there success at his office at North's Coffee House in King Street near Guildhall. Likewise those that have any of his share tickets drawn Prizes in the said Lottery, may have them exchanged for shares in the Hamburgh Lottery, or have money for them at his House or Office aforesaid; where Numerical Register Books and Tables for entring their Numbers are kept as formerly. N.B. The said Matthew West sells whole tickets in the Hamburg Lottery, and buys prizes in the Dutch."

Advertisement, 1723.—"The Cambrick Chamber is removed from St. Martin's le Grand to Mr. Thomas Atkins, up one pair of Stairs at the sign of Buchanan's Head, a Bookseller's Shop, the Corner of Milford Lane, over against St. Clement's Church in the Strand, where there is to be sold all sorts of fine Cambricks, fine Lawns, and good Hollands, by the Importer at reasonable rates. Attendance will be given from Morning till Night. N.B. There is a fresh Parcel of all the sorts above mentioned just arrived, superfine, good, and also very fine; and the prettiest Printed Cambricks and Hollands as yet made, to be sold very cheap. There is likewise at the same place, an extraordinary Parcel of Dutch Quills to be disposed of, of four sorts, newly landed."

EXTRACTS FROM STATE PAPERS.

Advertisement, 1724.—"William Barmby, at the "King's Arms," behind St. Clement's Church in the Strand, the only clergyman's warehouse in England that can furnish upon sight with gowns and cassocks, for judges, barristers, and students; livery gowns and for corporations. Likewise buys, sells, changes or furnishes by the year; also bands, roses, black cloths, prunelloes, Prince's black silks, and Bishop's square caps. He has the honour to work for fifteen bishops, where also the above mentioned goods are sold at reasonable rates. N.B. Any gentleman may be furnished with gowns and cassocks for what time they please, which will save them a great deal of trouble in bringing their own up to town."

"On Sunday night [January 9, 1743,] Mr. Emmerton, an eminent colourman, was knocked down in the Strand without being spoke to, by a street robber, who took his cane from him and endeavoured to pull his watch out of his pocket; but Mr. Emmerton having struggled some time with the fellow, a gentleman of Clement's Inn came up, and calling assistance, seized the villain, and secured him till Monday morning, when he was carried before Sir John Barnard, where the fact being plainly proved he was committed to Newgate by the name of Bryan Cooley.

"November, 1756.—On Saturday evening, about eight o'clock, as John Tracy Atkyns, Esq., and his lady came from Gloucestershire to their house in Cursitor Street, Chancery Lane, in a post chaise, their portmanteau was stolen from behind within a few yards of their own door; but a Hue and Cry being immediately made, the thieves were found out in St. Clement's Churchyard just as they were agreeing with a hackney coachman to carry the portmanteau, which was recovered, but the rogues found means to make their escape."

"Wednesday (April 11, 1764), a waiter at Mr. Andrews', the 'Crown and Anchor' in the Strand, was committed by Justice Fielding to the Gate-house for stealing a quantity of table linen and plate from that tavern, and money, the property of the other waiters; and likewise his sister, in Wych Street, for receiving them, knowing them to be stolen."

"September, 1765.—Last Wednesday morning, about two o'clock, four men carrying a large chest were taken up by the watchmen in the Strand, on suspicion of having been concerned in some robbery; and on their arrival at St. Clement's Watch-house, they were proceeding to inspect into the contents of the chest, but were prevented by a Custom-house officer who solemnly seized it in the King's name, saying he had dogged it a considerable way, and made not the least question but it was a valuable prize. At last both parties agreed to open it, when, instead of the booty, they expected, there appeared only the remains of a mangled dead body, supposed to have been in the hands of surgeons; during the dispute, the men took an opportunity to make their escape."

"1735.—Mr. Edwards chosen Curate of St. Clement Danes, in the room of Mr. Richardson, deceased."

"January, 1751.—His Majesty, according to annual custom, distributed £1000 among 9 parishes, viz.:—St. Margaret, St. John Evangelist, St. Anne's, St. James, St. Martin in the Fields, St. Mary le Strand, St. Paul, Covent Garden, St. George, Hanover Square, and St. Clemen Danes."

"January, 1678.—At the Musick School, in Essex Buildings, against St. Clement's Church in the Strand, will be continued a consort of vocal and instrumental musick, beginning at six of the clock every evening. Composed by Mr. John Bannister."

"Wich St., (so spelt) is described in 'Hatton's New View of London, 1708,' as 'a considerable street between the Angel Inn and Drury Lane, 230 yards, and 1,180 yards from St. Paul's Cathedral."

"Bromley's Catalogue of British Portraits mentions Hy. Smith, Minister of St. Clement Danes, London, ob. circa 1600 (prefixed to his sermons 1657, 4to. and 1660, 4to.,) engraved by T. Cross."

"March, 1634.—In the book of Acts of the Court of High Commn. for the exercise of Ecclesiastical jurisdiction—an original minute book of their proceedings—occurs the name of John Wells, of St. Clement's Street, in the brick building near the upper side of Lincoln's Inn Fields, Attorney for arresting the proctors concerned in the recent prosecution of Lord Davies."

EXTRACTS FROM STATE PAPERS.

"In a paper, in the State Paper Office, entitled 'Touching Ale Houses in Middlesex', dated 1632."

"St. Dunstan's prsh. for that pto. of Chancery Lane, in Midd:—

The number of the Ale Houses in Chancery Lane. A.D. 1630, amounted to	40
Whereof Sheere Lane then suppressed	25
And then licensed	15

The increase of the Ale Houses thus licensed since 1630, are five, and there remaineth still suppressed twenty.

"*To the Right Honble. the Lords of His Maties Most Hoble. Privie Councell.*

"At the Church House at St. Clement's Danes the 1st of June, 1631. Present: Sir William Slyngsbye, Mr. Dr. Bates, Mr. Laurence Whittacres, Mr. Thomas Shepheard, and ye Clarke of ye Peace.

"The humble certificate of Sir William Slyngsbye, Dr. Bates, Laurence Whittacres, and Thomas Shepheard, Justices of Peace in the County of Midds.

"That Mr. Shepheard had made former warrants (as by this Hoble Boarde was given in charge to the Justices of this Countie) to the Churchwardens of St. Clement's to levye upon presentments made before him for defective measures upon the victuallers, these penalties following, viz.:—

"Upon Thomas Hurley, Victualler	£4
Upon Willm Carpenter for the like	2
Upon Henry Hopkins	4
Upon Robert Hall	4
Upon John Brampton	4
Upon Harry Haycock	2
Upon Willm Hughes	2
In all	£22

"Sir Willm. Slingsbye did, upon the like presentments to him made, send forth his warrants to the Constables of the Libertie of the Duchy to levye -

"Upon the aforesaid Thomas Hurley	40s.
Upon the aforesaid Henry Hopkins	40s.
Upon the aforesaid John Brampton	40s.
Upon the aforesaid Robert Hamson	40s.
Upon the aforesaid George Sill	20s.
In all	£9.

"Soe, as the forfeitures by both these presentments is £31, direccons were formerly given to the Constables and Churchwardens to return their warrants and moneys levied for the penalties aforesaid at the time and place above mentioned, and that they should require the informers and parties accused to appear before us, whoe were all there present, and could not denye their fforfeitures presented. Nevertheless, for two botles of beere, for which the informers certified four defaults. Each bottle being sould for 2d., and under measure. We conceaved the meaning of the Statute to be that the selling of two botles was but two defaults, and therefore remitted halfe the penalty presented, and received only these somes following, viz.:—

"Of Thomas Hurley, for £6 presented	40s.
Of William Carpenter for 40s. presented	20s.
Of Henry Hopkins, for £6	40s.
Of Robert Hall, £4	40s.
Of John Bramton, £6	40s.
Of Henry Haycock, 40s.	40s.
Of William Hughes, for all	40s.
Of Robert Hampson, for 40s.	20s.
And of George Sill in all is	20s.

Soe as the forfeitures were £31, and the receipts but £14, out of which £14 there was then paid to the informers, allowing what Mr. Sheppherd had given them for their presentments to him, and for other fees for warrants and clarkes attending £3. 0s. 12d., so there shd. remayne as was tould upon the table £10. 19s. 0d, which some Sir Wm. Slingsbye desired might be left in Mr. Dr. Bates his hands untill the same were made up to £20, against the next monthes meeting upon other warrants of like nature granted for the levying thereof within the Libertie of Westminster, and then to consider how to employe ye whole to such charitable uses as should be thought fitt by the advices of the churchwardens and burgesses of that libertie, but Mr. Doctor refused to keepe the money, in respect of his present dwelling att Twyttnam, and Mr. William was desired to keep it till that time of meeting, the accompt and some being taken by Mr. Docter and Mr. Whittacris and by the Clarke of the Peace, which money and account is still reserved in a purse apart for that purpose and noe other.

"That meeting was diligently sollicited by Sir William Slingsbye in respect that for this division nothing had beene as yet raised to make a stock for reliefe of the poore by setting them to worke, or employed to binde apprentices; neither was there any certificate made to yor Lordship as was commanded, the impediment thereof being by reason of Mr. Dr. Bates his absence, whoe was enforced to leave his house and retyre with his ffamilly to Twittnam, the plague being at the next doore to his dwelling in Milford Lane.

"W. SLYNGSBYE."
"T. SHEPPARD."
"RO. BATES."

"By reason that I am commanded by his Matie to take the charge of the Lord of Reay in his lodging, I canot wthout leave attend yor Lopps., but I doe humbly certifye that I know that which is above written to be true.
"LAWR. WHITAKER."

"January 25, 1636-7, Charles I. (Vol. 344, No. 92}.—Petition of Churchwardens and Scavengers of the parishes of St. Clement's Danes, St. Mary, Savoy, to the Council.—Some inhabitants about 19 years since took a lease of a piece of ground in Long Acre, there being then no dwelling-houses near adjoining, about which they built a brick wall at the charge of £160, with a house for a laystall keeper, who gave bond not to suffer aught but street soil to be carried thereunto, the carrying whereof costs petitioners £95 p. ann. This laystall was never found legally to be a nuisance, till on information of the inhabitants of houses recently built near thereto, the Justices of Peace for Westminster in Sept. last condemned the same for a nuisance, and fforbade the carrying any more there under a penalty of £200, and committed the laystall keeper because he would not give bond not to suffer more soil to be carried there. The order of the Lords was, that as the houses came to the laystall and not the laystall to the houses, there is a greater nuisance, and ordered the houses to be pulled down, and the under Bailiff of Westminster to be committed to the Fleet for imprisoning the laystall keeper."

"Donishe, Charles II., 18th June, 1667 (Vol. 206, No. 59).—Warrant from Sec Morice to George Gilly, messenger of the Chamber, to apprehend Richard Langhorne, Councillor at Law in Shire Lane, and bring him before him to answer objections against him."

In the burial register of St. Dunstan's we find, '1604—Sir Arthur Atie, Knight, out of Shire Lane, Secretary to the great Earl of Leicester, attendant on the unfortunate Earl of Essex.

"Extracts from the Register (Hampstead)" (Lyson's Environs, p. 542'.—Sir Arthur Atey, who resided at Kilbourn Priory, was Principal of Alban Hall, and orator of the University of Oxford. He was Secretary to the unfortunate Earl of Essex, in whose ruin he was very near being involved and was obliged for a time to conceal himself. He was knighted on the accession of James I., and dying anno 1604, was buried (in his will he does not make any reference to where he wished to be buried), as Wood says, at Harrow.

ST. CLEMENT'S DANES IN 1734.

This parish of St. Clement Danes is large, well built, and inhabited by many persons both of the nobility and gentry, as well as rich tradesmen: Where also many noblemen's seats stood—as Essex House, Arundel House, &c.—though now pulled down and improved in rents, by building them into fair courts and squares.

To give the girt line, or present bounds of this parish, I must in abundance of places run through, or cross houses, nay long piles of buildings, as doth appear by the map of the parish. I shall begin at the west end of Portugal Row in Lincoln's Inn Fields, where the parish stone mark is set up; and from thence it runs cross the backsides of the houses in Portugal Row, taking in the playhouse, and the stablings into the new court in Lincoln's Inn almost to the pump placed at the pallisado pales by the garden; and from thence straight cross the court and the row of new buildings into Shear Lane, and down the same to the gate by Temple Bar; taking in all the west side thereof. Then it runs from Temple Bar, cross to the "Cock Alehouse" on the other side of the way, and so to the River Thames; taking in all the buildings except the Temple: which the Templers and barristers claim a jurisdiction unto. So that it passes from the "Cock Alehouse" in the street side, unto all the buildings to the Palsgrave's Head Court, which it takes in, and so down into Devereux Court, with all Essex Buildings on both sides, to the River Thames; then along the banks of the river from Essex Stairs unto Strand Bridge; and there it turns northwards taking in the east side, with part of the west side, at the upper end: where it joins to the garden wall of Somerset House. Which buildings it crosses, and so up to Three Helmet Court over against the "May Pole" in the Strand, and there it crosseth the High Street to the Stonecutters by the "Bell Inn." Thence through the said inn and crosses Wych Street to May Pole Alley; from whence it passeth by Craven House on the east side of Drury Lane to the Cheesemongers two doors on this side the Horseshoe Tavern; and there it crosseth the houses on the backside of Princess Street, and so cross Stanhope Street, and the Tallow Chandlers, with the other jetting out house, and then runs down the south side of Duke Street, unto the house where the parish stone mark is set up; and from this house it crosses the houses into Bear Yard, and so into Sheffield Street by Clare Market next the Oyl Shop; where it crosses the street to the Glaziers, and so through the houses; and again crossing by the sign of the "Black Jack," unto the parish stone mark, on the backside of Portugal Row, where I began. And this is the girt line of the parish, which lieth encircled together, as appears by the map. But there is a considerable part of the parish separate from the rest, and that part begins at Wimbleton House in the Strand, over against Duchy Lane and so runs to the corner of Exeter Exchange, and from thence up Burleigh Street, taking in Exeter Court, with Exchange Alley, and the back buildings against Exeter Street with all the East side of Burleigh Street except two or three houses by the corner of Exeter Street. Then again from the corner of the said Exchange it runs cross the Strand, taking in Fountain Court down to the River Thames, with all Beauford Buildings, and the east side of the new street called Cecil Street, built out of Great Salisbury House: all which said building it takes in, and this is the extent of this parish.

Now for the description of the streets, lanes, alleys, and courts in this parish, with their buildings of chief note. I shall first begin at Temple Bar, and so westward. And then the first is the Strand, on both sides to the "May Pole;" and here this street is not so broad as by and beyond the "May Pole;" but being so great a thoroughfare is well inhabited by shopkeepers. The "Cock Alehouse," adjoining Temple Bar, is a noted publichouse. Thence passing westward is Cross Key Alley, very small, the "Rose Tavern, a well customed house with good conveniences of rooms and a good garden. The next place that offers itself is the Palsgrave's Head Court, very handsome, large, well-built and inhabited, with freestone pavement, ascended by steps, which causeth it to lie dry and clean: it hath an outlet into the Temple with a door to it, and at the entrance out of the Strand, there is another door made open with iron bars, to shut up on occasion, for the security of the inhabitants and lodgers. Next to this is a small alley not worth the naming. Then through a small passage is an entrance into Devereux Court, which leadeth to the Temple back-gate. It is a large place with good houses, and by reason of its vicinity to the Temple, hath a good resort, consisting of publichouses and noted coffee houses; from this court is a passage into Essex Street.

Almost against St. Clement's Church is an open passage for coaches into Essex Street, or Building, being a broad, clean, and handsome street, especially beyond the turning into the Temple, where it crosseth Little Essex Street into Milford Lane; it consists of two rows of good built houses, well inhabited by gentry; at the bottom of which street is a pair of stairs to go down to the waterside, where watermen ply. This place, before its being converted into buildings, was a large garden with one great house, first called Exeter House, as belonging to the Bishops of Exeter. Afterwards it came to the Earls of Essex, and was called Essex House. Which name it retained, although afterwards possessed by Seymour, Marquis of Hartford. At length it was purchased by Dr. Barbon, the great builder, and by him and other undertakers converted into buildings as now it is: of late the passage into it out of the great street is widened, and made more convenient.

Out of this Essex Street westward is a small street or passage for carts, called Little Essex Street, which leadeth to Milford Lane, which openeth out of the Strand, against St. Clement's Church, and this lane runneth down on the backside of Essex Street to the waterside, a place much pestered with carts and carrs, for the bringing coals and other goods from the wharfs by the waterside. And therefore this lane is but ill inhabited, with old buildings, and the rather for that the entrance into it out of the Strand is so narrow. On the west side of this lane and opposite to Little Essex Street is Greyhound Court, a pretty handsome new built place, which hath a passage into Water Street on the back side of Norfolk Buildings. Then lower down in Milford Lane, near the wood wharf, is a small place called P——g Alley, a very proper name for it, and this alley goeth down to Milford Stairs, and also up into Water Street being ascended by steps.

Betwixt Milford Lane and Arundel Street is Crown Court, very small. Then betwixt Norfolk Street and Surrey Street in the Strand is Angel Court, containing two or three houses, and hath a freestone pavement. Then beyond Surrey Street is the "Talbot Inn," well resorted unto, which hath a passage into Surrey Street next to Mr. Foxe's house.

Strand Bridge goeth down to the Thames side, a place of some note, for its stairs to take water at ; the east side of this lane joins to Surrey Street, into which there is a passage up stone steps ; and the west side hath a brick wall belonging to Somerset House garden.

Beyond Strand Bridge towards Somerset House is a small court called Three Halbert Court. Which is the extent or out bounds of this parish westward

Now back to Norfolk Buildings, formerly the Bishop of Bath's Inn : which in process of time came to the family of the Howards, Dukes of Norfolk, the late Duke dwelling there. It then was a very large and old built house ; with a spacious yard for stablings, towards the Strand, and with a gate to enclose it, where there was the porter's lodge ; and as large a garden towards the Thames. This said house and grounds was some years since converted into streets and buildings, and contains four large streets graced with good buildings which are well inhabited and resorted unto by gentry ; three of which in a straight line from the Strand runs down to the River Thames : where there are good stairs for taking water, viz., Arundel Street, Norfolk Street, and Surrey Street ; and the fourth, viz., Howard Street, runs cross about the midst. The first of these streets eastward is Arundel Street, which hath the best buildings towards the Thames ; on the east side is a street called Water Street, chiefly for coaches and stablings, at the bottom of which is a pretty handsome house, with a garden towards the Thames ; and under the house there is a passage into the Thames for the watering of horses. Out of this street are two passages into Arundel Street, one of which is broad for coaches, and the other narrow, which is called P——g Alley. And out of this place there are two passages into Milford Lane, the one towards the bottom very small and bad, being descended by steps, very ill built and inhabited ; the other is called Greyhound Court already mentioned in the description of Milford Lane. At the upper end of this street is the "Crown Tavern," a large and curious house with good rooms and other conveniences fit for entertainment.

Norfolk Street, very large and spacious, lieth in the midst, and is esteemed the best both for buildings, and pleasantness of a prospect into the Thames.

Surrey Street, also replenished with good buildings, especially that of Nevison Fox, Esq.; towards the Strand, which is a fine, large and curious house of his own building; and the two houses that front the Thames; that on the east side being the house of the Honorable Charles Howard, Esquire, brother to Henry Duke of Norfolk, both fine houses with pleasant, though small gardens towards the Thames.

Howard Street, also a large open street, running cross as aforesaid, but not so well inhabited as the others.

The north side of the Strand begins at Temple Bar, from thence runneth to the Butcher Row, which goeth to the passage into St. Clement's Inn, thence to the "Angel Inn," and so on the backside of St. Clement's Church unto the "May Pole" in the Strand.

The parish church of St. Clement's is lately new built, a comely and curious structure, both as to its pillars, galleries, pews and pulpit within; and for its outward adornment, having a fine porch ascended by steps, and covered at the top cupulo-wise, and supported by freestone pillars. It also hath a fine steeple, with a good ring of bells, and chimes to them. To this church adjoins a fair churchyard, severed from the Strand by freestones set in the ground breast high, and handsomely shaped taperwise. On the east side are six parish almshouses.

Near unto this church, on the north side, is St. Clement's Inn, being one of the Inns of Chancery. It hath three courts one within another, all old buildings, except a row in the garden, which is well-built with a prospect in the garden, as also into that of New Inn adjoining to it, with a door to open into the said Inn at days, but shut at nights; and here is a back door which gives passage into Clare Market.

St. Clement's Lane comes out of Butcher's Row and fronts Clement's Inn. And near the gate is the "Lamb Inn" of some note and trade. Then passing by St. Clement's Inn and Boswell Court, it runneth northwards into Clare Market, and in its passage takes in St. Clement's pump or well, of note for its excellent spring water. A little above this pump is Plough Alley, which with three turnings, goes into a street by the Plough stables, which fronts the playhouse by Lincoln's Inn Grange, in little Lincoln's Inn Fields. More towards Clare Market, is Horshoe Court, a pretty handsome place, with a freestone pavement, having a prospect into St. Clement's Inn garden. And opposite to this court is Yates Court, not over good, nor large; and then nearer to Clare Market on the right hand, is a very small place, with a narrow entrance, called Pigmy Court.

Between Temple Bar and the turning into St. Clement's Inn on the north side of the Butcher Row, (so called from the butchers shambles on the south side) are several courts, most of which are but small. The first is Ship Yard, a throughfare into little Shear Lane, with a pretty broad passage; on the east side is an open place going into a small court, called Chair Court, with a fair freestone pavement.

This yard seems to take its name from the "Ship Tavern" at the entrance thereof. Next to Ship Yard are these courts: Swan Court, very small. Star Court, indifferent good and large with an open air. White Hart Court, long, but narrow. Lock Alley, but small. Windmil Court, very small, and inconsiderable. Crown Court hath an open air about the midst, and leadeth into little Shear Lane. Bear and Harrow Court, so called from such a sign, a noted eating-house, at the entrance into it. This court, (or rather alley, for its length and narrowness) runs into Boswel Court. Then beyond St. Clement's Lane is the "Angel Inn," a very large place and of a great resort, especially for the Cornish and west country lawyers. And near unto this inn is Knight's Court, a place of small account.

Hollowel Street, commonly called the backside of St. Clements, a place inhabited by divers salesmen and piecebrokers. This street runs up to the "May Pole" in the Strand, where is "Five Bell Tavern," which is a thoroughfare into the Wich Street; and near it is a small alley called Sallett's Alley, also with a passage into Wich Street. In this Hollowel Street is Lyon's Inn, another of the Inns of Chancery, which is but small and old. It hath a back door into Wich Street; and against the fore door is a small passage into the Strand, called P——g Alley, perhaps in contempt.

Wich Street begins at the Angel Inn, and so runs into Drury Lane; it is a street much taken up by upholsters for the sale of bedding and second-hand household goods. In this street is New Inn, another of the Inns of Chancery, and here the students of Strand Inn settled, when that house was pulled down in the reign of Edward the Sixth, for the building of Somerset House. This inn is of late much increased by the new buildings in the garden part; which is severed in with pallisades, and neatly kept with grass plats and walks, set with rows of trees, so that the chambers (which all front the garden) are very pleasant and airy. Through this inn there is a passage into Houghton Street, and another into St. Clement's Inn.

Near unto New Inn is Wickham Court and Wich Alley, both very small; and on the north side next to Lyons Inn is Ogdens Court, also but ordinary. Maypole Alley hath a narrow passage into Stanhope Street, but meanly inhabited, on the east side, and the west side is taken up by the back buildings of Craven House. And over against Houghton Street is Sherborn Court, which is but small and ordinary.

Drury Lane, so called from Drury House, now the seat of the Earl of Craven, which with the additions built by his Lordship, called Craven House, makes together a very large house, or which may be termed several houses; the entrance into this house is through a pair of gates which leadeth into a large yard for the reception of coaches, and on the back side is a handsome garden.

Blackmore Street, near unto Craven House, a street of no great account. In this lane, on the east side, which is in this parish, are these places of name: Clare Court, a very handsome open place with a passage into Blackmore Street;

and another into White Horse Yard; it hath very good new built houses fit for good inhabitants, and is handsomely paved with freestone. White Horse Yard hath a passage into Stanhope Street, being a place but ill built, nor over well inhabited. King's Head Court hath a passage down steps into Stanhope Street, an indifferent good court. Rain Deer Yard, but ordinary, and hath a passage into Stanhope Street, and Drum Court, or Alley, a small place.

Peter Street, but short and ordinary.

Houghton Street, also falling into the market, all of which three last streets are well built and inhabited; and from this street to Peter Street, there runs an alley without a name that crosses Holles Street and Clare Street.

Clare Street, a good open place fronting the market; here is White Horse Inn.

Holles Street, also fronting the market.

Stanhope Street, a pretty broad, well-built, and inhabited street; and besides the places which come out of Drury Lane, on the same side is Blue Boar Court, which is but small.

Vere Street comes out of Duke Street and falls into Clare Market,—a street well inhabited by tradesmen; on the east side is a passage into Bear Yard, which is a broad place with shambles and stalls built, as designed for a market place to join to Clare Market, but the project did not take; so of no use, and but ordinarily inhabited. Out of this yard is an alley which leadeth into Lincoln's Inn Fields against Portugal Row, and another passage into Shefford Street adjoining to the market, a place of some trade.

Clare Market, very considerable and well served with provisions, both flesh and fish; for besides the butchers in the shambles, it is much resorted unto by the country butchers and higglers, the market days are Wednesdays and Saturdays. The tole belongs to the Duke of Newcastle, as ground landlord thereof.

On the back side of Portugal Row, is a street which runneth to Lincoln's Inn gate, which used to pass without a name, but since the place is increased by the new buildings in Little Lincoln's Inn Fields, and the settling of the playhouse it may have a name given it, and not improperly, Playhouse Street. Fronting the playhouse, is a street which goeth to Plough Stables; which also had no name, unless one may call it Grange Street, from the "Grange Inn," a place of good note; nigh to which is the parish round house, on the back side of which is a churchyard also belonging to the parish.

The new buildings made by Sir Thomas Cook in Little Lincoln's Inn Fields, now make a large street with good built houses and before likewise had no name; but now may be called Lincoln's Inn Street; at the upper end of this street is Plough Alley and Stable Alley, already spoke of. Then Hooker's Court, a very fine large court, with very good buildings, well inhabited; it hath a passage down steps into Boswel Court, and to both passages or entrances are gates to shut up in the nights, for security of the inhabitants.

Boswel Court, chiefly for stablings and coach houses, except at the end towards St. Clement's Inn, where there are some houses; this court hath a passage into Little Star Lane; which is but narrow, and not over well built.

Hemlock Court, a neat court with a freestone pavement, lately new built with pretty good houses; it hath a passage into Lincoln's Inn, and fronts Ship Yard.

Shear Lane, very narrow towards Temple Bar, but upwards against Little Shear Lane it groweth wider, hath better buildings and well inhabited; of this lane, only the west side is in this parish, the other being in the Liberty of the Rolls.

Searles Street, hath on the east, the new row of buildings of Lincoln's Inn, and on the west that large pile of buildings which takes up the rest of Little Lincoln's Inn Fields; and in the midst of which is Cook's Court, which is a very handsome and cleanly place, with good buildings, very well inhabited.—*From Seymour's " History of the Parishes of London and Westminster."*

THE NEW COURTS.
(See also pages 1, 12, 119, 198, and 224-5).

In the House of Lords, on Tuesday, May 12th, 1868, Lord Denman rose to call attention to the uncertainty which prevailed as to the adoption of any plan for the new Courts of Justice. He said that large votes, amounting to a million and a half sterling, had been dedicated to that purpose. In one year £700,000 had been advanced for it, and £660,000 in another, leaving only £140,000 remaining. The Court of Exchequer and the Court of the Master of the Rolls had been mentioned as models, and he believed that if two or three good courts like them were constructed for the Probate and other courts, near Carey Street, they would answer every purpose. A certificate had been given that the expense of the new Law Courts would not be more than £1,500,000, but nothing could be more vague, and it was probable that by the time they were finished, on the scale proposed, the expense would not be much less than the cost of the Abyssinian war.

The Lord Chancellor.—I am not quite sure as to the information which the noble lord desires to have, but if I understand him correctly he wishes to know what is exactly the position of the contemplated buildings of the Courts of Justice. I believe I am right in saying that the difficulty which has for the moment suspended the choice of a plan is this:—A competition was invited, which was responded to by a certain number of architects—eight or nine—who sent in plans, which were publicly exhibited. Before they were sent in a memorandum was drawn up of the terms on which the exhibition was to be held, and it was that referees should be appointed by the Treasury who were to determine to which of the plans exhibited the award of superior execution ought to be given. The referees who were charged with this duty were unable to agree that any one of the plans exhibited in competition was the best, but they selected two, and made an award that they thought the interior plan of one of the competitors and the exterior plan of another were the best. That award having been made, some of the unsuccessful competitors objected to it as being beyond the power of the referees. They said, "We entered into competition each one against every other, but not into competition with the joint production of two others." In the memorandum of the terms of competition it was stated that any matter in dispute should be referred to the decision of the Attorney-General. That has been done, and I believe the reference is still going on, and until it is concluded it will not be in the power of the Commissioners for the erection of the Palace of Justice to take any steps in regard to the selection of any plan. I hope that before long the reference will be terminated, and that the Commissioners will then be allowed to proceed with the erection of the building.

In the House of Commons, on Friday, May 15th, 1868, Mr. Denman directed attention to the same subject, and said— Great difficulty, injustice and loss is inflicted by the delay upon persons whose premises may be required, and loss is incurred by the fund. An opinion is gaining ground in the legal profession that the Government have some notion of abandoning the present plan and site, and that this notion is a hobby of the late Prime Minister and the present Lord Chancellor. The Chancellor of the Exchequer said he thought the delay has been in one respect fortunate; for, the Judicatory Commission having since been appointed, it is desirable that the question what courts shall sit in the buildings shall be decided before the question what kind of buildings they shall sit in. (Hear, hear.) No suggestion for the change of site has come before the Government, or been made by any of its members. Mr. B. Cochrane begged the noble lord, the First Commissioner of Works, to consider whether it would not be better to erect the Law Courts on the Thames Embankment instead of the site at present chosen. (Hear, hear.) Mr. Alderman Lawrence observed that an estimate had been given of the amount of money required for the purchase of the site and other expenses for the New Courts of Law, and he wished to call attention in connexion with this subject to the importance of providing sufficient approaches to the New Palace of Justice. The estimate was for the site £1,000,000, and for the buildings £2,000,000. Here was an outlay of £3,000,000. The House could not too soon admit the fact that it would be necessary to make large and wide approaches to these Courts, yet nothing of the kind had yet been carried out. With the exception of setting back the main front in the Strand, this was the only part of the building where a sufficient width of space would be obtained. He trusted that the Government would not leave these approaches to be considered at the last moment; a comparatively small expenditure now would save a large outlay hereafter, for the public would not be satisfied that the New Courts of Justice, erected at an outlay of between £3,000,000 and £4,000,000, should be surrounded with narrow lanes and impassable streets. (Hear, hear.) Mr. M. Chambers was one of those who originally considered the site chosen to be a good one. He had since altered his opinion on account of the difficulty of access. An Act of Parliament ought to be at once passed empowering the Government to purchase the site of approaches, and it would also be well to consider whether the present site cannot be sold at a profit, so that a new site may be selected.

In Mr. Vice-Chancellor's Stuart's Court on Friday, May 29th, 1868, the following case was heard :—

CORBETT v. THE COMMISSIONERS OF HER MAJESTY'S WORKS AND PUBLIC BUILDINGS.

In the course of this case it appeared that a singular and serious difficulty has arisen on the title to the site of the proposed new Law Courts, and that now it is almost cleared, and the purchases have for the most part been completed, a considerable portion of the property, instead of belonging to the several vendors absolutely, is supposed to be merely leasehold for a term of years, created in the reign of Queen Elizabeth, which has now only a few years to run. Mr. Corbett, the plaintiff, was the owner of three houses in Horseshoe Court, and of a house in St. Clement's Lane, for the residue of terms, of which about 140 years are unexpired, the houses in Horseshoe Court being held by him under an agreement for a lease for 150 years from the 25th of March, 1854, from Mr. Cook, and the house in St. Clement's Lane for the same term, under a lease from Mr. Ballenden, dated the 3rd of December, 1858. In June, 1866, the Commissioners, who had been incorporated by the Courts of Justice Concentration (Site) Act, 1865, purchased the freehold of the houses in Horseshoe Court, the conveyance being expressed to be subject to the agreement with the plaintiff; and themselves entered into an agreement with the plaintiff for apportioning the rent between the houses in Horseshoe Court and some other property held by him from Mr. Cook. In November, 1866, they agreed to purchase the plaintiff's interest in the four houses for £900. The agreement was duly approved by the First Commissioner of Her Majesty's Works; the abstract was delivered, the requisitions sent in were answered to the satisfaction of the Commissioners, the plaintiff's title was accepted, a draught surrender of his interest was prepared by the solicitors to the Commissioners, was approved by the plaintiff's solicitors, and was actually engrossed for execution before any difficulty was raised. The objection then taken was as follows:—The Commissioners, in investigating the title to the "Plough Tavern," discovered a deed dated the 27th day of July, in the 21st year of the reign of her late Majesty Queen Elizabeth, and expressed to be made between Edward Clyfton of the one part, and William Crouch of the other part, by which "all that parcel and piece of ground then newly enclosed with a mud wall by the said William Crouch or his assigns, then or lately being parcel of a field commonly called or known by the name of Fyckett's Field, alias Fickatt's Field, abutting upon the east and south-east upon a parcel of ground wherein Mr. Bosvyle had then lately builded a house, then lately enclosed out of the said field called Fyckett's Field, and the west part thereof abutting upon Clement's-inn, and also that piece of ground parcel of the said field from the west corner of the brick wall of the said Mr. Bosvyle unto the east or south-east of the building of one Guy Andrews as it was then marked and set forth with a rigall, and all the estate and interest of him, the said Edward Clyfton, of and in the ditches and the soil of the same ditches enclosing the said piece of ground, and of and in all the way and ground beyond the said ditches westward, which said pieces of ground were situate lying and being in the parish of St. Clement Danes without the bars of the New Temple of London, and free ingress, egress, regress, and passage for all people and persons whatsoever with their carts and carriages whatsoever, and for horses and carriage, by horse, or otherwise, for all needful and necessary things and causes whatsoever in by and through a gate and way leading from Chancery-lane into the said field called Fickett's-field, and so by a way from the said gate through the said field to the said parcels of ground, which way through the said field should contain in breadth ten feet of ground at the least with the appurtenances" were leased to William Crouch, his executors, administrators, and assigns from the feast of the Nativity of St. John Baptist then last past before the date thereof unto the end and term of 300 years, at the yearly rent of £5 and under and subject to the covenants and conditions therein contained, and on the part of the lessee, his executors, administrators, and assigns to be performed and observed. The parcel of ground on which Mr. Bosvyle is mentioned to have then lately built a house was situate where Boswell-court now stands, and the said lease comprised a piece of ground extending from Boswell-court to Clement's-inn, and including the piece or plot of ground on which the plaintiff's four houses stood. It was contended by the Commissioners that as it had not been shown by the plaintiff that this lease had in any manner been surrendered or determined it must be assumed that his title was derived through some person claiming under the said William Crouch until the contrary is shown, and they stated that in fact claims had been made to the reversion of the piece or plot of ground comprised in the lease expectant upon the determination of the term of 300 years, and that a good title has, in fact, been shown to the reversion in part of the ground. Under the circumstances we have stated, the Commissioners were advised by the law officers of the Crown that it would be desirable that a Bill should be brought into Parliament for the purpose of facilitating the purchase of the land for public purposes, and to defer the completion of any pending purchases to which the Act would apply until it was obtained, and it was stated that a Bill on the subject was to be introduced early in the ensuing session. The Commissioners asked for an enquiry into the plaintiff's title, and it was stated on their behalf that they had offered to pay him the amount of rent he had formerly received pending the inquiry into the validity of the deed, but the offer was declined.

Mr. Greene, Q.C., and Mr. Lindley appeared for the plaintiff; Mr. Bacon, Q.C. and Mr. Field for the Commissioners.

The Vice-Chancellor, in giving judgment, said that the plaintiff had contracted with the defendants to sell them his interest in certain leasehold houses, of which they had previously purchased the freehold. By their previous dealings with him as owners of the freehold they had recognised the lease. The abstract and the requisitions were delivered, the title approved, and the deed engrossed before any objection was taken. The defendants' case was that since all this had been done they had discovered a lease nearly 300 years old, which overrode the plaintiff's interest; they did not, however, state that they had discovered whether any rent had been paid under that lease; whether the term was still subsisting; whether it had not been surrendered; or how it had been subsequently dealt with. The Commissioners contended the discovery gave them a right to an enquiry as to the plaintiff's title. But the Vice-Chancellor was of opinion that they had precluded themselves from any further inquiry. The Commissioners being a public body, and their advisers being the law officers of the Crown, were bound in the public interest to be cautious. But in the present case the plaintiff, whose property had been taken, was clearly entitled to compensation, and to have the agreement he had entered into with the Commissioners for its purchase specifically performed.

In the House of Commons on Friday, May 29th, 1868, Mr. Baillie Cochrane again called the attention of the House to the site of the New Law Courts, which elicited some lengthy discussion from Mr. Montague Chambers, Sir George Bowyer and Mr. Cowper, after which, Lord John Manners made the following reply:—He said that the hon. member had expressed a hope that the Government would not hastily decide on the site of the new Courts of Law. This question had, however, been decided years ago by both Houses of Parliament—not hastily, nor by one decision, but by repeated Acts of Parliament extending over a series of years. Ten years ago a Royal Commission was appointed to inquire into this very question of site. That Commission reported in favour of the present site. Parliament sanctioned the purchase, which was now virtually completed, and the whole legal profession were anxiously awaiting the proper steps to be taken to carry out the intentions of Parliament, yet at such a moment the hon. member had thought proper to raise the question of an entire change of site. No doubt much might be said in favour of the site of the Thames Enbankment, but the question had been definitively settled by the Legislature. The site had cost £789,000 up to the present moment, and there were additional purchases and contingencies, so that the total amount for the purchase of the site would amount in a very short time to £896,000. The hon. and learned member asked what they could sell the site for, two, five, or ten years hence. It was impossible to form anything but the most vague conjecture as to that. They knew what the site had cost; but what it would sell for if put into the market was a matter of speculation about which he could give no opinion offhand. Then it was said it was a drawback to the present site that the Strand was not on a level with Carey Street; but he thought it would be found that there was as great if not a greater slope between the Strand and the Thames Embankment. There could be no doubt that as far as the suitors were concerned the Carey Street site would be extremely convenient. That House had from time to time appropriated considerable funds for one of the best public buildings of which we could at present boast, namely,—the Public Record Depository, behind Chancery Lane. Including the sum of £60,000 sanctioned by the House the other day, during the last two years upwards of £200,000 had been expended on that building. It was of the greatest importance that the Public Records should be kept in immediate proximity to the Courts of Law; and that point ought also to be taken into view, when they were asked to place the Courts of Law on a different site from that which Parliament had decided upon. He did not think, therefore, that the present Government ought to take upon themselves the responsibility of changing a solemn decision of the Legislature on that matter, and he felt that if anything of that kind were now attempted not only would the greatest delay ensue, but in all probability there would be an immense outlay incurred, he did not altogether say of public money, because the fund applicable to that purpose was the Suitors' Fund, but there would be an immense demand made upon that fund, the result of which no human being could tell. Most probably, however, at the end of four, five, or six years, when the new site had been purchased and cleared, and when the Government of the day had selected the architect for erecting the building, other gentlemen would rise in the House and say that the circumstances were altered, that a still better site might be obtained in the east, the west, the north, or the south, the whole question would be left in suspense, and no final decision whatever would be come to. He agreed with the right hon. member for Hertford that the site already acquired was seven acres; and if the Courts of Law could not be accommodated on that space, their requirements must be very extraordinary indeed. Under those circumstances, as his hon. friend (Mr. Baillie Cochrane) had made no motion, he hoped he would be content with the discussion which had just taken place.

The difference of opinion respecting the site for the Law Courts was at length satisfactorily settled, and the decision arrived at by Parliament to have them erected adjacent to Lincoln's Inn was confirmed. The judges appointed to examine the designs for the new Palace of Justice, not being able to select any particular plan from those submitted, suggested that Mr. Street, A.R.A., and Mr. Edward Barry, A.R.A, should be jointly entrusted with the preparation of a special design in accordance with the original instructions. To this finding of the judges, however, exception was taken, and, at the request of the Commissioners, the Treasury called for the opinion of the Attorney-General. That learned gentleman's dictum was to the effect that the decision of the adjudicators on designs did not fulfil the obligations imposed on them, and was not binding on the Government. Her Majesty's Ministers thereupon decided—taking the whole of the circumstances of the competition into consideration—to appoint Mr. Street Architect of the new Law Courts.* The style of the new buildings is to be

---

* In the House of Lords, on June 19th, 1868, a discussion on the projected New Law Courts was opened by the Marquis of Salisbury, who inquired whether it was true that the Government had rejected the design recommended by the professional judges and judges of designs as the best for plan and internal arrangements, and adopted the one which had been recommended for elevation only; further, if the competitors were instructed that utility and convenient arrangement were to be preferred to architectural effect. Animadverting on the course which had been pursued in reference to this matter, Lord Salisbury complained that although the plan of Mr. Barry was superior in respect of all the points upon which the Government had insisted, that of

Gothic, or at least a mixture—of Lombard, such as may be seen at Como and Ravenna, of Gothic Renaissance, as may be seen at

Mr. Street, which was superior only in one point—that of elevation—had been selected. The Lord Chancellor, as president of the Law Courts Commission, said that the Government had neither rejected nor adopted any design. The terms of competition were arranged by a minute agreed on by the Treasury and submitted to and concurred in by the architects. In fact it was in the nature of a contract arrangement with those gentlemen; and it was a mistake to suppose it was ever intended that the competition should result in the selection of any particular plan. It was rather with a view to test the merits of the plans of the various architects, without pledging the Government to the adoption of any. The judges being unable to say which one of the competitors had been most successful, sent in their award to that effect; but putting the plans of Mr. Barry and Mr. Street together, they said they thought that Mr. Street's was the best for the external elevation, and Mr. Barry's the best for internal arrangements. Several of the architects objecting that they had not entered the lists to compete with two, and demurring to the award as technically unfair, the Treasury consulted the Commission, over which he (the Lord Chancellor) presided, who recommended that the opinion of the Attorney-General should be taken upon the point, and that opinion was that the reference had failed, and that, so far as the award was concerned, Mr. Barry and Mr. Street could not be regarded as successful competitors, and that the whole proceeding by competition had thus come to an end. It then became the duty of the Government to say who should be the architect for superintending the building of the Courts. At the same time another competition was now going on with respect to the National Gallery, which, singularly enough, miscarried just in the same way; but the judges pointed out that in this case the design of Mr. Barry exhibited the greatest amount of architectural excellence in the elevation, and the result was that they assigned to Mr. Street the task of erecting the Law Courts, and to Mr. Barry that of building the National Gallery. Upon the whole he believed that the course taken was the one most conducive to the erection of a building which would secure the objects that both Parliament and the public had in view.

On Monday, June 29th, 1868, Mr. J. Goldsmid called attention to the recent appointments of architects for the new public buildings in the metropolis, and moved for a select committee to inquire into the subject. The hon. gentleman proceeded to recount, step by step, each incident of the proceedings, from February, 1866, when five gentlemen had been appointed as judges of the designs for the Law Courts, to the present time, when the Treasury, acting under the advice of the Attorney-General, that as priority could not be given to the design of any one of the architects it was open to them to appoint whom they pleased, selected Mr. Street as the architect. There was, on the other hand, the petition of Mr. Barry before the House, praying for an inquiry into the matter, and this gentleman's design was pronounced by Messrs. Shaw and Pownall to be the best with regard to interior arrangement. Mr. Gregory seconded the motion. Mr. Gladstone, Mr. Lowe, Sir R. Palmer, Mr. B. Hope, Mr. Powell, Mr. Childers and Mr. Bentinck thought there was not sufficient reason for the appointment of a committee. Mr. Tite suggested that the Equity Courts should be built on the Carey Street site by Mr. Street, and that all the other Courts should be erected on the reclaimed land of the Thames Embankment by Mr. Barry. Mr. M. Chambers also stated that there was a growing opinion out of doors that the proper place for the erection of the Law Courts was in front of the River Thames. Mr. Pease said whatever celebrity Mr. Street possessed as an architect was in connection with church architecture, but this was not the style they required in the Law Courts. They wanted no "dim religious light" to be introduced there, but that the light of justice should illuminate the judgments to be delivered there. Mr. Winterbotham supported the motion for a committee, and complained that the contract entered into by the Government had not been religiously observed. After which, Lord J. Manners said

Ghent and Bruges, and of pointed and florid, as may be seen at Westminster.

Considering the greatness of the prize at stake, not only in money, but in that which many men value far more highly, fame, it was very natural that some amount of dissatisfaction and heartburning should have been caused by the decision arrived at by the Premier (for it is known to be his decision), but those who know the extent of the excitement and indignation which attended the appointment of the architect for the New Palace of Westminster, will be rather surprised at the mildness of the attack in the present instance, and will see in it an indication of what those who are well-informed on the subject know to be the fact, that the appointment of Mr. Street has given general and genuine satisfaction.

In a letter of Mr. George Gilbert Scott's, one of the architects who competed for the designs for the New Law Courts, inserted in the *Times* of July 2nd, 1868, he says:—" I cannot but rejoice that this great work has fallen into the hands of an architect of the highest class of talent, and in whom, without derogating from the talents of his competitors, we may feel full confidence that he will produce a building worthy of our age and country."

---

he understood the object of the hon. member for Honiton was not to obtain a committee to inquire into the subject-matter connected with the appointment of Mr. Street, but into the various appointments of architects for new public buildings within the last two or three years. He thought no such inquiry could be proceeded with at this period of the year. Mr. Barry had been appointed with reference to the National Gallery, Mr. Street for the Law Courts, Mr. Scott for the two public offices, the Home and Colonial, which were intended to complete the quadrangle in connection with the Foreign Office and India Office; and Mr. Waterhouse, whose appointment was made by the late Government, for the new buildings at South Kensington which were to receive the natural history collections from the British Museum. As he understood the right hon. member for Calne, his proposal was that nothing should be referred to the committee except to inquire whether there was not a contract between the Government and the competing architects, and whether the Government were not under some legal obligations. No more weight was to be attached to the opinion of Messrs. Shaw and Pownall than to the opinion since so weightily and remarkably endorsed. If the Government were not to start *de novo*, how could they be bound by a part of the award? Legally, the thing was at an end, and the Government sought to come to a decision fair to the competitors and safe for the country. They have arrived at such a decision, and the tone of the debate shows that the House is of that opinion (hear, hear, and cries of "Divide"). The House divided, and the numbers were—For the amendment, 45; against, 90; majority, 45. The amendment was therefore lost.

The following changes in the Commission have occurred since printing the list of Commissioners* (see page 3) :—

Right Hon. the Lord High Chancellor: Lord Cairns in the place of Lord Chelmsford. Right Hon. the Chancellor of the Exchequer: the Right Hon. G. Ward Hunt in the place of the Right Hon. B. Disraeli. Hon. Vice-Chancellor: Sir G. M. Giffard in the place of Sir W. Page Wood, now Lord Justice. The Solicitor-General: Sir William Balliol Brett, M.P., in the place of Sir C. J. Selwyn, now Lord Justice. President of the Law Society: John Henry Bolton, Esq., in place of Bartle J. Frere, Esq.

THE STRAND IMPROVEMENTS.

On Thursday, July 16, 1868, Mr. Alderman Lawrence asked the First Commissioner of Works whether notices would be served during the autumn on the owners of houses in Holywell Street, and also on the owners of houses in the line of a new street from the Strand to Lincoln's Inn Fields, on the west side of the proposed New Law Courts, in order that a bill might be brought in during the next Session of Parliament, to provide approaches to the site of the New Courts of Justice, by the removal of Holywell Street and the formation of a new street from the Strand to Lincoln's Inn Fields. Lord J. Manners said the Royal Commissioners did not recommend the removal of the property referred to by the hon. member for the approaches to the New Law Courts. And, however desirable it might be that these houses should be removed for metropolitan improvements, her Majesty's Government had no intention of giving the notices with a view of bringing in a bill for the purchase of the property next year.

---

* The difficulties with respect to some of the leases to which we have previously referred have now been overcome, and the Commissioners have resolved to clear the whole of the site by the end of the present year.

SHALL ANOTHER SITE BE PURCHASED FOR THE NEW LAW COURTS?

We extract the following from a leader in the *Times* of Wednesday, July 22, 1868.

"We are glad to see that in the matter of the site for the New Law Courts Mr. Baillie Cochrane has returned to the charge, and has for the second time this session given notice that he will urge upon Parliament the claims of the space on the South side of the Strand as superior to those of the area lately cleared on the North. He is now armed with a fresh argument, and, in our opinion, a very potent one. By common consent the time has arrived for the concentration of the Public Departments; already various plans for the purpose are afloat; three have been submitted to Parliament this session, though none as yet have been discussed; and of these one—that by Sir Charles Trevelyan—proposes to utilize the site of the Embankment beyond Somerset House for the Admiralty and War Office. Mr. Baillie Cochrane holds the opinion, in which we entirely concur, that this state of things affords a new reason why Government should stay the commencement of buildings upon the Carey Street site until they have reconsidered, or rather considered for the first time, the advantages of the site between Somerset House and the Temple. Were the New Law Courts the only public edifice now proposed to be erected, and were the sole object to provide a central site for the administration of justice, the choice of site would still be of national concern; much more so is it now, when there is an opportunity of making the new Courts part of a vast scheme for embellishing the metropolis, and of securing for the river an unbroken front of public edifices from Westminster Bridge to the Temple. Even in its present condition, the intervening space between the Middle Temple Library and Somerset House is unsightly enough, with its stone, timber, and coal wharves; but let it become an ugly break in a long line of noble buildings, a mere blot on a handsome river facade, and it will simply be intolerable. The country will have to invent a public building to put upon it."

"For ourselves, we are at a loss to comprehend how it is that the river facade, when once suggested as a site, was not immediately recognised to be of incomparable value. That the Law Courts, on the one hand, would look upon the river, would front a vast expanse of sky, and so be secure of abundant air and abundant light, and would, without being liable to the disturbances of dust or noise, command a prospect of the busy out-of-door life of the metropolis both on land and water; and, on the other hand, that they would stand out visible to the eyes, and therefore proclaim their object to all the inhabitants of the opposite shore, and the myriads navigating the stream, traversing the bridges, and circulating in what will then be one of the great metropolitan thoroughfares, the street parallel to the Embankment—these alone are advantages enough, in our opinion, to throw into the shade any other competitors, and to cover a multitude of drawbacks, if, indeed, they ever existed. From the vehemence of the advocates for the Carey Street site one might suppose there was as much difference between the North and South sides of the Strand as there was to Beau Brummell and his satellites between the East and West sides of Temple Bar. But can anyone seriously argue that the site between the Temple and Somerset House is one whit less central than the Carey Street site? It is certainly more spacious. It is also more accessible. For while the Strand is the common approach to both, Oxford Street, which is the northern boundary of the one, is, as a means of communication with the East and West of London, far inferior to the three thoroughfares, the river, the railway, and the Embankment, which run immediately on the south of the other. What, then, are the objections brought against the Embankment site? They seem to be reducible to three, which, after the fashion of Lord Salisbury, and for the sake of brevity, we will christen by the short titles of the Lincoln's Inn Objection, the Money Objection, and the 'Settled and done with' Objection.

"The Lincoln's Inn objection is put forward in the name of the profession. It is said that if the Courts are placed south of the Strand they will be removed from the chambers of barristers and the offices of solicitors, and that the ancient connection with the Inn will be utterly broken. Now, for the Society of Lincoln's Inn we have a sincere respect, and we shall be very sorry if the result of the change be at all to depreciate its property or to lower its importance. We cannot, however, but remember that in this matter the interest of Lincoln's Inn is not supreme, and if it clashes with the public advantage, the Society ought to give way, and, we are sure, will give way with a good grace. What Lincoln's Inn and Gray's Inn may lose the Middle Temple and the Inner Temple will gain. Much of that which will be lost to Lincoln's Inn must be lost to it whichever be the site adopted. Under the Carey Street scheme, equally with that of the Embankment, the Lord Chancellor will no longer hear causes in the ancient dining-hall of the Benchers, and the Courts of Equity will be held on the freehold of the nation, not of the Society of Lincoln's Inn. Again, though much will be taken, much will remain. The hall will be as available as now for dinners, lectures, and meetings; and as to the library, though for the purposes of reference by those engaged in the Courts it will be superseded by the public library open alike to barristers and solicitors, yet for members of the Inn desiring to pursue their legal studies continuously, it will become more convenient, because less crowded. Barristers will not suffer by the change. True, they must have their chambers close by the Court, and, in the event of a transfer of the

Courts to the southern side of the Strand, their present chambers in Lincoln's Inn might become inconveniently remote. These would have to be quitted, but they would be quitted without much regret. Those whose lot has been cast in Lincoln's Inn, or who have had to attend consultations there, know well what old-fashioned, tumble-down, ill-arranged buildings are the houses in Old Square and New Square. Whatever happens to the Courts, these houses must, before long, be pulled down and rebuilt. They have ceased to suffice; and for want of room in Lincoln's Inn, barristers are forced out into Chancery Lane on one side and Serle Street on the other. To give up such chambers as these is no sacrifice, if only others adjoining to the new Courts can be had in their stead, and, happily, this is a matter which does not admit of a doubt. Within a stone's throw of the suggested site of the Law Courts there is a space admirably fitted as building land for chambers, vacant, and already the property of the Commissioners of Public Works. We mean the space recently cleared between Carey Street and the Strand. Here might be erected handsome buildings specially designed for the use they would be intended to serve, and properly appointed with all modern improvements. The new chambers would be ready as soon as the new Courts, and the migration of the Bar might happen concurrently with that of the Judges. To solicitors it is likewise important, though by no means so important that their offices should be near the Courts. But if the Courts were placed, as proposed, between Somerset House and the Temple, there would be no need for solicitors to abandon that which is now their principal seat of custom, Lincoln's Inn Fields. That square would scarcely be further off from the new Courts than it is from those now existing. With Gray's Inn and Bedford-row it would be otherwise, but the accommodation now yielded by those localities would be found in Lincoln's Inn, which in proportion as it was vacated by barristers would be available for solicitors. In short, we are satisfied that there is no ground for any professional apprehension that proper chambers for barristers and offices for solicitors may not be found. The general effect would be that the entire world of Chancery—the buildings and the inhabitants thereof—would be removed a few hundred yards to the south, where there is ample space ready to receive them.

"The next is the Money Objection. 'What extravagance,' people say, 'first to buy one site at enormous cost, clear it of buildings, and then, just when all is ready for the architect, to take disgust, throw it up, and buy another. A million and three-quarters seemed a sufficiently handsome sum to pay for a single building; but now we are told a second site has to be bought, to cost we know not what—certainly more than the former one, because covered with superior houses instead of courts and alleys. And if we buy a second site who knows that we shall not be called upon to buy a third, at Westminster, for instance? Is London to be dealt with as the primæval forest by the settler, who, needing a few acres for tillage, sets fire to the wood at random, and so clears a waste from which he may choose a site at his leisure and change it again at discretion?' Well, by all means let us count the cost. We shall have to buy a new site, and pay for it, probably, a sum of nearly a million. But it does not follow that the old site is so much waste, or, indeed, any waste. On the contrary, as we have seen, it may be utilized in direct connection with the Law Courts, and in a manner absolutely remunerative. After all, too, the cost, great as it is, is not too great; and were it otherwise, it might be a reason for deferring the execution of the undertaking; but it could not be a reason for choosing an inferior site. A national work like this should be done in the best manner possible, or not done at all.

"Lastly, as to the 'Settled and done with' Objection. The argument is that the matter is concluded by the decisions of Commissions and of Parliament, which it is too late now to undo. But these decisions, so far as they bear upon the present subject, can carry weight only with those who are ignorant of the history of what has occurred.* They were decisions practically made *ex parte*, without even entertaining the claims of the Embankment site. The point never came before the Royal Commissioners of 1858. Their Report states that they had considered three sites—one the Lincoln's Inn site, another the Westminster site, and a third the Carey Street site, and that they recommended the last. The Embankment site is not so much as mentioned, and for an obvious reason—the Embankment was then a thing of the future. The object of the Bill of 1865, for the purchase of the Carey Street site, was to carry into effect the recommendation of the previous Commission; as it passed through Parliament, the claims of the Embankment site could not be completely overlooked, since the Embankment works were then already in progress; but it was most cursorily and imperfectly discussed, only to be discarded, not so much on the merits of the case as on the ground that if the Bill were thrown out the whole scheme for the concentration of the Courts would be indefinitely postponed, if not perish altogether. The Select Committee to whom the Bill was referred took no notice at all of the question of the site south of the Strand, and so the Act was passed. The Royal Commissioners of 1865 succeeded in giving effect to the Act; but they also had no instructions to enter upon the consideration of change of site, and, in point of fact, have not done so. Once only in the course of the present session has the question been raised by Mr. Baillie Cochrane, but no adequate debate followed, the arguments of the present and the late First Commissioner of Works having been very slight and unconvincing. It is impossible, therefore, to say that the matter has been subjected to that thorough investigation which as a national question it eminently deserves."

THE NEW LAW COURTS.

The following is extracted from a leading article in the *Standard* of Friday, July 23rd :—

"The question of the site of the New Law Courts, which we might reasonably suppose was settled three years ago, is once more, it seems, to be opened for discussion in the House of Commons. Mr. Baillie Cochrane is unremitting in his efforts to get the site changed from the north of the Strand to the banks of the Thames, and he has found an advocate in the press to take up his cause with singular zeal and fervour. It is declared, as some excuse for Mr. Baillie Cochrane's persistency, that he has acquired a new argument, said to be 'a very potent one.' The new argument is that 'by common consent the time has arrived for the concentration of the public departments,' that 'already various plans for the purpose are afloat;' that 'three have been submitted to Parliament this session, though none as yet has been discussed;' and that one of these three proposes to utilise the site of the Embankment beyond Somerset House for the Admiralty and the War Office. This state of things, it is affirmed, affords a new reason why the Government should suspend the construction of the building on the Carey Street site until they have reconsidered the advantages of the site between Somerset House and the Temple. The choice of site, it is argued, becomes a matter of special national concern now, when there is an opportunity of devising a vast scheme for the embellishment of the metropolis, and of obtaining for the Thames an unbroken front of public edifices from Westminster Bridge to the Temple.

"We cannot say that we are greatly impressed with the potency of this new argument with which Mr. Baillie Cochrane has armed himself, nor do we perceive in it a sufficient ground for re-opening a question which was determined upon its merits long ago. The consideration now put forth is certainly not new, and must have occurred to the Commissioners in 1865, if not in 1858. It has been ventilated and discussed any time during these three years, both in and out of Parliament. 'By common consent,' it is said, 'the time has arrived for the concentration of the public departments.' Whence do we gather this 'common consent,' and how is it that it comes now only for the first time? Admitting that it is desirable that the public departments should be concentrated, it does not follow that the Thames site is better than the Carey Street for the Law Courts. In the first place, the Law Courts are a department by themselves, not necessarily connected with the public offices, properly termed such. There may be a reason for joining the War Office to the Admiralty, and both to the Treasury or the Foreign Office; but there is certainly not the same reason for connecting the place where justice is administered with either of the above departments. We deny that the offices of law are a 'department' at all, in the sense required. Again, we maintain that whatever advantage there may be in having the Law Courts near the public offices is sufficiently secured by the Carey Street site. Allusion is made to some plan, already in existence, for constructing the new Admiralty and the War Office on the site beyond Somerset House on the Thames Embankment. Here, then, we have the concentration desired. Why not carry out Sir Charles Trevelyan's scheme, and thus occupy the ground between the Middle Temple and Somerset House? When this is done there will be little more than the width of the Strand between the principal public departments and the Law Courts—a proximity quite sufficient to meet the public convenience.

"Mr. Baillie Cochrane's new and potent argument being dismissed, there seems to be no other reason, but such as has been discussed a score of times, for changing the site of the Law Courts from Carey Street to the space between the Temple and Somerset House. We admit fully all that is said in praise of the Thames Embankment as a site for a public building. We deny only that it is a site specially suited to the Law Courts, or at least better suited than the site which has been fixed upon. It must be shown not only that the Thames Embankment site is good in itself, but that it is better than the one to which it is sought to be preferred. If they are equally good, then it is clearly not worth while to sacrifice all that we have done in the clearing of Carey Street and its neighbourhood, and to incur the delay perhaps of another two years, in going from the north to the south of the Strand. Not a single objection is brought forward to the Carey Street site in itself, and it is universally admitted to be central, accessible, and convenient. A building, such as is contemplated, would be not only admirably placed here for the purposes of justice, but it would tend to elevate and beautify what is at present one of the most prominently filthy portions of the metropolis. And surely if the interests of law and justice are sufficiently respected, we can afford to consider also the interests of one of the busiest and most popular thoroughfares in London.

"In favour of the Embankment site it is urged that the Law Courts would look upon the river, would 'front a vast expanse of sky,' and would command 'a prospect of the busy out-of-door life of the metropolis both on land and water!' that they would 'stand out visible to all eyes and proclaim their object to all the inhabitants of the opposite shore, and the myriads navigating the stream, traversing the bridges, and circulating in what will then be one of the great metropolitan thoroughfares—the street parallel to the Embankment.' A great deal of this is pure nonsense. What do the Law Courts want of 'a vast expanse of sky?' What is it to the judges or the lawyers to secure a prospect of the busy out-of-door life of the metropolis? What is the object in making the courts 'stand out visible to all eyes?' To carry out the impression which it seems by this theory that it is the function of our Palace of Justice to produce, should we not have a row of gibbets along the river front, with an ornament cunningly introduced in the architecture, suggestive of fine and penal servitude, a black cap surmounting the whole, and effigies of judges in their robes standing out visibly, for the better proclamation of the object of the building to the inhabitants of the opposite shore? Why should it be supposed that the Surrey side in particular requires this bodily presentment before their eyes of the form of justice? Why should the bargees be specially selected as the subjects of this curious architectural lesson? It puzzles us to discover any particular relation between justice and the river side. So far as the outside world are concerned, it certainly is not true that they are more liable to be struck with a building on a river bank than in a street. The Parliament Houses are a capital instance in point. What special advantages, architectural or otherwise, have been secured by building them with a river frontage? Can anyone deny that the building is ten times as interesting from the land side as from the water?

"There is no pretence whatever for saying that the claims of the Thames Embankment site have never been fairly discussed. Every one has allowed these claims, but not as superior to those of Carey Street, as a site for our new Law Courts. As for the 'Lincoln's Inn objection,' of that we take no account. The 'money objection' is scarcely more worthy of consideration. If it could be proved that the Thames Embankment site offers any advantages superior to those of Carey Street, it would be cheap to make the change, even after we have incurred the expense of clearing the ground to the north of the Strand. But we see no reason for any sacrifice at all either of the public money or the public time. The ground upon which it is proposed to build the New Law Courts is admirably suited to the purpose, and the improvement which will be made in this quarter of London by the erection of such a building as we look for from Mr. Street is of the utmost importance to the whole neighbourhood, both in a moral and architectural point of view. The Thames Embankment is a capital site for a range of great public buildings; and there are plenty of these projected to fill up this space and adorn the river."

In the House of Commons, on Thursday, July 23rd, 1868, in reply to Mr. Alderman Lawrence respecting the New Law Courts, the Chancellor of the Exchequer said that the plans of the New Law Courts will be settled by the Treasury with the advice of commissioners. With regard to the funds, the Act provides that £200,000 shall be voted by Parliament in consideration of the surrender to the Government of the building by the side of Westminster Hall now occupied by law courts. A million is to be contributed from the surplus interest of the Suitors' Fee Fund, and the rest is to come out of a fund to be provided by fees paid by suitors, other than those in the Court of Chancery, extending over a period of fifty years. He could not say whether the contracts will be submitted to Parliament this session, as the final plans have not yet been decided on.

On July 29th, the following letter from Mr. Baillie Cochrane was published in the *Times*:—

"Sir,—A severe indisposition and the late period of the session have combined to make me withdraw the notice I have given of my intention to call the attention of the House to the report of the Committee on the Reconstruction of the Public Offices; but while I am precluded from addressing myself to the House of Commons, perhaps you will permit me the favour of making a few observations on this important subject through the medium of your columns.

"When, some years since, the attention of the public was drawn to the inadequacy of the accommodation for the public offices, the idea of the Thames Embankment was only just originated; a portion of this magnificent design is completed, and will this week be thrown open to the public; the remainder is in progress, and it is obvious that in any new scheme for the improvement and embellishment of the metropolis the admirable site afforded by the Embankment should not be overlooked.

"In the debate on the New Law Courts, I presumed to lay down the principle that in all new buildings, light, air, space, and facility of access were the first considerations, and it is evident that no site can fulfil these conditions so well as the Thames Embankment.

"Three plans for the reconstruction of the public offices have been submitted to Parliament—1, that of the Government; 2, Sir Charles Trevelyan's; and 3, Colonel Clarke's. Of these three plans, the two latter keep in view the importance of the Thames Embankment; that of the Government passes it by. The expense of such scheme is much the same, something under four millions, for the erection of the new buildings, including the purchase of old houses and ground—a small sum to be paid for the economy and efficiency of the public services and the beauty of the metropolis when we consider that within the last ten years the city of Paris has raised forty millions, and the Spanish Government twenty millions for the embellishment of their respective capitals.

"It is not my desire to discuss the merits of these plans, which have been deferred to another Parliament. Lord John Manners is very sound and practical in his views, and has advanced excellent reasons for concentrating all the public offices between Charing Cross and George Street; but Sir Charles Trevelyan and Colonel Clarke both attach great importance to the Thames Embankment site, and consider beauty as well as utility in their designs; and as the æsthetic view may find most favour with the public, it is well to pause and consider before any irrevocable step is taken which may affect the scheme of general improvement.

"If the arguments which were brought forward the other day in favour of placing the New Law Courts on the site of the Thames Embankment, between Somerset House and the Temple, had weight at that time, they are still more important since the publication of this report; for, should either Sir Charles Trevelyan's or Colonel Clarke's plan find favour with the new House of Commons, the New Law Courts, placed on the Embankment, will form a magnificent feature in the general scheme. Here too, will be found all the requirements of light, air, space, and facility of access, every one of which is wanting in the Carey Street site.

"Here is an opportunity for embellishing the metropolis which, once lost, can never be regained. A million of money would be saved by the transfer of the site; for the space between Somerset House and the Temple may be purchased for the value of the houses which must be destroyed to afford access to the New Courts in Carey Street. The space afforded on the Thames Embankment is precisely double that on the north of the Strand. Here, instead of small Law Courts lit by skylights, dark passages, and confined rooms, there would be space for the accommodation of the Bar and of the public worthy of the capital of a great nation.

"And what is the one argument against the change of site?—That the matter has been too long delayed, and that the question is predetermined.

"My sincere trust, however, is that this view may still be modified. I am doing simple justice to Lord John Manners and Mr. Cowper in expressing my opinion that they have both gained great approval for the interest they have shown in the adornment of the capital. It can only be from the want of fuller consideration that the advantages of the Thames Embankment site for the New Law Courts are for the moment so entirely overlooked. Carrying out Sir Charles Trevelyan's plan, it is impossible to deny that the Thames Embankment from the Palace of Westminster will be unequalled in its beauty. The Admiralty and the War Office, placed on the Embankment next Westminster Bridge, will be followed by park-like ground, in which palatial edifices, such as Montague House, will be well-placed. It is then proposed to complete Whitehall according to a part of the original design. Between

Whitehall and Somerset House will be a large space for public buildings or noble private mansions; and to complete the whole the New Law Courts will replace the mass of dilapidated buildings which now deface the riverside. Thomson prophetically anticipated such a site and such a result when he described London as one day it would appear:—

> 'For kings and senates fit, the Palace see !
> The Temple, breathing a religious awe :
> E'en fram'd with elegance, the plain retreat,
> The private dwelling. Certain in his aim,
> Taste never idly working, saves expense,'

This is true. 'Taste never idly working, saves expense.' A thing of beauty is not only a joy for ever, but it is an economy. Beauty consists, not in extravagance, but in the combination of things pleasing in themselves, which lend to each an additional grace and charm. A grand Embankment is disfigured by defective buildings; noble edifices are lost in narrow streets. Place the palatial structure on the best site, and you add to the beauty of each. It has been well said of the Thames Embankment, that if we had not a suitable public building to place there we ought to invent one.

"I have the honour to remain, Sir, your most obedient servant,
"ALEXANDER BAILLIE COCHRANE."

"*Folkstone, July 29th.*"

In the House of Lords, on July 30th, 1868, Lord Denman rose to inquire of her Majesty's Government whether the Commissioners under the Courts of Justice Building Act had recommended any definite plan, and whether the Lords of the Treasury had adopted such recommendation and approved any contract as to a Palace of Justice. The noble lord expressed his opinion that the proposed concentration of the courts of law on one site would involve an expenditure of some four or five millions sterling, and that the measure was one of very doubtful expediency. He therefore hoped that no hasty step would be taken in the matter, but that the Government would consent to wait until the next session of Parliament before they entered into any contract with an architect for the erection of the projected buildings. The Lord Chancellor said that the Commissioners under the Courts of Justice Building Act had not yet actually recommended any definite plan to the Government, and therefore the Lords of the Treasury had not adopted any recommendation or approved any contract. At the same time, he was bound to add that the members of the Commission to which the noble lord had referred held a meeting a few days since, at which they agreed to a draught letter to the Treasury accompanying sketches of certain plans to be submitted for approval. That letter and the accompanying sketches of plans had not yet been despatched, but were about to be so; and that was the present state of the matter as between the Commissioners and the Government.

OPENING OF THE THAMES EMBANKMENT FOOTWAY.
(See pages 226 to 230.)

AT noon, on July 31st, 1868, the footway of the Thames Embankment, from Westminster Bridge to the Temple, was formally opened for public traffic. Killing two birds with one stone, the Metropolitan Board of Works appointed the same day for an official inspection of the Abbey Mills pumping station, the last great work connected with the main drainage system of the metropolis. Accordingly, about twelve o'clock, some three hundred gentlemen and ladies were admitted to the Embankment at Westminster under the guidance of Sir John Thwaites, the chairman of the Board, with whom were Lord John Manners, M.P., Chief Commissioner of Works, the Right Honourable W. Cowper, M.P., Major-General Seymour, Mr. Tite, M.P., Mr. Bazalgette, C.E., Colonel Hogg, M.P., Mr. Ayrton, M.P., Mr. Alderman Lawrence, M.P., Mr. Locke King, M.P., Lord Ebury, the Marquis Townshend, the Lord Mayor, Mr. Sheriff M'Arthur, Captain Shaw, Mr. Fowler, the Rev. Alton Hatchard, Mr. Lowman Taylor, Mr. Freeman, Mr. Newton, and nearly all the members of the Board of Works. Headed by the two gentlemen first named, the company walked in a slow, and indeed solemn manner, along the course of the footway lying between the two points of inauguration. Apart from the work itself, which is alike excellent in design and execution, and in that substantiality on which, as distinguished from meretriciousness, we as a nation are apt to pride ourselves, there was nothing to relieve the route from the staidness of an ordinary promenade. On the one hand lay the waste land which in due course will be levelled into a roadway, and on the other the broad expanse of the Thames, enlivened, as at all times the king of English rivers is, with many and various kinds of craft. Near the Temple end of the embankment road the appearance of one sergeant and two privates of the Royal Artillery standing behind half a dozen small carronades betokened that some kind of a demonstration was to be made. Two steamers had come up from Westminster, and while the company were stepping on board a wave of the hat by Sir John Thwaites was accepted as a signal by the artillerymen, and off went the small guns in by no means quick or regular succession. The reports brought down the street boys in force to the temporary pallisading which runs along the landside of the footway, but these, obedient to the powers that be, as represented by two or three policemen, did not attempt by an escalade to cause even a temporary excitement. And so, without even a cheer, the opening of one of the greatest works of modern London was celebrated.

A pleasant run down the river as far as North Woolwich brought the party to debarcation on the pier there, where a special train of the Great Eastern Railway stood in waiting, and by it the company were carried along through the bare, barren, and sparsely-populated districts of the Plaistow Marshes to the locality of the pumping station at Abbey Mills.

The pumping station of the northern main drainage works at Abbey Mills is by no means such a building as an ordinary-minded man would imagine such a place to be. The principal structure is in itself an architectural achievement of no mean order. It is mainly built of brick, the red and white being picturesquely arranged, is highly decorated with carved stone work, furnished with windows of plate-glass, and is surmounted by a cupola that might not unreasonably be mistaken for that of an observatory. The extreme length is 142 feet, with two arms of 47 feet each, making the building of the shape of a cross; and there are besides two boiler-houses of 100 feet in length by 62 in width. The height of the engine-house from the foundation is four stories, two of which to the depth of 38 feet are below ground; and two stories above measure 62 feet. Two chimney shafts of graceful construction, one on each side of the engine-house, rise to the height of 209 feet, and are of eight feet internal diameter throughout. The object of the pumping engines is to raise the sewage out of the main drain, which clears the greater part of North London, from a lower to a higher level, along which it flows by gravitation into the Thames at Barking. To this end machinery of commensurate magnitude and power has been erected in the houses just described. There, again, the visitor will be surprised at the highly decorative character of the interior. Iron galleries running round the house are supported by pillars and arches of the same metal, the pillars coloured with a groundwork of chocolate, the arches with a light mauve, picked out with gold stars and ornamented with gay designs. Gigantic wheels, enormous cranks, pistons and shafts in grand and regular motion, do the stupendous work that is effected in the noisome chambers far below; and so admirably is the purpose accomplished, that little or

THE THAMES EMBANKMENT. 313

no atmospheric taint, other than arises from the working of machinery generally, can be detected. The company were conducted through the works by Sir John Thwaites and Mr. Bazalgette, and were evidently highly astonished, as well as interested, at the working of this great sanitary scheme.

With reference to the two great works just inaugurated, it may be remarked, that although the idea of an embankment of the Thames was brought forward by Sir Frederick French and Mr. Martin, the painter, upwards of forty years ago, and though plans were at a later period prepared for the Corporation by Mr. James Walker, Mr. Page, and others, the 'designs for the present embankment were the production of Mr. Bazalgette, the engineer of the Metropolitan Board of Works. The northern embankment, between Westminster and Blackfriars Bridges, is 6,640 feet in length, and the cost of the works, as tendered for and commenced in 1864, was £875,500. The paved footway is 20 feet wide, with approaches to Villiers Street, Wellington Street, and Essex Street, Strand. The roadway will be 100 feet wide, including both footpaths, but is not to be formed until after the Metropolitan District Railway Company shall have completed their works, which will for a considerable length pass under the new road. The embankment road will be continued by a new street, which is now being formed, from Blackfriars Bridge to the Mansion House. About thirty-seven acres of land have been reclaimed from the mud banks of the river by the embankment, which will be laid out in approaches, ornamental grounds and gardens, as soon as the railway works have sufficiently advanced to admit of its execution.

As regards the sewage of the metropolis, now carried by the main drainage system far down the Thames, to the great purification of the river in London, it was found necessary to raise the whole from a lower to a higher level in the course of twelve miles through which the main drains run. For this purpose there are two pumping stations on the north side and two on the south side of the Thames. Of those on the south side, one is situate at Deptford Creek, of 500 nominal horse-power, and the other at the Crossness outfall, also of 500 nominal horse-power; the latter was opened by the Prince of Wales in April, 1865. That just opened on the north side, at Abbey Mills, is of 1,140 horse-power, and is by far the largest and most important. The fourth, of 240 horse-power, will be at Pimlico. The Abbey Mills pumps will lift the sewage of Acton, Hammersmith, Fulham, Shepherd's Bush, Kensington, Brompton, Pimlico, Westminster, the City, Whitechapel, Stepney, Mile End, Wapping, Limehouse, Bow, and Poplar, representing an area of 25 square miles, a height of 36 feet from the low-level to the high-level sewers, whence it will flow on by the side of the high-level gravitating sewers to the northern or Barking outfall, and thus it is there are no pumps at the northern as at the southern outfall. The maximum quantity of sewage and rainfall which it is estimated the eight steam engines at Abbey Mills will have to lift is 15,000 cubic feet per minute. A portion of the sewage of the north side of London has been very successfully applied to the irrigation of a farm of about 250 acres at Barking, where grass and root crops and fruit have been raised in luxurious abundance; and but for the difficulties which have been experienced in the Money Market during the last year or two, it is probable the whole of the sewage would ere long have been thus employed in the production of food for the London markets. The works have attracted the attention and gained the admiration of eminent engineers, both English and foreign, and have notably placed Mr. Bazalgette in the foremost rank in this department of his profession.*

On Friday, September 11th, 1868, the designs for the new Law Courts, which were deposited at the old Insolvent Debtors' Court, were removed by order of the Government to South Kensington Museum, for exhibition and for the purpose of study, according to the term of the contest, and will remain the property of the nation.

Clement's Inn.
(See also pages 127, 144, 197, 287.)

On September 3rd, 1868, Mr. Glasier sold by public auction for about £300, all that portion of the above inn which extends from the porter's lodge, just inside the gate, at the south end near the Strand, to the wall at the north end. Mr. Fairfoot, as one of the senior members of the Society, and as representing a firm which has occupied chambers there for nearly half a century, writes:—"The status of the Society as an Inn of Court is not affected, and the present members entertain a confident hope that a new and appropriate edifice will be erected on or near the very important site they still possess, where the Society, which has been in existence at least three hundred years, will continue to flourish for many future generations."

---

* On June 19th, 1868, at the Metropolitan Board of Works, the tenders for the construction of the Thames Embankment between the Temple and Blackfriars Bridge were opened. The highest was £179,000, and the lowest £126,000. The latter, that of Mr. W. Webster, was accepted.

The Late Sir John Dean Paul.

(See also pages 108, 249.*)*

This gentleman died at St. Alban's, on September 7th, 1868. We copy the following remarks from the *Standard* of September 14th, 1868.

The *Morning Star* says :—

Events crowd upon and obliterate one another so rapidly now-a-days that it is probable to many of our readers this name evoked no particular recollection and aroused no particular idea. And yet it is only thirteen years since London was ringing with the details of the frauds perpetrated by the deceased baronet and his partners, Messrs. Strahan and Bates. On the 29th October, 1855, the three partners were arraigned at the Old Bailey on the prosecution of a Dr. Griffiths, before Baron Alderson, Baron Martin, and Mr. Justice Willes, were found guilty, and sentenced by Mr. Baron Alderson to fourteen years' transportation. Few who were present will ever forget the scene in the court on that cold, grey, autumnal evening. Baron Alderson broke down several times in passing sentence, and was occasionally inaudible; the prosecutor, Dr. Griffiths, wept like a child; while the prisoners seemed completely stunned, and were unable to utter a word. Then Sir John Dean Paul passed out of the world's ken; rumours occasionally came of his good behaviour in prison, where he was engaged in basket-making; then his release was announced, and now we hear of his final release.

And the *Daily Telegraph* also says :—

That many of Sir John Paul's old friends and associates believed in his innocence to the end; at all events, they believed that his errors had not been the result of deliberate dishonesty. Even the severest censors of public manners will not be sorry to think that for the last half-dozen years of his life the sometime philanthropist and ex-banker lived peaceably in obscurity. If he sinned grievously, he also suffered cruelly; those who can now read that stern lesson most profitably amid the errors of the living, will also look back with the most charitable thought for the dead: and even those whom he most wronged may learn with satisfaction that he died neither friendless nor in gaol.

The paper called "The Tatler," conducted by Sir Richard Steele, and issued on alternate days, terminates on this day, January 2nd, 1711. "The hand that has assisted me in those noble discourses upon the immortality of the soul, the glorious prospects of another life, and the most sublime ideas of religion and virtue, is a person (alluding to Addison) who is too fondly my friend ever to own them; but I should little deserve to be his, if I usurped the glory of them." Who does not grieve, knowing that divisions afterwards embittered so genuine a friendship!

Sir William Cecil, the minister of Queen Elizabeth, is dignified with the Barony of Burghley, in Lincolnshire, on this day, February 25th, 1571; and in the next year he succeeded to the office of Lord High Treasurer, upon the decease of William Powlett, Marquis of Winchester, a man who lived prosperously under seven monarchs, and left behind him one hundred and three descendants, who had witnessed his garrulity.

The articles between Sir William Davenant and the players, comprising Bellerton, Nokes, and Underhill, erecting them to be a company publickly to act in any theatre in London or Westminster, November 5th, 1660. They began at Salisbury Court, then returned to the Cockpit, and afterwards removed to the new theatre "with scenes" in Portugal Row. (See pages 78, 202, 268.)

Shakspeare. The collected comedies, histories, and tragedies, of this "great heir of fame" are first published in Folio, November 8th, 1623. In the register, sixteen plays are mentioned to have not been formerly entered, and therefore (most probably) were now first printed. In February, 1624, there appears to have been a re-entry by the same proprietors. The edition is greatly prized by amateurs as it contains the only portrait which requires no evidence to support its authenticity. "Those who accuse Shakspeare to have wanted learning" (Dryden remarks), "give him the greater recommendation: he was naturally learned; he needed not the spectacles of books to read nature; he looked inwards, and found her there. I cannot say he is everywhere alike; were he so, I should do him injury to compare him with the greatest of mankind."

Milton. The funeral was attended by all the author's learned and great friends in London, not without a friendly concourse of the vulgar. "Fancy," says Johnson, speaking of this divine character, "can hardly forbear to conjecture with what temper he surveyed the silent progress of his work, and marked its reputation stealing its way in a kind of subterraneous current, through fear and silence. I cannot but conceive him calm and confident, little disappointed, not at all dejected, relying on his own merit with steady consciousness, and waiting, without impatience, the vicissitudes of opinion, and the impartiality of a future generation."

St. Clement. The pupil of St. Peter, Clemens Romanus, has left us an "Epistle" addressed to the Church of Corinth, which, although valuable for its antiquity, is now excluded from the Canon. His emblematical badge is an anchor.

Sir Wm. Cecil (Burleigh) receives his royal mistress, Queen Elizabeth, at supper within his "house in Strand, before it was fully finished; and she came by the fields from Christ Church," 1561.

"The Liberty of the Press." This celebrated toast was first given at the Crown and Anchor Tavern, Strand, at a Whig dinner, in 1795.

Madame Rachel, previous to the Bond-street mystery, resided in this parish, at 6, Clare Court, and the corner of Sheffield Street, Clare Market. On the 21st of September, 1868, she was tried at the Old Bailey for obtaining by false pretences very large sums of money from Mrs. Borradaile, under the pretence of effecting a marriage between her and Lord Ranelagh. The trial lasted five days, and ended in the jury finding a verdict of guilty. The judge, Mr. Commissioner Kerr, passed upon her the full sentence of the law—five years' penal servitude, remarking, that after she had robbed Mrs. Borradaile of all her property, and shut her up in a prison, she had concocted a scheme to blast her character, by saying she had been spending her money upon a paramour. (See also pages 96 to 114 for Life in St. Clements, High, Low, and Fast.)

Index.

A.

A few words about Westminster, 135
Abraham, Mr. H. R., 5
Academy of Music, 53
Ackermann, Rudolph, 151
Acland's Poll Book, 64
Addison, 168, 183
Advertisements, curious theatrical, 202
—————— old, 280
Advertising extraordinary, 251
African negro, 164
Akenside, 170
Albany Wallis, 182
Albemarle, Duchess of, 179, 192
Alderman Pickett in St. Clements, 115
Aldermen first elected, 117
Aldy, Colonel, 185
Ale houses in Middlesex, 282
"All Alive and Merry," 238
Alleyn, Edward, 79
Almshouses, 23
Alphabet, the, 113, 155
Amphlett, R. P., Esq., 4
Anchor of St. Clement, 139, 234
Ancient boundaries of St. Clement Danes, 43
—————— drama, 74 to 79, 201, 268
—————— hospitals, 32
—————— signs of taverns, 154
Anderson, W. G., Esq., 4
Anderson, Alderman, 188
Angel and Crown Tavern, 105
—————— and Sun, the, 259
—————— Court, 286
—————— Inn, 195, 259, 287
Anson, J. W., Esq., 79
Antigallican, the, 106
Aphorisms of Lord Burleigh, 92

Apollo Club, the, 251
Area of St. Clement Danes, 135
Arnold, Dr., 71
Artists' Club, the, 163
Arundel House, 182
—————— Palace, 89,
—————— Street, 150, 286
Ashmole, Elias, 214
Astley, Philip, 72
Atie, Sir Arthur, 283
"Atlas," the, 241
Authorities of St. Clement Danes, 38
Ayrton, Mr. C., M.P., 311

B.

Backside of St. Clements, 288
Bacon, Mr., Q.C., 294
Baillie, Dr., 49
Baker, Sir Richard, 177
Balfe, Mr., 71
Ballot Society, 63
"Ballot," the, 242
Barber Surgeons, 50
Barbon, Dr., 285
Barker's Panorama, 74, 253
Barnaby's Journal, 210
Barnard's Inn, 127
Barristers first appointed, 134
Barry, Sir C., R.A., 46, 227
Barry, Mr. Edward, A.R.A., 5, 297
Barrymore family, the, 106
Bat Pidgeon, 196
Bateman, Rowland, 81
Bath's, Bishop of, Inn, 89, 286
Bayford, A. F., Esq., 4
Bazalgette, Mr., C.E., 311
Bear and Harrow Court, 288
—————— Yard, 270

INDEX.

Beaufort Buildings, 151, 285
―― House, 151
Beaumont House, 118
Beddoe's Gift, 23
Beefsteak Club, the, 272
Beggars, 105
"Beggars' Opera," 77
Bell and Dragon Tavern, 199
―― Inn, 284
―― Yard, 11
"Bell's Life in London," 184, 240
Ben Jonson, 118, 251
Benett, W. M., Esq., 4
Benevolent Pension Society, 28
Bentinck, Mr. C., 6, 298
Berry, Lieut., 60
Betterton, 77
"Bible" Tavern, the, 105, 156
Bidgood, Henry, Esq., 67, 68
Birch, Dr., 183
Black girl, sale of a, 195
―― Horse Concert-room, 97
―― Jack, the, 35, 114, 207, 284
Blackmoor Street, 289
Blackstone, Sir William, 157
Bliss, H., Esq., Q.C., 4
Blue Balls, the, 202
Blyth, Mr. J. S., 32
Board of Guardians of the Strand Union, 41
Board of Works for the Strand District, 38
Bolton, J. H., Esq., 300
Boswell Court, 88, 287, 290
―――― New, 11, 100, 153
―――― Old, 11, 97, 152
Boundary of St. Clement Danes, 136
Bourke, Hon. Robert, 185
Bow-street runners, 101
Bowyer, Sir George, 295
Bracegirdle, Mrs., 164, 175
Bradbury, Rev. Thomas, 158
Bramston, autobiography of Sir John, 209
Brandon, Mr. R., 5
Brett, Sir W. B., M.P., 300
Brick Court, 11
Bright, Mr. 184
Bright, John, baptismal register of, 17

Brilliant Stars of our Law Courts, 120
"British Lion," the, 243
"―― Medical Journal," the, 244
Brokesby, Dr., Richard, 182
Brooke, G. V., 72
Brough, R., 259
Brougham, Lord, 120, 121, 122, 131
Brougham, Mrs., 73
Brown, Miss, 58
Browning, Miss, 198
Brownlow and White, Messrs., 9
Bruton, Daniel, Esq., 241
Bruce, Knight, 125
Buchanan's Head, the, 280
Bullock, Captain, 228
Bull's Head, 163
Bunning, Mr., 228
Burdett, Sir Francis, 61, 64, 250
Burford, Robert, 253
Burges, Mr. W., 5
Burke, 172
Burial Ground Committee of Saint Clement Danes, 81
Burleigh, Lord, ten precepts of, 92, 316
―― street, 284
Burnet, Mr. W., 7
Butcher's Row, 116, 192, 287
Byron, Mr. H. J., 274.

C.

Cadgers' Hall, 105
Cairns, Lord, 125, 300, 310
Calvert's Museum, 254
Cambrick Chamber, the, 280
Campbell, Lord, 121
Canary House, the, 276
Capes and Harris, Messrs., 10
Carey Street, 11, 154
―― widening of, 39
Carlisle House, 151
Carved woodwork, sale of, 196
Castles, Robert, 109
Cato Street conspirators, the, 114
Cecil, Sir Robert, 90, 160
Cecil, Sir William, 91, 316
―― Street, 160, 285
Celeste, Madame, 72

INDEX. 319

Chair Court, 218, 287
Chambers, Mr. M., 292, 295, 298
Chambers, Tom, 109
Chancellor, title of, 122
Chancery Lane, 210
————— alehouses in, 282
Chapel of the Holy Ghost, 178
Chapman, Mr. T., 81
Chapone, Mrs., 157
Charities of St. Clement Danes, 21
Charity children in the Strand in 1713, 220
————— schools, 25, 26, 31, 178, 219, 271
"Charlies," the, 101
Chatto, Mr. J., 47
Chelmsford, Lord, 120
Chester Inn, 126
Chetwood's History of the Stage, 141
Child, G. B. Esq., 79
Childs' Bank, 251
Childers, 298
Church, 13, 53, 114, 139, 234, 258, 287
Church (old), 42
Churchill, R., Esq., 79
Churchill, Lady Mary, and the Kit-Cat Club, 217
Churchill, Lord Alfred, 184
Churchyard and vaults of St. Clement Danes, 80
"City's Pride" Lodge, 57
Clare Family, 197.
——— Market, 79, 103, 160, 222, 284, 289
————— butcher boys, the, 79, 163, 222
————— Chapel, 19
————— Concert Room, 103
————— Ragged Schools, 271
——— Street, 289
Clarke, Colonel, 308
Clarke, Mr. J. F., 245
Clement's Inn, 127, 144, 197, 287, 314
————— Lane, 12, 44, 58, 59, 90, 96, 168, 287
Clifford's Inn, 128
Coach, the first made, 179
Coaches introduced by Earl of Arundel, 89
Coal Hole, the, 111

Cobbold, J. C. Esq., M.P., 185
Cobden, Richard, baptismal register of, 17
Cobden, Mr., 184
Cobbett's Register, 244
Cochrane, Mr. B., 292, 295, 301, 304, 308, 309, 310
Cock Alehouse, 284, 285
Cockburn, Sir Alexander, 5, 120
Codrington, Sir William, Bart, 185
Coffee first imported, 87
Coke, Sir Edward, 181
Coldbath Field's Prison, first prisoner at, 207
Combe, Alderman, 188
"Comedy of Plautus," 75
Commissioners of New Law Courts, 3
Commons, Debate in House of, as to site of New Law Courts, 291, 295
Company of Parish Clerks, survey made by, 42
Coneygarth, the, 130
Congreve, William, 77
Conservative Benefit Building Society and United Land Company, 184
Conservative Franchise Society, 184
Conspirators in Milford Lane, 177
Cook, Mr., 206
Cook's Court, 290
Cookson, W. S., Esq., 4
Coombes, Bob, 109
Copeland, Mr. Alderman, 48, 199
Copper Holmes, 110
Corbett v. Commissioners of H.M.'s Works and Public Buildings, 293
Cornwall, Duchy of, 192
"Cosmopolitan," the, 241
Country mouse and City mouse, the, 186
Court of Chancery Funds, 10
Courts of Justice Concentration Court, 206
Coverley, Sir Roger de, 182
Cowper, Right Hon. W., 5, 6, 295, 309, 311
Coxhead, Rev. Mr. 220
"Craft," the, 109
Cranworth. Lord, 3
Craven, Earl of, 29

INDEX.

Craven Head, the, 114, 180
—— House, 179, 284, 179
—— Lord, 179
Crockford's, 108, 256
Cross Key Alley, 285
Crossley, Mr., 28, 58
Crown and Anchor Tavern, 53. 54. 55, 141, 250, 254, 316
—— Court, 197, 286
Cruikshank, Mr. G., 55
Cubitt, Sir William, 228
Cunningham Peter, 239
Currie, Mr., 185

D.

"Daily News," the, 245
"Daily Telegraph," the, 238
Dale, W. W. Esq., 79
Danegelt, 143
Danes in St. Clements, the, 143
Darling, Mr. Vincent, 184
Davenant, Sir Wm., 76, 316
Davenport, Miss, 73, 76
"Day," the, 243
Day and Martin, 27
Deaf waterman, a, 110
Deane, Mr. T. N., 5
Deate, R. D. D., tablet to, 14
Deaths, number of, in St. C. D., 193
Defective measures, fines for, 282
Delafield, Mr., 73
Denham, Sir John, frolics of, 105
Denman, Lord, 290, 310
—— Mr., 291
Dennie's Gift, 25
Dens of St. Clements, 107
Dent, Mr., 41
Denzell Street, 113, 169
Designs for New Law Courts, 5, 7, 297, 314
Devereux Court, 170, 284, 285
Devil Tavern, the, 251
—— the, outwitted for once, 168
Devonshire, Duchess of, 61
Dibdin, Charles, 172
Dickens, Mr. 12, 74

Dick's Coffee House, 215
Dickson, Colonel, 185
Discovery of leases 300 years old, 295
Distressed Beggars, 105
Dobby, Mr. J. H., 81
Donne, Dr. John, 237
Dramas and theatres, 201
Drum Court or Alley, 289
Drury family, the, 179
—— House, 179, 288
—— Lane, 179, 288
—— Theatre, 180
—— Ward, 44
Duckett's Charity, 23
Duchy Lane, 284
Duke Street, 284
"Duke of York," the, 260
Duke of York's Column, 138
Duke's Theatre, the, 76
"Dunciad," the, 178
Dust-hole, the, 84
Dutch lottery, the, 280

E.

Ebury, Lord, 311
Egerton, Mr., 72
Eldon, Lord, 120, 121
Elliston, Robert, 72
Embden, Mr., 73
Eminent lawyers, 120
"Engineer," the, 240
Englefield, Mr. R., 65
English opera, the first, 77
—— Company, 71
—— theatres, earliest, 76
Enon Chapel, 83
Entertainment in the Strand, 255
Epitaph to Joe Miller, 33
Essex Buildings, 255, 284
—— concerts in, 255
—— Street, 171
—— Chapel, 19
Evans, C. Esq., M.D., 37, 39
Evans, General Sir De Lacy, 61 to 69, 146
Exeter Change, 197
—— Court, 284

INDEX.

Exeter Hall, 137
—— House, 89, 171, 197, 285
—— Street, 285
Exchange Alley, 284
Excuse for a late appearance, 76
Exhibitions and entertainments, 253
Extraordinay craft, an, 110
—————— Men, 114

F.

Farlow, Ensign, 60
Fascinating actress, 175
Fallowfield, Mr. 182,
"Famous" Bell, 213
Farrah, Mr. 243
Farren, Mr., 73
"Farthing Post," the, 238
Fechter, Mr., 72
Feckett's Field, 146, 208
Feet-washing by Kings of England, 45
Female players, the first, 77
Fenton, Miss Lavinia, 202
Ferrer's, Earl, Execution, 51
Field, Mr. 294
Field, Roscoe, Field, and Francis, Messrs., 9, 206.
First M.P.'s for Westminster, 70
—— shop lighted with Gas, 252
—— Lord Mayor, 117
Fitzgerald, Lord Gerald, 60
Five Bell Tavern, the, 288
Fleet Street, 11
Flower, Mr. W. H., F.R.S. 49
Franklin, Benjamin, 208
Freeman, Mr., 311
Fry, Mr. G. F. 39
Foot-race round St. Clement Danes, 196
"Forrex and Porrex," 75
Forty days' poll, the, 62
Fountain Court, 111, 174, 285
—————— Club, 173
—————— the, Clare Street, 104
Four Alls, the, 155
Fowler, Mr., 311
"Fox, here's another!" 61
Furness, Mr. George, 229
Furnival's Inn, 133

G.

Galleria della Belle Arti (Brucciani) 236
Gamblers and Swindlers, 112
Garling, Mr. H. B., 5
Garrick, David, 71, 86, 182
Gates of London, 149
Gee, Nat, 259
George, Mr. 68
Gibbons, Charles, 267
Gibson, Mr. John, 5
Giffard, Sir G. M., 300
Gilbert, Mr. Thomas, 65
"Gilt Tub," the, 161
"Giovanni in London," 72
Gisborne, Mr. Lionel, C. E., 227
Gladstone, Right Hon. W. E., 5, 298
Glasier and Sons, Messrs. 224
Goldsmid, Mr. J., 298
Goldsmith, 172
Goodson, J. Esq., 185
Gordon Riots, the, 270
Grange Tavern, the, 154
Graves of St. Clement Danes, 80
Gray, Rev. T. D., 13
Gray's Inn, 133
—— Inns appertaining to, 133
Great City Lotteries, the, 189
—— Rebellion planned, 114
—— Salisbury House, 285
Greene, Mr., Q.C., 294
Green Ground, Portugal Street, 80
Gregory, Mr., 74, 298
Greyhound Court, 286
Griffin, the, 105
Grimaldi, Joe, 223
Grosvenor, Earl, M.P., 60
Grosvenor, Capt. the Hon. R. W., M.P., 70
Gruneisen, C. L., Esq., 184, 185
Gunpowder Plot, the, 112
Gwynne, Nell, 77
Gye, Mr., 72

H.

Hackney coaches, first stand for, 179
Halls, Dimensions of, 132
Half-moon Passage, 257

INDEX.

Half-moon, Sign of, 181, 257
Halfpenny and farthing newspapers, 238
Ham, Rev., J. P., 19
Hammond, Mr., 74
Hardwicke, R., Esq., 244
Harper, Bishop, 195
Harold, King, burial-place of, 18
Harriott, Mr., 232
Harrison and Lewis, Messrs. 153, 185
Harrison, S. Esq., 63
Hart, Mr. Ernest, 244
Hatchard, Rev. A., 311
Hatmakers' tradition, 142
Hatton, Miss Sarah, 58
Hatton, Sir Christopher, 218
Haunts of gamblers and swindlers, 112
Havelock (48th Middlesex) Rifle Volunteers, 55
Hemlock Court, 102, 290
Hemmerde, Mr. G. R., 249
Henley, the orator, 162
Henry IV., charter of, 18
Heycock's Ordinary, 184
Hill's Gift, 23
Hilton, Mr. John. F.R.S., 47
Historical sketch of St. Clement Danes, 139
———— the Strand, 147
———— Temple Bar, 149.
Hockley, Major, 56
Hogg, Col., M.P., 311
Holborn Estate Charity, 25
Holcroft, Mr., 74
Holes and corners, 104
Hooper, D. Esq., M.D., 37
Holles Street, 177
Holmes, Mr. T. H., 185
Holloway, Professor Thomas, 251
Hollowel Street, 288
Holy Rood Palace Tavern, 156
Holroyd, Mr. S., 53
Holy Well, the, 18, 181
Holywell Street, 174
———— Street menagerie, 112
———— Ward, 44
Honygold, George, 165
Hook, Theodore, 214
Hooker's Court, 289

Hope, Mr. Beresford, 6, 298
Hope Tavern concerts, 103
Hopeful family, a, 106
Horne, Mr., 198
Horseshoe Tavern, the, 284
———— Court, 11, 287, 293
Houses, number of, in 1708, 196
———— and families, numbers of on site of New Law Courts, 11
Houghton Street, 288
Howard Street, 175, 286
Huggett, Mr. George, 65, 81
Hungerford Market, 137
Hume, G., Esq., 4
Hunt, Right Hon. G. Ward, 300
Hunt, H. A., Esq., 4
Hunter, John, 47

I.

"Illustrated London News," the, 238
"Illustrated News of the World," the, 243
"Illustrated Times," the, 238
"Index," the, 241
Indulgences, &c., granted to Brethren, &c., of St. Clement, 234
Infamous houses, 100
Infant parish poor of London and Westminster, 193
Ingestre, Viscount, 185
Ingram, Herbert, 238
Inner Temple, the, 127
———— Inns appertaining to, 127
Innes, G. R., Esq., 27
Inn yards, plays acted in, 267
Inns, liability of to poor-rates, 197
———— of Court, the, 125
"Inquirer," the, 243
Insolvent Court, the old, 204
Institutions of St. Clement Danes, 46
Ireland, T., 110, 183
Irish compliment, an, 61
Isaacson, J. F., Esq., 27, 60, 184

J.

Jackanapes Lane, 214
Jack Sheppard, 35, 105, 113, 114, 163 273

INDEX. 323

Jenkins, Mr. T. M., 39
Jerrold, Mr. Douglas, 53, 242
Jerrold, Mr. Blanchard, 242
Jervis, Colonel, M.P., 185
Joe Miller, life and times of, 33, 114, 200
Johnson, Dr., 85, 173, 182, 253
——— tablet to, 14
Jolly young watermen, 108
Judge Best, 213
Judges of Designs, the, 5
Jump, the, 35

K.

Katt, Mr. Christopher, 173, 263
Kean, Charles, 174
Kean, Edmund, 174
Keane, D. D., Esq., Q.C., 4
Keeley, Mrs., 72
Keeley, Robert, 72, 157
Kelly and Co., 152
Kelly, C., Esq., M.D., 37
Kelly, Miss, 71
Kelligrew, Thomas, 78
Kilner, Mr. James, 41
Killick, Rev. R. H., 13, 20, 58
King, Mr. Locke, M.P., 311
King of Clubs, the, 54
——— Exeter Change, the, 197
King's College Hospital, 31
Kit-Kat Club, the, 216, 261
——— Portraits, the, 264
Knick-Knacks from the Natal Book, 316
Knight's Court, 288
Knights of the barrow, 102
——— toast, 261
Knollys, Common Serjeant, 188
Knox, Colonel, 185
Koran, translator of the, 267
Kossuth, Louis, 241
Kynaston, 76

L.

Lady Middleton's Charity, 21
Lamb Inn, the, 287
Lane, Mr. W., 65, 81
"Lancet," the, 244
Large halls, dimensions of, 132

Law, Mr. Commissioner, 206
Law and Equity Stores, 154
"Law Reports," the, 243
Lawrence, Mr. Alderman, 292, 300, 307, 311
Lawrence's Gift, 22
Leach, Mr., 228
Lee, Nelson, Esq., 79
Lemon, Mark, 238
Lewis, C. E. Esq., 184
Lewson, "Lady," 172
"Liberty of the Press," toast of, 316
Library of College of Surgeons, 49
License, theatrical, of James I., 76
——— ——— Queen Elizabeth, 76
Lindley, Mr., 294
Life in St. Clement Danes, 96
Lightermen's and Watermen's Arms, 109
Lincoln's Inn, 130
——— Chapel and Preachers, 131
——— Hall and Library, 132
——— Inns appertaining to, 133
——— Fields, 210
——— Executions in, 213
——— Theatre, 202
Liston, 73, 259
Little Essex Street, 285
——— Lincoln's Inn Theatre, 78
Livett, Mr. Charles, 58
Living of St. Clement Danes, 95
Littlecot, Rev., F. G., 13
"Lloyd's Gazette," 242
"Lloyd's Weekly Newspaper," 242
Lock Alley, 288
Lockwood, Mr. H. F., 5
"London Telegraph," the, 238
London and Westminster Bank, 249
——— Life, 113
——— Dens, 113
Lord Chancellors', list of, 123
——— Chancellor, office of, 122
——— Keepers, list of, 123
——— Mayor's Show, 117
Lords, Debate in House of, as to site of New Law Courts, 290
Lost Charities, 24

INDEX.

Lottery for building Pickett Street, 187
——— the first, 191
"Love for Love," comedy of, 77
Lovelace, Lord, 53
Lovelock, Mr. S., 52
Lovers' trips, 110
Lowe, Mr., 298
Lower Serle's Place, 216
Lyceum Theatre, 71, 271
Lyndhurst, Lord, 120, 121
Lyon's Inn, 112, 126, 180, 288
Lyttleton, Sir Edward, 88, 258

M.

Mail Coaches, 195
"Mail Coach Adventures," Entertainment, 71
Mackay, Dr., 238
Mad Duchess, the, 192
"Magnet," the, 242
Magpye Lane, 180
Malcolm, Sarah, 218
Malins, Vice-Chancellor, 125
Mallock, Mr. David, 65, 68
Manchester Unity, Independent Order of Odd Fellows, 57
Man-hunting Club, the, 167
Manners, Lord John, 6, 295, 298, 300, 309, 311
"Mark Lane Express," 240
Marlborough, Duke of, 184
Marriage in St. Clement's, singular, 258
Marston, Westland, Esq., 246
Mason, Henry, Esq., 27
Marvell, Andrew, 186, 215
Mathews, C., 259
Maundy Thursday ceremonial, 45
Maynard, Serjeant, 200
Maypole Alley, 178, 284
——— erection of, 178
——— the, 284
Maxwell, Sir W. S., Bart., M.P., 5
McArthur, Mr. Sheriff, 311
"Medical Times," the, 245
Members of the Inns of Court, 134
Merry Wives of Windsor, the, 75
Metropolitan Police, 101
Meyrick, Colonel, 185

Merivale, Hermann, Esq., 241
Middle Exchange, the, 160
——— Serle's Place, 215
——— Temple, the, 128
———, Inns appertaining to, 129
——— Ward, 45
Middlesex Registry, Office of Deeds, 206
Milford Lane, 177, 285
Mill, J. S., Esq., M.P., 70
Miller, Joe, 33, 200
——— Mrs., 200
Milled money, punishment for passing, 196
Miller, G. M., Esq., 185
Milton, funeral of, 316
Mission House, St. Clement's Lane, 58
"Morning Advertiser," the, 244
Mortimer, 182
Mortimer, John H., 258
Mortimer's, supper at, 258
Moseley, R. Esq., 20
Mortlake, Dick, 109
Most celebrated parish in London, 119
Motteaux, Antony, 114, 192
Mountain Sylph, the, 71
Mudford's Gift, 23
Murphy, Mr. Commissioner, 205
Museum of the College of Surgeons, 47
Musick School, Essex Street, 281

N.

Nan Clarges, 179
"National Magazine," the, 246
National Gallery, 137
Nat, Lee, 113
Neele, poet and lawyer, 259
Nelson's Column, 137
Nelson, Mr. 68
Nelson, Robert, 221
Neville, Mr. H., 74
New Court Chapel, 157
Newcastle Court, 100
——— Street, 178
Newcomen, Mr. 185
New Inn, 129, 274, 287
——— Buildings, fire at, 275
New Law Courts, the, 1, 119, 198, 224, 290 314

INDEX. 325

New Square, 131, 208
"News of the World," the, 239
Newspaper, first in England, 239
NEWSPAPERS, &c.
    Atlas, 241
    Ballot, 242
    Bell's Life in London, 184, 240
    British Lion, 243
    British Medical Journal, 244
    Christian World, 158
    Cosmopolitan, 241
    Day, 243
    Daily Telegraph, 238, 315
    Daily News, 245
    Engineer, 240
    Hunt's London Journal, 245
    Illustrated London News, 238
    Illustrated Times, 238
    Inquirer, 243
    Lancet, 244
    Law Reports, 243
    Lloyd's Weekly Newspaper, 242
    Law Magazine, 124
    London Directory, 152
    London Medical Gazette, 245
    London Telegraph, 238
    Magnet, 242
    Medical Times, 245
    Medical Times and Gazette, 246
    Mark Lane Express, 240
    Morning Advertiser, 244
    Morning Star, 315
    National Magazine, 246
    News of the World, 239
    Notes and Queries, 113
    Observer, 240
    Penny Newsman, 243
    Pharmaceutical Repertory, 246
    Pharmaceutical Times, 246
    Provincial Medical Journal, 244
    Solicitor's Journal, 243
    Sporting Times, 243
    Standard, 243, 305
    Times, 299, 301, 308
    Tablet, 240
    Tomahawk, 243
    Weekly Advertiser, 244
    Weekly Chronicle and Register, 243
    Weekly Notes, 243
    Weekly Reporter, 243

Newspaper press in St. Clement's, 238
Newspapers first stamped, 239
Newton, Sir Isaac, 170
Newton, Mr., 311
Nicoll, Burnett and Newman, Messrs., 153, 224
Nightingale, Miss, 32
Nobility of St. Clement Danes, 88

Noble, Mr. T.C. 224
"No flies !" 98
Norfolk Buildings, 286
Norfolk, Duke of, 60
——— Giant, 114
——— Street, 182 258, 286
Noted Houses in the Strand, 249
Noteworthy things, 256
Notorious Robbers, 113

O.

"Observer," The, 240
Ogden's Court, 288
Ogilby's book lottery, 78, 270
Ommaney, Sir Francis, 184
Old Black Jack, 35, 114, 207
——— Buildings, 130
——— Dog Tavern, the, 181
——— Hall, the, Lincoln's Inn, 130
——— Mission House, 58, 169
— — Parr, 150
——— Poor House, 41
——— Signs and Tokens in St. Clement's, 275
——— Trumpet Tavern, 215
Olympic Theatre, 72
Oranges, curious custom with, 198
Osborne, Mr. Bernal, 184

P.

Pageant in the Strand, 256
Page, Mr. 227
Palk, Sir Lawrance, Bart, M. P., 185
Pall Mall, first street lighted with gas, 252
Palmer, Sir Roundell, 5, 19, 298
Palmer's Charity, 21
Palsgrave Head, 186
——— Court, 284
——— Place, 186
Parish Register, 16
Parish, J., 110
Partridge, Dr., 160
Parry, Mr. Sefton, 274
Pass, the, 116
Pastors of New Court Chapel, 159
Patent, theatrical, of Charles I., 76

Paterson's Auction-room, 255
Paul, Sir J. D., 108, 249, 315
Payne, Howard, 259
Pease, 298
Peel, Sir Robert, 205
Penn, William, 182
"Penny Newsman," the, 243
Percival, murder of, 153
Pest House Field Charity, 28
Peter Street, 289
—— the Great, 183
Pett, T., the miser, 166
P——g Alley, 286, 288
Phillips, Mr., 196
——, Mr. J. S., 37
——, Mr. Commissioner, 204, 205
Pickett, Alderman, 115, 117, 187
—— Street, 11, 187
Pigmy Court, 287
Pillory in the Strand, 258
"Plautus," comedy of, 75
Play-bill, the first, 77
Playhouse Street, 199, 289
Playhouses, old, 201
Plough Alley, 287
—— Court, 11, 96, 102
—— Tavern, 102, 154
"Plumpton Correspondence," the, 195
Poetic butcher of Clare Market, 223
Police, the Thames, 231
Pope, 168
Population of St. Clement Danes, 19
Poor of St. Clement Danes, 40
Poor rates levied in St. Clement Danes, 41
Pop-gun plot, the, 207
Portugal Row, 284
—— Street, 199
Pouncy, Gilbert, 65
Pownall, G., Esq., 5, 8, 184
Powell, 298
Precepts of Lord Burleigh, 92
Prior, Mathew, 265
Professional comedians in London, 75
Prout, John, Esq., 65
Prout, Thomas, Esq., 63
Prout, tablet to, 146
"Provincial Medical Journal," the, 244
Prynne, George, Esq., 241

Public Dispensary, the, 37, 165
Public-house, first license for, 215
"Public Intelligencer," the, 239
Punch's Playhouse, 74, 253

Q.

Quarrington, Mr., murder of, 105
Queen Elizabeth's leases, 293
"Queen of Bohemia," the, 179
Queen's (Westminster) Rifle Volunteers, 60
Quin, 77

R.

Rachel, Madame, 316
Radstock, Lady, 20
Raimondi, W., Esq., 27
Ragged School Shoeblack Society, 218
Ralli, Mr. P. P., 32
Ranelagh, Viscount, 184, 185
Rate Books of St. Clements, 160
Rayner, Mr., 74, 253
"Recruiting Office," comedy of, 77
Reddish, John, Esq., 79, 183
Reed, Rev. Andrew, 118
Reindeer Yard, 270
Religious Plays, 75
Residents of Butcher Row, 118
Retreat, the, 105
Rich, John, 77, 167
Riche, Mr. G. T., 240
"Richard II.," 76
Ripon, W., first coachmaker, 179
Riston, Mr. A. W., 229
Ristori, Madame, 72
Robberies in the Strand, 281
Robin Hood Society, 171
Robson, Mr. F., 73
Rochester, Earl of, 200
"Rochester," play of, 72
Rogers, Mr. J., 74
Rogers, Mr. W. G., 196
Rogers, P. W., Esq., 4
Rolls Court and Chapel, 126
Rolt, Vice Chancellor, 125
Roman Spring Bath, 265
"Romeo and Juliet," 76

INDEX. 327

Rose, Rev. F., 19
Rose Tavern, the, 285
Rothery, H. C., Esq., 4
Royal College of Surgeons, England, 46
—— Diversion, 231
—— Farmers' and General Insurance Company, 183
—— Globe Theatre, the, 274
—— license, the first theatrical, 75
—— Ward, 45
Russell, Lord William, 205
Russell, Rev. Dr., 83
Russell's Gift, 24

S.

Sainsbury, Mr. S., 65
Sale, George, 267
Sams, W. R., Esq., 79
"Sam's" Club, 85
Saunders, John, Esq, 246
Saunders, Mr., 228
Savage Club performances, 72
Salisbury, Marquis of, 56
Salvator Rosa, the English, 182
Savings Bank, 52, 183
Savoy Ward, 45
Scenery first introduced on the stage, 76
Scott, Mr. G. G., R.A., 5, 299
Scott, Charles, 267
Scrivener, T. P., Esq., 52. 60
Seddon, Mr. J. P., 5
Sedley, Sir Charles, 90, 214
Sergeants' guard at theatres, 77
Serjeants' Inns, 125
Serle's Coffeehouse, 210
—— Court, 208
—— Place, 214
—— Street, 208, 290
Seven Stars, the, 280
Seymour, Major-General, 311
Seymour's parishes of London and Westminster, 290
Seymour Place, 89
Shakspear, first published, 316
Shakspear's Head, the, 275
Shakspearian Forger, the, 110
Shalmer's Gift, 21
Shaw, Captain, 311

Shaw, J., Esq., 5
Shaw, Sir James, 188
Shaw's Gift, 24
Sheer Lane Ward, 44
Shear Lane, 284
Sheffield Street, 284
Shelley, Sir J. V., Bart., 70
Shepherd and his Flock Club, 163
Sherborn Court, 288
Sheriffs, first, 117
Sheridan, 172
Shields, Mr., 228
Ship and Dolphin, the, 255
—— Inn, the, 275, 288
—— Yard, 11, 107, 218, 287,
Shipp, Tressillian P., Esq., 249
Shire Lane, 104, 259
Shock Jem, 104
Shoppen, Mr. W., 182, 263
Shorthouse, Dr., 243
Signs of Taverns, 154
Silvester, Recorder, 188
Sloman, Charles, 111
Smashing Lumber, the, 107
Smith, C. M., Esq., 4
Smith, W. H., Esq., 19, 69
Smith, W. H. & Son, 247
Soane's Museum, 213
Somerset House, 288
Songs and Suppers at the Cole Hole, 111
"Solicitors' Journal," the, 243
Southwark, City magistrates in, 105
"Siege of Rhodes," the, 76
Sigoursy, Mrs., 58
Site of New Law Courts, 11, 198
Skirrow, C. F. Esq., 4
Southgate, T. Esq., Q.C. 4
Spectator, 272
Speeding. J. Esq., 184
Spiller, epitaph on, 223
Spillers' Head, the, 163, 223
Spilsbury, Mr. W. H., 132, 134
Spooner, Sergeant-major, 56
"Sporting Times," the, 243
Spring musical clock, a. exhibited, 255
Spy, treatment of a, 106
Stansfield, Mr. M.P. 246
Stainton, J. J., Esq., 79

INDEX.

"Standard," the, 243,
Stanhope Street, 219, 289
Staple Inn, 133
Star Court, 11, 288
State papers, extracts from, 277
Steven, R. Esq., 185
Stone, Mr. T. M., 50
Storr, Mr. 65
Strahan, Paul, and Bates, 249
Straits of St. Clement, 116
St. Agnes, legend of, 156
Strand the, 147, 224 to 259
—— signs and tokens in, 276
—— improvements, 300
—— Bridge, 265, 284, 286
—— Fishmongers, the, 256
—— Hotel Company, 180, 274
—— Inn, 288
—— Lane, 109, 265
—— noted houses in the, 249
—— noteworthy things about, 256
—— pillory in the, 258
—— Theatre, 74, 253
—— Steamboat Pier, 230
—— Union, 41
St. Clement Danes, 13, 21, 38, 42, 46, 71, 80, 85, 88, 96, 115, 119, 135, 139, 234, 238

The Charities belonging to St. Clement Danes

Comprise Backhouse, Beddoe, Benevolent Pension Society, Bissell, Bridgman, Dennie, Duckett, Forster, Hester, Hill, Holborn Estate, Holford, Jacob, Jale, Lawrence, Lowman, Middleton, Mudford, Northumberland, Duke of, Palmer, Pest House Field, Price, Read, Russell, Shaw, Shoren, Shalmer, Salisbury, Earl of, Schools, Warner, Webb, and Wraxall Charities (*See page 21*).

The present Church, erected, 13, 237
Pulpit, 237
Tablets, 14, 146
Dr. Johnson's pew, 14, 85
Vaults crowded with dead, 17
Churchyard, 42, 80
Register from, 1558, 16
Richard Cobden and John Bright christened in St. Clement Danes Church, 17
Singular marriage, 258
Marriage in high life, 145
Old Church, 16, 18, 42, 139, 145 234
State of Streets round the Old Church, 16

The New Law Courts in
Commissioners, 3
Judges of Designs, 5, 298
Number and list of houses and places required, also families removed, 11
Temple of Justice, 119
Cost of purchasing houses on the site, 198
Clearance of Houses, 224
Sale of old buildings on the site, 224, 314
Cost of building Law Courts, 10, 290
Decision of Vice-Chancellor Stuart respecting leases granted in the reign of Queen Elizabeth, 293
Appointment of Architect, 297
Shall another site be purchased, 301
The Lincoln's Inn objection, 302
The Money objection, 303
The Settled and done with objection, 304
St. Clement's, Epistle of, 316
——— in 1734, 284
——— Well, 197
St. Martin-in-the-Fields, Church of, 138
Steelids, the ; or the Tryal of Wit, 263
Stone Buildings, 132
Stilwell, J. G., Esq., 19, 220
Stilwell, Mrs., 20
Stocks, last in London, 104
——— Market, the, 257
St. Paul's School, petition from, 75
Streets, and places of St. Clement's Danes 150
Street, Mr. G. E., A.R.A., 5, 297
Street nigger minstrels, 97
Stuart, Vice-Chancellor, 295
Surgeons' Hall, 50
Sun Tavern, 105
Surrey Street, 267, 286, 287
Survey of St. Clement Danes, 42
Sussex, Duke of, 165
Swan Court, 288
Swanborough, Miss, 74
Swanborough, Mrs., 74
Swift, Dean. 168
"Tablet," The, 240
Tablet to Dr. Johnson, 14
Talbot Inn, the, 286
"Tatler," the, 215, 260, 316
Taylor, Mr. L., 311
Tea, introduction of, 87
Temperance Hall, Portugal Street, 20
Templars' Field, 146
Temple Bar, 149, 225, 233
——— Bar Stores, 105

INDEX. 329

Temple Bar Ward, 44
—— Church, 129
—— of Justice, 119
Thames Embankment, the, 226, 230, 311
——————, proposed for site of new Law Courts, 292
Thames Police Ship, 230
—— Watermen, 108
"That's the Ticket!" 34
Thavies' Inn, 127, 133
Theatres, ancient, 268
—————— of St. Clement Danes, 71
Theatrical costumes, 77
—————— critics of the 17th century, 78
"The Ship without Temple Bar," 218
Thieves' Club and Cross Gents, 99
—— Colony, a, 107
Thompson, Major-General, 63
Three Halbert Court, 286
—— Horse shoes, the, 108
"Three Kings," the, 254
Thurlow, Lord, 120
Thwaites, Sir J., 311, 313
"Tim-buc-too," 164
"Times," the, 299, 301, 308
Tite, Mr., 298, 311
Toasts, custom of drinking, 262
"Tomahawk," the, 243
"Tom and Jerry; Life in London," 108
Tom Thumb, 271
Tombstone of Joe Miller, 33
Tom's Coffeehouse, 170
Townshend, Marquis, 311
Tonson, Jacob, 264
Tragedy, the first perfect, played, 75
Treasury, 307, 308
Tressillian, P. Shipp, Esq., 249
Trevelyan, Sir Charles, 301, 309
Trevor, Sir John, 88
Trimmer, Mr. E., M.A., Cantab, 47
Trumpet Tavern, the, 259
Tuller, Jacob, 109
Turner, Lord Justice, 124
Tuxford, Mr., 240
Twining, F., Esq., 58
Twining, Miss, 20
Twining, R., Esq., 28, 37, 52
Twining, S. H., Esq., 27
Twining's Bank, 249
Twining's Tea Warehouse, 250

V.

Varney's Eatinghouse, 182
Vauxhall Gardens, 108
Vere Street, 267, 289
Vestris, Madame, 73
Vestry Hall of St. Clement Danes, 192
Vestry, select, 42
Vice-Chancellors, the, 124
Vickers, Messrs. G. and H., 258
"Voltigern," 111
Voting, slow mode of, 61

W.

Waithman, Alderman, 165
Wakley, Dr. J. G., 245
Walker, Mr. Samuel, 8
Walker, Mr. G. A., F.R.C.S., 81, 84
Walker, Mr., 228
Walmsley, Mr. Edward B., 227
Walpole, Sir Robert, 182
Walton, W. H., Esq., 4
Walsh and Nisbett, 189
Wards of St. Clement Danes, 44
Watchhouse, the parish, 200
Waterfield, J., Esq., M.D., 37
Waterhouse, Mr. Alfred, 5, 299
Waterloo Bridge, 137
Watermen's churchyard, 110
Watts, Mr., 73
Waylett, Mrs., 74, 253
Weale, John, 259
Webb's Gift, 22
Webster, B., Esq., 79
"Weekly Chronicle and Register," 243
Wellesley, Marquis, 112, 131
Wellington Street, 271
Williams, T., Esq., 79
Westbury, Lord, 120, 122
Westminster, a few words about, 135
—————— Abbey, 138
—————— Bridge, 137
—————— Elections, 61
—————— Hall, 138
—————— Liberal Registration Society, 64
—————— Paving Act, 118
—————— School, 137
Whatley, Mr., 10
White Horse Yard, 164

2 T

330 INDEX.

White Lion Passage, 273
Whitehurst, E. C., Esq., 63
Whiting and Co., Messrs., 151
Whittington Club, 53
" ——— listening to Bow Bells," 53
Wigan, A., 73
Wild, George, 73
Williams, T., Esq., 79
Will's Coffeehouse, 200
Wilton, Miss Marie, 74
Williams, Mr., 198
Wilson, John, 241
Winchelsea, Earl of, 184
Winstanley, 185
Winter, Thomas, confession of, 112
Winterbotham, 298
Wodderspoon and Co., Messrs., 200
Woking Cemetery, 81
Wollaston, Dr., 160
Woman with horn, exhibition of a, 255
Wonders in the Sun, the, 262

Wood, J., Esq., 37
Wood, Sir Wm. Page, 4, 125, 300
Wooden Houses of St. Clement Danes, 116
Wood's "History of Clerkenwell," 193, 201
Workhouse dietary, St. Clement's, 40
Wraxall's Gift, 22
Wrench, 71, 259
Wright, Mr. A., 65
Wright, conspirator, 112
Wych Alley, 288
——— Street, 90, 113, 273, 284, 288

Y.

Yates Court, 9, 11, 44, 287
Yonge, J., LL.D., monument to, 126
Young, J., Esq., 4
Younge, Rev. W. C., 158
Young's "Night Thoughts," 246

INNS, STREETS, LANES, COURTS, ALLEYS AND OTHER PLACES REFERRED TO IN THIS WORK.

Those marked thus (*) form the site of the New Law Courts.
Those marked thus (†) are the names of places formerly in the Parish of St. Clement Danes.
All others (except otherwise expressed), are now in the Parish of St. Clement Danes.

Angel Court, 45, 286
Arundel Street, 45, 150, 286
*Bailey's Court (out of St. Clement's), 11
†Baker's Yard and Tweezers' Alley, 45
Barnard's Inn (out of St. Clement's), 127
Beaufort Buildings, 45, 151, 285
†——— Street, 45
*Bear and Harrow Court, 44, 283
——— Yard, 44, 270, 284, 289
*Bell Yard, part of, (out of St. Clement's), 11
Bennet's Court, 44
Blackmoor Street, 44, 103, 162, 288
†Blue Boar Court, 289
†Boswell Court, 88, 287, 290
*——— Old, 11, 44, 88, 97, 152, 290
*——— New, 11, 100, 153
*——— Yard, 11
†Bowling Alley, 270
*Brick Court, (out of St. Clement's), 11
†Burleigh Court, 45
——— Street, 45, 285

†Butcher Row, 44, 113, 116, 118, 171, 275, 287
*Carey Street (part of), 11, 39, 44, 58, 154, 243
†Carpenter's Court, 44
Cecil Street, 45, 90, 160, 285
*Chair Court, 11, 218, 287
Clare Market, 44, 79, 103, 113, 160, 167, 284, 287, 289
——— Street, 44, 104, 289
——— Court, 44, 288
*Clement's Court, 11
*——— Inn (part of) 11, 114, 127, 144, 197, 287, 294, 314
*——— Foregate, 11
*——— Passage, 44
*——— Lane (part of), 11, 44, 88, 90, 96, 168, 293
Cook's Court, 44, 55, 290
Covent Garden (out of St. Clement's), 61, 78
Craven Buildings, 44
——— Passage or Yard, 44
*Cromwell Place, 11

STREETS, LANES, AND OTHER PLACES. 331

†Cross Keys Alley, 45, 285
*Crown Court, 11, 44
*——— Place, 11
†Cucumber Alley, 44
†Cup Fields, 214
 Denzell Street, 113, 169, 271
 Devereux Court, 45, 89, 170, 284
†Dirty Lane, 45
†Drum Alley, 44
†——— Court, 289
 Drury Lane (part in St. Clement's) 44, 161, 179, 284, 289,
 Duke Street (part in St. Clement's) 44, 284, 289
†Dutchy Lane, 45, 284
†Essex Buildings, 255, 284
 ——— Street, 19, 45, 171, 241, 244, 246, 285
 ——— Little, 45, 285
†Exeter Court, 284
†——— Exchange, 197, 284
 ——— Street (out of St. Clement's), 239, 242, 285
†Exchange Alley, 284
†Feckett's Field, 146, 208, 214, 294
*Fleet Street (part of, and out of St. Clement's), 11, 238, 246
 Fountain Court, 45, 111, 174, 285
 Furnival's Inn (out of St. Clement's), 133
 Gilbert's Passage, 44
 Grange Court, 44
†——— Street, 289
 Gray's Inn (out of St. Clement's), 133
 Greyhound Court, 45, 286
†Green Arbour Court, 45
 Half Moon Passage, 257
*Hemlock Court, 11, 102, 290
‡Herbert's Passage, 45
†High Street, 115, 265, 284
 Holles Street, 44, 177, 289
 Holywell Street, 44, 112, 174, 288
†Hooker's Court, 289
*Horseshoe Court (part of), 11, 287, 293
*——— Little, 11
 Houghton Street, 25, 44, 288
 Howard Street, 175, 286, 287
 Hungerford Market (out of St. Clement's), 137
†Jackanapes Lane, 214
†Jesuits' Ground, 45
†King's Arms Court, 44
†——— Head Court, 44, 289
†Knight's Court, 288
 Lincoln's Inn (part of), 131, 133
 ——— Fields (out of St. Clement's), 46, 161, 210, 213, 284, 287, 289
†Lock Alley, 288
†Lyon's Inn, 112, 126, 180, 288
†Magpye Lane, 180
 Maypole Alley, 44, 178, 284, 288
†Middle Exchange, 160
 Milford Lane, 25, 45, 108, 177, 285
†Naked Boy Court, 45
*New Court, 11, 44, 157
†——— Market, 160
 Newcastle Street, 110, 178, 180, 240
*——— Court, 11, 44, 100

 New Inn, 110, 129, 274, 287
 ——— Buildings, 275
 ——— Passage, 26, 44
 ——— Square (part of), 131, 208
†Norfolk Buildings, 286
 ——— Street, 45, 90, 110, 182, 258, 286
†Ogden's Court, 288
†Palsgrave's Head Court, 284
 ——— Place, 186
†Peach Tree Court, 44
†Peter Street, 289
*Pickett Street (part of), 11, 187
*——— Place, 11, 197
†Pigmy Court, 287
*Plough Court, 11, 96, 102
†——— Alley, 287
†——— Stables Alley, 44
 Portugal Street, 20, 44, 80, 104, 199, 207
†——— Row, 199, 200, 284, 289
 Portsmouth Street (out of St. Clement's), 35, 114, 207
 Princess Street (out of St. Clement's), 284
 Queen Street (out of St. Clement's), 213
†Reindeer Court, 270, 289
*Robinhood Court, 11
†Rogues' Lane, 214
†Sadlers' Court, 45
 Salisbury Street (out of St. Clement's), 90, 160
*Sawyer's Yard, 11
 Serjeant's Inn (out of St. Clement's), 125
†Serles Court, 131, 208
*——— Place, 11, 214,
*——— Lower, 11, 104
*——— Middle, 11, 215
 ——— Street, 44, 208, 290
 Sheffield Street, 284
*Ship Yard, 11, 44, 107, 218, 287
*——— and Anchor Court, 11
*Shire Lane, 44, 104, 156, 214, 259, 284, 287, 290
†Stable Alley, 289
 Stanhope Street, 44, 195, 279, 284, 289
 Staple Inn (out of St. Clement's), 133
*Star Court, 11, 44, 288
*Strand (part of, and part in St. Clement's) 11, 45, 53, 108, 147, 220, 224, 276, 285, 287
 ——— Lane, 45, 265
 Surrey Street, 45, 267, 286
†Swan Court, 288
 Temple, 128
 Thavies Inn (out of St. Clement's), 127, 133
†Three Helmet Court, 284
†——— Halbert Court, 286
†Tweezers' Alley, 45
 Vere Street, 44, 57, 267, 289
†Water Street, 45, 286
 Wellington Street (part of), 71, 271
†Wickham Court, 288
†Windmil Court, 288
 Wych Alley, 44, 288
 ——— Street, 39, 44, 72, 90, 113, 273, 284, 288
 White Horse Yard, 44, 289
 ——— Lion Court, 45
†Worcester Ground, 45
*Yates Court (part of), 9, 11, 44, 287

A LIST OF THE STREETS, LANES, COURTS AND PLACES WITHIN THE PARISH OF ST. CLEMENT DANES.—NOVEMBER, 1868.

Almshouses, near Clement's Inn
Angel Court, near Surrey Street, Strand
Arundel Street, Strand
Bear Yard, Nos. 5 to 12, 14 to 19
Beaufort Buildings, Strand
Blackmoor Street, Clare Market
Carey Street, Nos. 24 to 53
Carting Lane, Strand
Cecil Street, Strand, Nos. 1 to 27
Chapel Court, Clement's Inn
Clare Court
—— Market, North of the Passage leading to Gilbert Street
—— South of ditto
—— The Western side, between Clare Street and Houghton Street
—— Passage, Denzell Street
—— Street, Nos. 1 to 25
Clement's Inn
—— Passage
—— Lane, Nos. 20 to 23, East side
—— Nos. 34 to 53, West Side
Colonnade, Clare Market
Cook's Court, Carey Street
Craven Buildings, Drury Lane
Danes Inn
Denzell Street, Clare Market
Devereux Court, Strand
Drury Lane, Nos. 93 to 121
Duke Street, Lincoln's Inn Fields, Odd Numbers only, Nos. 3 to 27
Essex Street
—— Little
Eversley Court, late Brown's Buildings
Fountain Court, Strand
Gilbert's Passage, Clare Market
—— Street, Clare Market, East side from Gilbert's Passage, passing Northward
—— West side from Gilbert's Passage, passing Southward
Golden Buildings, Strand
Granby Place, Drury Lane, formerly called Bennett's Court
Grange Court, Carey Street
Greyhound Court, Milford Lane

Half Moon Court, Stanhope Street
Harford Place, Drury Lane
Herbert's Passage, Strand
Holles Street, Clare Market
Holywell Street, Strand, Nos 1 to 25, North side
—— Nos. 28 to 53, South side
Horse Shoe Court, Clement's Lane
Houghton Street
Howard Street
Maypole Alley, Newcastle Street
Milford Lane, Strand, East and West sides
Nag's Head Court, Drury Lane
Newcastle Street, Nos. 1 to 31
New Inn
—— Buildings
—— Passage
—— Square, Lincoln's Inn, Nos. 5 to 11
Norfolk Street, Strand
Palsgrave Place, Temple Bar
Portugal Street
Sadler's Court, Milford Lane
St. Mary's Buildings, Wych Street
Serle Street, Lincoln's Inn, Nos. 3 to 16
Sheffield Street, Clare Market, Nos. 3 to 10, and part of 11
Somerset Street
Stanhope Street, Nos. 2 to 63
Strand, Nos. 85 to 106, 161 to 197, 199 to 235, 261 to 304, 310, 351 to 359
—— Lane
Surrey Place, Strand
—— Street, Strand
Temple Pier
Thames Police Ship, on the Thames
Thanet Place, Temple Bar
Tweezer's Alley, Milford Lane
Vere Street, Clare Market
Wellington Street, Strand, Nos. 10, 12, 14, 17 and 19, and part of 21
White Horse Yard, Drury Lane
—— Lion Court, Wych Street
Wych Alley
—— Street, Nos. 1 to 54
Wycham Court
Yates Court, Carey Street

DIPROSE & BATEMAN, PRINTERS, 13 AND 17, PORTUGAL STREET, LINCOLN'S INN.

www.ingramcontent.com/pod-product-compliance
Lightning Source LLC
Chambersburg PA
CBHW030304240426
43673CB00040B/1059